Nothing but the truth

Nothing
but the
truth

Brian H. Edwards

 EVANGELICAL PRESS

EVANGELICAL PRESS
12 Wooler Street, Darlington, Co. Durham, DL1 1RQ.

© Evangelical Press 1993
First published 1978
Second edition 1993

British Library Cataloguing in Publication Data available

ISBN 0 85234 305 1

Unless otherwise indicated, Scripture quotations in this publication are from the Holy Bible, New International Version. Copyright © 1973, 1978, 1984, International Bible Society. Published by Hodder & Stoughton.

Quotations marked NASB are from the New American Standard Bible © The Lockman Foundation 1960, 1962, 1963, 1971, 1972, 1973.

Quotations marked NKJV are from the Holy Bible, New King James Version, ©1984 Thomas Nelson Inc.

Printed in Great Britain by the Bath Press, Avon.

This book is dedicated to the elders, deacons and members at Hook Evangelical Church in Surbiton.
They have never begrudged my wider ministry and without their fellowship, prayer and encouragement my writing would not be possible.

Acknowledgements

I must express my sincere gratitude to those whose particular expertise has proved invaluable in the production of this second and revised edition of *Nothing but the Truth*.

My secretary Jenny Wigginton and Peggy Rowbotham, before her unexpected death, between them typed the whole of the first edition onto computer and Jenny typed the extra chapters and the indexes for me. Andrew Anderson from Bristol read the draft and made valuable comments regarding both accuracy and presentation. The Evangelical Library in London, as always, provided much source material, with the librarian, Stephen Taylor, and his staff researching for me and Norah Sayer acting as my courier! Above all my wife Barbara has given her total support and with her considerable experience and accuracy in proof-reading has made a vital contribution.

All these, together with the staff at Evangelical Press, who coped with an ever-growing volume, and the members at Hook Evangelical Church, Surbiton, to whom this book is dedicated, are part of a team. With the exception of any errors and shortcomings, which are my responsibility alone, this is *our* book.

Brian H. Edwards
Hook Evangelical Church, Surbiton, Surrey, England
May 1993

Contents

List of illustrations

1.
Whatever happened to our Bible?

The Bible is the textbook of Christianity, and in every area of life it is generally agreed that a textbook must be free from errors if it is to be trustworthy. Unless it is a textbook for the experts only, it must also be simple to understand. There may be some difficult subjects within it and a few parts that require special care if the true meaning is not to be lost, but taken as a whole, a textbook intended to inform ordinary readers must be clear and straightforward. If those ordinary readers are to be found in a variety of cultures, from the nomadic tribesman to the university professor, spread over four thousand years of man's history, then the textbook must be unusual in the plainness of its message, powerful in the effect of its message and universal in the attractiveness of its message.

The Bible stands alone among all the books ever written in meeting these requirements.

The Bible also stands alone among books not only by reason of its long history and great popularity, but because of the enemies it has attracted to itself. All through its history, even during the days when it was being written, its enemies have tried to destroy it. It has been burned, banned and people have been punished for reading it. This is still the situation in parts of the world today.

But why is this? Certainly not because it is a book of low moral standards that encourages people to rebel against governments and rulers. In fact, it is generally accepted that no book ever written by man maintains such a consistently high standard of morality over such a long period. The writing of the Bible was spread over a period of about fifteen hundred years, and it always encourages men to be loyal to those in authority, however godless the leaders might be. Why then has the Bible been so bitterly attacked?

One answer to this question lies in the fact that the Bible makes great claims for itself. It claims to be the Word of God and therefore to carry the authority of God with its every sentence and line. It claims to be the only infallible rule to govern men's lives, and this word 'infallible' means not merely that the Bible is *found to be without error*, but that since it is God's Word *it is not possible for it to contain error*.

The Bible claims that its laws and statements, because they come from God, are higher and more important than those of governments or churches. It also claims that its history, geography, and any other subject it deals with, are accurate and more valuable than any of the theories of men. The Bible claims to reveal the only reliable truth about man and God and to point mankind to the only way of salvation. The Bible never claims to be one holy book among many, but *the* holy book above all. It therefore claims to be a good textbook and completely reliable, but, more than that, it claims to be God's textbook, and as such it is not possible for any part of it to be unreliable.

In addition to all this is the incredible fact that literally millions of true Christians, for the past two thousand years, have taken this book as their rule and guide for life. They have gladly obeyed it, and willingly died for it. Philosophy and religion may reform, but only the Bible can transform.

Such claims as these are not popular. For a thousand years the church of Rome feared the power of the Bible to guide men and women into the truth and, in order to protect its own beliefs from being tested by Scripture, the church forbade ordinary people to read the Bible. From the year 1401 it was illegal to own a copy of the Bible, and the penalty for disobedience was often death.

In spite of this, during the fourteenth century John Wycliffe translated the Bible from Latin into English, and then he sent out volunteer preachers, carrying their handwritten copies with them, to proclaim God's Word all over England. Such a revival of true Christian faith followed that, more than a century later, Sir Thomas More, a great enemy of the gospel, was grumbling about the fact that you could not meet two men on the road without discovering that one of them was a 'Wycliffe'!

Early in the sixteenth century, manuscripts of the Greek New Testament were brought to the West, and by 1522 Martin Luther had translated the New Testament into German. Four years later William Tyndale's English New Testament was circulating, and whilst many copies were eagerly bought and read by the people, others were burnt by the bishops.

The Protestant Reformation of the sixteenth century restored the Bible to its rightful position at the centre of the Christian life and the life of the church. Doctrine and practice were referred to the Bible and were reformed according to its teaching. The principle of the Reformation was *Sola Scriptura* — Scripture alone. This was the view of men like Martin Luther in Germany and John Calvin in Switzerland. Luther claimed, 'It is impossible that Scripture should contradict itself.' He believed the actual words and phrases came from God: 'Not only the words which the Holy Spirit and Scripture use are divine, but also the phrasing.' This view, Luther claimed, was the historic view of the Christian church held, for example, by the great church leader Augustine who lived from A.D. 354-430. Luther commented: 'St Augustine, in a letter to St Jerome, has put down a fine axiom [truth] — that only Holy Scripture is to be considered inerrant.' Consequently Luther himself allowed his conscience and life to be governed by the Bible: 'I am bound by the Scripture ... and my conscience has been taken captive by the Word of God.'

John Calvin spoke of Scripture in the same way: 'Moses and the prophets did not utter at random what we have from their hand, but, since they spoke by divine impulse, they confidently and fearlessly testified, as was actually the case, that it was the mouth of the Lord that spoke ... it has proceeded from him alone, and has nothing of man mixed with it.'

Neither of these men had to defend the Bible from the kind of attacks made against it in our day, but they were great Bible teachers, scholars and theologians, and they held a high view of the authority and inspiration of Scripture. In fact they, and the other Reformers with them, were not introducing some new idea into the life of the churches, but were restating exactly what the early church leaders had believed.

Tertullian, a bishop in Carthage in the second century, had insisted that the whole Bible is true and trustworthy and that we must believe and obey it all. At the same time Clement of Alexandria was teaching that in the Bible we hear the voice of God which is more reliable than anything else. Similarly, the great preacher at Antioch towards the end of the fourth century, John 'Chrysostom' (called this because of his preaching — his name means 'John the golden-mouth'), was constantly urging his congregation to get and read their own copies of the Scriptures. At the same time Augustine in North Africa described Scripture as 'the highest pinnacle of divine authority'. In fact, so certain were the early church leaders during the first four centuries that the Bible was the voice of God, that the danger they were most likely to fall into was ignoring the value of the human writers altogether.

The Reformers were therefore men with a long history behind them of trust in the authority of the Bible. The conviction that the Bible was wholly trustworthy in every part was not, as some would have us believe, the invention of Christians under siege during the eighteenth-century 'Age of Enlightenment' when all values were being challenged. We shall return to this subject in more detail in chapter 3.

In 1530 Sir Thomas More, Lord Chancellor to Henry VIII, arrested a Reformer, Thomas Hilton. More found letters on Hilton, 'written from evangelical brethren here unto evangelical brethren beyond the sea'. That was enough to condemn poor Hilton and he was burnt at the stake in Maidstone, Kent, in March of the same year. The word 'evangelical' had been used to refer to the Reformers in 1523 by the great Dutch scholar Desiderius Erasmus, and as early as 1519 he had complained, 'No word is heard of evangelical doctrine in the schools of theology.'

Although the word 'evangelical' is taken simply from the Greek word for 'good news', we have seen that by the early sixteenth century it distinguished those who spoke of Scripture as their only infallible guide, and who governed their life and beliefs by it. We must never allow that word to lose its meaning.

For two centuries following the Reformation, the position generally remained like this, and those who criticized the Bible or denied its authority were a small minority. Then, during the latter half of the eighteenth century and throughout the nineteenth century, four influences began to change the attitude of many towards the Bible.

Influences against the Bible

Discovery

Men were finding new frontiers in philosophy, science and geography. It was the age of discovery; man was coming of age.

Philosophy means 'the love of wisdom'. Men felt they were

growing up in wisdom and they wanted to free themselves from anything that limited their freedom. Two German philosophers, Immanuel Kant, who died in 1804, and Albrecht Ritschl, who died in 1889, doubted the supernatural and all statements of authority and certainty, insisting that experience is the only proper basis to judge anything; they were thoroughgoing sceptics — doubting everything. A third German philosopher-theologian, Friedrich Schleiermacher, published a book in 1821 with the innocent-sounding title, *The Christian Faith*. In it he stressed the importance of subjective feelings, over against authoritative statements, as the way of arriving at a knowledge of the truth. Doctrines and infallible statements had no place in these philosophies. Similarly, Soren Kierkegaard, a Danish philosopher born in 1813, taught that an individual's experience was what carries authority and meaning, and not external standards of belief or practice. These philosophies had a great influence on the way people began to view all authority. The Bible was under attack.

This attempt to be free from rules and authority went in company with a strong confidence in the ability of man to reason out things for himself. Although the Scottish philosopher David Hume had died as early as 1776, his thoroughgoing rationalism, which exalted man's reason above everything else, dispensed with the supernatural and therefore the miraculous. The nineteenth century was the age of invention and discovery. Steam power, electricity and the telegraph, for example, made men proud of their achievements. The Industrial Revolution would lead man to the golden age of prosperity. Everything, including God and his laws, could now be judged by man's intellect and reason. During this time atheistic humanism grew stronger, replacing God by man, who was quite capable, so it was thought, of working out his own future.

It was also the age of colonialism, and the European countries were fighting to extend their territory. In Britain it was the dawn of the golden era of Queen Victoria's empire, on which the sun never set. After the Battle of Waterloo in 1815 men felt that the 'thin red line' of the British regiments was unbeatable in the field, and even the disastrous Crimean war in the middle of the century did not shake this confidence in British supremacy. The philosophy was that man — especially the Englishman — could do anything and he did not need God to guide him. The Bible was the greatest enemy of this kind of thinking and therefore it had to be attacked.

History

The nineteenth century was also an age of renewed interest in the
past. Men wanted to know about the origins of everything and so,
'Libraries were ransacked for hidden documents and the earth itself
for the remnants of lost civilizations.' During the middle of the
century British and French archaeologists were working in Egypt.
In 1865 the Palestine Exploration Fund was set up, and in 1880 the
Egyptian Exploration Society commenced. The Middle East and
Asia were being ransacked for pottery, inscriptions and all the
rubbish left behind by long lost civilizations. Archaeology was
coming into its own as a science. Now we could find out the truth,
or otherwise, behind the Bible stories.

Many history books were written, such as *The History of Civilization in England,* published in 1858 by the historian Henry Buckle,
and in 1876 George Adam Smith published Assyrian and
Babylonian accounts of creation and a flood, and later a *Historical
Geography of the Holy Land.*

This is a very small sample of what was happening at this time,
but the effect of it all was to persuade men that the Bible was just
another ancient history book which was very interesting but could
be right or wrong. It was the task of the historian and archaeologist,
so it was thought, to discover where the Bible could be trusted and
where it could not.

Geology

In 1830 a Scottish lawyer turned geologist, Sir Charles Lyell,
published *Principles of Geology,* in which he claimed to have found
evidence that the earth was much older than the Bible seemed to
imply. In 1844 another book, this time anonymously written and
called *Vestiges of the Natural History of Creation,* denied biblical
creation and suggested a gradual development of the earth and
universe under divine guidance. Then in 1859 Charles Darwin
published his *Origin of the Species* in which he claimed that new
species developed by cross-fertilization and mutations and that this
was a natural but very slow process within nature taking place over
millions of years. Certain qualities, Darwin taught, are favourable
to survival, like strength, speed and colour, and animals lacking
these will die. By various changes, known as mutations, new
abilities are developed, such as wings, legs or lungs.

This process of 'natural selection' was the foundation of Darwin's theory of evolution. It was very popular and soon included the whole of man's existence. Morality and religion were said to have 'evolved' from that which is simple and primitive to that which is detailed and complex. The Bible was seen merely as a book reflecting man's growth from a primitive religion to a complex Christianity. In 1869 T. H. Huxley popularized Darwin's views and coined the word 'agnostic' to refer to those who believe that there is no evidence for the existence of God. The word simply means 'without knowledge'.

The result of all this was that scholars, and sadly many ordinary Christians also, began to think that the plain statements of Scripture could no longer be trusted. The philosophers told men to test everything by reason and to avoid authoritative statements. The historians and archaeologists claimed to have discovered sufficient information about ancient civilizations, and the way in which stories were passed down from one generation to another, to be able to question the accuracy of the Bible. At the same time, the scientists were certain that they knew how the world began, which, they said, was not at all like the biblical account. The Bible should now be read just like any other book: in parts it is good and accurate; in parts it is not. By the end of the nineteenth century there were apparently enough scholars to tell us which parts were which. At this point the fourth and most dangerous influence came onto the scene.

Theology

In Germany, at the University of Tübingen, a school of theologians had already begun to read the Gospels and Acts, not as historical accounts of what actually happened, but as what they called 'the product of communal imagination', which roughly means 'how the early Christians would like it to have happened'. Two university professors, Baur and Strauss, used the word 'myth' to refer to the gospel stories. (Strauss later renounced Christianity altogether.) They admitted that Christ was historically real, but claimed that all the stories were made up to illustrate the way the early Christians thought about him. The task of the scholar was to strip away this myth to find out the real truth at the centre. This was called 'demythologizing', a term later used by the Bible critic Rudolf Bultmann; it was like peeling off the outer layers of an onion in order to discover the truth at the heart of the story.

We need to understand that the word 'myth', for theologians then and now, does not mean lies or fairy tales, but serious stories made up to illustrate spiritual truths. Those who say that the Bible contains myth are not suggesting that the early writers set out to deceive us, since, in the view of these theologians, they never intended their history to be taken as literally true; they were merely presenting spiritual truths in a picture form. Apparently they thought we all knew this! Of course, only the scholars were capable of stripping off these myths for us, and ordinary Christians were expected to wait until the professors of Tübingen in Germany or Oxford in England told them what they could believe! To a greater or lesser extent this was the critical approach to the New Testament: the supernatural and miracles were abandoned and most of the New Testament writers were robbed of the books they claimed to have written.

Julius Wellhausen was the Old Testament counterpart of Baur. In 1878 he published his *History of Israel,* which is still the basic textbook of what is known as 'higher criticism' (see pages 16-17). Wellhausen believed that the first five books of the Bible, known as the Pentateuch, were written by several different authors and, at a very late date, were put together by one or more editors. David was robbed of most of the psalms, at least two different men wrote Isaiah, and all Old Testament prophecy was assumed to have been written as late as possible to avoid the embarrassment to the unbelieving critic of fulfilled prophecy.

Wellhausen was followed by Samuel Davidson and many others in England. As with the New Testament, these scholars assured the public that the Bible, though interesting and valuable, was nothing more than another ancient book, full of contradictions and errors.

Evangelical reaction

Since these influences which brought pressure upon those who trusted the Bible in the nineteenth century, the storm has not slackened. In fact, the opponents of Bible inerrancy have become more bold and vigorous in their sustained onslaught against the trustworthiness of Scripture. We can identify four responses by evangelical Christians to bring us to the present day.

Hesitation in the late nineteenth century

By the 1880s it was claimed, 'No periodical is complete without an article in which Christianity is defended or attacked.' Many Christians refused to look carefully at the statements and they simply accepted the conclusions of the Higher Critics. But others, like Alfred Cave in England, tried to begin with the principles of the Higher Critics and argue back to an evangelical position. This proved impossible, however, because you cannot put up a strong building on poor foundations. With some notable exceptions, evangelicals were timid and lacked the intellectual vigour to combat the academics in Tübingen and Oxford. Preaching lost its importance in the churches and consequently spiritual life and church attendance began to decline. The High Church movement erected impressive church buildings in a vain attempt to win back the disillusioned, and tragically many evangelicals lost their belief in the Bible as a book without error, or they retreated into a stubborn resistance without knowing how to answer their critics.

Very few realized what was happening until it was too late. Among those who did see the danger was Charles Haddon Spurgeon, England's greatest preacher of the nineteenth century, whose regular Sunday evening congregation in London numbered around 6,000 people. Spurgeon refused to accept either the principles upon which the critics worked or the conclusions to which they came, and he urgently warned evangelicals to hold fast to their belief in the inerrancy of Scripture; he was certain that time would prove many of the principles and conclusions of the critics to be wrong. In this Spurgeon was right, but few leaders listened to him. Seeing the downgrading of Scripture within the Baptist denomination, Spurgeon resigned from the Baptist Union in 1887.

Capitulation in the early twentieth century

At first evangelicals had few scholars to defend the inerrancy of the Bible and those who did were largely ignored. By 1909 a series of articles was being published in North America under the title *The Fundamentals*. These defended the true evangelical view of Scripture and the term 'fundamentalist' was first used. In America men like Benjamin Warfield and Gresham Machen were defending

Charles Haddon Spurgeon

biblical inerrancy, and in 1929 some of them left Princeton University to found Westminster Theological Seminary as a protest against the American downgrade. In England the influence of a new philosophy hastened the slide into a lack of confidence in the Bible. 'Logical Positivism', taught by men like Wittgenstein, Schlick and A. J. Ayer, in his book *Language, Truth and Logic*, published in 1936, asserted that unless you can prove a statement true or false, it is meaningless. Since many of the great claims of the Bible concerning God and salvation are unprovable in scientific terms, much of the Christian faith was considered to be nonsense.

Gradually almost all the major denominations slipped into the fashion of denying full authority to the Bible. Church attendance slid even further and there was very little literature from an evangelical standpoint to stem the tide of unbelief. One man, among others, who was aware of this twentieth-century downgrade in Britain was E. J. Poole-Connor. As a pastor, mission leader and theologian, he had a firm grasp of what was happening in the evangelical world. In

1933 he published a little book under the title *The Apostasy of English Non-Conformity* in which he exposed the denominational leaders who had capitulated to critical views of the Bible.

In 1925 Dr Reaveley Glover, the incoming president of the Baptist Union, had reflected on Spurgeon at the time of his leaving the union and concluded: 'Gout, conscience and Satan make queer alliances in us all.' He further rejoiced in modernism, the name for the critical attitude to the Bible, as a glorious 'holding open of the door for new conceptions of truth', and claimed that the idea that the whole Bible was inspired by God was a 'monstrous belief'. Dr Glover also denied the atonement of Christ and justification by faith as understood by the Reformers.

Dr Arthur Samuel Peake, president of the Free Church Council in 1929 and a Primitive Methodist, published a Bible commentary which was a thorough surrender to modernism. Dr Fairbairn, a leading Congregational scholar, followed the same road.

By the end of the first quarter of the century not one free church denominational theological college in England was free from critical views of the Bible. Yet evangelicals still often failed to appreciate what was happening; Dr Fullerton, a conservative evangelical, spoke of Reaveley Glover as a 'prophet whom God has sent us'.

Aspiration in the mid-twentieth century

From the end of the Second World War there was a new evangelical intellectual vigour. Through the influence of Dr Martyn Lloyd-Jones' preaching at Westminster Chapel in London, some evangelicals took heart and fought back. The Inter-Varsity Fellowship (now the Universities and Colleges Christian Fellowship) and its associated publishing company Inter-Varsity Press captured the minds of many Christian students; the Banner of Truth Trust reprinted long-forgotten Puritan books; the London Bible College set out to train ministers and missionaries, and the research study centres at Tyndale House and Rutherford House provided opportunities for evangelical research. All this appeared to promise a new and bright future for evangelicalism. Each of them stood firmly for a Bible without error.

Evangelicals set out to take the ground away from critical scholars and redeem it for a high view of the authority of the Bible. Gradually throughout the 1960s and '70s evangelicals found places within the theological and biblical departments of national universities; they were to be found in all the disciplines, including archaeology. These were men of high intellectual ability and the motive was good: to meet modernism on its own ground — and to win.

Across the Atlantic, a similar attempt was being made to meet the challenge of the critics as evangelicals emerged from their 'fortress of faith' from the mid-1930s onwards. Graduates from Harvard entered the world of respectable academics, aided by the organization of the Institute for Biblical Research, and by publishing companies like Eerdmans with its Bible commentary series.

Flirtation towards the year 2000

Some years ago J. B. Phillips, whose paraphrase of the New Testament in English was read by millions, wrote a book entitled *Ring of Truth*. In it he claimed, 'I should like to make it quite clear that I could not possibly hold the extreme "fundamentalist" position of so-called "verbal inspiration"... There still survives a minority who passionately believe in verbal inspiration... Any man who has sense as well as faith is bound to conclude that it is the truths which are inspired and not the words which are merely the vehicles of truth' (p.15). Yet many evangelicals considered this to be an excellent book and Christian bookshops made great displays of it. J. B. Phillips is, of course, entitled to his opinion and to publish it, but it is completely opposed to the evangelical doctrine of the inerrancy of Scripture.

Similarly, evangelicals read and recommend the Bible commentaries by William Barclay who, though frequently expressing a high regard for the Bible as the Word of God, had no commitment to inerrancy, and was free to deny the recorded miracles, downgrade Paul's authority and doubt much of the Old Testament history. Pious erosion is very dangerous. Today many evangelical books are denying evangelical doctrine by accepting liberal views.

The philosophy of Logical Positivism was replaced by that of Linguistic Analysis which encourages us to believe that all statements are open to new interpretations. Modernism, now referred to as 'liberalism', did not feel threatened by the new breed of evangelicals, but welcomed their rich perspectives to add to the ongoing debate about the Bible. Perhaps without realizing it, but certainly to gain credibility with the academic world, evangelical scholars began to flirt with modernism.

The first to notice this shift were the liberal scholars themselves! James Barr, a Scots theologian, and John Robinson, a respected New Testament scholar whose book *Honest to God* was a best-selling theological disaster in the 1960s, rejoiced at the new 'openness' to critical approaches amongst evangelicals. Robinson commented how glad he was to see among evangelicals 'an open and not merely half-hearted acceptance of critical scholarly disciplines as entirely compatible with the authority of Scripture'. For this reason Robinson described one important evangelical publication as 'a breakthrough'.

In their flirtation with liberalism, many evangelicals began subtle shifts of terminology. They talked about the Bible as 'infallible' but not 'inerrant'. Infallibility, they said, refers to the truth of Scripture statements, whilst inerrancy refers to its facts and history. There may be inaccuracies in the second, but never in the first. However, this is a false distinction. The two words should never be opposed like this. Of the two, infallible is the stronger word but only because it contains inerrancy within it. Something can be inerrant without being infallible, but nothing can be infallible without being inerrant. Occasionally a newspaper report is accurate to the point of being without error, but no one would claim that the article was infallible! Besides, the *Oxford Dictionary* definition of the word 'infallible' begins: 'Incapable of erring'!

Others committed themselves to the position that, even if 'minor discrepancies' were to be found in Scripture, this would in no way upset their confidence in the Bible as the Word of God. They could write of 'a basic historical core' in the Bible, and the fact that the historical accuracy of certain narratives 'should perhaps be held with certain reservations' (Kenneth Kitchen, *The Bible in its World*). Bruce Chiltern, an evangelical New Testament scholar writing in *Themelios* in April 1970, asserted that 'None of the documents which make up the New Testament would pass as history in the modern sense.'

Professor Bernard Ramm scored an unintentional 'own goal' by writing of the humanity of Scripture in this way: 'We must also have a doctrine of the Scriptures which is of the same heartbeat as the theology of the cross... God's written word ... shares the brokenness, the servanthood, the masking of the divine glory as the incarnate son...' Thus, he concluded, the Bible has the stamp of man and his fallibility upon it. Our professor seems to have forgotten that Christ was both perfectly God and perfectly man and as such was without error or sin!

In a similar fashion, two American theologians, Professors Rogers and McKim, maintain that in the Bible God accommodated himself to human limitations of understanding when he spoke to us in human language. He never expected us to look to the Bible for accurate detail in historical and scientific statements, but to discover salvation truth in Jesus Christ. Rogers and McKim conclude that the writers of the Bible were not interested in detailed accuracy, and the 'small errors' that trouble evangelicals today did not in the slightest bother them; they were not intentionally, or even knowingly, inaccurate, but because of their human weakness they inevitably made mistakes in recording events. The argument concludes that Christ and his salvation message is the authority of the Bible, not its accurate words.

A close bedfellow of this is the view that some miracles are to be understood as the misunderstanding of pre-scientific man. James Dunn and Graham Twelftree from Nottingham, writing in the *Churchman* in 1980, conclude: 'Some of the cases of demon possession in the Gospels can be demythologized at least to some extent. In particular Mark 9:14-26 is probably a good example of pre-scientific man attributing to demon possession a malady whose physical mechanism we have since learnt to identify and largely control', by which they meant epilepsy. By way of concession they add, 'though not wanting to eliminate the spiritual dimension of this or any illness'.

Some have written about the 'doctrine of intention', suggesting that perhaps the Gospel writers did not intend us to take all that they wrote as historically accurate. Or, as James Dunn expressed it in the *Churchman* in 1982 during a vigorous attack upon the views of Benjamin Warfield, 'What if it never was the fourth evangelist's intention that the extended discourses of the fourth gospel should be understood as uttered by Jesus during his ministry on earth?' It is not sufficient to say, as one evangelical leader did when under pressure in an interview, 'The Bible is true in the sense in which its authors intended it to be understood as true.' From one point of view this is correct, but it is not very helpful unless explained. After all, according to 1 Peter 1:10-12, some of the Old Testament prophets did not know what they intended!

Arguments of this kind certainly please the liberal critics of the Bible. It is what they have been saying for years!

Flirting is often very subtle, and so are these shifts in evangelical emphasis. To speak of the Bible, as some do, as trustworthy and reliable 'in those matters which it prescribes as all-important', or 'infallible in all that it affirms', leaves open a wide door of interpretation in what actually is 'all-important' and what the Bible 'affirms' and what it does not. This led the evangelical theologian Francis Schaeffer to refer to the Bible as 'true truth', to make it clear that what the Bible said was all to be taken as reliable. Perhaps without realizing it, evangelicals are accommodating to the language of liberalism. When Bruce Chiltern, writing in *Themelios* in 1978, suggested that 'The gospels are historically grounded considerations of the significance of Jesus in the mind of faith,' he was using language that many modern critics would have been proud to have thought of first!

Today's liberalism does not ridicule the Bible: it speaks of revelation, inspiration, the Word of God, the authority and truth of the Bible and even occasionally uses the word 'infallibility'. This is extremely dangerous because many evangelicals do not realize that this language, as used by critics of Bible inerrancy, is only twentieth-century flesh over nineteenth-century bones.

Many evangelicals have failed to distinguish between scientific facts and theories. Evolution, for example, is a theory that no scientist can prove. But some evangelicals feel compelled to accept that Genesis chapters 1 to 3 are not statements of fact but are merely poetic. They forget the sound principles of interpreting the Bible that we shall look at in a later chapter, and overlook Paul's theological arguments, in Romans 5 for example, based upon the view that the Fall actually happened as the Bible says it did. We have no need to change the long-accepted view that Genesis 1 is history, simply because some scientists hold a theory that contradicts it.

It is a sad thing to read of evangelicals referring to the Bible as the 'nearest' to a final authority that men can find, and to be told by them that whether or not the story of Jonah and the fish is historical fact is unimportant, for it is the 'divine authoritativeness' of the message that really matters. This is exactly the reasoning of many liberal critics of the Bible; they are willing to accept the truth of the Bible but not its accuracy. Karl Barth was a Swiss theologian-pastor who taught just this. Barth exercised a great influence during the first half of this century and denied that the Bible is the Word of God, but he taught that it becomes God's word to a man when it speaks to him. Barth had no interest in discussing whether or not the Bible was without error. He was sure it wasn't, but he believed its authority did not depend upon its factual trustworthiness.

To give natural explanations for biblical miracles, or even to allow the possibility of errors in the Bible, is to begin on the critical road. Some evangelicals have gone so far towards accepting critical views that they are referred to as 'neo' or 'new' evangelicals. Perhaps it is only a new wave of liberalism but the concept of 'liberal evangelicals' is a contradiction in terms. Writing in the *Christian Graduate* in 1980, Oliver Barclay commented wisely, 'You cannot sit both wholeheartedly under the authority of God and his Word and also allow that it can be rejected when its teaching seems unacceptable to the modern mind or to the current fashion in scholarship.'

Criticism, criticism and more criticism

It may be helpful to define some terms here. Some of them will be needed later on, and others you may never hear about again! They are included here simply to illustrate how vast is the world of Bible criticism, and to acquaint those who wish to be 'in the know' with some of the current issues discussed among Bible scholars. Not all of these approaches are bad — indeed some of them are indispensable to our understanding of Scripture; but all of them can become destructive if used without due care and attention.

Textual Criticism

Textual Criticism, or 'Lower Criticism', is the study of the texts of the manuscripts and documents of the Bible to discover the best and most accurate text to translate. We shall look again at this in chapter 12 because it is an important subject in our study of Bible authority.

Literary Criticism

Literary Criticism, or 'Higher Criticism' as it is more commonly called, builds on the results of Textual Criticism (thus it is 'higher') and is the study of the way the Bible stories have been put together and how reliable the claims and stories really are. It is concerned with the structure, date and authorship of the books of the Bible, and the literary style (whether it is history, poetry and so on). Higher Criticism is a phrase that was first used by the German scholar J. G. Eichhorn in the preface to his second edition of *Old Testament Studies* in 1787. Eichhorn rejected the reliability of the Old Testament. Even before Eichhorn, in 1753 Astruc suggested the idea that Genesis was compiled from two sources, one using the name Jehovah for God and the other using the name Elohim. This view was taken up and expanded by Wellhausen. The term 'Higher Criticism' does not necessarily imply a liberal criticism of the Bible, but since in practice it almost always has done, the term is commonly used to refer to those who deny the trustworthiness of Scripture. Some of the following 'criticisms' can be seen as subdivisions of Literary Criticism.

Source Criticism

Source Criticism is the study of the material that supposedly lies behind the Bible stories. It asks where the writers obtained their material, how much of it is original and how much is 'borrowed' from other sources. The discussion about which of our four Gospels was written first, who borrowed what from whom, and whether there is a mysterious source known as 'Q', is all part of Source Criticism. There is a value in Source Criticism, but its danger has been in the readiness of critics to assume that the Bible writers merely copied ideas from other religions and cultures: Moses 'cribbed' his laws from the Hammurabi Codes, the Jews 'borrowed' their ceremonies from surrounding nations, the prophets 'stole' their visions from contemporary culture, and so on. This denies the unique authority of God's revelation in the Bible. One of the earliest 'hunting grounds' of the Source Critics was the first five books of the Bible. The critics believed these books were compiled by a mixed multitude of sources known as J, E, P and D, depending on whether a passage contained the divine name 'Jahweh' (J), the normal word 'Elohim' for God (E), or whether it contained priestly information about sacrifice and ceremonies (P) or the laws of Deuteronomy (D). Inevitably the critics rarely agreed with each other.

Form Criticism

Form Criticism builds on all this and asks why the stories are in the form they are, and in what form they were passed on before being committed to writing. The Form Critic wants to know what the original story was before all the bits and pieces of the story-tellers' imagination or bias was added. For example, liberal Form Critics assume that the Gospels were written in the second century and then try to discover, in the form of the writings, whether we can identify the actual words Jesus may have uttered. One of the tests the Form Critics use is that of 'dissimilarity'; this assumes that if a statement in the Gospels is unlike anything we expect of the second-century church, and unlike anything the Jews taught, and so on, then it might be the actual words of Jesus!

Rudolf Bultmann, a professor at the University of Marburg in Germany before his death in 1976, used Form Criticism in a devastating way in the New Testament. Bultmann was an 'expert' in demythologizing, and assumed that all we have in the Gospels is the Jesus of the wishful imagination of the second or third-century church as stories were passed from generation to generation. In his book *Jesus and the Word* Bultmann concluded: 'We can know almost nothing about the life and personality of Jesus.' But never mind, he continued, what matters is the Christ of faith, not the Jesus of history!

Redaction Criticism

Redactor is another word for editor. The discussion is about how the Gospel writers, for example, adapted their material to suit their theme. In one sense we all use Redaction Criticism when we come to understand the Gospels. For example, Matthew and Luke differ from each other in the precise order of the last two temptations of Christ; our usual answer is that since neither claims to present an exact order, each is free to close with the temptation best suited to his theme — Matthew presenting Christ as king, and Luke presenting him as man. However, a more liberal approach to Redaction Criticism assumes that the editors have changed historical facts to fit in with their theological purpose.

Historical Criticism

There are two parts to Historical Criticism. The first is the need to understand the Bible in its original historical context. In other words, we need to appreciate the culture and customs of the age in which the Bible writer lived. So far so good. We all accept the need for this. However, there is a further step that is taken by Bible critics.

It is frequently assumed among some scholars today that in recording history the ancients paid little attention to accuracy of facts. As one evangelical writer has expressed it, 'None of the documents which make up the New Testament would pass as history in the modern sense. Edward Gibbon and Leopold von Ranke were not about at the time to write it.' We may therefore discover where the biblical writers played with historical accuracy to fit their purpose; you can see that this is a main argument for Redaction Criticism.

However, this widespread assumption cannot be accepted. In the first place the two modern historians mentioned are both biased in their presentation of history and are hardly models for unprejudiced and wholly reliable reporting. Secondly, there were some first-rate historians in the ancient world who placed a high premium on accuracy. Among Greek writers, Herodotus, who lived about the same time as Ezra and Nehemiah, allowed some freedom in reporting speeches, but not in narratives. In the second century A.D. Lucian of Samosata demanded that 'History cannot admit a lie, even a tiny one... The historian's sole task is to tell the tale as it happened.' He referred to Thucydides in the fifth century B.C. as one who gives us the model. Thucydides was not always able to give the speeches he heard word for word, but he did claim to adhere 'as closely as possible to the general sense of what was actually spoken'.

We shall see later in this book that the New Testament writers laid particular claim to careful accuracy, and the early church was insistent that only those with apostolic authority could be trusted to give us the Scriptures. Besides, we shall see also what the Bible teaches us about its own inspiration.

Canonical Criticism

Canonical Criticism is interested not so much in the material that goes to make up the contents of the books of the Bible (that is the job of Source and Form Criticism), but it looks at the reasons why the completed books were accepted as authoritative in the life of the Old Testament or New Testament church and the effect this had upon the community. It looks at how the community shaped what was accepted, or why it rejected it. The word 'canon' means a rule or standard, and we shall return to the subject of the 'canon' of Scripture in chapters 10 and 11, but our use of the word there will not include Canonical Criticism.

The New Hermeneutic

The word 'hermeneutic' refers to our way of interpreting Scripture. Again, this is a very important study, and in chapter 14 we shall look at how we should understand the Bible; that is the study of hermeneutics. However, the New Hermeneutic (notice the word is used in the singular) is different. It is especially concerned with the way the Bible 'speaks' to a modern reader. The New Hermeneutic sees every application of the text of the Bible as an event to be experienced by the modern reader or listener. The foundation of Historical Criticism, understanding the world of the Bible, is helpful, but that may leave us with a dry and sterile book that merely relates things about history. We must somehow make every act of interpreting Scripture a living experience.

So far so good! But the New Hermeneutic critics assume that for the dynamic relationship between the text and the interpreter to be meaningful, there may be many meanings of the text, each different according to the identity and situation of those interpreting it. We therefore cannot expect to find just one universal meaning for a passage of Scripture. The effect of this is that ultimately we can make the Bible say anything that appeals to us and there is no final and correct understanding of any text. According to the New Hermeneutic we are not looking for the meaning of the words or statements in the Bible so much as for their effect upon us. That is a far cry from an evangelical view of Scripture because it confuses the clear voice of the authority of God that we find in his Word. Truth is not what I make it, but what God said.

Contextualization

For all its length, the word sums up a very simple issue facing the church today and we can summarize it like this: how do we convey what God has said in his Word, by men who lived in an ancient cultural context, to those who live in a very different one, through translators or preachers who live in a culture that is different from the other two? There are therefore three cultures involved! Making a faithful and meaningful 'tri-cultural' communication of biblical truth is an issue of great importance today.

The danger is to avoid the hard work that is needed to communicate the Word of God faithfully to another culture and to allow that culture to dictate how we understand the Bible. This has led to a number of distortions: for example, a 'prosperity gospel', which makes the Word of God say what a capitalist society wants it to say, or a 'black theology', which takes the Bible as a charter for positive discrimination, and the 'theology of liberation' which forces the Bible to give support to active terrorism simply because the oppression and corruption in a particular culture seem to call for this. We are all in danger of making the Bible say what our culture wants it to say, and that is an abuse of contextualization.

Where do we go from here?

This brings me to explain the purpose and plan of this book. The purpose is to restate the true evangelical doctrine of Scripture with particular reference to biblical inerrancy. This will be done, not to defend evangelicalism, but to make clear what the Scripture says about itself. The first thing that is essential when anyone begins to read the Bible is to know what it claims for itself. We must start there. From this point each of us must decide whether or not we will trust and obey it as God's Word, but we must be in no doubt what the Bible says about itself. This will be our concern in the first part of this book.

However, the doctrine of Bible inerrancy raises problems, and these must be faced honestly. For this reason the scope of this book covers such subjects as, 'Just how accurate is the Bible?' 'Who decided how many books there should be in the Bible?' 'How our Bible was written and passed down through the centuries,' and 'How we should interpret the Bible'. Two chapters provide reasonable answers to many of the supposed errors and contradictions of the Bible.

The purpose of this book must be clearly understood. It is not a technical handbook for the minister or advanced student of

Scripture. What is needed today is a book that covers the whole subject of the evangelical view of Scripture written with the ordinary Christian in mind. To this end I have tried to make understandable even the more difficult subject of textual criticism!

Evangelical Christians in our churches are frequently overawed by supposed scholarship—a process that even the liberal critic John Robinson admitted was 'the tyranny of untested assumptions'. We are told that scholars say this and scientists say that, and the ordinary Christian is given the impression that only great minds can really understand the issues that lie behind criticisms against the Bible. The purpose of this book is to open the door of that world to any Christian and to encourage him or her not to be intimidated by 'scholarship'. In recent years Dr Robert Funk in America made the incredible claim: 'New Testament scholars have established beyond any reasonable doubt that the Jesus of the early Christian documents is to some extent a figment of the Christian imagination.' Dr Funk should be warned: a century ago the German scholar Julius Wellhausen wrote confidently about 'the assured results of scientific criticism' to support conclusions that have long since been thrown into the waste-bin of scientific rubbish!

Technical words and phrases are only used where they are essential or where they will certainly be met in any further reading on this subject and they are always explained. Today the scholar's delight is to intimidate the reader by academic language. He uses words and sentences that need to be read many times before they can be understood. So he will write of the 'conceptual inappropriateness of the disjunctions', when he really means, 'I don't think his distinctions fit.' Or he may speak of 'Dominican kingdom logia', when all he means is 'Jesus' teaching about the kingdom'. Or again, 'The insufflation is missiologically orientated' probably just means, 'The direction of thought is geared towards missions'!

All this is a kind of academic defence, and it may even be dishonest, for if few can understand then few can criticize. In this book I have tried to use simple language and the words employed are intended to have their plain and obvious meaning. Similarly, to avoid the appearance of a 'heavy' theological textbook, quotations from other publications have been kept to a minimum. There are no footnotes; everything is in the text! For those who want an in-depth study of particular subjects, there are better books than this one!

Without doubt, the loss of faith in the complete trustworthiness of Scripture has robbed many ministers of their Bible, many churches of Christians and many Christians of a living and powerful faith in Christ. This much is admitted even by some of those most critical of the evangelical faith. Throughout the world it is a fact that the living, growing Christian church is the evangelical section committed to the inerrancy of Scripture. But even that is in danger, and it is the prayer of both publisher and author that this book may help to call Christians to stand for 'the faith that was once entrusted to the saints', and to give them good reasons for standing there.

2.
How God makes himself known

'If God has something to say to man, then let him say it.' This seems to be a fair comment and we would expect that the God who made everything would have a pattern and plan for the way his creation should work. Anything that is made by men, whether it is a bicycle, a transistor radio, or a jet plane, comes with a set of instructions. We call these 'the maker's instructions', and if they are not obeyed then the machine will not work properly. If we choose to ignore the maker's instructions, then we cannot blame the maker when the machine breaks down. If there is a God who made everything, it is reasonable to expect that he knows best how everything should work; and if he does know best and wants us to gain the best, then it is also reasonable to expect that he will give us his instructions.

Man's spiritual blindness

We might think that man would know how he should live and what he should do to please God. After all, the birds know how to migrate and animals know how to look after their young, and nobody gives them a set of instructions. But man is different. Something has happened to his knowledge of God and of right and wrong.

In Genesis 3 the Bible tells us how man first disobeyed the Maker's instructions and allowed sin to spoil everything. At first Adam and Eve lived in perfect fellowship with God and complete obedience to his will. There seemed nothing, in all creation, to spoil that relationship. Then Adam and Eve disobeyed God's first command and they fell into sin (see Genesis 2:17; 3:1-7). The immediate result of this Fall was that man broke fellowship with God: 'The man and his wife ... hid from the Lord God among the trees of the garden' (3:8). Adam and Eve wanted to avoid God and what he had to say to them. The second result of the Fall was that God took away their privileges in the Garden of Eden: 'He drove the man out' (3:24).

Because of that first sin, it is as though a curtain was drawn across man's mind, and all generations from Adam have been ignorant of God and his plans. As a black storm cloud hides the clear brightness of the sun, so sin caused man to lose sight of God, and he has lost his way in life also. The Bible calls it a spiritual blindness: 'The god of this age has blinded the minds of unbelievers, so that they cannot see the light of the gospel of the glory of Christ' (2 Corinthians 4:4).

'… so sin caused man to lose sight of God'

Man's natural condition, apart from Christ, is seen also as spiritual darkness. The Christian has been 'rescued from the dominion of darkness' (Colossians 1:13) and 'called out of darkness into his wonderful light' (1 Peter 2:9). Since man's mind, heart and will have all been spoiled by sin, he manages to spoil almost everything good that God gives him. The clearest picture of the condition of our present world is found in Romans 1:18-32, which begins like this: 'The wrath of God is being revealed from heaven against all the godlessness and wickedness of men who suppress the truth by their wickedness, since what may be known about God is plain to them, because God has made it plain to them. For since the creation of the world God's invisible qualities — his eternal power and divine nature — have been clearly seen, being understood from what has been made, so that men are without excuse.' That is the result of ignoring the Maker's instructions.

Because man is spiritually blind and in a darkness of ignorance and disobedience, if he is to know anything about God then it must be God who takes the first step. God must draw back that curtain. He must remove the thick cloud. He must reveal himself and his will to man.

What is revelation?

The word 'revelation' comes from a Latin word, *revelatio,* which means 'to make something known that is hidden'. We reveal what is unknown when we tell a neighbour that we have discovered a good bargain in the market and we encourage him to go and find it too, or when the teacher instructs his students in an area of knowledge completely unknown to them before. We draw back the curtain; we uncover that which is hidden. Most important of all is the fact that when we talk of God's revelation we mean God reveals *himself* to man. It is not so much God revealing how he acts, or what he thinks; still less is it just a matter of God telling us what he wants or how men in the past have lived. All this is important, but most important of all, revelation is God showing us who he is. He shows us that he is the eternal God who created all things, the one who is holy and hates sin and yet will have mercy upon sinners. Therefore the Bible is first and foremost a book about God. We must never forget this.

The purpose of God revealing himself to man is to restore man to true fellowship with himself. Revelation is God reaching into man's darkness and drawing back the curtain to show us the truth about himself in order that we might come to love, worship and obey him. Revelation must therefore be true and reliable, or else it is meaningless.

God's general revelation to everyone

There is a general revelation, sometimes called 'natural revelation', which is there for all men to see. Not all will see it, but none will have any excuse for ignoring it, because God has made it plain. General revelation comes to us in at least three ways.

Revelation in nature

In the Old Testament we read of David, who spent much of his time as an outlaw. He lived in the desert and was constantly trying to escape the army of King Saul. David often walked out into the hills alone and looked up into the sky. There, in the sun, moon and stars, he could see the work of a great God:

'The heavens declare the glory of God;
  the skies proclaim the work of his hands.
Day after day they pour forth speech;
  night after night they display knowledge.
There is no speech or language
  where their voice is not heard.
Their voice goes out into all the earth,
  their words to the ends of the world'

(Psalm 19:1-4).

The whole of creation has a voice that 'speaks' about God and presents a picture that describes him and, according to the psalmist, the whole world can hear this voice and see this picture. No one is excused for not listening and looking and then worshipping.
This revelation in nature speaks about man also:

'When I consider your heavens,
  the work of your fingers,
the moon and the stars,
  which you have set in place,
what is man that you are mindful of him,
  the son of man that you care for him?'

(Psalm 8:3-4).

The witness of God's marvellous creation is there for anyone and everyone to see. The stars that we can see in the clear night sky, and the many more that lie beyond our sight, are called a galaxy. It is estimated that there are one hundred billion stars in our galaxy and that there are one hundred million galaxies in the whole of known space. Some modern scientists go further and tell us that known space is one billionth part of what is possibly all space. With the naked eye you can see about 4,500 stars on a clear night. A small telescope will reveal almost two million, whereas a radio telescope

The Milky Way
(Reproduced by courtesy of the Science Museum)

will show us thousands of millions. It is estimated that there are thirty thousand million stars in the Milky Way alone — that great splash of tiny stars closely packed together in the night sky.

All of this should tell us something about the greatness and majesty of the God who made it all. We should agree with the prophet who wrote, 700 years before the coming of Christ,

> 'Who has measured the waters in the hollow of his hand,
>   or with the breadth of his hand marked off the heavens?
> Who has held the dust of the earth in a basket,
>   or weighed the mountains on the scales
>   and the hills in a balance?'
>
> (Isaiah 40:12).

Creation certainly tells us something about the greatness and power of God!

No generation, no tribe, no nation has ever been left without a revelation of God. Speaking at Lystra 1900 years ago, Paul could preach about 'the living God, who made heaven and earth and sea and everything in them ... he has not left himself without testimony' (Acts 14:15-17). Paul presents the same truth when writing to the Christians at Rome. In Romans 1:19-21 the apostle claims that 'What may be known about God is plain to them, because God has made it plain to them. For since the creation of the world God's invisible qualities — his eternal power and divine nature — have been clearly seen, being understood from what has been made, so that men are without excuse.' However miserable their condition, or however hard their lot, Paul says everyone is without excuse.

However, in spite of this clear revelation by God of himself through nature, man's spiritual blindness is so great that he will never find God by this means. It is not the revelation that is at fault, but man's mind and heart (Romans 1: 21-32).

Revelation in man's heart

Wherever we find people, we find them worshipping and believing in life after death. They may worship evil spirits, idols, or even their ancestors, and they may fear death or some may look forward to it gladly. But they are worshipping; they do believe in a god or gods, or something. Until the collapse of the Soviet Union, communism

spent vast sums of money trying to educate their people not to
believe in God. In his heart man believes there is something,
somewhere, bigger and more powerful than himself, and he feels
that he must worship. Why is this? Animals do not pray, nor do they
fear death. Why is man different?

'Man ... feels that he must worship'

King Solomon once tried hard not to believe in God. He tried to
shake off religion like a dog shaking off the water from its hair. But
Solomon discovered that he could never get God and a belief in
eternity out of his mind. The dog may shake himself dry, but the river
is still there. Solomon was wise enough to know the reason for all
this: '[God] has set eternity in the hearts of men' (Ecclesiastes 3:11).
Man is made to worship God, but sin has so spoiled his mind and soul
that instead of worshipping the Creator, he worships the creature; he
exchanges the glory of God for an image of creation (Romans 1:23).
Once again, it is not the revelation that is at fault, but man's heart and
mind.

In the same way, everywhere that we find people, we find them with a knowledge of right and wrong. Some things are generally held to be wrong all over the world, like murder and stealing. This is not always true because sin has so spoiled man's conscience (1 Timothy 4:2) that he sometimes learns to call good evil and evil good, but there are still generally accepted standards of right and wrong, good and evil. Although man does not keep to what his conscience tells him, he is at least aware that he is doing wrong. Once again Paul put this very clearly in Romans 2:14-15: 'When Gentiles, who do not have the law, do by nature things required by the law, they are a law for themselves, even though they do not have the law, since they show that the requirements of the law are written on their hearts, their consciences also bearing witness, and their thoughts now accusing, now even defending them.' This knowledge of right and wrong is also part of God's revelation, but because of sin it is unreliable. Yet, once more, it is not the revelation that is at fault, but man's heart and mind.

Revelation in providence and history

The history of man can only be understood properly in the light of God and his purpose for the church. In the Old Testament the Lord revealed himself as the God of Israel, and the Jews came to know him as the 'God who brought you out' from Egypt (Exodus 6:7). The history of the Exodus was a revelation of God.

In Acts 17:26 Paul declared to the men of Athens that both history and geography belong to God: 'From one man he made every nation of men, that they should inhabit the whole earth; and he determined the times set for them [history] and the exact places where they should live [geography].' Immediately Paul went on to give the reason: 'God did this so that men would seek him and perhaps reach out for him and find him' (v. 27). God's purpose in revealing himself in the providence of history is to lead men to himself.

Similarly, just as our Lord pointed to the kindness of God in allowing both the evil and the good, the righteous and the unrighteous, to enjoy his sun and rain (Matthew 5:45), so Paul reminded the citizens of Lystra: 'He has not left himself without testimony: He has shown kindness by giving you rain from heaven and crops in their seasons; he provides you with plenty of food and fills your hearts with joy' (Acts 14:17). God's good gifts of sun and rain, the seasons of the year, health and strength, beauty and love, are all part of God's revelation of himself.

Of course, not everyone will have equal portions of God's general revelation. For example, some may see little of his providential love and care because of their desperate circumstances of famine or poverty, and others, through the loss of sight, may not even see the stars or sun. But the Bible makes it clear that all men have sufficient evidence of God, even if it is only that voice of conscience that tells them there is a God. The tragedy is that men and women suppress the truth about God (Romans 1:18) and for this reason they need to hear of Christ. Paul's argument in Romans 10:13-14 clearly shows that if people are to know God, they must hear of Christ, believe in him, and call upon God.

The greatest example of God revealing himself in history is, of course, the cross and the coming of Christ. God had spoken of this right at the dawn of history in Genesis 3:15. He confirmed it to Abraham in Genesis 12:3 and according to Galatians 3:8 the promise was fulfilled in Christ. We can never understand history before the coming of Christ unless we see in it God preparing the world for 'when the time had fully come', which was when 'God sent his Son' (Galatians 4:4). Similarly, we cannot understand history after the coming of Christ unless we see in it God working out his purposes for his people. History is 'his story'. But once again, fallen man cannot reliably see God through history and he will reject what he does see. It is not the revelation that is at fault, but man's heart and mind.

God's special revelation

In addition to God's general revelation, which is there for all men to see, there are some particular and special ways in which God has revealed himself.

Appearances, visions, dreams and miracles

During the Old Testament period there were occasions when the Lord appeared in a visible form to his people. This is called a 'theophany' and the word comes from a Greek noun meaning 'God' and a verb meaning 'to appear'. This appearing of the Lord is often spoken of as 'the angel of the Lord'. Hagar met with the Lord (Genesis 16:7-13) and so did Abraham just before the destruction of Sodom and Gomorrah (Genesis 18). Jacob met a stranger by the river Jabbok whom he identified as the Lord, and said, 'I saw God face to face' (Genesis 32:22-31). Joshua (Joshua 5:13-15), Gideon (Judges 6:11-24) and Manoah (Judges 13:2-23) had similar experiences, as did the three friends in the fiery furnace (Daniel 3:25). In a theophany, God the Father was revealing himself through his Son even before Christ's birth at Bethlehem.

Dreams and visions were also used by God to reveal himself and his plans. Jacob saw something of the Lord in his dreams during that first restless night when he fled from his brother's revenge (Genesis 28:13). In the year of King Uzziah's death the prophet Isaiah went into the temple and there saw the glory of the Lord (Isaiah 6); from John 12:41 it is clear that this was Christ's glory. There are at least six accounts of God speaking through dreams and visions in the Acts of the Apostles, including Peter's vision in chapter 10.

Even godless kings like Pharaoh, Nebuchadnezzar and Belshazzar received revelations of God's purposes either through dreams (Genesis 41:1, 25; Daniel 2:1), a direct voice from heaven (Daniel 4:31), or some other appearance (Daniel 5:5).

Miracles, in both the Old and New Testaments, had only one main purpose and that was to reveal God. Moses was sent to Pharaoh to perform miracles, 'that you may know that I am the Lord' (Exodus 10:2), and Christ's first miracle was to 'reveal his glory' (John 2:11).

But such was the darkness of man's mind that many ignored or misunderstood the love of God in the revelation. Once again, it was not the revelation that was at fault, but man's heart and mind.

Christ the Word

John in his Gospel refers to Christ as 'the Word' (John 1:1) because it is chiefly by words that we reveal ourselves to each other and communicate with each other. You will recall that David said even the stars in the sky seem to have 'words', for they 'speak' about God. But when God wanted to reveal himself as fully as sinful man could ever bear or understand, he spoke through Christ, his only Son. Christ is God's greatest 'Word' to mankind. He fully and perfectly reveals the Father: 'Anyone who has seen me has seen the Father' (John 14:9). Writing to the Hebrew Christians the apostle made the incredible claim that: 'In these last days [God] has spoken to us by his Son... The Son is the radiance of God's glory, and the exact representation of his being...' (Hebrews 1:3). What could be more clear? There is no greater visible revelation of God than Jesus Christ. But since Christ is no longer visible to man, how can we be sure of this greatest revelation?

Scripture

The book we call the Bible is God's collected revelation. It contains all we need for our knowledge of God and his saving love. In God's general revelation we saw that man's sin and spiritual blindness draw a curtain across his understanding. God reveals himself clearly and without error, and if men were not sinful then the beauty and the wonder of creation would be sufficient to lead men to true worship. But since men always wrongly interpret God's general revelation, God has given something simple, clear, sufficient and, like all of his revelation, perfect and without error. He has given us the Bible. Fallen man would not know reliably about God, Christ, himself or salvation without the Bible.

The Bible is not just another way in which God gets his message across, nor is it merely the means by which we learn of salvation. The Bible is part of God's way of salvation. It is not merely a witness to God's revelation; it *is* God's revelation. It is God breaking through the barrier of sin and revealing himself and his salvation in the simplest and most sufficient way possible. The Bible does not *contain* God's Word; it *is* God's Word. Nor does the Bible become God's Word when it speaks to us; it *is always* God's Word, whether we acknowledge this or not. The Bible is never dependent upon man's response to it for its authority. The laws of a nation do not depend for their authority upon the obedience of every single citizen; on the contrary, the laws carry the authority of the government regardless of our obedience. So God, as the highest authority, has given us his Word, the Bible, and it carries the fullest possible authority regardless of anyone's response.

Similarly, the Bible does not simply contain stories of God's love; it is in itself an expression of God's love. It does not merely contain God's offer of salvation; it is part of God's act of salvation.

Because of all this the Bible must be a book beyond error; if it is not, then God's final and clearest revelation of himself today is less reliable than the stars in the sky.

In every area of life, communication is a vital ingredient. Whether in the family or society, in the classroom or boardroom, on the sportsfield or battlefield, it is essential that those with instructions are able to communicate clearly and accurately so that the important information they have to pass on is not jumbled beyond recognition. Nowhere is this more important than when the Sovereign God communicates with sinful man. It is to the subject of how carefully and accurately God has communicated his words to man that we now turn.

3.
What we mean by 'inspiration'

The Bible's claim for itself

From here on it is God's revelation in the Bible that is our concern
and if, as we have already claimed, the Bible is without error, we
must begin to support such a big statement with some evidence. To
do this, we have to begin with the Bible itself!

But to say that the Bible is the Word of God and therefore without
error because the Bible itself claims this is seen by many as an
argument in circles. It is rather like saying, 'That prisoner must be
innocent because he says he is.' Are we right to appeal to the Bible's
own claim in settling this matter of its authority and inerrancy? How
can we defend our trust in this 'self-witness' of the Bible?

Self-witness ought to be sufficient

If men were not sinners, witness to oneself would be enough. In John
5:31-32 our Lord agreed with the principle that self-witness is
normally not sufficient: 'If I testify about myself, my testimony is
not valid. There is another who testifies in my favour, and I know
that his testimony about me is valid.' Later, in John 8:13, the
Pharisees took up this point when Jesus claimed, 'I am the light of
the world.' They corrected him by saying, 'Here you are, appearing
as your own witness; your testimony is not valid.' In defence our
Lord showed that in his case, because he was the Son of God, self-
witness is reliable: 'Even if I testify on my own behalf, my testimony
is valid...' (v.14), and the following verses make clear our Lord's
position that self-witness is reliable where sin does not interfere.
Because Christ was never found to be a false witness and no one
could prove him guilty of sin (John 8:46), his words could be trusted.

In the same way, since the Bible is never found to be a false witness we have a right to listen to its own claim about itself.

Some truths can never be known without self-witness

This self-authentication, as it is often called, is used frequently in our daily experience. When a man writes his own life story, much of it can never be checked because it would never be known unless the author revealed it. He may write about his childhood fears or memories and we must take his word for these things. We either believe what he says or call him a liar. The same is true when I relate a dream I had recently; no one can possibly confirm or deny my account since I am the only witness. In this case you rely entirely on self-authentication and you either trust me or you don't — depending upon how trustworthy you have proved me to be. This is exactly Paul's argument in 1 Corinthians 2:11 when he writes, 'Who among men knows the thoughts of a man except the man's spirit within him? In the same way no one knows the thoughts of God except the Spirit of God.'

Much of the Bible's story is such that unless God had revealed it we could never have known it. There are many scientific theories telling us how the world came into being. Some of these theories differ only slightly from each other, but others are contradictory. This only shows that men can never really be sure about such matters because no scientist was there when it all happened. Unless God, who was there, had revealed it, we would never have known it. The same is true for all the great Bible doctrines. How can we be sure of God's anger against sin, or his love for sinners, or his plans to choose a people for himself, if God himself had not told us?

There must be a final court of appeal

When men want to confirm that what they are saying is true, they appeal to someone or something greater than themselves. They swear on a holy book or say, 'God is my witness.' God had no one greater than himself to confirm his Word, and therefore he appealed to his own character: 'When God made his promise to Abraham, since there was no one greater for him to swear by, he swore by himself...' (Hebrews 6:13).

'… the final court of appeal'

In law, the final court of appeal, whether it is a judge, governor, prince, president or king, must be the final authority; there is no higher authority. Therefore if the Bible is God's Word it must be its own witness. There is no higher authority than God to witness to its truth. Hilary of Poitiers, a fourth-century theologian, once claimed, 'Only God is a fit witness to himself.' No one can improve on that!

We should test authority by its results

This was the principle our Lord left us in John 10:37-38: 'Do not believe me unless I do what my Father does. But if I do it, even though you do not believe me, believe the miracles, that you may learn and understand that the Father is in me, and I in the Father.'

This principle ran through the Old Testament also: 'You may say to yourselves, "How can we know when a message has not been spoken by the Lord?" If what a prophet proclaims in the name of the Lord does not take place or come true, that is a message the Lord has not spoken' (Deuteronomy 18:21-22).

If the Bible can be proved true wherever we can test it, then we are right to accept its word in those areas where we cannot test it. It is therefore essential that the Bible is seen to be accurate in its

history, geography and prophecy — areas that we often can test —
in order for us to trust its doctrine, which is an area we cannot test.
A prisoner on trial is more readily believed when he says things we
cannot check, if he has been proved right in the things we can check.
If the author, writing his own life story, is proved wrong on many of
his supposed facts then we are hardly willing to trust his word for
those childhood fears and memories either.

The accuracy of the Bible in its facts helps to prove its own claim
to be a God-given book.

The witness of Christ and the Holy Spirit

During his lifetime our Lord witnessed to the inspiration of the Old
Testament, a subject we shall return to in chapter 4, and the Holy
Spirit witnesses in the mind of the Christian. So often a young
Christian accepts the authority of God's Word without being told he
must. It was through that Word he became a Christian and that same
book speaks with a living power to his mind and heart each day. To
deny the claim of Christ and the witness of the Holy Spirit is to make
God a liar. The Bible is a book that speaks for itself.

What is meant by 'inspiration'?

We shall begin by a study of 2 Timothy 3:16: 'All Scripture is God-
breathed...'

The phrase 'God-breathed' is found only in this verse in the
whole of the Bible. It is just one word in the Greek and is often
translated by the word 'inspired'. Usually the word is explained as
the divine 'inbreathing' into a man by God's Holy Spirit, with the
result that the man speaks, or writes, with a quality, insight, accuracy
and authority that are possible in no other form of human speaking
or writing. The word *may* be defined in this way, but it ought not to
be!

'Inspire' is an old French word and it was not used to refer to the
Scriptures until the Reformation in the sixteenth century. The Greek
word is *theopneustos,* which literally means 'God' *(theos)* and
'breathed' *(pneustos).* Our word 'theology' comes from the Greek
word for 'God'; theology is the study of God. Our words 'pneu-
monia' and 'pneumatic' are derived from the Greek word for

'breathed'; they refer to breath or air. To be accurate, 2 Timothy 3:16 does not mean 'breathed *into* by God' but 'breathed *out* by God'. There is a big difference between breathing into something and breathing out — inspiring and expiring!

In this verse there is really no reference to the human writer at all. Another passage in the Bible tells us about the human writer: it is 2 Peter 1:20-21 and we shall look at that later. But in 2 Timothy 3:16 there is no reference to the method by which we received the Scripture, but to its origin, where it came from. It is not breathed into man, but breathed out by God. That is a very big claim.

Benjamin Warfield was a brilliant biblical scholar in the United States earlier this century and he carefully studied this word, *theopneustos,* in all its uses outside the Bible. In chapter 6 of his book, *The Inspiration and Authority of the Bible,* he shows that it is always used in a passive sense, something that is breathed out, and never in an active sense, breathing into something. The emphasis is on where the words came from — they were breathed out by God— and not on what happened to the human writer, God actively breathing into him his words. If I say to a man, 'How did you get that new car I see in your garage?' he may reply, 'It was sold to me by a friend of mine.' Or he may say, 'I drove it home from my friend's house.' Both answers are correct, but the first tells me where the car came from; you notice the passive use of the verb: 'It was sold to me.' On the other hand, the second answer tells me how the car came to be in my friend's garage: 'I drove it home,' and that is an active use of the verb. *Theopneustos* is passive, it tells us where the words came from. The word 'inspiration' is therefore misleading and not strictly scriptural. However, it has become a technical term and we shall have to continue to use it, though with the correct understanding. 'God-breathed' is an excellent translation of the word *theopneustos.*

How much of the Bible is inspired?

If 'inspired' really means 'God-breathed', then we must accept that all Scripture, being God-breathed, is accurate, without error and can therefore be trusted completely. God would cease to be God if he breathed out errors and contradictions, even in the smallest part. So long as we give *theopneustos* its real meaning, we shall not find it hard to accept the full inerrancy of the Bible.

However, some people do find it hard to accept this, as we saw in the first chapter. Many have a very liberal view of Scripture and they will not accept the supernatural, such as miracles, nor will they trust the words of Moses, Paul, or even our Lord himself. Others accept the words of our Lord but believe that Paul, John or Peter were not always correct. Still others believe that the doctrines revealed in the Bible are reliable and so are most, but not all, of the historical facts. A view held by many today is that the words of God are not to be found in the Bible at all; the Bible becomes the Word of God when it speaks to man. This was the dangerous modern view put forward by the Swiss theologian Karl Barth to whom we referred in chapter 1. To various extents each of these views denies the true meaning of *theopneustos*.

Plenary and verbal inspiration — a new approach

These two words are sometimes used to explain what evangelicals really mean when they speak about the Bible as God's Word. 'Plenary' comes from the Latin *plenus,* which means 'full', and refers to the fact that the whole of Scripture *in every part* is God-given. 'Verbal' comes from the Latin *verbum* which means 'word' and emphasizes that even *the words* of Scripture are God-given.

By definition plenary and verbal inspiration means that the Bible is God-given (and therefore without error) in every part (doctrine, history, geography, dates, names and so on) and in every single word. But unfortunately some evangelicals today use these words 'plenary' and 'verbal' but mean something different. They say there are errors in the Bible, just small ones here and there, but these need not be counted against plenary and verbal inspiration because the facts that the Bible intended to state are what matters.

An example of this is found in 1 Chronicles 21:12 where David experienced three years of famine as a result of his disobedience. In 2 Samuel 24:13 it is referred to as 'seven years' (see NIV footnote). We are told not to waste time trying to resolve the problem; the fact of a famine lasting a few years is what God intended, and in that the Bible is absolutely right and completely reliable. Just how we can resolve this particular problem is discussed in chapter 17.

Of course, there is a proper use of discovering what the Bible intends to say, and we shall look at this in chapter 14, but to use 'intention' to cover up possible errors is incorrect. It is like a football team discounting all goals scored against it by the argument that it was never its intention to let the ball into the net. Such reasoning may satisfy its supporters, but certainly not its opponents! A witness to a crime may give a lot of details to the court, but if many of them are proved to be completely false the witness cannot be allowed to plead, 'Well, what I intended to say was that I saw the crime, and in that everyone agrees I am right.' The fact is that he has lied, or at best has proved himself an unreliable witness, and no court will listen to him further.

We must watch for those who use the terms 'plenary' and 'verbal' but only in a limited way. This new thinking by some evangelicals is the top of a slippery slope into full liberalism. After all, liberalism first started by allowing just a little acceptable error here and there in the Bible. History is just repeating itself. To talk of an infallible Bible in spite of its errors is a misuse of plain words and simply dishonest. The only safe and consistent attitude to the Bible is to see it as a book without error.

Why is inerrancy important?

Is this whole debate about whether or not the Bible contains nothing but the truth merely a theological quibble? Certainly not! The question of ultimate authority is of the highest importance for the Christian, and for a number of good reasons.

Inerrancy governs our attitude to the truth of the gospel

We cannot offer the world a reliable gospel presented in an unreliable Scripture. How can we be sure of truth on any issue if we are suspicious of errors everywhere or anywhere? An airline pilot will ground his aircraft even on suspicion of the most minor of faults because he is aware that one fault destroys confidence in the complete machine. If the history contained in the Bible is wrong how can we be sure that the doctrine or moral teaching is correct? The answer is that we cannot be sure. Some theologians claim that it is the real message of the biblical writer that is important and that if the writer is incorrect in a number of facts, or even makes them up, it does not at all alter the truth of his message. But in no other area of life would we accept this argument.

A farmer, wishing to sell his cow to a neighbour, may describe in great detail its size and weight, food intake and milk output, its age and characteristics, and then add that it is brown in colour. If, on the following day, he arrives with a black and white cow, his neighbour will quite rightly distrust all the important details given the previous day. Either it is a different cow or the farmer does not know his animals. When I collected my car from a service, I noticed that although the list of items to be checked included refilling the windscreen wash bottle, the mechanic clearly had not done so. The foreman suggested it was a very small item, but I pointed out that if they missed something so obvious and simple, I had good reason to question what else of greater importance they might have overlooked.

The gospel of salvation may sound wonderful, but if the history in which it is all said to have happened is not correct, then how can we trust the gospel itself? The heart of the Christian message is rooted in history. The incarnation — God becoming a man — is proved by the virgin birth of Christ. Redemption — the price being paid for man's rebellion to be forgiven — is obtained by the death of Christ on the cross. Reconciliation — the privilege of the sinner becoming a friend of God — is gained through the resurrection and ascension of Christ. If the recorded events are not true, how do we know that the theology behind them is true?

Inerrancy governs our attitude to the value of Christ

We cannot have a reliable Saviour without a reliable Scripture. If, as many suggest, the stories in the Gospels are not historically true and the words of Christ are occasionally inaccurate, how do we know what we can trust about Christ? Must we rely upon the conflicting interpretations of a host of critical scholars before we know what Christ was like, or what he said? If the Gospel stories are merely the result of the wishful thinking of the church in the second or third centuries, as many suggest, or even the personal views of the Gospel writers, then our faith no longer rests upon the historical Jesus but upon the opinions of men. Who will want to trust an unreliable Saviour for their eternal salvation?

Many today doubt the reality of the resurrection of Christ but then claim that such an unbelief does not stop us from believing in Christ as a life-giving spirit. We are told that one-third of Church of England bishops do not believe in the virgin birth of Christ or his resurrection and Bishop David Jenkins of Durham has called the resurrection 'merely a conjuring trick with bones'. I can only reply that since the Bible is so plain, straightforward and insistent in its claim to the literal truth of Christ's resurrection, if it is wrong at this point we must all despair of ever understanding what it means about anything.

Inerrancy governs our response to the conclusions of science

We shall consider the Bible and science again in chapter 16, but the matter can be stated very simply here. If we believe the Bible contains errors, then we will be quick to accept scientific theories that appear to prove the Bible wrong. In other words, we have allowed the conclusions of science to stand in judgement upon the Bible. On the other hand, if we believe in inerrancy, we will not be prepared to accept the hasty theories that often come to us in the name of science, but will test those theories by Scripture. A belief in inerrancy means that we will allow Scripture to stand in judgement upon scientific theories. A Bible in error is at the mercy of the wisdom of the current opinions of science, but an inerrant Bible submits to no man's judgement.

Inerrancy governs our attitude to the interpretation of Scripture

If we believe that scriptural inerrancy is a higher principle than scientific theories, then we will be prepared to accept those passages that are written as history but which may seem to be contradicted by some scientific views. We will have no trouble in accepting the account of creation, or Jonah and his big fish, or any of the miracles in the Bible; they are plainly written as history and we will readily accept them as such. Only when we doubt inerrancy do we have to invent new principles for interpreting Scripture that for convenience turn history into poetry and facts into myths. One of the first questions a man must answer when he turns to a passage of the Bible is this, 'How reliable is this passage?' Only then will he be able to decide how to interpret it.

Inerrancy governs our attitude to the preaching and authority of Scripture

A denial of biblical inerrancy always leads to a loss of confidence in Scripture both in the pulpit and in the pew. It was not the growth of education and science that emptied churches, nor two world wars, but the cold deadness of theological liberalism. If the Bible's history is doubtful and its words are open to dispute, then people understandably lose confidence in it. Must every preacher first check with the latest view of critical scholarship before he can claim any authority for a passage from the Bible? If he has to discover whether a particular verse is what Christ actually said, or what Matthew thought Christ said, or what the second-century church wanted Matthew to say that Christ said, then he is not likely to have much confidence in what he himself eventually says! Besides, most congregations have better things to do than listen to this sort of nonsense. People want authority. They want to know what God has said. Where inerrancy is denied there is no longer clear authority. A church without authority is like a crocodile without teeth; it can open its mouth as wide and as often as it likes, but who cares?

Inerrancy protects the honour of God

Almost all theologians agree that Scripture is in some measure God's revelation to man. But to allow that it contains error implies that God has mishandled inspiration and has allowed his people to be deceived for centuries until the twentieth-century scholars disentangled the confusion. The alternative is that God has revealed himself plainly and without error in words that carry his eternal authority and by their trustworthiness reflect his honour and glory.

Does the Bible claim to be God-breathed and without error?

The answer to this question is certainly 'Yes'. Some of the strongest critics of the Bible, who themselves deny inerrancy, have admitted that this was clearly the belief of our Lord and the apostles. The German theologians Adolf Harnack (1851-1930) and Rudolf Bultmann (1884-1976) are examples of this. F. C. Grant, of Union Seminary in the United States of America, a very liberal critic of the

Bible, has written of the New Testament: 'Everywhere it is taken for granted that what is written in Scripture is the work of divine inspiration and is therefore trustworthy, infallible, and inerrant.' He then added: 'What is described or related in the Old Testament is unquestionably true.'

We shall look at the biblical position very briefly here and return to it in later chapters.

The view of the Old Testament writers

The Old Testament writers saw their message as God-breathed and therefore utterly reliable.

God confirmed this to Moses and future prophets in Deuteronomy 18:18: 'I will raise up for them a prophet like you from among their brothers; I will put my words in his mouth, and he will tell them everything I command him.' This was also Jeremiah's experience at the beginning of his ministry: 'Then the Lord reached out his hand and touched my mouth and said to me, "Now, I have put my words in your mouth"' (Jeremiah 1:9).

'The prophets frequently identified themselves with God'

The Hebrew word for prophet means 'a spokesman' and the prophets' message was: 'This is what the Sovereign Lord says.' As a result they frequently so identified themselves with God that they spoke as though God himself was actually speaking. Isaiah 5 reveals this clearly. In verses 1-2 the prophet speaks of God in the third person, 'he', but in verses 3-6 there is a change, and Isaiah speaks in the first person, 'I'. Isaiah has become the actual voice of God. It is little wonder that King David could speak of the word of the Lord as 'flawless' (2 Samuel 22:31 and see also Proverbs 30:5).

The New Testament agrees with the Old

Peter and John saw the words of David in Psalm 2 not as the opinion of a king of Israel, but as the voice of God. They introduced a quotation from that psalm in a prayer to God: 'You spoke by the Holy Spirit through the mouth of your servant, our father David' (Acts 4:25). Similarly, Paul accepted Isaiah's words as God himself speaking to men: 'The Holy Spirit spoke the truth to your forefathers when he said through Isaiah the prophet...' (Acts 28:25).

So convinced were the writers of the New Testament that all the words of the Old Testament Scripture were the actual words of God that they even claimed, 'Scripture says,' when the words quoted came directly from God. Two examples are Romans 9:17: 'For the Scripture says to Pharaoh,' and Galatians 3:8: 'The Scripture ... announced the gospel in advance to Abraham...' In Hebrews 1 many of the Old Testament passages quoted were actually addressed to God by the psalmist, yet the writer to the Hebrews refers to them as the words of God.

Our Lord believed in verbal inspiration

Clearly our Lord believed that the words of the Old Testament were God-breathed. Here are three examples:

In John 10:34 (quoting from Psalm 82:6) our Lord based his teaching upon a phrase: 'I said, "You are gods."'

In Matthew 22:32 he based his teaching upon the words, 'I am', in Exodus 3:6. Our Lord was in conflict with the Sadducees who denied the resurrection of the body. If God had said to Moses, 'I was the God of Abraham, Isaac and Jacob,' or even if he had meant, 'I am the God who was worshipped by Abraham, Isaac and Jacob,' then Christ had established nothing by quoting this verse from Exodus. In fact the present tense 'I am' is all important here and forms the basis of our Lord's argument. In its Old Testament context the verb is understood as God saying to Moses, 'I am still the God of Abraham, Isaac and Jacob. I am not the God of dead men, but living men; their death has been conquered and their resurrection is certain.' We should note here as a matter of accuracy that the Hebrew of Exodus 3:6 does not contain a verb, only the personal pronoun 'I'. However, in such a case the present tense is understood. The Septuagint, which is the Greek translation of the Old Testament, does contain the present tense of the verb and our Lord certainly used the present tense in Matthew 22:32. In all this, he settled an issue by reference to one word in the Hebrew Old Testament!

In Matthew 22:43-44 our Lord quoted from Psalm 110:1 and emphasized a single word, 'Lord'; and here he was seeking to show himself to be the Son of God.

Paul believed in verbal inspiration

In a very significant passage Paul based an argument upon the fact that a particular word in the Old Testament is singular and not plural. Writing to the Galatians, Paul claimed that in God's promises to Abraham God does not say, '"and to seeds", meaning many people, but "and to your seed", meaning one person, who is Christ' (Galatians 3:16). Paul was quoting from Genesis 12:7; 13:15; 22:18 and 24:7. In each verse our translators use the word 'offspring' and the Hebrew word is in the singular. Paul's argument here is that God's chief purpose is not to refer to Israel as the offspring of Abraham, but to Christ. You may rightly say that the singular of this particular word can also have a plural meaning; in English also the word 'offspring' can refer to one or many. It is also true that in Galatians 3:29 Paul used the word (in this case 'seed' instead of 'offspring') with the plural meaning. What is significant, however, is the way Paul drew attention to the fact that the Hebrew word in Genesis is singular when God could have chosen a plural word. As far as Paul is concerned God chose the singular for a special purpose because it emphasized that the greatest descendant of Abraham was Christ (singular) and that by faith in him many become descendants.

This is a belief in verbal inspiration; it mattered to Paul whether

God used a singular or plural in these passages of the Old Testament. It is therefore not surprising that in Romans 3:2 Paul gives as one advantage of being a Jew the fact that 'They have been entrusted with the very words of God.'

The method of inspiration

We have already seen that 2 Timothy 3:16 should rightly be translated, 'All Scripture is God-breathed.' This verse tells us of the origin of Scripture. It comes from God and its accuracy and authority are therefore plenary, covering every part, and verbal, covering even the words themselves. But there is one more question we must ask: 'How was the Bible inspired?'

2 Peter 1:20-21 will help us answer this question: 'No prophecy of Scripture came about by the prophet's own interpretation. For prophecy never had its origin in the will of man, but men spoke from God as they were carried along by the Holy Spirit.'

The Scriptures came through men

The claim of the Bible's critics is that since it was men who wrote down the words of Scripture, the light from heaven was broken up and spoilt by human error. This is the argument of the 'humanity of Scripture' that we referred to in chapter 1. To show that the words of God are marred by man, the critics use the illustrations of the pure rays of the sun broken and shaded as they filter through the trees of a thick forest, or the clear sunlight becoming a kaleidoscope of broken colour through the stained glass window. But we may use the same illustration with an opposite purpose! Suppose the Creator so designed the leaves and the trees that the light and shade falling across the forest floor are exactly what he intended? Or suppose the craftsman planned the window exactly as he wanted the colours to be reflected?

The Scriptures came from the pen of men prepared by God. God did not choose Paul as the most suitable man. He formed and equipped Paul for his sovereign purpose. If a commanding officer has an important message to relay to his troops, he will take every precaution to make sure the exact message he wants to communicate gets through. Armies spend time and money to make sure their

'The light and shade falling across the forest floor are exactly what he intended'

communications network is of the highest possible standard of accuracy. It is possible today for a soldier who has become lost to gain a satellite bearing on his location to within a few feet of accuracy; the expense of time and technology for that information is colossal. But God has something far more important to say to us and his accuracy is greater than that of any man-made system.

In Galatians 1:11-24 Paul gives his testimony. Among his claims are two of great importance. First: 'The gospel I preached is not something that man made up. I did not receive it from any man, nor was I taught it; rather, I received it by revelation from Jesus Christ' (vv. 11-12). Second: 'God set me apart from birth and called me by his grace' (v. 15). This was exactly the experience of the prophets Isaiah (49:1-2,5) and Jeremiah (1:5); and this is what Peter was talking about in 2 Peter 1:20-21, particularly when he claimed that 'No prophecy of Scripture came about by the prophet's own interpretation.'

The Scriptures did not come by the prophets' own interpretation

It is wrong to think of the human writers of the Bible as co-authors with God. Certainly they reflected their own personality and employed their own style of writing, but they had nothing at all to do with the *origin* of the message; that belonged to God alone. However, although they wrote the God-breathed message in God's words, they were personally *involved in* the message. An officer may send warning to a platoon of some danger that threatens it. The messenger is given a carefully prepared message which he delivers faithfully and exactly. The message is not his own, but the urgency of his voice and the excitement of his gestures are his own. The message has become part of his thinking and action. He feels the urgency, and although everyone knows he passes on the very words of the commanding officer's warning, the soldiers can rightly claim, 'That man's message is very important.' So it is with the human writers of the Bible. In origin it is not their message; they received it from God. It was not written for them on a sheet of paper like our military messenger, but in their minds, and it became so much a part of their thinking that it was their own message. They spoke it or wrote it with all the force and enthusiasm they could. It was exactly God's message, given by men. Similarly, Peter assures us that the human writers were not free simply to interpret the message God gave to them. No officer allows his vital communication with the front-line troops to be interpreted by the soldier into a message he thinks the forces will best understand — or enjoy!

Three times in the Bible this relationship between the human messenger and the God-breathed message is spoken of as the writer 'eating' the words of God. One of these is in Jeremiah 15:16: 'When your words came, I ate them; they were my joy and my heart's delight.' The other two are in Ezekiel 2:8 to 3:4 and Revelation 10:8-11. As a result, the prophets often preached a message they did not fully understand; they preached God's words, not their own. This is Peter's claim in 1 Peter 1:10-12.

In contrast to all this, false prophets were described as those 'who prophesy out of their own imagination' (Ezekiel 13:2). No commanding officer wants a messenger like that!

The Scriptures came by men 'moved' by the Holy Spirit

The Greek word used here in 2 Peter 1:21 is *phero,* which means 'to bear' or 'to carry'. It was a familiar word to the sailor, referring to the sailing ship carried along by the wind; and remember that Peter was a fisherman on the Sea of Galilee. The human writers of the Bible certainly used their minds, but not to make up the message. The Holy Spirit carried them along in their thinking so that only his God-breathed words were recorded. The apostle Paul set the matter plainly in 1 Corinthians 2:13: 'This is what we speak, not in words taught us by human wisdom but in words taught by the Spirit.'

A summary therefore, is that 2 Timothy 3:16 tells us where the Scriptures came from, that is, the origin of the Bible: it came *from God*. 2 Peter 1:20-21, on the other hand, tells us how the Scriptures came to us, that is, the method by which we got our Bible: it came *through men*. This same distinction is seen also in the Old Testament. In Nehemiah 8:1 we read of 'the Book of the Law of Moses' and immediately we are informed, 'which the Lord had commanded for Israel'. This is the same as Peter's 'Men spoke from God'.

Two errors to be avoided

In answering the question, 'What was God's method of inspiration?' we must be aware of two extremes.

Mechanical inspiration

This view makes the human writers mere dictating machines or typewriters. They were not thinking, but simply wrote down letters and words as God dictated them. Admittedly such a view of the Bible would emphasize it as the Word of God, but it is inaccurate for a number of reasons.

Firstly, it ignores the obvious preparation of the man by God. If God is merely dictating, the writer's only necessary qualification would be the ability to write neatly!

Secondly, it ignores the fact that the various writers in the Bible reveal their own character, style and culture, to such a degree that at times we can recognize characteristics of Paul's letters or John's Gospel in much the same way that people can recognize our own phrases and style from our letters.

Thirdly, it ignores the fact that some writers used the results of their own research into documents available. Long lists of family histories (genealogies) and official letters were almost certainly reproduced from government records. Some of the lists of names in Chronicles are 'records from ancient times' (1 Chronicles 4:22). See also, for example, 1 Kings 11:41; 1 Chronicles 29:29-30; Ezra 4:11-22 and Luke 1:1-4.

General inspiration

This is the most widely held view by critics of the Bible. Admitting that the Bible is a very special book with a unique message, they claim that the writers were merely prompted by God to a deeper spiritual understanding than most men. They were very understanding of life in general. But then, the argument runs, so were the English poet Shakespeare and the French philosopher Voltaire. These men too were inspired. Many of their ideas were good, but we must not say that their words are infallible. In the same way, say the critics, the Bible writers were capable of error and at times were either too extreme, or too loose in their statements. We must bring our own reason and common sense to the Bible to remove the errors, just as a gardener prunes off the dead and unwanted wood from his trees and bushes in order to get better fruit.

Such a view wholly ignores the Bible's claim for itself, a claim that Shakespeare and Voltaire never made for themselves. It also overlooks the fact that the only way to convey the truth is through words. If God has a message for mankind but his words cannot be trusted, then without doubt the truth is unreliable as well. When a man is learning a new language, he will often get his words wrong. He knows exactly what he wants to say, but he fails to communicate his message because he does not use the right words. If the words of the Bible are not exactly right then, however 'inspired' and well meaning the writers may have been, we may as well give up all hope of finding the whole truth. Besides, this view of general inspiration assumes that the scholar who removes the error and discovers the truth is more 'inspired' than the original writer!

A definition of inspiration

The Holy Spirit moved men to write. He allowed them to use their own style, culture, gifts and character, to use the results of their own study and research, to write of their own experiences and to express what was in their mind. At the same time, the Holy Spirit did not allow sin to influence their writings; he overruled in the expression of thought and in the choice of words. Thus they recorded accurately all that God wanted them to say and exactly how he wanted them to say it, in their own character, style and language.

The inspiration of Scripture is a harmony of the active mind of the writer and the sovereign direction of the Holy Spirit to produce God's inerrant and infallible Word to mankind.

From the apostles onwards

Today a lot of printer's ink is spent on the question of whether or not the evangelical view of Scripture represents the mainstream of Christian thought throughout the history of the church. Understandably evangelicals are convinced that it does. Writing in *Scripture and Truth,* Professor Geoffrey Bromiley concludes: 'That the Fathers [the leaders of the church during the first few centuries] accepted the divine inspiration of the Holy Scripture, whether as the Old Testament or the New, may be demonstrated with the greatest of ease' (p.204).

The first five hundred years

Clement of Rome, writing to the church at Corinth in the first century, reminded them: 'You have studied Scripture [he was referring to the Old Testament] which contains the truth and is inspired by the Holy Spirit. You realize that there is nothing wrong or misleading in it.' In a similar way Justin Martyr, in his *Dialogue with Trypho,* a Jew he was seeking to win for Christ, claimed, 'I am entirely convinced that no Scripture contradicts another.'

Tertullian led the church in Carthage, North Africa, in the second century and argued that whatever the Scripture teaches is true and binding upon us, and Clement of Alexandria called it the first principle of instruction because in it we hear the voice of the Lord. Irenaeus represented the Greek church in the second century and wrote, 'The Scriptures are indeed perfect, since they were spoken by the Word of God and his Spirit.' Expressing his confidence in Luke as a historian Irenaeus continued: 'No person of common sense can permit them to receive some things recounted by Luke as being true, and to set others aside as if he had not known the truth.'

Augustine represented the western church two hundred years later and claimed that the Bible books are 'free from error', and whilst he acknowledged some difficult places in Scripture, he allowed 'variations but not contradictions; diversities but not contrarieties'. John Chrysostom, the 'golden-mouthed' preacher from Antioch in the fourth century, declared that even the most trivial statement in the Bible has more than superficial value since it all came from God, and he urged his congregations to obtain and read a copy of the Scriptures. In the same way Athanasius, the fourth-century champion for the truth, recorded that 'The Sacred and divinely inspired Scriptures are sufficient for the exposition of the truth.' He spoke also of 'the plain authority of the Scriptures' and 'the divine Scriptures'.

If anything, the conclusion must be that the early church leaders, in their desire to lay full emphasis upon the divine inspiration and infallibility of the Scriptures, fell into the danger of overlooking the importance of the human authors and of leaning at times to a dictation view of inspiration. If they do not use the word inerrancy it is because they were not confronting the issue of those who call Scripture 'the word of God' and then proceed to demolish its authority by debating its accuracy. In the first five centuries at least, for Jews and Christians alike, if the Scriptures were the Word of God they must be true and free from error. Today we have been forced to 'fine-tune' our definitions because of the modern critics both inside and outside the ranks of so-called evangelicals.

The Reformation and beyond

Despite claims to the contrary, there can be little reasonable doubt that the Reformers in the sixteenth century also followed the position of the early church leaders. Not only was the watchword of the Reformation *Sola Scriptura*, Scripture alone, but it was a Scripture that, according to Martin Luther, 'cannot err'. Unfortunately Luther sat loosely to this at times, as is evident in his commentary on Zechariah in 1528, when he raised the question why Matthew should attribute Zechariah 11:13 to Jeremiah (see Matthew 27:9) and concluded with the possibility that Matthew 'is not quite correct about the name'. Elsewhere, however, he maintains: 'It is impossible that Scripture should contradict itself; it only appears so to senseless and obstinate hypocrites'! Luther also refers to the Scriptures 'which have never erred' and claims that 'One letter, even a single title of Scripture, means more to us than heaven and earth. Therefore we cannot permit even the most minute change.' Slackness in the occasional comment was due not to a low view of scriptural accuracy, but to carelessness at a time when hardly anyone was taking issue with inerrancy; the reliability of the Bible was in fact the one thing that both Luther and his Catholic opponents, Desiderius Erasmus and John Eck, had in common.

The sixteenth-century Swiss Reformer John Calvin was clear: the Bible is the 'pure word of God' and 'the infallible rule of his holy truth'. Edward Dowey, one of the opponents of inerrancy today, admits: 'To Calvin the theologian, an error in Scripture is unthinkable.' In fact the same writer suggests that Calvin's mistake was his constant harmonizing and explaining to avoid the possibility of error anywhere. Even the Matthew 27:9 passage that Luther dismissed as 'not quite correct', Calvin resolves by assuming the name of Jeremiah 'crept in' through a copyist's error. (See chapter 17 for a more reasonable solution.) Just one quotation from Calvin must be sufficient: 'It is not even enough to believe that God is trustworthy, who can neither deceive nor lie, unless you hold to be beyond doubt that whatever proceeds from him is sacred and inviolable truth.'

Later Reformers and Puritans followed the same line but with one noticeable difference. Until the end of the seventeenth century there was little dispute among either Catholics or Protestants regarding biblical infallibility. The eloquent John Eck advised his friend: 'Listen, dear Erasmus, do you suppose any Christian will patiently endure to be told that the evangelists in their Gospels made mistakes?' and Archbishop James Ussher calculated the year of creation as 4004 B.C. on the basis of the absolute reliability of biblical dates. However, with the Age of Enlightenment, free thinking led to scepticism and the Protestants began to tighten their terms of reference. William Whitaker, a Cambridge scholar, published his *Disputation on Holy Scripture* in 1588. He believed unquestionably in biblical inerrancy and he demonstrated that this was the view of the Church Fathers in the early centuries. Whitaker claimed: 'We must maintain intact the authority of Scripture in such a sense as not to allow that anything is therein delivered otherwise than the most perfect truth required.' Whitaker was a typical Puritan and believed that this infallibility related to the original documents written by the biblical writers. He was followed by William Ames in *Marrow of Sacred Divinity* in 1624.

By the eighteenth century evangelicals were in no doubt. 'If there be one error in Scripture,' concluded John Wesley the preacher and evangelist, 'there might as well be a thousand. It would not be the truth of God.' A. A. Hodge and B. B. Warfield, the Princeton theologians of the late nineteenth and early twentieth century, were no inventors of new things when they spelt out the detail of biblical inerrancy and offered clear scriptural reasons for the doctrine; they were simply following a long history of mainstream Christianity. Professor Kirsopp Lake at Harvard University can be permitted the final word on this question of how old is the evangelical view of the Bible: 'It is we [the liberals] who have departed from the tradition.'

4.
Christ and his Bible

The Bible for Jesus and the Jews was our Old Testament, and whatever doubts men may have concerning the value and trustworthiness of the Old Testament, those doubts were not shared by our Lord.

A young man asked how he could obtain eternal life, and Jesus pointed him to the Old Testament (Matthew 19:16-22). A lawyer questioned Christ about the law, and in reply our Lord quoted directly from the Old Testament (Matthew 22:34-40). The Pharisees tried to trap him with hard moral questions about divorce, and again Christ directed them to the Old Testament (Matthew 19:3-6).

Christ used the Old Testament all the time. He used it to introduce himself (Luke 4:16-21), to fight Satan (Luke 4:1-12), to silence his enemies (Matthew 15:1-9), to instruct his hearers (John 6:25-34), to warn his disciples (Matthew 26:31) and to teach salvation (John 3:14). He used the Old Testament on the cross (Matthew 27:46) and after his resurrection (Luke 24:27). He constantly quoted it and without question accepted its accuracy and authority.

The way Christ introduced the Old Testament

The Gospels record quotations by our Lord from at least thirty-six different passages in the Old Testament, taken from thirteen Old Testament books. In addition there are many more occasions when he referred to the Old Testament but did not quote the actual words.

These indirect references or allusions to the Old Testament are like the colourful threads in a piece of cloth. They are woven into his teaching so regularly that they help to make it the strong and attractive material that it is. Without such an accurate knowledge of the Old Testament as our Lord and his hearers possessed, we can

'The Old Testament ... woven into his teaching like the threads in a
piece of cloth'

often miss these 'threads'. For example, Mark 4:29, 'As soon as the
grain is ripe, he puts the sickle to it, because the harvest has come',
reflects Joel 3:13: 'Swing the sickle, for the harvest is ripe.'

Similarly, the phrases 'The meek ... will inherit the earth' in
Matthew 5:5, and 'the pure in heart' in verse 8, are clearly reflections
of Psalm 37:11 and Psalm 73:1. The parable in Matthew 21:33-41
is our Lord's application of Isaiah 5, and the terrible warning of
Luke 19:44 echoes Psalm 137. In a single verse, Matthew 24:31,
there are allusions to Exodus 19:16; Zechariah 2:6; 9:14; Daniel 7:2
and Deuteronomy 4:32!

No one who has any knowledge of the Old Testament can doubt
that Christ's thinking was full of its words and phrases: he used them
all the time, indirectly or directly, and never did he give his approval
to anything other than the words of the Old Testament. Most of the
direct quotations were introduced by a special phrase that under-
lined the authority of what he was about to say. In particular he used
the phrase 'It is written' on eighteen different occasions. When
Christ employed this phrase, or other phrases such as 'the Scriptures', 'the Law', 'the Prophets' and 'the Law and the Prophets', he
was always introducing the Old Testament. He never used these
phrases except to refer to the Old Testament.

The Jewish rabbis, the religious teachers of Jesus' day, had added
613 laws of their own to God's law. 248 of these were positive and
365 were negative. Many of them were ridiculous. The Jewish
Talmud, a second-century A.D. collection of writings of the rabbis,
contained twenty-four chapters on the subject of keeping the Sabbath holy, and one rabbi spent two and a half years studying one
chapter alone! In trying to decide what 'burden' a man could or
could not carry on the Sabbath they concluded that a forbidden

burden would be equal to the weight of one dried fig; but two halves of a dried fig could be carried in two journeys. Similarly, if a man moved a sheaf of corn in his field it was forbidden labour; but he could move it if he put a spoon on top since this was a tool for eating. A 'Sabbath day's journey' was 2000 cubits, just under one mile, from a man's 'dwelling place', but if the day before the Sabbath he placed two meals at the end of the two thousand cubits then he could go on for another two thousand, for those meals were considered a 'dwelling place'. The crowning folly was the serious instruction that if a man kept a hen for the benefit of her eggs and she foolishly laid one on the Sabbath, he could not eat it because the hen was working — laying eggs was her occupation; however, if he was fattening her for the table and she laid an egg on the Sabbath, he could eat it because that was not her chief occupation!

Our Lord gave no authority to such nonsense as this, and never at any time did he discuss or quote approvingly the foolish teaching of the rabbis. But on an even more serious note he refused to accept the way the Pharisees misinterpreted and abused Scripture. In Matthew 5:21,27,31,33,38 and 43 Christ introduced six Old Testament passages by the phrase, 'You have heard that it was said'. He did not say, 'It is written', not because he rejected the authority of those passages, but because he refused to accept the Pharisees' abuse of them. Our Lord never introduced Jewish laws or traditions with those special phrases he reserved for Scripture alone.

In Matthew 4:4 Christ reminded Satan of the value of the whole of Scripture: 'Man does not live on bread alone, but on every word that comes from the mouth of God.' In fact he was quoting from Deuteronomy 8:3, but it is particularly important to notice what this verse actually says. In the first place God used the singular 'word', not 'words', and then added 'every' to reinforce his point. Our Lord was prepared to accept the authority of every single word that God had given. In the second place these words are described as coming 'from the mouth of God'. It is this that gives the words of Scripture their special authority. We could hardly have expected a clearer statement of inspiration than this, for the phrase 'comes from the mouth of God' is only another way of explaining the word *theopneustos*, 'God-breathed', found in 2 Timothy 3:16, which we discussed in the previous chapter. In this verse our Lord accepted without question that every word of Scripture had come from God. This is a belief in verbal inspiration.

Matthew 5:17-19 reads: 'Do not think that I have come to abolish the Law or the Prophets; I have not come to abolish them but to fulfil them. I tell you the truth, until heaven and earth disappear, not the smallest letter, not the least stroke of a pen, will by any means disappear from the Law until everything is accomplished. Anyone who breaks one of the least of these commandments and teaches others to do the same will be called least in the kingdom of heaven, but whoever practises and teaches these commands will be called great in the kingdom of heaven.' Notice that our Lord emphasized the eternal and binding authority of Scripture. He warned against abolishing or cancelling the law. The word means to loosen the force of a law and make it not binding. When Christ said that he came to 'fulfil' the law he meant that he came to carry it out in every detail. His obedience to the law is our example, and he clearly had no doubt that the law was binding for ever.

The way Christ used the Old Testament

'Jesus agreed always with the scribes of his time in accepting without question the authority of the [Old Testament] Law... Jesus did not attack the Law but assumed its authority and interpreted it.' These words were written by Rudolf Bultmann in 1934, in his book *Jesus and the Word* (p.61). Bultmann, who was mentioned in the previous chapter, was a New Testament scholar who denied the miracles recorded in the Bible, and most of its history. Yet even he was compelled to admit that, although he personally did not accept the inerrancy of Scripture, it is plain that Jesus did. Here are some examples of the way our Lord emphasized the authority of the Old Testament:

'God said, "Honour your father and mother..."' (Matthew 15:4). In quoting from Exodus our Lord did not say, 'Moses said', but 'God said'.

In Matthew 19:4-5 Christ introduced the words of Genesis 2:24 with the phrase, 'The Creator said...', but in Genesis the words are not directly the words of the Creator. Bultmann would say they are merely the words of the human author, but our Lord said they are the words of God.

Quoting from Psalm 110:1, Christ commented, 'David himself, speaking by the Holy Spirit declared...' (Mark 12:36).

When our Lord claimed, 'The Scripture cannot be broken' (John 10:34-35), he used the same word as that found in Matthew 5:19. In John 10:34 the quotation is from Psalm 82:6 and Christ introduced it by the phrase: 'Is it not written in your Law... ?' Therefore the Psalms were given the same authority as the law that came through Moses.

Three times our Lord countered Satan's temptations in Matthew 4:1-10 with the response: 'It is written'. He then quoted from Psalm 91 and Deuteronomy 6. For our Lord, when Scripture speaks there is nothing more to be said.

Did Christ ever contradict the Old Testament?

Six times in Matthew 5:21-43 our Lord quoted a verse from the Old Testament and then added, 'But I tell you'. From this many have concluded that Christ was contradicting the Old Testament statements. There are two simple answers to this.

In the first place we should go back and read what our Lord has said in that same chapter in verses 17-20. There, as we have seen, he underlines the eternal value of the law and he is not so foolish as to contradict himself in the next breath.

Secondly, as we have already noted, our Lord was not condemning those Scriptures but the abuse of them by the Pharisees. He was saying, 'You have so twisted them and torn them out of context that you have turned God's law into your own traditions; you have used God's words but have completely missed what God was saying. I will not therefore say of them, "It is written", but "You have said".' In just the same way the reader could take seven words from the earlier part of this section and claim that the author has stated, 'Christ was contradicting the Old Testament statements.' Those are, in fact, my words but that is certainly not what I said!

The way Christ used the history of the Old Testament

Some would agree with all that has been said so far in this chapter but then point out that we can accept our Lord's view of the authority of Scripture without admitting the accuracy of every historical detail. We have already met this approach; the argument is that the moral teaching and doctrine are inspired, but the history is open to error. What was our Lord's approach? Did he accept the story of Adam and Eve as fact or fiction? Are Noah and the flood and Jonah and the fish to be taken as myths only?

A myth, remember, is a made-up story to illustrate the supernatural or religious. Many twentieth-century theologians, like Rudolf Bultmann, insist that although the Bible stories are mythical (not historical) they are nevertheless true. They claim the stories may be loosely based upon historical facts but bear little resemblance to those facts; however, they believe the stories are mythical in that their message and purpose tell us something true about God. But this is playing with words. Our concern here is not what liberal theologians think about the stories of the Old Testament, but what our Lord thought of them. Was our Lord teaching deep spiritual truths in stories that have little or no fact in history? It is true that in Christ's day the Jews were fond of making up stories, but nowhere do we find him using those stories. The Old Testament is written as plain history and that is exactly how the Lord used it. Not once did he cast the smallest doubt upon the historical facts of the stories to which he referred.

In every Old Testament story used by Christ two things should be noticed in particular.

1. Christ never doubted the historical accuracy of the account

Those who deny that Christ was God will maintain that he was as ignorant of the true facts as were the Jews themselves. This amounts to a claim that it requires the wisdom of modern scholarship to reveal the truth to us. We need not delay on this line of argument, for the attack here is really directed towards the character of Christ himself. If he was not God, it follows that nothing he said can be trusted, and our hope of eternal life is therefore robbed of real meaning. If Christ was not God, all his claims are without foundation.

But others, who are prepared to accept that Christ was truly God, remind us that he took upon himself certain limitations when he came to earth. For example, he could only be in one place at a time, and he required food and sleep. More important still, on his own admission our Lord consulted with his heavenly Father before he spoke. In John 14:24 we read: 'These words you hear are not my own; they belong to the Father who sent me' (see also John 8:26,40). Similarly, he admitted that he did not know the time of the end of the

age: 'No one knows about that day or hour, not even the angels in
heaven, nor the Son, but only the Father' (Matthew 24:36). Is it not
therefore reasonable to conclude that Christ did not know the truth
about the Old Testament history either?

Our answer to this is that the only limitation of knowledge that
our Lord ever admitted, and that only whilst he was the Son of Man
on earth, was the time of the end of the world. But this did not involve
him in any falsehood either intentionally or unintentionally. To
suggest that Christ was ignorant of the historical facts behind Old
Testament stories, and therefore continued to relate myths, makes
him party to untruths, whether intentionally or not. It attacks the
character of Christ and his teaching to suggest that he ignorantly
taught untruth while he was claiming to be 'the way and the truth and
the life' (John 14:6). Besides, he claimed to be 'a man who has told
you the truth that I heard from God' (John 8:40), and to question the
accuracy of his words therefore makes both God the Father and his
Son Jesus Christ liars.

However, some still respond that Christ merely accommodated
himself to the ideas of the Jews around him. He knew the Old
Testament was largely myth, and that the recorded history was very
inaccurate, but it suited his purpose not to attack the Jewish view of
the Old Testament but simply to base his teaching upon it. His
teaching is therefore right even if the history he quoted is wrong.
This is the least defensible position of all, for it makes Christ quite
intentionally party to a lie. We can hardly be expected to trust the
words of a man who gave the clear impression that he believed
something to be true which he knew perfectly well to be wrong. We
are left wondering where else he has misled us in areas where even
modern scholars have not yet found him out!

2. *He always used the Old Testament to teach important truths*

In every instance of his use of Old Testament history our Lord was
not merely retelling stories to amuse his hearers; he was seeking to
prove or illustrate important Christian truths. If the stories were
false, how can we trust the teaching? You cannot prove a truth by a
lie.

For example, in Matthew 12:40, in order to show that his
resurrection would be the greatest sign of his authority, Christ could
say, 'For as Jonah was three days and three nights in the belly of a

huge fish, so the Son of Man will be three days and three nights in the heart of the earth.' If the story of Jonah and the fish is not historically true, but a myth to illustrate important truths, then we are at liberty to deny the fact of the resurrection also, as many do. This would bring us into conflict with Paul's teaching in 1 Corinthians 15.

Similarly, in Matthew 12:41 our Lord used Jonah's preaching to Nineveh, and the repentance of that city, to warn his hearers that one day those very people in Nineveh would stand in judgement upon all who reject the gospel of Christ. If the story of Jonah is nothing more than a myth, then Christ's serious warning about judgement is based upon a prophet who never lived, and a people who never heard the preaching he did not give and who therefore did not respond to the warning they never received! This has as much value as a prosecution lawyer standing up in court and, in order to secure the conviction of the man on trial, inventing a story of a crime for which he was accusing the poor man. We are hardly likely to take the lawyer seriously in the future, and we would lose respect for any court that bothered to listen to him.

Here is a list of our Lord's use of Old Testament history, and you will notice that in each instance he is not telling a story but illustrating or proving a significant issue.

Reference	History	Old Testament reference	Teaching
Matt. 19:4-5	Adam and Eve	Gen.1:27;2:24	Marriage
Luke 11:51	Cain and Abel	Gen. 4:8	Judgement
Luke 17:26-27	Noah and the flood	Gen. 6-8	Second coming of Christ
John 8:56-58	Abraham	Gen. 15-25	Deity and eternity of Christ
Luke 17:28-32; 10:12	Sodom and Gomorrah and Lot's wife	Gen. 19	Second coming of Christ
Matt. 8:11	Isaac and Jacob	Gen. 25	Heaven and hell
Mark 7:9-10	Moses and theTen Commandments	Exod.20: 12; Lev. 20:9	Family duty
John 6: 31-51	Manna in the wilderness	Exod. 16	Eternal life

Reference	History	Old Testament reference	Teaching
John 3:14	The serpent of brass	Num. 21	Salvation
Mark 2:25-26	David and the consecrated bread	1 Sam. 21	Sabbath
Matt. 12:42	Solomon and the Queen of Sheba	1 Kings 10	Judgement
Luke 4:25-26	Elijah and the widow of Zarephath	1 Kings 17	Miracles
Luke 4:27	Elisha and Naaman	2 Kings 5	Miracles
Luke 11:51	Murder of Zechariah	2 Chron. 2	Judgement
Matt. 12:39-41; 16:4	Jonah and the fish	Jonah	Resurrection of Christ and judgement.

The way Christ applied the Old Testament to himself

At the beginning of his ministry our Lord sat in the synagogue at Nazareth, quoted two verses from Isaiah 61 and declared: 'Today this Scripture is fulfilled in your hearing' (Luke 4:16-21). Later, whilst he was teaching in the temple courts, Christ quoted the first verse of Psalm 110 and challenged his listeners to explain who it was that David was writing about; he himself spelt out David's clear implication: if David called the Messiah 'my Lord' then the Christ must be much more than simply a descendant of the great Israelite king himself.

At the end of his earthly ministry our Lord walked beside two unhappy disciples on the road to Emmaus. They had heard of the crucifixion and could hardly believe in the resurrection; life seemed at an end. All their hopes were gone. The stranger began by rebuking their stupidity and unbelief. He told them that they should have known the Old Testament prophets spoke of the Messiah and that therefore it was inevitable that the Christ would suffer as he had.

Then he opened the Scriptures: 'And beginning with Moses and all the Prophets, he explained to them what was said in all the Scriptures concerning himself' (Luke 24:25-27). He might have said only, 'Here I am, alive!' but he chose rather to persuade them with the authority of Scripture.

A short while later, he did the same with the rest of the disciples: 'This is what I told you while I was still with you: Everything must be fulfilled that is written about me in the Law of Moses, the Prophets and the Psalms... He told them, "This is what is written..."' (Luke 24:44-47).

Again and again our Lord claimed that the Old Testament Scriptures foretold the details of his life and death. See, for example, Mark 14:27,49 and John 13:18; 17:12. His chief use of the Old Testament was put to the Jews in two simple phrases: 'These are the Scriptures that testify about me... Moses wrote about me' (John 5:39-47). Our Lord based the authority of his life and ministry upon the authority and inerrancy of the Old Testament Scriptures. It is little wonder, therefore, that Christ claimed that ignorance of Scripture was the chief cause for ignorance about himself (Matthew 22:29).

Conclusion

If a critic of the Bible like Rudolf Bultmann could accept that Christ believed in the inspiration and authority of the Old Testament, no one can have good cause to deny that that is what Christ did believe. But Bultmann considered Christ was mistaken in this belief. We are left with one remaining question: 'Do we take Christ, or a German theologian, as our final witness to the inerrancy of Scripture?'

5.
The apostles and their use of the Old Testament

Writing in *Revelation and the Bible*, chapter 9, Roger Nicole claims to have counted in the New Testament 224 direct quotations from the Old Testament introduced by such definite phrases as 'Scripture says,' or 'It is written'. In addition he finds seven occasions when a second quotation follows on from the first, nineteen occasions when a summary or paraphrase is used rather than a direct quotation, and forty-five when no claim to be quoting from the Old Testament is made but where a passage is clearly in mind. Roger Nicole maintains that, if anything, this underestimates the number. However, it gives us 295 references to the Old Testament contained in 352 verses of the New Testament. That is nearly four and a half per cent of the total number of verses in the New Testament, or one verse in every twenty-two and a half! Only nine books of the Old Testament are not quoted in the New Testament. They are Ruth, Judges, Song of Solomon, Ecclesiastes, Esther, Ezra, Nehemiah and 1 and 2 Chronicles.

In the light of these frequent references to the Old Testament, it is particularly interesting that in the New Testament there is not one reference to a book of the Apocrypha. The Apocrypha is a group of Jewish religious books that were written after the close of the Old Testament and before the start of the New Testament. In other words the Apocrypha comes historically between Malachi and Matthew. In chapter 10 we will discuss the place of the Apocrypha.

This constant use of the Old Testament is very impressive and we must ask the question: 'Exactly how did the apostles use the Old Testament?' We have already seen our Lord's use of it, but what did the apostles think when they wrote their letters to the young churches? Part of the answer to this question has already been given in chapter 3, but there are a number of facts that we can add here.

God is considered the author of the Old Testament

Fifty-six times the New Testament refers to God as the author of the Old Testament, and even where the human writer is known, the divine authorship is often stated instead. We shall look at just two of many examples we could have quoted.

In Hebrews 1:5-13 quotations are taken from 2 Samuel 7:14; Psalms 2:7; 104:4; 45:6-7; 102:25-27; 110:1. The human writers are ignored entirely and five times the apostle introduces a quotation with the phrase: 'He [God] says'.

Similarly the same writer quotes from Jeremiah 31 with the simple introduction: 'The Holy Spirit also testifies to us about this...' (Hebrews 10:15).

Divine authorship is added to the human writer

It is not always true that the human writers are ignored. The apostles were well aware of the men who wrote the Old Testament and yet when they referred to them they often felt the need to emphasize the divine authorship as well. Here are four obvious examples.

In Acts 1:16 Peter is quoting from Psalm 41:9 and he introduces the verse in this way: 'Brothers, the Scripture had to be fulfilled, which the Holy Spirit spoke long ago through the mouth of David...'

Similarly in Acts 4:25 the apostles prayed, 'You spoke by the Holy Spirit through the mouth of your servant, our father David...'

In Acts 28:25 Paul introduces Isaiah 6:9-10 to his Jewish hearers by saying, 'The Holy Spirit spoke the truth to your forefathers when he said through Isaiah the prophet ...'

Finally, in Romans 9:25 Paul begins a quotation from Hosea 2:23 with the words: 'As he [God] says in Hosea...'

There can therefore be no doubt in our minds that Peter and Paul understood the words of the Old Testament writers to be those of God the Holy Spirit speaking through men.

Scripture is identified with God

The phrases 'Scripture says' or 'the Law says' are often used when in the Old Testament passage we are in fact told that God is speaking. The implication from this is not that the Scriptures are God, but that whenever Scripture speaks, it is God speaking and thus these expressions are the same as saying, 'God says'.

In Romans 7:7 Paul writes, 'The Law ... said, "Do not covet",' and he then quotes from Exodus 20:17, but Exodus 20:1 distinctly says, 'God spoke all these words.'

In Romans 9:17 Paul introduces the words of God to Pharaoh found in Exodus 9:16 with the phrase: 'The Scripture says to Pharaoh...'

In Galatians 3:8 Paul claims, 'The Scripture ... announced the gospel in advance to Abraham,' and he continues with Genesis 12:3 where we are told in verse 1: 'The Lord said to Abram...'

These are just three of many examples and we cannot avoid the conclusion that 'Scripture says', 'the Law says', and 'God says' are all the same in the apostle's mind.

The term 'law' is used for the whole of the Old Testament

We have just seen that 'the Law says' is the same as 'God says' in the minds of the apostles. But the term 'Law' does not cover merely the Ten Commandments. Everything in the Old Testament has the force of law. Although the Jews generally divided the Old Testament into three parts, the Law, the Writings and the Prophets, they frequently referred to the whole of the Old Testament as 'the Law'. Therefore our Lord, speaking to the Jews and quoting from Psalm 82, which was part of the Writings, could say, 'Is it not written in your Law?' (John 10:34). This was the view of the apostles also; every part of the Old Testament carried the authority of God's law.

In Romans 3:19 Paul places a number of Scriptures under the general heading of 'Law', but he has just quoted from five psalms and the prophet Isaiah!

Similarly, in 1 Corinthians 14:21 the apostle claims, 'In the Law it is written...' and then continues with a quotation from Isaiah 28:11-12.

The Old Testament Scriptures are the 'words' of God

On two occasions the Greek word *logion,* or 'word,' is used with reference to the Old Testament. This word *'logion'* is similar to, but not identical with, the commonly used word '*logos*', or 'word', and it has a very special meaning. Outside the Bible it often referred to a short statement from the gods; this is why some versions translate it by the word 'oracle'. In Acts 7:38 Stephen claims that the Ten Commandments came by Moses, who 'received living words to pass on to us', and in Romans 3:2 Paul tells us that the Jews were 'entrusted with the very words of God'. There are only two other uses of this word in the whole of the New Testament. In Hebrews 5:12 it refers to the summary of Christian doctrine and in 1 Peter 4:11 the Christian teacher is to speak 'as one speaking the very words of God'.

It is interesting to note that the Septuagint, which is the Greek translation of the Old Testament completed between approximately 250 and 150 B.C., uses this word *logion* thirty-six times, and nineteen of these uses are in Psalm 119, which has a direct reference to God's Word in all but five of its 176 verses. According to the American Bible scholar Benjamin Warfield, apart from three references, *logion,* as used in the Septuagint, always refers to 'a sacred utterance of the Divine Being [God]'. Stephen, Paul and Peter were all familiar with the Septuagint and they would therefore use the word in the same way. Certainly many of the leaders of the church, writing shortly after the close of the New Testament, used the word '*logion*' in exactly this way, to refer to a sacred word from God.

The Old Testament is God-given, authoritative and relevant

Although we shall return to this in the chapters concerning the authority and sufficiency of Scripture, we should recall that from 2 Timothy 3:16 and 2 Peter 1:21 we have already seen how committed the New Testament writers were to the divine authorship of the Old Testament. In addition, they were aware of the fact that everything in the Old Testament was relevant for the first century A.D. When the New Testament used the expression, 'It is written', to introduce a quotation from the Old, the writers were not merely finding a convenient way of introducing their reference; on the contrary, the phrase was significant in that it registered the fact that what follows is part of the written and unbreakable Word of God. The phrase 'It is written' occurs eighty-six times in the New Testament; forty of those are in the Gospels, chiefly used by Christ himself.

Speaking to the Jews at Pisidian Antioch, Paul quotes from Isaiah 49:6 and declares, 'This is what the Lord has commanded us' (Acts 13:47). Similarly, the writer to the Hebrews quotes Proverbs 3:11-12 and introduces it with the challenge, 'You have forgotten that word of encouragement that addresses you as sons' (Hebrews 12:5-6).

There was nothing merely historical about the Old Testament for the apostles; it was a book of authority and relevance and the apostles placed themselves under its commands. Paul could honestly claim before the governor Felix: 'I believe everything that agrees with the Law and that is written in the Prophets...' (Acts 24:14). Similarly he could write to the Christians at Rome: 'Everything that was written in the past was written to teach us...' (Romans 15:4).

Paul's use of the Old Testament in 1 Corinthians 15 is typical of the New Testament writers. He was concerned to demonstrate the historical fact of the physical resurrection of Christ because some in the church at Corinth had denied this. Paul had many arguments to make and many eyewitnesses to offer, but his first reason for asserting the truth of the resurrection of Christ was that it was based upon the Old Testament. Christ's death and resurrection took place 'according to the Scriptures' (vv. 2-3).

The apostles' use of the Septuagint

More often than not, when the New Testament writers wanted to quote from the Old Testament they used the Septuagint. It was only natural that they should use this translation since they spoke Greek and so did all their readers; Greek was the common language of the first-century Roman Empire, not Latin or Hebrew! The problem is that sometimes they used the Septuagint in places where it was not a very good translation of the Old Testament Hebrew — and they didn't bother to correct it. Some suggest that this presents a problem for those who believe that the Holy Spirit guided the New Testament writers to keep them free from error. There are two answers to this accusation.

First, we must make it clear that never did the New Testament writers try to support an argument by a bad translation. Therefore they had no need to correct the Septuagint, even if they had known it was not the best translation. As an illustration of this, a preacher today will have a modern translation in front of him as he preaches. A verse he wants to refer to in the course of his sermon may not be the best possible translation, but if it is adequate for his purpose he will not bother to correct it; to do so would only divert the attention of his congregation away from the main purpose. There is no error in using the Bible in this way. At times a preacher may cover a whole passage of Scripture with his own free paraphrase; this does not imply any weakness in his view of biblical inerrancy.

The apostles did not assume that the Septuagint became an inspired translation whenever they used it; it was simply a translation, and was only authoritative in so far as it faithfully represented the Old Testament Hebrew. Their use of it is infallible, certainly, but this does not imply infallibility in the whole or any part of the Greek translation. The valuable lesson we can learn here is that God can speak through a translation of his Word, even though the translation may not be perfect.

Second, the apostles did not have the advantages of the modern writer in the use of punctuation, quotation marks, brackets and so on; these aids for the writer just did not exist. Therefore we have no way of knowing when they stop a direct quotation and begin their own paraphrase of an Old Testament passage. For example, Romans 3:10-12 is a free paraphrase of Psalm 14:1-3, and in the next six verses Paul sprinkles in parts of Psalm 5:9, Psalm 140:3, Psalm 10:7, Isaiah 59:7-8 and Psalm 36:1. It would be quite wrong to accuse Paul of inaccuracies because he chooses only to pick out parts of the verses.

New meanings for the old

It is also alleged that the New Testament writers are sometimes too free in their application of an Old Testament passage, giving it a meaning that is not clearly there in the original. Again there are two answers to this.

First, Professor C. H. Dodd, who was no supporter of the evangelical view of Scripture, maintained that 'In general...the writers of the New Testament, in making use of passages from the Old Testament, remain true to the main intention of their writers.' That should be sufficient as an answer, although you will notice he says, 'in general'. So, what about the few times when they are more free than we would be in the way they apply the Old Testament? We come to our second response.

Second, if the doctrine of the Scriptures as the 'God-breathed' word is true, then we can safely assume that where the New Testament writers understand an Old Testament passage in a less than obvious way, or apply it in a way we would hesitate to do, this is because God has more light to reveal to us through the apostles. Here are some examples of the ways New Testament apostles provide us with new meanings for the Old.

1 Corinthians 10:1-5. We may not all see the rock from which water came for the Jews in the wilderness as a picture of Christ, but clearly Paul did.

1 Corinthians 15:27. The Hebrew text (Masoretic Text), and the Greek translation of the Old Testament (Septuagint) of Psalm 8:6, both use the second person singular: '*You* put everything under his feet...', whereas Paul uses the third person 'he' (God) and 'his' (Christ). Is Paul quoting, or just using the language of the psalm? The answer is that in Psalm 8 we read of man in his created state before the Fall; in 1 Corinthians 15:45-47 Paul claims that Christ is the second Adam, so Psalm 8 is given Messianic meaning by Paul.

Romans 1:17; Galatians 3:11. The Masoretic Text of Habakkuk 2:4 has 'The righteous will live by *his* faith', and the Septuagint has 'The righteous will live by *my* faith.' Paul omits both and states simply; 'The righteous will live *by faith*...' Since faith is a gift of God, he chooses to refer to it as neither belonging to God nor man.

Galatians 3:16. The Hebrew and Greek word for 'seed' (as in the English also) can be either singular or plural. But Paul, by insisting upon the singular, is drawing out a deeper meaning and reading Christ in all the Scriptures (Luke 24:27).

1 Corinthians 9:9; Deuteronomy 25:4. Paul is not saying that Deuteronomy has no relevance for animals but his word 'surely' in verse 10 means that God is more concerned for us.

All this is what is known as the *sensus plenior*, the fuller sense of Scripture. But we must be careful. The Alexandrian School of interpreting Scripture, led by men like Clement and Origen in the third century A.D., virtually discarded the literal meaning altogether. As we shall see in chapter 14, we do not have the right to go beyond the apostles in our attempts to understand the Scriptures.

Scriptures for every occasion

In his chapter in *Revelation and the Bible* (p.140), Roger Nicole summarized the apostolic use of the Old Testament in these words: 'The New Testament writers used quotations in their sermons, in their histories, in their letters, in their prayers. They used them when addressing Jews or Gentiles, churches or individuals, friends or antagonists, new converts or seasoned Christians. They used them for argumentation, for illustration, for instruction, for documentation, for prophecy, for reproof. They used them in times of stress and in hours of mature thinking, in liberty and in prison, at home and abroad. Everywhere and always they were ready to refer to the impregnable authority of Scripture...'

That seems to be a bold assertion. Can we actually find instances to prove the claim of Roger Nicole? Certainly we can. Here is a list of all the categories he mentions with an example, in each case, of how the New Testament writers made a habit of quoting the Old Testament Scriptures.

Sermons. In Peter's sermon on the Day of Pentecost, Acts 2:17-21 is a direct quotation from Joel 2:28-32.

Histories. Stephen, just before his martyrdom, went through the history of Israel, and in Acts 7 he referred to Genesis, Exodus, Deuteronomy, Numbers, Isaiah, Amos and a psalm.

Letters. Peter wrote to Christians scattered throughout the Roman Empire. 1 Peter contains quotations from Leviticus, two psalms, Proverbs and Isaiah.

Prayers. With the arrest of Peter and John, the Christians went to prayer, and in Acts 4:24-26 they used Psalms 146:6 and 2:1.

Jews. Paul preached to the Jews at Pisidian Antioch where, according to Acts 13:33-35, 41, he referred to two psalms, Isaiah and Habakkuk.

Gentiles. At Lystra Paul and Barnabas were mistaken for Greek gods. According to Acts 14:15, Paul took his text from Exodus 20:11.

Churches. In the letter to the church at Rome there are fifty-three quotations from the Old Testament, and Romans 15 alone contains quotations from three psalms, Deuteronomy, Isaiah and 2 Samuel.

Individuals. Paul wrote to Timothy, who was ministering at Ephesus, and in 1 Timothy 5:18 quoted from Deuteronomy 25:4.

Friends. Because of his experiences in the town Paul must have counted the Christians at Ephesus among his closest friends. Ephesians 4:8 is a quotation from Psalm 68:18.

Antagonists. Paul faced opposition from Jewish leaders at Rome and in Acts 28:26-27 turned his accusers to Isaiah 6:9-10.

New converts. Galatians was probably Paul's first letter and the young Christians were already slipping from the truth. Galatians 3 contains references to Genesis, Leviticus, Deuteronomy and Habakkuk.

Seasoned Christians. Timothy, though young, had proved himself an experienced worker. 2 Timothy 2:19 quotes from Numbers 16 and Isaiah 26.

Argumentation. The great debate at Jerusalem was settled by James, who in Acts 15:16-18 reminded the council of Amos 9.

Illustration. Paul illustrated the bondage of law and the liberty of Christ by reference to Hagar and Sarah. Galatians 4:27,30 are taken from Isaiah 54 and Genesis 21.

Instruction. Paul taught the Roman Christians about Israel and evangelism, and Romans 10 contains quotations from Leviticus, Deuteronomy, Isaiah and Joel.

Documentation. The writer to the Hebrews listed some of the great saints of the past, and his familiar eleventh chapter is packed with references to the Old Testament and contains direct quotations from Genesis 15 and 21.

Prophecy. Paul turned to the Old Testament for a prophecy of the resurrection and supported his position in 1 Corinthians 15:54-55 with quotations from Isaiah 25 and Hosea 13.

Reproof. The Hebrew Christians had forgotten the benefits of discipline, and Hebrews 12:5-6 is taken from Proverbs 3:11-12.

Stress. Peter and John were on trial before the Jewish rulers but the record of their response in Acts 4:11 is a quotation from Psalm 118.

Mature thought. The eighth chapter of Romans is often considered to be Paul's greatest theology, and Romans 8:36 comes from Psalm 44:22.

Liberty. Peter's second sermon after Pentecost was given at a time when nothing could hold the disciples back from evangelism. Acts 3:22-23 is taken from Deuteronomy 18.

Prison. John was a prisoner on the island of Patmos and his vision received there and recorded in the book of Revelation

'The New Testament writers used the Old … in liberty and in prison'

contains at least fourteen quotations and paraphrases from seven books of the Old Testament.

At home. James wrote from his home town of Jerusalem and the second chapter of his letter contains quotations from Leviticus 19; Exodus 20; Genesis 15 and Isaiah 41.

Abroad. Paul wrote 2 Corinthians from Macedonia. 2 Corinthians 6:2 comes from Isaiah 49:8.

6.
The authority of the Bible

In 1521 Martin Luther stood before the Emperor Charles V, in the town of Worms in Germany. Luther was on trial for insisting upon the authority of Scripture as opposed to the traditions of men and the decrees of the popes. Towards the end of the debate the great Reformer challenged his accusers: 'I am bound by the Scriptures and my conscience has been taken captive by the Word of God, and I am neither able nor willing to recant, since it is neither safe nor right to act against conscience. God help me. Amen.' The trial immediately ended in confusion!

Luther was not the only one to make this stand. Before him and since, evangelical Christians have accepted the authority of Scripture as full and final and they have appealed to Scripture to settle every issue of their faith and their practice. But why do they do this? Those who do not believe the Bible sometimes argue that this God-given authority has been imposed upon Scripture: that is to say, the Bible never considered itself as having special and final authority, but that evangelical Christians have pressed this claim upon it as the centuries passed.

Perhaps the chief part of our answer to this charge has already been given in chapters 3, 4 and 5. If all that is true, then it would be little short of blasphemy to claim anything other than a God-given authority for the Bible. But there is more that we can say, and we must discover what the writers of the Old and New Testaments thought about their own writings. Did they believe their words carried divine authority or not? After all, it is a very serious matter to expect people at the dawn of the twenty-first century to allow their lives to be governed by the words of a book some of which was written more than three and a half thousand years ago!

Even today Christians give their liberty and lives for their belief in this book. Christians all over the world gladly submit to its authority and allow it to guide them in the very details of how they should live and what they should believe. But what is the basis of this trust? How far should we accept its authority, and how far does it reach into every problem and situation that faces people today? These questions are really concerned with the authority, sufficiency and finality of Scripture. In other words, must we trust it, is it all we really need, and is it God's last word to man before the return of Christ? It is the authority of Scripture that concerns us in this chapter.

Throughout this chapter remember what we are setting out to prove. We are only seeking to show that the writers of the Old Testament, our Lord himself and the apostles all believed quite firmly that they spoke with the authority of God. A man may say that they were wrong and misguided — he is entitled to that view — but, as we shall see, what no man must ever say is that the writers of the Bible did not think they were giving messages with the authority of God, because they certainly did.

The claim of the Old Testament

The prophets' claim to divine authority

The prophets knew themselves to be governed by the Spirit of God.

Nearly 4,000 times in the Old Testament, and around 500 times in the first five books alone, we read such expressions as 'The Lord spoke', 'The Lord commanded' or 'The Lord said'. None of the prophets spoke on his own authority. Micah contrasted himself with the false prophets and claimed, 'But as for me, I am filled with power, with the Spirit of the Lord' (Micah 3:8). Zechariah spoke for both himself and the prophets who had come before him when he accused Israel of ignoring 'the words that the Lord Almighty had sent by his Spirit through the earlier prophets' (Zechariah 7:12).

Even David, who was a prophet, and who gave us many of our Old Testament psalms, declared in his dying speech, 'The Spirit of the Lord spoke through me; his word was on my tongue. The God of Israel spoke, the Rock of Israel said to me...' (2 Samuel 23:2-3).

Their experience of receiving the message from God

The prophets never thought of their message as originating in their
own minds or with their own ideas. In fact their description of the
false prophets was that they were men who prophesied 'out of their
own imagination' (Ezekiel 13:2). On the contrary, the true prophets
knew that their words were given directly by God. Jeremiah described his call to the prophetic ministry in this way: 'Then the Lord
reached out his hand and touched my mouth and said to me, "Now,
I have put my words in your mouth..."' (Jeremiah 1:9). Isaiah
recorded the same divine preparation in Isaiah 51:16; 59:21. Similarly, God promised Moses that his successor would speak with the
same authority as Moses himself: 'I will raise up for them a prophet
like you from among their brothers; I will put my words in his
mouth, and will tell them everything I command him' (Deuteronomy 18:18). Certainly this verse has an ultimate fulfilment in the
coming Messiah, but it also covers the immediate successors of
Moses.

However we understand these words, it is clear that the prophets
knew that they received the words of their prophetic ministry in an
unusual manner, which was completely different from the ideas that
came to them in normal conversation. As a consequence they saw
themselves as God's spokesmen (Ezekiel 3:4).

Perhaps even more startling is the expression that the prophets
actually *saw* their message. Whether this was a seeing with the eye
or with the mind is not always clear, but what is clear is that the
prophet received his message in such a vivid and real manner that
it could be described in no other way than 'seeing'. Isaiah introduces a message with the statement: 'This is what Isaiah son of
Amoz saw concerning Judah and Jerusalem' (Isaiah 2:1). Amos 1:1;
Micah 1:1; Habakkuk 1:1 and Revelation 1:19 all record the same
experience.

This experience of 'seeing' his message in a vision or dream led
to the prophet being called a 'seer' on at least twelve occasions in
the Old Testament: for example, 1 Samuel 9:9; Amos 7:12; and
1 Chronicles 26:28, where Samuel is called 'the seer'. Even in the
time of Isaiah the rebellious people are aware of the significance of
this word: 'They say to the seers, "See no more visions!", and to the
prophets, "Give us no more visions of what is right! Tell us pleasant
things, prophesy illusions"' (Isaiah 30:10).

Their responsibility to speak only the words of God

Standing in this special relationship with God, the prophets could not speak beyond the words God gave them.

The view of Amos was typical of all the prophets of the Lord; they knew themselves to be in an unusual relationship with God and they appreciated the solemn responsibility of this. Amos could record, 'Surely the Sovereign Lord does nothing without revealing his plan to his servants the prophets' (Amos 3:7). In consequence of this, the prophets not only had to speak the words God gave them, but were unable to say anything more or less than that which God commanded them. So Amos declares: 'The lion has roared — who will not fear? The Sovereign Lord has spoken — who can but prophesy?' (Amos 3:8).

Even the rebellious prophet Balaam could do no other than remind King Balak, who was trying to bribe Balaam to curse the people of Israel: 'Even if Balak gave me his palace filled with silver and gold, I could not do anything of my own accord, good or bad, to go beyond the command of the Lord — and I must say only what the Lord says' (Numbers 24:13). It is hardly surprising therefore that again and again the prophets began their message with the words 'Hear the word of the Lord' (see for example Isaiah 1:10; Jeremiah 10:1; Micah 6:1).

This clear sense of accountability to God is seen in the warnings that came through the prophets not to add to God's words. Moses passed on to the people the solemn warning from God: 'Do not add to what I command you and do not subtract from it...' (Deuteronomy 4:2). A similar warning is conveyed through Proverbs 30:6: 'Do not add to his words, or he will rebuke you and prove you a liar.'

Although there is some uncertainty about the original meaning of the word for a prophet, which is *'nabi'* in Hebrew, it is generally agreed that it refers to a spokesman on behalf of another. This is illustrated in the episode recorded in Numbers 12:1-8 where Miriam and Aaron rebelled against the authority of Moses. They ask, 'Has the Lord spoken only through Moses? Hasn't he also spoken through us?' God's reply is to remind Moses' sister and brother that he reveals himself to his prophets through visions and dreams, but that Moses stands in a special relationship with God; he was one to whom God revealed himself 'face to face'. Moses, like all the prophets, stood as a spokesman for God and should not be opposed.

This is exactly how the Jews understood the ministry of all the Old Testament writers. When Moses came down from Mount Sinai he gathered together the elders of Israel and gave them 'all the words the Lord had commanded him to speak'. The immediate response of the elders showed their complete trust in Moses as the voice of God: 'We will do everything the Lord has said' (Exodus 19:7-8). All through history the sincere Jews accepted this view of the Scriptures as the Word of God.

The authority of the words

The words of the Old Testament were all considered to have God-given authority.

This thought runs throughout the Old Testament and is woven into it like the strands of a piece of cloth. Nowhere is it found more clearly than in Psalm 119, which consists of 176 verses and only five contain no direct reference to the Word of God. It is not claiming too much to say that verse 160 is a summary of the Old Testament's view of itself: 'All your words are true; all your righteous laws are eternal.' As a consequence of this, there was no doubt in the minds of the Old Testament writers that every word of God was 'flawless' (Proverbs 30:5-6). The word translated 'flawless' comes from a root verb meaning 'to refine metal'; similarly the Greek translation means to burn with fire or purify. The passive use in Proverbs 30 means that the words have been tested and proved true; because of the agency of the Holy Spirit any flaw, any impurity, has been taken out.

The claim of the New Testament

In chapter 3, we looked at two important verses in the New Testament: 2 Timothy 3:16 and 2 Peter 1:21. In their immediate context, of course, they refer to the Old Testament, because this was the Bible of the New Testament Christians. What we now need to show is that the same authority the New Testament writers saw in the Old Testament, they also claimed for themselves, and for each other.

The claims of the writers to divine authority

The New Testament writers claimed to speak and write by the Holy Spirit and with the authority of God.

When Paul wrote to the Corinthian Christians he found it necessary to defend his authority as an apostle against those who had refused to accept his ministry. Paul's argument was that he wrote and preached, 'not in words taught us by human wisdom, but words taught by the Spirit' (1 Corinthians 2:13). Before this is dismissed as a claim to nothing more than a wisdom a little above the average, it must not be forgotten that prior to his conversion Paul was an educated leader of the Jews and he was well aware that a claim like this was almost identical to the claim of the Old Testament prophets.

In exactly the same way, Peter could encourage the young churches to 'recall the words spoken in the past by the holy prophets and the command given by our Lord and Saviour through your apostles' (2 Peter 3:2). Our translators have handled fairly well an unusual form of Greek here; the emphasis is not that the apostles merely passed on the commands that Christ had given during his earthly ministry, but that they now spoke with the voice of Christ himself. A reasonable translation would be: 'the commandment of the apostles of the Lord Jesus'.

Peter not only gave equal authority to the words of the prophets and apostles, but also declared his belief that the Lord and Saviour now revealed his commands to his church by the apostles. In his first letter Peter is even more plain. He first made the statement, familiar to many of his readers, that the Old Testament prophets spoke of the coming of Christ by the power of 'the Spirit of Christ in them' (1 Peter 1:11). Peter then turned his attention to the apostles 'who have preached the gospel to you by the Holy Spirit sent from heaven' (v. 12). Clearly, then, to Peter's thinking, what the Holy Spirit was to the prophets, so he was to the apostles; the authority of the one is equal to the authority of the other. Similarly in Revelation 22:6 John claimed that the God who controlled 'the spirits of the prophets' also revealed the contents of John's revelations to him.

If ever a church tested Paul's patience it must have been the church at Corinth; against no other church did he have to defend his apostolic authority so much. But it is useful for us that he had to do so. In 1 Corinthians 14:37 Paul made it quite clear that his words carried with them the authority of Christ himself: 'If anybody thinks he is a prophet or spiritually gifted, let him acknowledge that what I am writing to you is the Lord's command.'

Similarly, the apostle could remind the Thessalonians: 'You know what instructions we gave you by *the authority of* the Lord Jesus' (1 Thessalonians 4:2). The words in italics are not part of the original Greek, and have been unnecessarily added by our translators! Earlier in that same letter Paul reminded his readers how they had first responded to Paul's message: 'When you received the word of God, which you heard from us, you accepted it not as the word of men, but as it actually is, the word of God...' (2:13).

Because Paul was convinced that his teaching carried with it the authority of God, he was not ashamed to claim that his preaching was the standard of the truth and that other preachers could be tested and measured by it. In Galatians 1:6-12, Paul claims that anyone preaching contrary to his teaching, even he himself if he ever dared to change the content of his gospel, should be cut off from God. The reason is that Paul's gospel was not 'according to man', (NASB) but was received 'by revelation from Jesus Christ'(v.12). Galatians chapter 1 must convince even the most casual reader that Paul saw the gospel that he preached as God-given, and not something that 'man made up'.

For this reason obedience to the apostles' teaching became a condition of fellowship, as we can see from the following two pasages: 'If anybody thinks he is a prophet or spiritually gifted, let him acknowledge that what I am writing to you is the Lord's command. If he ignores this, he himself will be ignored' (1 Corinthians 14:37-38). 'In the name of the Lord Jesus Christ, we command you, brothers, to keep away from every brother who is idle and does not live according to the teaching you received from us... If anyone does not obey our instruction in this letter, take special note of him. Do not associate with him, in order that he may feel ashamed' (2 Thessalonians 3:6, 14).

For the apostles, inspiration, in the sense of the true meaning of *'theopneustos'* (God-breathed) that we saw in chapter 3, was the same as revelation. Paul makes this clear in Ephesians 3 where he insists that his message was 'made known to me by revelation' (v. 3) and 'revealed by the Spirit to God's holy apostles and prophets' (v. 5). Whether the 'prophets' here are the Old or New Testament prophets is a matter of discussion among Christians today, but either way the apostles and prophets have the authority of God-given revelation through the Holy Spirit.

There are a few phrases used by Paul that, quite unnecessarily, present problems to some Christians. When the apostle claims in 1 Corinthians 7:10: 'I give this command (not I, but the Lord)' he means nothing more than that on the particular subject he is dealing with, Christ had already spoken during his earthly ministry — see for example Matthew 19:1-9. On the other hand, when Paul declared in verse 12: 'To the rest I say this (I, not the Lord)' he means that on this part of the subject Christ had nothing direct to say. In this way we can understand verse 25 also. The phrase, 'I think that I too have the Spirit of God', found in verse 40, is not a statement of doubt. Paul is either making a sarcastic jibe at those in Corinth who claimed to be full of spiritual gifts and wisdom (you will find these people in 14:37), or else he is simply making a positive statement in much the same way as we might affirm the truth of a statement with the positive claim: 'I think I know what I am talking about.'

How their letters were to be received

The writers of the New Testament expected their letters to be read and received as carrying great authority.

'Paul did not expect his letters to be read once and then thrown away'

Paul did not expect his letters to be read once and then be thrown away. The letter addressed to the Colossian church was to be read and then passed on to the church at Laodicea, and similarly the letter he had written to Laodicea, though we do not possess any other record of this letter, was to be read at Colosse (see Colossians 4:16). The apostle was so insistent that his letter to the Thessalonian church should be read by everyone that he placed them under an obligation to the Lord himself to make sure that 'all the brothers' had it read to them (1 Thessalonians 5:27). There is a particular blessing promised to those who read and obey the words of John's Revelation (Revelation 1:3).

The words of Christ equal with the Old Testament

Paul gave the words of Christ recorded in the Gospels equal authority with the Old Testament.

In 1 Timothy 5:18 Paul is arguing that proper payment should be given to those who lead, preach and teach in the church. To prove his point the apostle quotes first from Deuteronomy 25:4: 'Do not muzzle an ox while it is treading out the grain' and then he quotes a phrase that is found only in Luke 10:7: 'The worker deserves his wages.' What is important here is the fact that in 1 Timothy 5:18 Paul introduces both quotations with the statement: 'The Scripture says…' Therefore Paul recognized the words of Christ in Luke's Gospel as Scripture equally with the words of Moses in Deuteronomy. It is quite plain also that when Paul is dealing with the same subject in 1 Corinthians 9:9,14 he has these two quotations in his mind.

The writings of the apostles as Scripture

Peter gave Paul's letters the same authority as the Old Testament Scriptures.

We all have some sympathy with Peter's admission that some things in Paul's letters are 'hard to understand'! (2 Peter 3:16). But when Peter continued, 'which ignorant and unstable people distort, as they do the other Scriptures,' it is clear that Peter considered Paul's letters carried the same authority as the Old Testament Scriptures and could therefore rightly be called 'the Scriptures'.

Therefore, when we refer the 'all Scripture' in 2 Timothy 3:16 to both Old and New Testaments, we are only doing what the apostles themselves had begun to do before the close of the New Testament.

The authority Christ gave to his disciples

The passage in Matthew 16:18-19 has often been the cause of debate and argument, but there is a particular phrase in verse 19 (found also in Matthew 18:18) that is very relevant for our present chapter: 'I will give you the keys of the kingdom of heaven; whatever you bind on earth will be bound in heaven, and whatever you loose on earth will be loosed in heaven.' When we understand the Jewish background to this verse it presents little difficulty; in fact the binding and loosing referred to have nothing to do with the forgiveness of sins. That is referred to in John 20:23, but not here.

The scribes of Israel were thought of as stewards of the treasures of divine wisdom (see, for instance, Matthew 13:52) and when admitted to this office a scribe received, as a symbol, a key of knowledge (there is a reference to this in Luke 11:52). The duty of the scribe was to interpret the law of God to particular cases. He would

'A scribe received, as a symbol, a key of knowledge'

inform a man whether a certain law applied to him or not. Therefore, when the scribes bound a man they placed him under the obligation of the Scriptures; he was prohibited from doing something. When they loosed a man, they released him from the obligation.

Our Lord had been training his disciples to be stewards of the treasure of the new covenant, the gospel. In this promise in Matthew 16:19, he is referring to their future writing and preaching: it will have the authority of God's law. They will be the true scribes of the new covenant. Our Lord promised his disciples special help in writing the New Testament. In John 14:26 Christ gave his disciples two promises. One was a divinely aided understanding, and the other was a divinely aided memory: 'The Counsellor, the Holy Spirit, whom the Father will send in my name, will teach you all things and will remind you of everything I have said to you.' John 16:13 adds to this a divinely aided knowledge: 'He will tell you what is yet to come.' Therefore, in order that the disciples might recall accurately all Christ had said and done, instruct the Christian church in the way of truth, and write of things yet to come, Christ promised the help of the Holy Spirit. The apostles would be writing with no less authority than the Old Testament prophets. This is confirmed in Revelation 22:6: 'The angel said to me, "These words are trustworthy and true. The Lord, the God of the spirits of the prophets, sent his angel to show his servants the things that must soon take place."'

The authority of Christ himself

Finally, our Lord always saw his own teaching as holding a position of authority no less than that of the Old Testament prophets. His declaration that 'I gave them the words you gave me...' (John 17:8) reminds us of the claims of the prophets. Similarly, on the Mount of Transfiguration God's own voice gave approval to his Son's teaching with the words: 'This is my Son, whom I have chosen; listen to him' (Luke 9:35).

Nowhere did Christ more plainly express his belief in the authority of Scripture, an authority that would remain until heaven and earth pass away, than in Matthew 5:18: 'I tell you the truth, until heaven and earth disappear, not the smallest letter, not the least stroke of a pen, will by any means disappear from the Law until everything is accomplished.' Later in his ministry our Lord applied the same authority to his own words: 'Heaven and earth will pass away, but my words will never pass away' (Matthew 24:35).

Conclusion

In 1632 the Italian scientist Galileo published a book in which he supported the view of Copernicus a century earlier that the earth is round and that the sun is the centre of our solar system. The church authorities disagreed and his book was banned. Galileo was forced to change his views under threat of death by the infamous Inquisition. In fact Galileo was right and he knew he was right; merely declaring him to be in error and forcing him to change his views altered nothing of the truth. Today any schoolchildren who learn about Galileo know what the great mathematician and astronomer really believed.

In the same way we cannot read the Bible honestly without coming to the conclusion that what it claims for itself is an authority that nothing else can match. No other writings, no other documents, and the views of no other teachers or philosophers are ever referred to in the Bible as carrying the same authority. Some of our great philosophers and religious leaders were alive in Bible times, including Plato, who was born 400 years before Christ, and Gautama the founder of Buddhism, who was born a century before Plato, but they are never mentioned and certainly never quoted in Scripture. To the human writers of the Bible, both in the Old and New Testaments, there is only one authoritative Scripture.

Like the authorities in Italy who punished Galileo for telling the truth, men may not like what the Bible says about itself; they may even consider it to be wrong. But what they must never do is to pretend it does not claim such a clear authority for itself. Men may twist its words and change its meaning but, like the views of Galileo, all the world will know what the Bible really teaches about itself. Ignorance or fear of accepting the claims of the Bible can never change the truth of them.

7.
The Bible: sufficient and final

When the General Assembly of the Church of Scotland met on 27 August 1647 it approved what is now known as the *Westminster Confession of Faith*. This is a detailed statement of Christian belief and it rightly begins by affirming the authority and sufficiency of Scripture. In chapter 1, section 6, the following sentence is found: 'The whole counsel of God, concerning all things necessary for His own glory, man's salvation, faith, and life, is either expressly set down in Scripture, or by good and necessary consequence may be deduced from Scripture: unto which nothing at any time is to be added, whether by new revelations of the Spirit, or by traditions of men.'

This statement in seventeenth-century language means simply that God's Word for man, covering every area of what we believe about God and salvation and how we live, is found in the Bible either in direct statements or in principles that can be applied to various situations. The Bible is not to be added to by any other words which claim the authority of God.

So far in this book we have shown that the Bible is God's Word, with God's authority, and that it is completely reliable in all its statements, whether they concern doctrine, history, geography or practical Christian living. The question we must now answer is this: 'Is the Bible sufficient? Is it all we need to guide us in life? Is it enough?'

A definition of 'sufficient and final'

When we speak of the sufficiency and finality of Scripture we mean that in the Bible Christians in every century have all the infallibly given words of God that they need on any subject, and that in matters of what God expects us to believe about our Christian faith and how God expects us to live our Christian life, we do not need to know any more.

You will notice there are two parts to this definition. First, on every subject the Bible contains the only words from God that we need; we may need to know more, and we may be able to discover more as the history of man's thinking and discoveries develops, but God will not give us any more Scripture on the subject. The second part of our definition says that on issues of what we believe about God, that is, Christian doctrine or theology, there is nothing else that we need to know; the Scripture says it all. There are things we may want to know, but there is nothing else we need to know, and nothing else we can know. In contrast to God's revelation in the Bible, all other views of God and man and salvation are unreliable. Similarly, the Bible contains all that we need to know about how to live to please God. No other words can speak to us with the same authority and completeness and there can never be any more words from God added to the Bible.

Does the Bible teach sufficiency and finality?

There is an interesting warning that appears three times in Scripture. It is found in Deuteronomy 4:2 (repeated in 12:32), in Proverbs 30:6 and finally in Revelation 22:18-19. In the first God warns: 'Do not add to what I command you and do not subtract from it.' In the second we are told: 'Do not add to his words, or he will rebuke you and prove you a liar.' In the third a severe judgement is threatened to those who either add to or take away anything from the prophecies in the book of Revelation. It is not enough to claim that these warnings have to do only with the books of the Bible in which they are found. Clearly God has placed these three passages at three strategic places throughout his word, the beginning, the middle and the end, as a constant reminder that nothing can be added to his infallible verbal revelation.

When our Lord promised the disciples that his Holy Spirit would guide them into 'all truth', it was a promise that they would be given infallible aid in the writing of Scripture. A more accurate translation of what our Lord said to his disciples would be: 'But when he comes, the Spirit of truth, he will guide you into *all the truth*.' In other words, not only would all that they wrote be truth, but all that they wrote would be all the truth that is needed. God may give his people more light on the truth in later generations of the church, but he will not give them any more truth.

According to Paul in 2 Timothy 3:16-17, the Scripture is 'useful for teaching, rebuking, correcting and training in righteousness, so that the man of God may be thoroughly equipped for every good work'. The words 'thoroughly equipped' translate one small Greek word that Paul used, which means 'complete'. In other words, the Scriptures can make a Christian 'complete' for the service of God. The picture is that of the soldier fully equipped with all that he needs to do battle. The Scriptures are therefore sufficient and nothing else is required.

In 1 Corinthians 4:6 Paul reminded his readers: 'Do not go beyond what is written.' He appears to be quoting from the Old Testament, although there is no phrase exactly like this in the Old Testament. However, he may well have been using a common phrase among the Christian churches, which at least reflected Deuteronomy 4:2, and which reminded them not to add anything to what God had already spoken in his Word.

In a similar way, Jude 3 encourages the Christians to 'contend for the faith that was once entrusted to the saints'. Clearly Jude had in mind the fact that the content of the Christian gospel had been finally given through the apostles, and nothing more could be added. Significantly the word 'once' means 'once for all', and the same word is used in Hebrews 9:28 of the once-for-all death of Christ for sin.

How sufficient is sufficient?

In this section we shall go back over the definition we have given and work out the implications in more detail.

Sufficient about everything?

To say the Bible is sufficient may tell us very little because we then need to ask, 'Sufficient about what?' If we imply that the Bible tells us all we need to know about everything, then we at once put a stop to all scientific research and we cease asking questions about anything not directly mentioned in the Bible. But the Bible is a relevant book, not a ridiculous book, and therefore such a view cannot be accepted. God has given men minds and skills and both are to be used to benefit the human race. Job speaks of man's enquiring mind and his amazing discoveries and achievements (see especially Job 28) and nowhere does he even hint that these things are wrong. Clearly there are many subjects upon which the Bible is silent: for example, it has nothing to say directly about the technical problems of space travel or the control of dangerous viruses, but scientists are not wrong to study these subjects.

On the other hand, if we say the Bible is sufficient in the subjects about which it does speak, have we really helped very much? After all, the Bible does say something about business dealings (see, for example, James 4:13), building construction (Matthew 7:24-27; Luke 14:28), farming (2 Timothy 2:6) and shepherding (John 10), but no one would claim that it says everything there was to be said about these activities at the time it was written, let alone today.

Therefore sufficiency does not mean that the Bible is all we need to know about everything. This is why we said earlier that in the Bible we do not have everything we need to know about everything, but we have *everything that God wanted infallibly to tell us* about everything. You may need to read that sentence again!

Sufficient for the main purpose

What is the purpose of the Bible? If its chief purpose was to be a complete handbook for the space engineer or the micro-biologist, the business salesman or the building contractor, the farmer or the shepherd, then we would expect it to say everything and could rightly criticize it for anything it left out. But in fact the Bible is first of all a book about God. It tells us all we need to know, and all we shall ever need to know, about God: who he is, what he is like, what he does and, of course, how we can know him. In this area it is sufficient; it is enough.

The Bible is also a book about man and salvation. It tells us accurately and in detail what man is like, not physically — because the body is only a part, and the least important part, of man — but spiritually, in his soul and character. It tells us where and why man has gone wrong, and where and how he can be put right. On these subjects the Bible is sufficient because it leaves nothing for us to guess or make up. In this area God cannot leave man to discover the answers for himself because man's mind and soul are so spoilt by sin that by human knowledge and wisdom man will never find God. Paul reminds us of this in 1 Corinthians 1:21: 'The world, through its wisdom, did not know him.' In fact, as the same apostle makes clear in Romans 1:21, although men should be able to know God through the revelation of creation they 'neither glorified him as God nor gave thanks to him, but their thinking became futile and their foolish hearts were darkened'.

What we are now saying is that on the subject of doctrine (theology) of what we should believe about God, man and salvation, the Bible leaves no areas unclear that we need to know about. There are many things that the Bible has not revealed even in these areas and we must therefore conclude that we do not need to know about them. Moses realized this when he reminded the people of Israel: 'The secret things belong to the Lord our God, but the things revealed belong to us and to our children for ever' (Deuteronomy 29:29). On the subject of doctrine the Bible is both clear and sufficient; it is enough.

Sufficient principles

We have not yet exhausted the word 'sufficient'. The Bible has a great deal to say about many other subjects besides doctrine. It is amazing how many areas of daily life and practical Christian living are mentioned in the Bible. In each of these areas we would not claim that the Bible says everything that could be said, but we do claim that it says everything that needs to be said from God for us to know just how we should govern our lives. As a handbook for Christian morality and citizenship the Bible is sufficient; it is enough. Where there are not specific statements to govern a particular situation, there are general statements (principles) that we can apply. These principles will be found in the Scriptures and can be worked out in many different circumstances.

In the world of medicine there is a principle that sterilization kills germs and prevents infection; that is the general statement or principle, but how we actually apply that principle will differ according to the situation. A dressing or a surgical knife can be steam-sterilized at a temperature of 120° Centigrade, but a different method is needed to sterilize a dirty wound! However, we can rightly claim that the principle of sterilizing to avoid infection is sufficient. In the same way when our Lord was asked whether or not it was right to pay taxes to a pagan ruler, his answer, 'Give to Cæsar what is Cæsar's, and to God what is God's' (Matthew 22:21), dealt not merely with that particular question but gave us a principle that can be applied in many different situations.

'Render to Cæsar the things that are Cæsar's'
Denarius of Tiberius Cæsar,
reproduced by courtesy of the British Museum

The Christian does not dare to live without constant reference to the Bible, because, whilst the standards and principles of the world are constantly changing, those of the Bible never change. Here, in the Bible, are principles that are both sufficient and completely reliable for all Christians in every age and culture.

A belief in the sufficiency of the Bible both for doctrine and for living, for what we believe and how we live, does not mean that we have an answer to every question that confronts us. A frequent question put to the Christian is this: 'What happens to an infant who dies before reaching an age when it could reasonably be expected to respond to God's offer of salvation?' Many Christians immediately say, 'Oh, it goes to heaven, of course.' But nowhere in the Bible are we told this. The Bible is silent on this subject; it is one of those secrets not revealed to us. What is our answer then? Lacking a clear statement from Scripture we do not guess or make up an answer but we look for a principle that will guide us; and we find one in Genesis 18:25: 'Will not the Judge of all the earth do right?' That must settle it. We do not know for certain what happens to the infant who dies, but we know that God is just and right in all that he does and we can safely leave the problem there.

The Scripture is therefore sufficient not only on matters of doctrine, but also for practical Christian living, because there are principles in Scripture that will guide us in any and every situation.

Contrary to Scripture or not in Scripture?

Historically the church of Rome taught that whatever Scripture does not forbid it allows; the Reformed churches taught that whatever Scripture does not command, it forbids. Who is right?

There do seem to be some subjects on which God has spoken, but not in a way so clear as to avoid differences about them among Christians. For instance, there are many things we do in our churches that have no direct scriptural support and there are many areas of understanding the Bible where Christians, equally committed to the full inspiration and authority of Scripture, are in fairly radical disagreement. In the light of this can we therefore still hold to the sufficiency of Scripture? If it is sufficient, why do we not all agree about everything?

There are two answers to this. In the first place, even the Christian has a mind that has been heavily influenced by sin, and as a result we often impose on the Bible our own understanding of what it is saying; we all come to the Bible with our prejudices and preferences and that affects how we understand it. The fault lies in us, not in the Bible. In the same way we must humbly admit that our fallen mind cannot always grasp the great and deep things about God that are revealed in the Bible; there will be some things that, though revealed to us, are beyond our ability to understand fully. Given these limitations we should be grateful that nevertheless God has given us a complete Bible. You can imagine how much nonsense men would add to it if it was incomplete; in fact you don't have to imagine; there is plenty of evidence from those who have added to the Bible, even though it is complete! But the second answer is that although God has told us clearly what we need to know, there are many details he allows us to work out according to the conditions of our local situation. We must always distinguish between something that is contrary to Scripture and something that is not in Scripture; a thing may be non-scriptural without being against Scripture. We are allowed to do things not specifically mentioned in

Scripture provided they are not contrary to Scripture; that is, provided they are in harmony with scriptural principles.

Scripture itself is sufficient to tell us which is which

Some Christians talk about 'the regulative principle', an expression which means that the Scriptures must regulate or control all that we do in our own lives and in our churches. This is true, but the phrase, 'the regulative principle', must never be taken to mean that we cannot do something unless we can find a specific mention of it in the Bible. The writer to the Hebrews resolves this issue for us. In Hebrews 5:14 he encourages his readers: 'Solid food is for the mature, who by constant use have trained themselves to distinguish good from evil.' We may ask, 'Constant use of what?' The answer is found in the previous verse, where the writer refers to 'the teaching about righteousness'. In other words, the Christian must learn to use the Bible as the source book from which principles will be found that speak to us in every area of life and faith.

If we take an example from the area of organizing the local church we can see this difference between things that are legitimate, but not specifically mentioned in Scripture, and those that are clearly against the principles of Scripture. A church may keep a formal list or register of those who are members of the church. Nowhere is this practice explicitly found in Scripture, but in order to follow the principle of doing things properly and in an orderly manner (1 Corinthians 14:40) and to know who is committed to the church and who is allowed to help make important decisions, it is a sensible and practical idea. It is not contrary to Scripture in that there is nothing in Scripture that says or implies that such a practice is wrong.

On the other hand, suppose the church decides to make a charge for membership amounting to one week's pay each month. The Scripture gives us clear principles to guide our giving and one important principle for the Christian is that giving should be done freely and willingly and from the heart. Paul's principle in 1 Corinthians 16:2 and 2 Corinthians 9:7 would seem to be clearly against any forcible membership fee. We can therefore conclude that such a forced charge to members is not merely non-scriptural but actually against Scripture; it is against the principles laid down in Scripture.

This is a very important distinction that we should never forget. We can still see that even in these areas Scripture is sufficient; it is our guide to whether or not something should be done. It is sufficient to tell us whether we must do something, whether we may do it, or whether we must not do it.

A summary of sufficiency

To sum up what has been said, the sufficiency of Scripture does not mean that Scripture says everything we need to know on every subject. It does mean, however, that it says everything we need to know on the chief subjects of the Bible, such as what we should believe about God, man and salvation. In all other areas, such as living the Christian life in a modern world, or organizing a local church, Scripture gives us principles that are sufficient to guide us in any and every situation. Whatever subject it speaks about, the Bible gives us all the revelation from God that we need to have.

Where the Bible appears to be unclear on an issue, we must ask ourselves, 'Is my proposed action clearly against Scripture or simply not in Scripture?' Even here Scripture is sufficient. All matters of doctrine and life are to be brought to the final test of Scripture. There are no subjects upon which Scripture has nothing to say either by direct command or direct principle — and this is what is meant by the sufficiency of Scripture.

The Bible is also sufficient to help us understand its own message. Valuable as books and commentaries may be, they are not essential to a correct understanding of the Bible. A humble and spiritually wise mind is quite capable, by reading thoughtfully and comparing Scripture with Scripture, of understanding its message and applying it relevantly to life.

What are the alternatives offered?

We have established that the Bible is all that we need as a reliable and authoritative guide and that there will be no more Bible added to it. However, in the history of the so-called Christian church this has not been the conclusion of everyone.

The Roman Catholic view

Alongside the Bible, the Roman Catholic Church has placed a host of human traditions, including the Apocrypha (see chapter 10), the writings of church leaders in the first few centuries A.D. and a collection of decrees and statements given by popes and church councils down the centuries. In 1546 the Council of Trent declared that all this extra material is to be taken as equal in authority to the Bible. This is still the official position of the Roman church. Therefore the Roman Catholic Church does not believe in the sufficiency of Scripture.

The liberal view

If the Roman church adds to the sufficiency of Scripture, the liberal theologian, who denies both the accuracy and authority of the Bible, subtracts from it. The liberal approach to Scripture doubts that the Bible is reliable in its statements about history, denies the reality of miracles and other supernatural experiences and declares all Bible doctrine to be a matter of personal opinion that we may accept or reject as we like. Of course, not all liberal critics of the Bible are as extreme in their views as this, but very many are, and some are much worse. To them the Bible is largely irrelevant for the modern world, and it has little to say to help us with the issues of today. Therefore liberal theology does not believe in the sufficiency of Scripture.

The view of the cults

Almost all modern heresies that have formed themselves into strong organizations have added to the Bible in one way or another. The Mormons have the *Book of Mormon, Doctrines and Covenants* and *The Pearl of Great Price*, all written by Joseph Smith and all considered to be equal in authority with the Bible; in addition they claim their international president can speak with infallibility, in much the same way as Roman Catholics believe the pope can when he is speaking as Peter's representative. The Mormons, therefore, do not allow final authority to any of the statements of the Bible. The Christian Science movement claims divine authority for *Science and Health* by Mary Baker Eddy. Many, though not all, of the

Christadelphians believe that *Elpis Israel* by John Thomas is the final understanding of the Bible and therefore the Bible is incomplete without it. This is certainly implied by Robert Roberts, a leading Christadelphian who, in 1874, claimed: 'To the charge of holding that the knowledge of the Scriptures in the writing of Dr Thomas has reached a finality, we plead guilty.' Similarly, no teaching is allowed among the Jehovah's Witnesses without reference to the Watchtower Society literature. Seventh Day Adventists believe that the teachings of their founder Ellen G. White are essential to a proper understanding of Scripture.

Such claims show that the cults do not believe the Bible to be sufficient in itself without the aid of their own writings. It is therefore doubtful whether any of the cults really believes, or at least practises, the sufficiency of Scripture.

The view of some charismatics

Many of those who belong to what is known as the modern charismatic movement deny the sufficiency of Scripture, though often this is unintentional. They believe in its authority and its inerrancy, but deny its sufficiency. This is certainly not true of all, but it is sadly true of many. Charismatic Christians lay great emphasis upon the gifts of 'prophecy' and so-called words of wisdom and knowledge, dreams and visions, as ways by which God speaks to his church today through infallible words of revelation. These are seen as necessary for the growth and life of the church.

Writing in the magazine *Renewal* for October 1990, David Pawson makes this very clear: 'Once its divine inspiration has been fully established, prophecy carries the same authority as Scripture, since both carry the authority of the same Lord who has spoken and is speaking. Both are to be obeyed.' Admittedly David Pawson then tries to guard his view of the Bible by stating that modern prophecy is not an addition, or an alternative, or an advance on Scripture and that 'In all matters of faith and practice Scripture is both final and universal', but we must wonder what is left beyond 'faith and practice'! Clearly Scripture is not quite sufficient and the church requires more revelation from God for her normal life and growth. Something more is needed.

In her book *Something More* Catherine Marshall stated this clearly. 'When he, the Spirit of truth, comes, he will guide you into all [the] truth' (John 16:13) is taken to mean: 'He will lead you into further truth', and is seen as a promise for modern-day Christians. On page 281 of this book she writes, 'In fact, it seemed to me that Jesus' promise of "further truth" gives us clear reasons to believe that not all the truth and instruction Christ has to give us is contained in the canon of the Old and New Testaments. How could it be? He who is Truth will never find the people of any given century able to receive everything He wants to give.' It is therefore clear that charismatic Christians who accept this view deny the sufficiency of Scripture.

The liberal view of some evangelicals

In Chapter 1 we saw that some liberal 'evangelical' Christians have begun to question how reliable the Bible is; they accept its authority on matters of doctrine but doubt whether it can be trusted on facts of history. They suggest that we do not need to think that on any and every subject facing the Christian we should go to the Bible for advice. They believe there are many things in the life of the modern Christian that find no mention in Scripture, either by direct statement or principle, and much of our church life and private or business life can be planned and lived in a Christian way without reference to the Bible. These evangelicals are really following the views of liberal critics of the Bible. Whilst they claim to have a very high view of Scripture and will talk about the authority of God and inspiration, they do not believe in the sufficiency of Scripture.

How do we know the Bible is sufficient and final?

We have seen that there are many who deny the sufficiency of Scripture, from the liberal critic who denies almost everything in the Bible to many charismatics and liberal 'evangelicals' who nevertheless believe in the inspiration and authority of the Bible. Why, therefore, are we so insistent that the Bible is sufficient and that it is all the verbal revelation we need from God? We have already seen that the Bible itself teaches this, but we can add some further points.

There is no reference in Scripture to something more

As with all the questions that face us, we must turn to the Bible itself for our answer. The Scripture always refers to itself as final, and nowhere is there even a hint that further revelation will be found

somewhere else at some future time. Catherine Marshall's understanding of John 16:13 as 'further truth' is just not possible as an
accurate translation of the words our Lord actually used, and it is a
dangerous thing to twist the words of the Bible to make it say what
we want it to say. In this passage our Lord was giving his disciples,
and no one other than his disciples, a promise that the Holy Spirit
would guide them into 'all the truth'.

If someone accuses me of saying something that I am quite sure
I have never said, then it is his responsibility to prove that I said it,
by giving the time and place. There is no way I can prove my
innocence other than by demanding: 'Tell me exactly when and
where I am supposed to have said such a thing.' In the same way the
complete silence of the Bible as to the possibility of more revelation
and new inspired words from God must be the final proof until
someone can show that it teaches otherwise. Human reasoning
about Christ not being able to find people 'able to receive everything
he wants to give' is quite irrelevant as proof against the finality and
sufficiency of Scripture.

The Scriptures speak with finality

By this word 'finality' we mean that the Bible, and particularly the
New Testament, always speaks as if it is the last and final word on
a subject and that nothing more can or will be added later.

When our Lord was speaking to his disciples in John 14-16,
some of what he promised was especially for them, and we cannot
apply it to every Christian in every age. He promised the apostles
that the Holy Spirit would 'teach you all things and will remind you
of everything I have said to you' (John 14:26). He did not limit the
'all things' to things necessary just for the first hundred years of the
church. He meant all things necessary for his people in all ages.
Similarly, in John 16:13-15 our Lord promised the apostles that his
Spirit would give to them all the truth necessary for the church for
ever. This is not simply doctrinal truth, but practical truth also.

Because of this Paul could remind the Ephesian Christians that
the church is built upon the teaching of 'the apostles and prophets,
with Christ Jesus himself as the chief cornerstone' (Ephesians 2:20).
Once again there is a finality; no one else is mentioned as part of this
foundation. There will be no more apostles and no more prophets.
There is an interesting development through the New Testament
which must be significant: less and less reference is made to prophets

and prophecy as the New Testament develops, and more and more emphasis is placed upon preaching and teaching. In fact the only references to New Testament prophecy are found in 1 Corinthians 12-14, three times in Ephesians, where Paul says it is foundational, and one each in Romans, Thessalonians and in 1 Timothy, where it refers to something that happened thirteen years earlier. However, when Paul gives his final instructions to Timothy he urges him to pay attention to 'the public reading of Scripture' (1 Timothy 4:13) and to 'preach the word' (2 Timothy 4:2). In 2 Peter 2:1, Peter compares the false *prophets* in the Old Testament with the false *teachers* in his own day. The New Testament letters are full of instructions about teaching and preaching, and yet they have very little to say about prophecy and revelations. The reason is surely clear: God's plan for his church was changing as he brought his verbal revelation to a close and continued to lead his church through the faithful teaching of what he had already said. In other words, as the New Testament progresses there is a clear shift from revelation to proclamation.

When Paul wrote to the Corinthians he had experienced some difficulty with that church's attitude to his authority as an apostle. In the course of explaining that he was secure in his apostleship, whether or not they judged him correctly, Paul reminded them of the expression: 'Do not go beyond what is written' (1 Corinthians 4:6). Although we are not aware of any wording quite like this elsewhere, clearly Paul and his readers were, and the phrase 'what is written' is a common enough way in which Paul referred to the Old Testament Scriptures; he uses it sixteen times in his letter to the Romans alone, and more than thirty times in all. Therefore, as Dr Leon Morris concludes in his commentary on Corinthians, 'We may fairly conjecture that "Not beyond what is written" was a catch-phrase familiar to Paul and his readers, directing attention to the need for conformity to Scripture.'

We have already seen earlier in this chapter that Jude 3 settles the matter of the finality of Scripture by using the same word that is used elsewhere of the once-for-all death of Christ. There can be no more Scripture, just as there can be no more sacrifice of Christ.

The Scriptures condemn the traditions of men

In the time of Christ the Jews had gathered a great amount of teaching from the rabbis and this was placed alongside Scripture and sometimes given the same authority as Scripture itself. Much of this

teaching was nonsense, but some of it was good and profitable.
However, our Lord never allowed any of it to stand beside Scripture
and warned the Pharisees against it: 'Why do you break the command of God for the sake of your tradition?' (Matthew 15:3).
Reminding them of Isaiah 29, Christ accused the Jewish leaders:
'You nullify the word of God by your tradition' (Mark 7:13). These
warnings should be enough to make a Christian reject immediately
any suggestion that we can still add to the inspired Word of God.

Qualifications for those who claim to give the Word of God

It has long been accepted that all who gave us the New Testament
Scriptures were qualified in a way that is not possible for anyone of
a later age. When the eleven apostles were looking for someone to
take the place of Judas Iscariot there were two essential qualifications they demanded: he must be a man who had been in company
with Christ throughout the three years of his ministry and who had
actually seen him after the resurrection (Acts 1:21-22). It was from
men who fulfilled these conditions that the whole of our New
Testament came. We shall look again at this subject in chapter 11.
Paul was an unusual apostle, as he himself admitted in 1 Corinthians 15:8-9, and he had to defend his right to speak and write as an
apostle against those who doubted that he had really seen Christ (see
1 Corinthians 9:1-2). Both Peter (2 Peter 1:16-18) and John (1 John

'Paul was an unusual apostle, as he himself admitted'

1:1-3) emphasize their qualification of having seen Christ and having lived with him. These were the men who gave us the verbal revelation from God and no one can fulfil these conditions today. It is a bold Christian who will place himself or herself alongside the authority of Paul or John or Peter.

The alternative: confusion

If the Bible is not sufficient and final, then confusion results.

The converted eighteenth-century slave trader John Newton wrote of the assistance the Holy Spirit gives with reference to the Scriptures: 'He has not promised to reveal new truths, but to enable us to understand what we read in the Bible; and if we venture beyond the pale of Scripture, we are upon enchanted ground, and exposed to all the illusions of imagination and enthusiasm.'

We would expect God to make his Word clear and final and not to leave us to the illusions of imagination and enthusiasm. No military officer or government lawyer would give an order that invites others to add to it as they pass it down the line of command; the result would be complete confusion. In fact this is exactly what we find among those who deny the sufficiency and finality of Scripture. If we take those who deny sufficiency on the grounds of it being unreasonable to trust the Bible completely, then we find these liberal critics constantly criticizing one another over how the Bible should be understood! They have no clear standard of morality or faith to put in its place. Almost anyone can pull a building down, but it requires a skilled architect and builder to put one up. Millions of words and thousands of books have been produced over the last one hundred and fifty years by those who deny the Bible and its authority and sufficiency, but still the critics disagree among themselves about almost everything. That is confusion, not order.

Similarly, the Roman church is faced with serious and embarrassing contradictions among her popes, teachers and 'saints', each of whom has added to Scripture. For thirty years towards the end of the fourteenth century there were two popes, one at Rome and the other at Avignon; each excommunicated the other and each claimed to be the true successor of Peter. For a year there were even three popes! This state of affairs, together with the mass of contradictory teachings from the various schools of doctrine, makes nonsense of any attempt to claim that Rome has added a consistent tradition to the Bible. Once more it is a picture of complete confusion.

The same is true of the false cults who deny the finality of the Bible. To prove that the Bible prophesies the coming of the *Book of Mormon*, the Mormons point to the two sticks referred to in Ezekiel 37:15-23! Christian Scientists believe that *Science and Health* is the 'little book' of Revelation 10:2, and Mary Baker Eddy is the woman of Revelation 12! In 1925 the London Convention of the Jehovah's Witnesses was ignored by the press, and the movement at once decided that London was the 'throne of the beast' referred to in Revelation 16:10! These are tragically amusing illustrations of how not to interpret the Scriptures, but they also show the ridiculous confusion among those who add to the Bible or claim an infallible interpretation of it.

The situation is no better when we look at the modern charismatic view of prophecy. Books, articles and long debates have tried to settle the thorny problem of how we can tell which modern-day prophecies are from God and which are not, and when they are, what their precise authority is. Should Christians be disciplined by their church leaders for disobeying modern prophecies in the same way that they would be for disobeying the Bible? To claim that the Bible is sufficient and final 'in all matters of faith and practice' whilst still allowing prophecies that 'carry the same authority as Scripture' leaves us wondering what remains for us beyond faith and practice! Catherine Marshall's position of 'more truth' opens the door for anything, including new doctrine. More recently evangelicals have debated the possibility of two levels of prophecy — one for the Bible and another for today!

Conclusion

When we need to know the will of God, a belief in the sufficiency of Scripture will direct us to find our answer from the statements and principles of God's final verbal revelation, and nowhere else; we will train ourselves to use God's Word rather than to seek easy answers elsewhere. When we need to test the claims of the cults or, for that matter, evangelical traditions, we shall know immediately where to go. A belief in the sufficiency of Scripture is humbling, for it reminds us that there are some things we would like to know, but on which God has not chosen to give us an answer. There is a reverent agnosticism that does not try to invent a reasonable Christian response but recognizes that 'The secret things belong to the Lord our God, but the things revealed belong to us and to our children for ever, that we may follow all the words of this law' (Deuteronomy 29:29).

Sufficiency means also that we must not add to Scripture nor take from it and that, as a consequence of this, we must never demand anything that is not found directly or by implication in Scripture — that is Pharisaic legalism. But we should not expect less either. In other words, we must believe and live the true balance of Scripture.

History shows that wherever the sufficiency and finality of Scripture are denied, confusion is always the result. True evangelical Christians believe firmly, and from the teaching of Scripture itself, that, with the close of the New Testament, God's inspired revelation came to an end. After the book of Malachi at the end of the Old Testament, God gave no more verbal revelation until the coming of Christ at his incarnation; in the same way, after the close of the New Testament God has no more verbal revelation until the coming of Christ in glory. The book we call the Bible is God's final word to mankind until Christ returns. It is the authoritative Word of God and it is a sufficient guide for every aspect of Christian belief and practice.

8.
Unity and prophecy in the Bible

The Bible was written by approximately forty different authors over a period of some fifteen hundred years. The writers therefore lived in greatly differing cultures: some during the Egyptian civilization and others in the time of the Assyrians, Syrians, Babylonians, Persians or Romans. Some writers were kings and princes, others were priests and prophets, farmers and fishermen, civil servants and soldiers. These facts alone are sufficient for us to make the claim that the Bible is a unique book. But what makes it all the more amazing is that the Bible has one great story running from its beginning to its end, and that story unfolds with unerring accuracy. Never, through all its long history, does any part of the Bible contradict another part, never does it leave us with the idea that we are just reading another book of ancient history, and never does it turn aside from the unfolding plan that runs from beginning to end.

The purpose of this chapter is to show that the Bible has a unique accuracy in its story, or if you prefer, in its theology. What the Bible says about God and man and salvation is consistent from start to finish. Given the long period of time over which it was written, and the longer period of history that it covers, that is an incredible fact that can only be accounted for by a firm belief in the divine origin of the Bible.

What is the Bible all about?

The fact that the New Testament is about Christ is self-evident. A large part of the New Testament is devoted to his birth, life, death and resurrection, and the remainder is concerned with the history of his church and the instructions that he gave to his church through his disciples. But what about the Old Testament?

The Old Testament is more than a history book. It too is all about Christ. Are we really interested in the details of how the Jews offered their sacrifices or what the priests wore? Does it really matter about the construction of Solomon's temple or the family history of a poor widow called Naomi? What is the value today of knowing the story of a wandering nomad called Abraham, or reading the fiery preaching of a prophet called Isaiah, or the strange visions of a man called Daniel? If the Old Testament is just history, even history with a religious slant, then it will have little relevance to today's world.

There is only one answer to the question: 'What is the Old Testament all about?' It is all about Christ. God has not wasted half a million words just to tell us interesting stories about the long history of three million people who lived in a tiny piece of land in the Middle East.

One reason why we can claim the Old Testament is all about Christ is because Christ himself said so. After his resurrection he joined two disciples as they walked home from Jerusalem. Not realizing who it was who had joined them on their walk, they shared their miseries with him and to their surprise he took their bad news as good news: 'And beginning with Moses and all the Prophets, he explained to them what was said in all the Scriptures concerning himself' (Luke 24:27). When they found out who the stranger was, those two disciples returned to Jerusalem and told the other disciples their story. Whilst everyone was chattering in excitement, Jesus himself stood among them and continued to teach them the meaning of the Old Testament. He said, 'Everything must be fulfilled that is written about me in the Law of Moses, the Prophets and the Psalms' (Luke 24:44).

According to Christ that is the purpose of the Old Testament. Moses for the Jew meant the first five books of the Bible; all the prophets take up twenty-five per cent of the Old Testament; the Psalms take up seven per cent more, and 'all the Scriptures' covers the rest! The entire Old Testament has something to say about Christ.

All this means that when we read the Old Testament we should be looking for Christ. However, we must be careful to read Christ *out of* the Old Testament and not *into* it. That distinction is very important. Reading Christ out of the Old Testament means looking for the places where God is intending to point us to his Son. Reading Christ into the Old Testament means imagining we have found a reference to Christ where no such reference is intended by God.

Because the Old Testament is all about Christ, it is God's unfolding story of salvation — how God planned to solve the problem of our sin. That is what makes the Old Testament such an exciting and interesting book. We must never think of it merely as a collection of stories and biographies of great men and women who trusted God in the centuries before Christ came. It is that, but it is much more than that. To help us follow through God's unfolding plan about Christ, there are two things to look out for as we read the Old Testament: we must watch the promise and watch the people.

Right at the beginning of the Bible God made a promise and that promise keeps coming into focus throughout the unfolding story that follows throughout the Old and New Testaments. But in order to keep his promise, God chose a special people, and the story of those people forms a major part of the Bible.

The promise

You may have read about the different 'covenants' God has made with man. People write about the covenant with Adam, the covenant with Noah, the covenant with Abraham, Isaac and Jacob, and the covenant with Moses, and of course, the new covenant in Christ. Then they discuss whether these are two, three, or four different covenants. I want to cut the knot of that problem quite simply. There is only one covenant God has made with man. It began with Adam and right up to the coming of Christ God kept on renewing it and adding a little more of his plan of salvation.

The word 'covenant' is often used in the Bible. For example, it occurs twenty-five times in Genesis and nineteen times in Hebrews. It simply means a binding agreement, a definite promise. Generally, in a covenant there are four ingredients. There are the

> Parties concerned — those who sign the agreement;
> Promises made — the benefits of the agreement;
> Penalties involved — the conditions of the agreement and
>   what will happen if one side breaks it;
> Pictures to seal it — the legal documents.

For thousands of years men have been making covenants or promises to each other; but earlier than all, God has made a covenant with man. Some covenants are two-sided, with both sides agreeing to do something for each other. This is like the contract to buy and sell a house. One side agrees to hand over the house and the other side agrees to pay the money. Other covenants are one-sided, with one side doing all the giving and the other, having nothing to give, doing all the receiving. God's great covenant with mankind is one-sided. Whilst there are two parties involved — Almighty God and sinful mankind — God makes the promises and signs the covenant. His great promise does not depend upon man's signature at all. It is exciting to trace this through the Old Testament.

The promise made in Adam's day

Genesis 3:15 is the first place where God's plan for sinful man is mentioned. This is the promise referred to in the Old and New Testaments and it is to this covenant promise that we are referring throughout this chapter whenever we speak of 'the promise'. God had created man and woman and placed them in a beautiful garden. Everything was just right and day after day Adam and Eve enjoyed fellowship with God. It was a perfect world, a wonderful creation. Then Satan came onto the scene and, pretending to be a snake, tempted Adam and Eve into sin. When they broke God's law it was the end of man's unbroken fellowship with God and the beginning of sin.

God had to punish disobedience and in Genesis 3 we have a description of God's judgement upon the devil, the woman and the man. But even at this time, when the devil had vandalized God's creation and written his own graffiti across man's mind, God came with his great promise of salvation: 'I will put enmity between you and the woman, and between your offspring and hers; he will crush your head, and you will strike his heel' (Genesis 3:15).

That is one of the most important verses in the Old Testament, because the rest of the thirty-nine books in the Old Testament is God showing how he keeps his promise. In fact, we cannot understand the Old Testament unless we understand this verse. The verse is not about snakes and men, but about Satan and God. Although God is addressing a snake, that snake is the mouthpiece of the devil. So God is speaking to Satan. And he is speaking to Satan simply because man is not listening and because the great enemy of God is not man but the devil. Man has been, and is still being, deceived by the devil.

In that verse God begins by apparently saying, 'There will be constant warfare between you [the devil] and the woman [Eve], and between your offspring [the devil's angels or demons] and hers.' We would expect the woman's offspring to refer to all the generations of men and women born from Eve, thousands of millions of them, but there is a sudden and unexpected change in this verse. Instead of saying, '*They* will crush your head and you will strike *their* heel,' God says, '*He* will crush your head and you will strike *his* heel.'

This promise is not about millions of demons against millions of men, but about the devil against one man. What is more, we are told that although the devil will hurt this man, 'You will strike his heel', this man will finally 'crush your head'. Satan will give a wound, but in return he will receive a crushing death-blow.

To discover just who this person is who will deliver the final knock-out to Satan we move on to Paul writing in the New Testament. In Romans 16:20 the apostle wrote, 'The God of peace will soon crush Satan under your feet' — a clear reference to the promise. But how will he do that? John gives us the answer in 1 John 3:8: 'The reason the Son of God appeared was to destroy the devil's work.' Clearly Christ is the fulfilment of God's great promise given at the moment of the fall into sin. The party to the promise is God. He says, 'I will', and he doesn't ask man to sign the agreement: it is something God promises to do unconditionally. The promise is that Satan, who so spoiled and defaced God's perfect creation of man, will one day be defeated and all his evil work destroyed. God will never break his agreement.

The picture God uses to illustrate his promise at this point in his unfolding story of salvation is nothing more than a *snake*. When we look at a snake we are expected to remember God's promise. A long time after the Fall, God's special people had disobeyed him and they were being punished for it; when their leader Moses pleaded with God to forgive the people, God told him to put a brass snake on a pole for all the people to see (Numbers 21:4-9). That was not intended as a new god for them to worship, but as a reminder of that first sin and, by implication, the first time God made his promise of salvation. So, the story of salvation begins in Genesis 3:15.

In this key verse of the first book of the Bible, there are three actors on stage: the woman, the snake and God, as the one who makes the promise of the Offspring. In the last book of the Bible we are presented with a picture in which the same three characters appear. In Revelation 12 we are told of a woman who gives birth to a child, and of a dragon who is ready to destroy him at the moment of birth. However, 'Her child was snatched up to God and to his throne' (v. 5) and the chapter includes a song of victory:

'Now have come the salvation and the power and the
  kingdom of our God,
  and the authority of his Christ.
For the accuser of our brothers,
  who accuses them before our God day and night
  has been hurled down.
They overcame him
  by the blood of the Lamb
  and by the word of their testimony...'

(Revelation 12:10-11).

The chapter closes with the warning that although the dragon knows his ultimate destruction is near, he will try to do as much damage as possible to the church before the end comes. Here is a remarkable instance of the theme of the Bible which is opened up in the first book continuing right through to the last book, with at least fifteen hundred years between the writing of each.

The promise confirmed in Noah's day

By the sixth chapter of Genesis man had become so evil that God planned to start all over again — almost. Noah and his family went into the ark and after one year and seventeen days he, his family of seven and the floating zoo came out into the new world as the only survivors of the universal flood. God immediately gave orders to Noah and renewed the covenant promise. The first use in the Bible of the word 'covenant' is found in Genesis 6:18: 'I will establish my covenant with you.' God is saying, 'I will keep my promise with you, Noah.' Remember, this is a promise to the whole of mankind; it is a promise of salvation.

Now, however, there is a new sign. It is described in Genesis 9:12-13: 'This is the sign of the covenant I am making between me and you and every living creature with you, a covenant for all generations to come: I have set my rainbow in the clouds, and it will be the sign of the covenant between me and the earth.'

The fact that the *rainbow* is a sign from God that he will never

again flood the whole earth has led many to believe that this is a
different promise altogether, completely unrelated to the promise of
Genesis 3:15. In fact this new sign or picture (the rainbow) and the
new form of the promise (no more flood) is only the great promise
renewed; it is a little more of God's plan unfolded. If God ever
blotted out the whole world with a flood then he could not keep his
promise of Genesis 3:15. But this promise is with 'every living
creature', because according to Paul in Romans 8:21, when Jesus
Christ comes again in glory, 'Creation itself will be liberated from
its bondage to decay and brought into the glorious freedom of the
children of God.' Every part of God's creation was spoilt when
Satan tempted Adam and Eve into disobeying God; ever since then
it has been 'groaning as in the pains of childbirth right up to the
present time' (Romans 8:22). All the natural disasters and misery in
the world are the result of the fall into sin by man. When Christ
finally crushes Satan there will be new heavens and a new earth, the
home of righteousness (2 Peter 3:13).

The rainbow is therefore not simply a reminder about a flood,
any more than the snake is just a reminder about Adam's sin. Both
are intended as pointers or signposts to the future. God is saying, 'I
have plans for sinful mankind; I have not forgotten my promise.'

The promise confirmed through the patriarchs

In Genesis 12 we meet with Abraham, and God takes another step
forward in unfolding his promise. In Genesis 12:2-3 God promised
Abraham that from him would come a special people (the Jews) in
a special land (Israel); later, in chapter 17, God added a special sign
(circumcision). But why was God bothering so much with Abraham
and his family? The answer will be found in Genesis 12:7: 'To your
offspring I will give this land.' At first we might simply think this
refers to the Jews who were all descended from Abraham, but we
must not forget that the same word 'offspring' was there in Genesis
3:15: 'your offspring and hers'. We know that in Genesis 3:15 this
was a reference to Christ. So the promise to Abraham is all about
Christ!

Once again, if we turn across two thousand years of history from
Abraham to Paul, we discover that this is exactly what the apostle
says. Writing in Galatians 3:16, Paul is playing with words. 'Offspring', like 'seed', can be both singular and plural. If I talk about

leaving my money to my 'offspring' you do not know whether I have one, two, three or any number of children. In the same way I can have a 'bag of seed' meaning many seeds, or I can hold one 'seed' in my hand. In Galatians 3:16 Paul writes, 'The promises were spoken to Abraham and to his seed. The Scripture does not say "and to seeds", meaning many people, but "and to your seed", meaning one person, who is Christ.'

That should be clear enough. The promise to Abraham was the same as that to Noah and to Adam; it was the promise of Christ coming to destroy the works of the devil. First the reminder was a snake, then a rainbow and now a *special people* in a special land. If you have never seen this before, you will now be watching the incredible unity of the Bible story unfolding.

You will notice that the promise always refers to a person. Now comes the next amazing reference to this promise. In Genesis 49 we have the story of the patriarch Jacob, or Israel as he was later called, blessing his twelve sons just before he died. This was an important occasion in the ancient world but it was deeply significant in the life of a patriarch because he gave a prophecy about one of his sons in particular that went far beyond his own expectation. Verses 8-12 in this chapter concern the future of his son Judah who became the father of the tribe of Judah; in time this tribe gave its name to the true people of God. If you read this passage you will immediately see that it points forward in time. But before we come to its fulfilment, notice that it is greater than all the other promises given to Israel's sons, and that fact alone is interesting.

As the best of all the promises Israel gave, it is contrary to custom. The best was normally given to the firstborn, but Judah was fourth in line after Reuben, Simeon and Levi. It was also contrary to Israel's natural preference, since his favourite son was Joseph and not Judah. Similarly it was contrary to what we would expect, since Judah was by no means the best of the sons; it was he who suggested selling Joseph to the traders (Genesis 37:26), and one whole chapter (38) is taken up with Judah's loose and unfaithful way of life. In spite of all this, the promise is given to Judah.

The key verse in this passage is verse 10. Notice once again the personal pronoun 'he'. Just as we found in Genesis 3:15, so here we have a reference to a particular person who is yet to come; and it is said of him that the 'sceptre' belongs to him. A sceptre was the orn-ate staff held by royalty that represented their power and authority;

we find it in the Persian court in Esther 4:11, for example. The one who is promised will have rule and authority over the nations. The references to the donkey and his robes washed in blood (Genesis 49:11) have a very obvious ring about them to our New Testament ears. Remember that sceptre, we shall meet with it again.

These are not just occasional stories thrown together to make interesting reading, or to tell us a little about God or ancient civilizations. In the Old Testament we have a perfect plan as God unfolds the great promise he has made; this is taken up in the New Testament as the writers understand exactly to whom it had all been pointing. But now the picture becomes even more clear.

The promise confirmed to Moses

After Abraham, God confirmed his promise in the same way to Isaac and Jacob also. In the days of Jacob, whose name was changed to Israel, his family went to live in Egypt, where they grew to a large company of people and gradually became slaves. 430 years after God confirmed his promise to Abraham, the Israelites were groaning under their slavery. But God had not forgotten them: 'God heard their groaning and he remembered his covenant with Abraham, with Isaac and with Jacob' (Exodus 2:24).

This time it was Moses to whom God confirmed the same promise with a new sign. Exodus 12 tells the story of how the Israelites left Egypt. One night they were told that each family must take a male lamb from the flock; it had to be a first-born lamb, one year old, and without any blemish. The lamb was to be killed and some of the blood sprinkled on the doorposts of their houses. During that terrible night God's angel of death came to Egypt and killed the first-born in every home. Only where the angel of death saw the blood of the lamb on the doorpost did he 'pass over' and spare that family. God said to Moses and the people, 'The blood will be a sign for you' (Exodus 12:13).

Blood is the new sign. As a matter of fact it was not completely new. Because this new sign was such an important step in God's plan, he had already prepared the way for it. Abel offered a lamb as a sacrifice (Genesis 4:4) and Noah was told that from now on people were never to eat blood (Genesis 9:4). Noah, Abraham, Isaac and Jacob all offered sacrifices, but now, with Moses, it was going to become very clear why.

From the time of Moses throughout the rest of the Old Testament, thousands upon thousands of sacrificial animals were killed. A special group of people, called priests, offered these sacrifices on behalf of the Jews, and a special part of Israel's family (the descendants of Levi) was set aside to look after all the events or ceremonies that went along with sacrifices. God gave detailed instructions about the ceremonies. This is called the ceremonial law — how the Jews were to worship. The other part of the law was called the moral law, which told them how they were to live.

This ceremonial law and the blood sacrifices were not the final fulfilment of God's great promise in Genesis 3:15, but just the next stage in God unfolding his plan. Galatians 3:17 is an important verse in the New Testament, and here it is with some explanation added in brackets: 'The law [the ceremonial law], introduced 430 years later [i. e. with Moses, 430 years after Abraham], does not set aside the covenant previously established by God [with Abraham] and thus do away with the promise [Genesis 3:15].' Leaving out Noah, here are three big steps: the promise (Genesis 3:15), the covenant (with Abraham) and the law (the ceremonial law with Moses).

What was the purpose of all this? We should know the answer by now, but Paul makes it clear for us as he continues in Galatians 3:19: 'What then was the purpose of the law? It was added because of transgressions until the seed to whom the promise referred had come.' The 'seed to whom the promise referred' is Christ.

Just in case any of his readers have still missed the point, Paul adds in Galatians 3:24: 'So the law was put in charge to lead us to Christ.' This is the law Paul is referring to when, in Romans 6:14, he reminds us we are 'not under law, but under grace'. The law of Jewish ceremony led us to Christ, but we no longer need it now that Christ has come. The Christian is completely free from binding ceremonies and ritual to gain salvation. When Christ came, they all went. He is the 'Lamb of God, who takes away the sin of the world' (John 1:29) and is spoken of repeatedly in the New Testament as the final sacrifice without whom none of the Old Testament sacrifices had any meaning (see especially Hebrews 9:11-15). Christ did not come because the old ceremony of sacrifice had failed: on the contrary it was never expected to succeed; the old ceremony was simply a signpost, and only by the blood of Christ's sacrifice could the Old Testament men and women of faith be forgiven. This is clear when we understand the promise and its fulfilment.

These signs, therefore, are like signposts. A signpost is not a destination; it is only a pointer. The snake, the rainbow, the special people, the special land, the Jewish ceremonies and shed blood, are all signposts that say, 'This way to the promise'.

In addition to the sacrifices, God gave another reminder of his promise in the time of Moses. In Deuteronomy 18:15 God renewed his promise in this way: 'The Lord your God will raise up for you a prophet like me from among your own brothers. You must listen to him.' At first we may be looking for any one of the Old Testament prophets to fulfil this verse, but according to Deuteronomy 34:10, 'No prophet has arisen in Israel like Moses.' So, to whom does this promise refer?

In Matthew 17:5, on the mount of transfiguration, God said of his Son: 'Listen to him.' The fact that the Jews took this reference in Deuteronomy as a prophecy of the coming Messiah is evident from the New Testament. Our Lord once said, 'If you believed Moses, you would believe me, for he wrote about me' (John 5:46). After the feeding of the great multitude, the crowds were debating who Christ was and some concluded: 'Surely this is the prophet who is to come into the world' (John 6:14). When Philip came to bring Nathanael to Christ he declared: 'We have found the one Moses wrote about in the law' (John 1:45). Even the Samaritans knew that the Messiah would explain everything to them (John 4:25), and both Peter and Stephen quoted this verse from Deuteronomy and applied it to Christ (Acts 3:22-23; 7:37). Clearly Deuteronomy 18:15 is another step in God's unfolding revelation of his promise.

The promise confirmed by an unexpected source

The next time God spoke of his promise, the evidence comes from an unexpected quarter. Balaam is better known for what his donkey said than for what he himself said! As a false prophet he had been hired by the King of Moab to curse the great army of the Israelites as they marched through the wilderness on their way to the promised land. Unfortunately for the king, Balaam found that he could not speak anything other than the words of God on this occasion. As he stood on the hill overlooking the Israelites, these were his words, recorded in Numbers 24:17:

'I see him, but not now;
  I behold him, but not near.
A star will come out of Jacob;
  a sceptre will rise out of Israel.
He will crush the foreheads of Moab,
  the skulls of all the sons of Sheth.'

Balaam sees someone coming with power and authority (a sceptre) from the line of the patriarchs (out of Jacob) — but not yet.

The time of David

Many of the psalms written by David are what we call 'Messianic' psalms. This refers to the fact that they are prophecies pointing forwards to the coming of God's great promise. Here is just one of them:

'Your throne, O God, will last for ever and ever;
  a sceptre of justice will be the sceptre of your kingdom'
(Psalm 45:6).

There again is that sceptre promised!

The promise confirmed by the prophets.

Abraham, Jacob, Moses and David were all prophets of the Old Testament, and so was John the Baptist; and that covers two thousand years! Some of the prophets are named within the stories of the Old Testament, whilst others have a Bible book named after them. We will call this latter group the 'book prophets'. Probably the earliest of the book prophets was Obadiah. Writing about 850 years before Christ, he condemned Edom, the descendants of Esau, for standing aside and rejoicing when enemies attacked Jerusalem. Then, in a half-hidden reference to the promise, Obadiah declared:

'But on Mount Zion will be deliverance;
  it will be holy,
and the house of Jacob
  will possess its inheritance'
(Obadiah 17).

The prophets began in this veiled way but gradually their prophecies became more and more clear. A hundred years after Obadiah, Isaiah was preaching in a way every Jew should have understood. He spoke of a suffering Saviour who was still to come:

'He was despised and rejected by men,
    a man of sorrows, and familiar with suffering.
Like one from whom men hide their faces
    he was despised, and we esteemed him not'

                                       (Isaiah 53:3-7).

A hundred years on from Isaiah, another great prophet, Jeremiah, continued the same theme:

'"The days are coming," declares the Lord,
    "when I will raise up to David a righteous Branch,
a King who will reign wisely
    and do what is just and right in the land.
In his days Judah will be saved
    and Israel will live in safety.
This is the name by which he will be called:
    The Lord our Righteousness"'

                                     (Jeremiah 23:5-6).

Notice the 'seed' becomes a 'Branch' here. Isaiah also refers to the promise in terms of the Branch and, another hundred years after Jeremiah, so does Zechariah: 'Listen, O high priest Joshua and your associates seated before you, who are men symbolic of things to come: I am going to bring my servant, the Branch' (Zechariah 3:8).

These quotations from the prophets Obadiah, Isaiah, Jeremiah and Zechariah are what we call 'Messianic' prophecies; they point forward, like signposts, to the coming of Christ, who is the Messiah or Anointed One. These four examples, covering only three hundred years, are a small part of the very many Old Testament prophetic references to the promise. Whenever you read one of the book prophets, watch for the promise. Sometimes it is hidden and you may miss it, but sometimes it is plain for us to see.

Christ was referring to himself when he said, 'This is the blood of the covenant, which is poured out for many for the forgiveness of sins' (Matthew 26:28). He was saying, 'My blood is what all the

Old Testament was pointing to.' Paul called it the 'new' covenant (1 Corinthians 11:25). It was not new because it was a different promise, but new because it did away with all the old ceremonies and signs of the same promise.

As you read the Old Testament, therefore, you should watch for the promise. That is what it is all about. When Christ came and died on the cross, the promise of Genesis 3:15 began to be kept. I say, 'began to be', because on the cross Satan dealt a blow against Christ and Christ by his death and resurrection began to bind Satan. Christ snatched people away from Satan's grasp and made a new nation of Christians, but the final crushing blow to Satan has not yet been given. We are looking forward to the day when Christ comes again in glory and power and the devil will be thrown into hell, where he will be tormented day and night for ever and ever (Revelation 20:10). This will be the final crushing blow to Satan, and the promise will have been fulfilled by God. Revelation 15:3-4 gives us the song of praise in heaven for the ultimate victory of God and the triumph of his Son's sceptre:

'Great and marvellous are your deeds,
  Lord God Almighty.
Just and true are your ways,
  King of the ages.
Who will not fear you, O Lord,
  and bring glory to your name?
For you alone are holy.
All nations will come
  and worship before you,
for your righteous acts have been revealed.'

The people

The best way to read the Old Testament is to trace the promise through the stories and events. Another, and equally thrilling way to read it, is to trace the line of the special people through whom God was planning to fulfil his promise. The promise was going to benefit all kinds of people, all over the world, but because the promise was about a person, Jesus Christ, he had to come from a family. Christ did not just appear from heaven; he was born into a family, and that family had a very special history. So now we shall survey the Old Testament watching for the special people, the family from which Christ came.

Our journey starts in Genesis 4:26 with the statement: 'Seth also had a son, and he named him Enosh. At that time men began to call on the name of the Lord.' After the disobedience of Adam and Eve they had children and these children in turn had families. As men began to move across the world they also moved spiritually further and further away from God. Sin had taken root. Adam had been created 'in the likeness of God' (Genesis 5:1) and that meant he was perfect; but Adam had children 'in his own likeness' (5:3) and that was a likeness spoiled by sin. Men and women drifted downwards into more and more sin.

At this time there began a terrible division in the world. It was not a division of geography, colour or race; it was a tragic spiritual division — one that is still with us: there were those who called upon God, and those who did not.

Genesis 4 begins the list of those who did not call upon God. These were the descendants, or family, of Cain, the godless man who killed his brother Abel. You can see by their lifestyle that the family of Cain had no interest in God. Cain lost his temper, killed his brother and 'went out from the Lord's presence' (Genesis 4:16). Lamech was the great-great-great-great-grandson of Cain and he was a man of pride and violence (4:23-24). Among Cain's descendants in this chapter there is no reference to God.

On the other hand, Genesis 5 introduces us to a family who began to call upon God. It started with Seth, who was the son born to Adam after the death of Abel. Seth starts the line of the special people. You can see by their lifestyle that the family of Seth knew God. Not only did Seth call upon God, but Enoch 'walked with God' (5:22), and Noah, a descendant of Enoch and Seth, 'was a righteous man, blameless among the people of his time, and he walked with God' (6:9). Here is the beginning of the line leading to Christ; the special people through whom God was preparing to carry out his great promise. Cain wanders off the stage and God turns our attention to Seth.

The interesting fact about this family line — Adam, Seth, Enoch, Noah, and all the others in between — is that it does not follow the line of the first-born son. Seth was not the first-born son, and Seth was 105 years old before Enosh, the next in the line, was born! Enosh was ninety before Kenan was born, Methuselah was 187 before Lamech was born, Noah was 500 before Shem was born and, according to Genesis 10:21 Shem certainly was not the oldest son of Noah. God did not choose the line of the first-born for his special people, but he chose spiritual men, converted men, Old Testament Christians. Another important fact is that when God renewed his promise, he always did so with his special people. For example, he renewed the promise with Noah.

After the flood, Noah stepped out on dry land and his three sons came out with him: Shem, Ham and Japheth. These three sons were to be the start of the new world, and everybody today comes from them. But we are only really interested in Shem as we watch for the people of God's promise. Ham and Japheth leave the stage but God turns our attention to Shem. You can follow Shem into Genesis 11:10. From Shem came the man called Abraham. It was with Abraham that God renewed his promise. He told Abraham that a great nation would come from him and all the world would be blessed by his offspring, who, as we have seen, is Christ. God renewed this promise to Abraham's son Isaac. Isaac had twin sons, but Esau was just a little older than Jacob, yet it was Jacob whom God chose to continue the line leading to Christ. God said to their mother, 'Two nations are in your womb, and two peoples from within you will be separated; one people will be stronger than the other, and the older will serve the younger' (Genesis 25:23). Esau leaves the stage and our attention is focused upon Jacob.

As we have already seen, Jacob had twelve sons, but only one of them could lead us to Christ. The one God wants us to watch especially is Judah, although he was not the first-born:

'The sceptre will not depart from Judah,
    nor the ruler's staff from between his feet,
until he comes to whom it belongs
    and the obedience of the nations is his.
He will tether his donkey to a vine,
    his colt to the choicest branch;
he will wash his garments in wine,
    his robes in the blood of grapes'

(Genesis 49:10-11).

This was nearly two thousand years before Christ was born, and already God was talking about a ruler who will be given obedience from all nations; and he spoke of a donkey, a colt, wine and robes dipped in blood! It all points forward to Christ. Five hundred years before the birth of Christ, the prophet Zechariah gave the people a reminder of this promise when he too spoke of the coming king, 'gentle and riding on a donkey, on a colt, the foal of a donkey' (Zechariah 9:9).

When the twelve sons of Jacob went to Egypt they were to form the nation of God's special people and amongst that special nation was one family or tribe named after their ancestor Judah. Fifteen hundred years later, in Revelation 5:5, Christ is actually called the 'lion of the tribe of Judah'. In Egypt, Pharaoh tried to exterminate God's special people (Exodus 1:8-22), but that was just not possible. God's promise depended upon him looking after his people.

Moses led the people out of Egypt and for forty years God looked after them in the wilderness before Joshua led the victorious army of the Israelite tribes into the promised land. During these years God had told his people how to live (the moral law) and how to worship (the ceremonial law).

For many years the family from which the promise would come is lost from sight. We know the family is there, even during the long, sad years of the judges when often everyone did what was right in his own eyes, but we cannot see them. Then suddenly, in the tiny book called Ruth, God shows us that he has been looking after that family all the time. Set somewhere in the period of the judges, the book of Ruth is the story of how Boaz married Ruth. Why was God so interested in the story of one small family? Because Boaz came from the family of Judah and he was the great-grandfather of King David. The one who fulfilled God's promise was descended from David. God shows us how he was protecting the special family. The family tree, or genealogy, recorded in Ruth 4:18-22 is very important.

When David eventually became king about nine hundred years before Christ, he had many sons. Solomon was not the oldest, but he was the one chosen to continue the line leading to Christ. In the days of Solomon's son Rehoboam, the whole nation of the Jews divided into two. Humanly speaking, it was all the fault of Rehoboam, but God was once again narrowing our vision to one part of the twelve tribes of Israel. Ten tribes chose their own king and set up their headquarters in Samaria, about fifty-six kilometres (thirty-five miles) north of Jerusalem. Two tribes, Judah and Benjamin, remained loyal to the line of David and stayed in Jerusalem. The breakaway kingdom was now called Israel, and the loyal part based on Jerusalem was called Judah. We must watch Judah, of course; these are the special people. The kings of Judah were the line leading to Christ.

For two hundred years these two kingdoms were sometimes fighting each other and occasionally friendly. At last in 722 B.C. Israel was crushed by the armies of Assyria and 135 years later Judah was crushed by Babylon. The Jews were scattered all over the known world and it might seem impossible for us to find the family leading to Christ. Because God showed us how he was looking after the family once before in the time of the judges, we can trust that he was doing it again.

When, by the command of Cyrus, King of the Medio-Persian empire, the Jews were allowed to return to Jerusalem and rebuild the city and temple in 537 B.C. the tribe of Judah was quick to send men to the work (Ezra 1:5). Along with the men from Judah came one particular family, that of Zerubbabel son of Shealtiel (Ezra 3:2). According to Matthew 1:12, Christ was born from this family. Luke agrees with this (3:27), but from Zerubbabel onwards Luke follows the line to Mary, rather than Joseph.

During this period there was a determined effort once again to exterminate all the Jews. The story is told in the book called Esther. The outcome was never in doubt. God's promise was at risk so he rescued the special people and therefore, somewhere among them, the family of Zerubbabel which was to lead to Christ.

During the four hundred years after the close of the Old Testament we know nothing of this family from whom Christ was to come. Matthew gives us the list of names in his Gospel (1:13-16) and when he concludes, 'of whom was born Jesus, who is called Christ', the unbroken line from Seth is complete. The promise given to the people is preserved in the family until Christ came.

Prophecies and more prophecies

Earlier we looked at the way God used his prophets to prepare for the coming of his great promise. We need to turn to the subject of

prophecy once more because it is so important in the Bible. It has
been calculated that there are more than three hundred prophecies
in the Old Testament that refer to Christ, and that twenty-nine of
them were fulfilled in the final twenty-four hours of his life. Here are
a few to illustrate the point:

Old Testament reference	*Prophecy*	*New Testament reference*
Zech. 13:7	He would be deserted by his disciples	Mark 14:50
Ps. 35:11	He would be falsely accused	Matt. 26:60
Isa. 50:6	He would be brutally beaten	Matt. 26:67
Isa. 53:7	He would not retaliate	Matt. 27:14
Isa. 53:12	He would be executed with criminals	Matt. 27:38; Luke 23:32
Ps. 22:16; Zech. 12:10	His hands and feet would be pierced	John 19:34
Ps. 34:20	Yet his bones would not be broken	John 19:33
Ps. 22:18	They would gamble for his clothes.	John 19:23-24

There is an amazing parallel between Psalm 22 and Isaiah 53 and the
events at the crucifixion.

This sample refers only to the closing hours of Christ's life and
the fulfilment is unbelievably precise. It would have been impossible for him to 'manipulate' events to suit these prophecies and the
chances of coincidence are too impossible to waste time discussing.
The manner of his conception in the womb of a virgin (Isaiah 7:14),
the very place of his birth (Micah 5:2) and the triumphant journey
into Jerusalem (Zechariah 9:9) are also among the many prophecies
of Christ's birth, life and death. That these passages we have quoted
from the Old Testament were written centuries before Christ was
born is beyond any doubt. So how can we account for the incredible
accuracy of fulfilment if it is not one more evidence of the Bible as
a book with a divine author?

Impressive as these promises of the coming of Christ may be,
they are no more significant than the hundreds of prophecies in the
Old Testament that were fulfilled before the close of that part of our
Bible. Again and again God warned his people, and sometimes the

surrounding nations, of events that were to come. The usual re-sponse of the critic, in fact the only response available to him, is to assume that the prophecies were actually given long after the events they predicted! This at least admits that the Bible is either a book of incredible accuracy or near-total fraud. We cannot here detail all the Old Testament prophecies, but one example may prove helpful to illustrate the way critical scholars are compelled to twist the obvious in order to justify their position.

One of the most outstanding kings of Judah was Josiah, the fifteenth in line from Solomon. His sweeping reforms were unpar-alleled in the history of the kings of the Old Testament. Tragically, however, the change was only in the heart of the king and not in the hearts of the nation. As soon as Josiah died at the age of thirty-nine the nation returned to a godless way of life and suffered the consequences. There were three significant prophets preaching during the reign of Josiah: Zephaniah, Jeremiah and Habakkuk. Each of these three prophets preached a message of doom and destruction that was quite contrary to what appeared at the time to be the future for Judah, since the massive, far-ranging reforms and genuine piety of the king promised well for the nation.

We are therefore to assume, if the critics are to be believed, that the Scripture plainly deceives us when it records the prophecies given by these three men because the critics tell us that these passages must have been written *after* the events were fulfilled; how could they give such terrible and accurate warnings if they were written at a time when the nation was more reformed than at any time in its history? One of the three might perhaps have hazarded a guess as to what would happen, but when three prophets are all so accurate it can only be assumed that they wrote after the events!

For a moment let us place ourselves in the position of the three prophets if they were indeed writing after the events. How would we plan our deceit? One thing is certain, and that is that we would draw attention to the reforms, admit they were impressive and then warn the nation not to think that these things would take away the anger of God. The simple fact is that, apart from a very brief reference in Jeremiah 22:15-16, not one of the prophets even hints at the reforms under Josiah. Why? Because each prophet was writing in the middle of the best reforms and everyone was aware of what was going on. They deliberately ignored the reforms and startled the nation by their warnings.

One of the amazing aspects of Habakkuk's prophecy was his reference to the rise of the Chaldeans as the future masters of the world (1:6-11). At the time when he was prophesying, the Chaldeans were a fairly insignificant group in Babylon, though they were always trying to infiltrate into power, and the father of Nebuchadnezzar was a Chaldean. Babylon was itself under the domination of Assyria, who had a succession of strong kings and had already burnt Babylon in the lifetime of the prophet. Thus Habakkuk was prophesying the future role of a fifth column in a second-rate nation. In fact Assyria's world supremacy seemed secure. Next to Assyria it was Egypt, not Babylon, that was flexing its war muscles. If Habakkuk had been writing after the event, it would have been natural for him to make reference to Assyria, Egypt and Babylon in order to highlight his 'success' as a prophet; in other words we would expect him to say, 'You think these are the world tyrants? You are wrong, watch the Chaldeans.' In fact he makes no reference to Assyria, Egypt or Babylon. The prophet knew that his message was almost unbelievable (1:5), but he simply stated the facts and left the future events to prove him right.

The harmony of Old and New Testaments

This has been a brief survey of the way God made and kept his promise that he would send a Saviour to defeat the work of Satan. There are other ways we could trace God's unfolding plan in the Old Testament. We could look at the nations and see how God led his people through domination by Egypt, Assyria, Babylon, Persia and finally Rome, and how in each case his prophets warned of the nation that would next come onto the stage of world power, sometimes when it appeared most unlikely.

Alternatively we could look for the ways Satan employed the hatred of men and nations to try to destroy the family line that would lead to the birth of the Messiah. Perhaps the first large-scale record of this is in the plan of the Pharaoh of Egypt to destroy the male children of the Israelites (Exodus 1:15-16). In the dark days of the judges of Israel, God guarded the line by a godly man in an ungodly age in the story recorded in the book of Ruth. On more than one occasion David almost lost his life by the hand of King Saul (1 Samuel 19:9-10), and years later the queen mother, Athaliah, slaughtered all the royal children in a vain attempt to protect her throne; she unknowingly left just one offspring of David alive — Joash, who would later destroy her and continue the line of the Messiah (2 Kings 11). Esther is yet another story in the Bible of an attempt to exterminate the entire Jewish nation, and almost the final throw of Satan came at the birth of Christ (Matthew 2:16). However, the cross and the resurrection finally led Satan captive (Ephesians 4:8) and the promise of God waits for the total and inevitable destruction of the power of Satan (Revelation 20:7-10). Here again the perfect unity of the story of the Bible is clear.

The New Testament writers never doubted the unity of the Old Testament, and they saw their own writing as continuing the great story of salvation. When their Lord claimed that he had not come to abolish the law or the prophets 'but to fulfil them' (Matthew 5:17), he provided them with their theme. Far from contradicting the Old Testament or abolishing it, the New Testament writers knew that their Gospels and letters were fulfilling all that God had revealed to the prophets. Paul's explanation of justification by faith in Romans 4 is rooted in the Old Testament story of Abraham, who is used not as an illustration but as an example of salvation by faith alone. Similarly the apostle's letter to the Hebrews assumes that everything under the old ceremonies and sacrifices was there to prepare for Christ — a point made forcefully by Paul in Galatians 3:24. Peter was similarly aware that the gospel he and his fellow apostles preached and wrote was that which God first gave to the prophets, who were told, 'They were not serving themselves but you' (1 Peter 1:12).

In this way the New Testament is an extension of the Old and the completion of it. In Acts 17:11 we are told that the Bereans were able to check out Paul's teaching simply by referring to their Old Testament; the New does not contradict or correct the Old. The character of God, the nature of man and his sin and the way of salvation by faith alone through the sacrifice and atonement of Christ are all consistently taught throughout the unfolding revelation of the Scriptures both in the Old and New Testaments.

By looking at the plan of God to keep his promise and protect his people, we can see how unique the story unfolded in the Bible really is. There is no other story, and therefore no other book in the world, to compare with the Bible. Far from it being a jumble of ancient legends all thrown together haphazardly, we have a perfect plan

that is pressed forward a little further with each book in the library
that makes up our Bible. Everything points forwards to Christ and
we are therefore not surprised to find him, at the beginning of his
ministry, reading from the prophet Isaiah in the Jewish synagogue
in his home town of Nazareth and then declaring, 'Today this
scripture is fulfilled in your hearing' (Luke 4:21). Nor are we
surprised to find him, just before his return to heaven, opening the
minds of his disciples to 'understand the Scriptures' so that they
could see how the Law of Moses, and the Prophets and the Psalms
were all fulfilled in him (Luke 24:44-45).

Within this story of God's plan of salvation we have a totally
consistent view of the character of God and the spiritual state of man
since the Fall; not one statement ever contradicts another and never
are we presented with a conflicting view of the world or its history.
The harmony of the various Bible books, as they each press forward
the plan of God, is remarkable; and it must stand as one of the
greatest witnesses to the divine authorship not only of the book
itself, but of the story it relates.

9.
The accuracy of the Bible

'You surely don't believe the Bible to be true! It's a book of fables and myths and everyone knows that it's full of contradictions. The Bible isn't meant to be taken seriously as an accurate book of history.'

This is a common challenge to those who believe in the verbal inspiration of Scripture, and the impression is always given that real scholarship and intelligent study lie on the side of those who deny the accuracy of the Bible. J. B. Phillips revealed this attitude in his book *Ring of Truth* when he dismissed those who believe that the Bible is reliable in every part and contrasts them with those who have 'sense as well as faith'. James Barr, a contemporary liberal theologian, similarly ridicules the evangelical position as 'a pathological condition of Christianity', and claims that he cannot accept any of the intellectual arguments for inerrancy 'except in very minor respects' (*Fundamentalism,* p.9). In fact, he goes further and believes that it is his and not the evangelical position that really respects the Bible and accepts its authority. The claim is that evangelicals have imposed their view of inerrancy upon the Bible and so are making claims for the Bible that it does not make for itself.

We have already seen that the evangelical Christian believes in the truth and historical accuracy of the Bible in all its statements, and that this is what our Lord and the apostles clearly taught. The challenge of many critics of the evangelical position is that to believe that the Bible is God's errorless Word and that it contains within its pages nothing but the truth is simply an anti-thinking position which is impossible to maintain if we have 'sense as well as faith'. Admittedly there are problems and difficulties of 'apparent' contradictions and errors, and these will be dealt with in chapters 16 and 17, but the purpose of this chapter is to establish that true scholarship is not on the side of critical views of the Bible but, on the contrary, that it supports the evangelical confidence in the absolute trustworthiness of Scripture.

In 1990 Dr Eta Linnemann published a book called *Historical Criticism of the Bible: Methodology or Ideology?* Such a title would not normally attract the interest of any except those dedicated to academic theology, but in this case the book was of unusual interest. Eta Linnemann is Professor of New Testament in the Philipps University at Marburg in Germany and has written a number of best-selling books; she has spent years destroying the confidence of her readers in the Bible as the inerrant Word of God. It was her conviction that the Bible was inaccurate as a book about history and unreliable as a book about God and that it was her mission to prove this.

Slowly, however, the proud professor at Marburg and dedicated student of Rudolf Bultmann became disillusioned with her own method of study. She writes, 'I became aware of what folly it is to maintain that the miracles of the New Testament never took place... It was clear to me that my teaching was a case of the blind leading the blind. I repented for the way I had misled my students.' In this latest book Dr Linnemann regards everything she has ever taught and written as rubbish. She declares that she has thrown some of her most popular and critical books into the bin and advises her readers: 'I ask you sincerely to do the same thing with any of them you have on your own bookshelves.' In her case the force of truth had triumphed.

During this century a number of scholars have come to the defence of Bible accuracy with a learning and skill that have still not been answered. When criticizing the Bible people usually ignore these people; we are all in danger of ignoring those things we cannot understand or answer. From the long list of those who have ably defended the detailed accuracy of the Bible, I have chosen just two in this chapter. One represents the Old Testament and the other represents the New Testament. But before we look at their work and conclusions one or two points need to be made.

First of all, these two men were acknowledged to be leading experts and scholars with first-class minds. There was nothing casual or lazy about their methods of study. They were men searching for truth and, though one of them began with a commitment to the inerrancy of the Bible whilst the other did not, both claimed that they were forced to agree that the Bible is completely reliable in its history. We need never be afraid to refer to these men since they had few equals, if any, in their own day. Their work has been added to in recent years as new discoveries have been made, but we may claim without any fear of contradiction that nothing has yet been put forward that alters their general conclusion regarding the complete accuracy of the Bible.

Secondly, and this is very important, a chapter like this can only prove that a belief in the accuracy of the Bible is a perfectly reasonable and intelligent position. What this chapter does not attempt to do is to prove that the Bible is true to a man who will not believe. Our belief in the Bible is a matter of faith, not merely reason. We believe that God is true and cannot lie. That is where we began our study. All that this chapter proves is that our faith is not unreasonable. Sense and faith are not opposites.

The Old Testament:
Professor Robert Dick Wilson, Ph.D., D.D.

Earlier this century it was assumed that the evangelicals, like a tiny David, were being overwhelmed by the Goliaths in the universities. Professors Ewald and Wellhausen, at Göttingen in Germany, and Doctors Driver and Gray, at Oxford in England, were names that stood for great scholarship, brilliant intellect and careful research. Between them they denied the accuracy of the Bible and their views, though altered by modern critics, still form the basis of arguments against its inerrancy. How could the evangelical David, possessing only 'faith without sense', resist the liberal Goliath with all his learning and skill?

Robert Dick Wilson was Professor of Semitic Philology (the languages and literature of the Middle East) at Princeton Theological Seminary in the United States of America, during the 1920s. In 1929 he left Princeton with others to form the Westminster Theological Seminary. Wilson's scholarship, though little spoken of today, excelled that of the learning of the great critics at Göttingen and Oxford. He was born in 1856 and during his student days in Germany, Wilson worked out a programme for his life. He planned to spend fifteen years in language study, fifteen more in the study of

Professor Robert Dick Wilson

the Old Testament text in the light of these languages and, finally, fifteen years in publishing his findings. Those first fifteen years were amazing!

He learned a few languages by filling the odd moments of time: Greek, Latin, French, German, Hebrew, Italian, Spanish, Portuguese, biblical Aramaic, Syriac, Arabic — and a few more! Wilson then moved to Heidelberg in Germany to study Babylonian. To these he added Ethiopic, Phoenician, all the Aramaic dialects, Egyptian, Coptic, Persian and Armenian. These were the 'semitic' languages. During those first fifteen years Robert Dick Wilson became familiar with some twenty-six languages and dialects; many of these languages he studied under the leading professors of his day.

Throughout the following fifteen years, Wilson collected over 100,000 quotations from these languages to illustrate basic facts proving the accuracy of Scripture. Among his many books and papers, in 1922 Wilson published a book *Is the Higher Criticism Scholarly?* in which he claimed, 'I try to give my students such an intelligent faith in the Old Testament Scriptures, that they will never doubt them as long as they live.' The results of his vast research enabled Professor Wilson to conclude, 'I have now come to the conviction that no man knows enough to assail the truthfulness of the Old Testament.' When this man ridiculed the arguments and questioned the scholarship of the 'higher critics', he did so from a greater height than they ever attained. Here are just a few examples of his work.

The date of Ezra, Nehemiah and Chronicles

The critics demanded a very late date (around 300 B.C.) for these three books on the ground that they use an expression 'King of Persia', which, the critics claimed, was 'unnecessary and contrary to all contemporary usage'. Who could argue with such great scholars? Wilson gathered a mass of quotations and references, particularly from Babylonian, Persian, Susian and Egyptian sources, and showed that from 400 B.C. down to Augustus in A.D. 14, 'It was the custom in all times, languages, and kingdoms, to use titles similar to this,' and that this exact title was used by Nabunaid of Babylon to refer to Cyrus in 546 B.C., seven years before its first use in the Bible. Wilson revealed that this title, so 'contrary to all contemporary usage', was employed thirty-eight times, by eighteen different authors, representing six different languages, between 546 and 365 B.C.!

Why, asked the evangelical, had not the learned professors read these sources for themselves? Then Wilson challenged the infallibility of Ewald, Wellhausen, Driver and Gray: 'Having read carefully and repeatedly what these critics have to say on this title, I have failed to find any hint indicating that they have ever appealed for their information to any original sources outside of Greek, Hebrew and Aramaic.' Perhaps this was because they could not easily read beyond these three.

Abraham's expedition in Genesis 14

The German critic Wellhausen read the account of the raid of Chedorlaomer against the Kings of Sodom and Gomorrah and his subsequent defeat by Abraham (Genesis 14), and for various reasons concluded these accounts 'are simply impossibilities'. Wilson showed that such expeditions were not uncommon at that time, that the names given to the kings in the Bible account are also found in

literature of the surrounding nations, and that Abraham is mentioned in such literature as early as 1950 B.C. Without any evidence,
the critics could only claim that an unknown Jewish archaeologist,
somewhere between 900 and 300 B.C., had invented the story in
honour of Abraham by using names he had discovered!

This instance is so typical of the critical approach to Scripture
that perhaps we should have Wilson's own words taken from *A
Scientific Investigation of the Old Testament,* published in 1926:
'Against the historical character of this narrative we have the
assertion of Wellhausen and other critics of our times (only about
4,000 years after the supposed expedition!) that the expedition was
"simply impossible", and that it is probable that the account may
have been fabricated (or forged) by some person unknown, at some
time unknown, for reasons unknown. Not one item of evidence in
the way of time, place, logic, psychology, language, or customs, has
been produced against the trustworthiness of the document... But a
German professor says it is "simply impossible", English followers
echo "simply impossible", and the Americans echo again "simply
impossible". And this assertion of "simply impossible" is called an
"assured result of scientific criticism"!' (p.22).

The accuracy of the Old Testament copyists

It is a commonplace argument that over the centuries a great number
of mistakes must have been made in the Scriptures as they were
copied and recopied from generation to generation. It is certainly
true that this is what we might expect, but is it in fact what we find?
This is a subject we shall turn to again in chapter 12, but Robert Dick
Wilson illustrated the careful accuracy of the Old Testament in the
following way.

Twenty-six foreign kings are referred to in the Hebrew Old
Testament, and in all but three instances the spelling is identical with
that found in inscriptions made by these kings themselves. For
nearly four thousand years the names were copied with unswerving
accuracy to the extent that the 120 consonants involved in these
names are all in exactly the right order.

In contrast to this biblical accuracy an Egyptian priest wrote a
history somewhere around the year 280 B.C. He gives 140 names of
kings of Egypt and only forty-nine are clearly recognizable when
compared with the relevant monuments and inscriptions! Similarly,

Ptolemy, the great astronomer-geographer of the second century A.D. whose conclusions were accepted without question for thirteen centuries, listed eighteen kings of Babylon and most of these bear no resemblance to the names on monuments and inscriptions! In spite of these facts critics of the Bible almost always assume that pagan historians are correct when their records disagree with the Bible. Surely a man who has been proved to be wise and honest has the right to be believed when a liar or fool disagrees with him!

There are more than forty kings of Israel and Judah listed in the Bible. Each is found in the correct order and references to the kings of surrounding nations are all accurate when checked with the records of those nations. By any fair critic the Bible must be seen to be an amazingly accurate book. If there is such care over the spelling and order of names is it not reasonable to expect a similar care in recording the words and actions of these kings?

The use of foreign words and customs in the Old Testament

In any collection of documents written over a long period of time, we would expect to find the use of foreign words reflecting the influence of the nation that held world power at that time. This would prove the date and order of the documents, for it would be almost impossible for an author of a later date to insert words and customs unfamiliar to him. For example, it would be extremely difficult for a present-day author to write a play or a novel based upon a family who lived five hundred years ago, unless he had first undertaken a great amount of research to ensure that the words and customs were exact.

Wilson has shown that the customs and words used in the Old Testament reveal each book to have been written at the time it claims to have been written. We find foreign words in the Old Testament just where we would expect to find them. The early chapters of Genesis contain a number of Babylonian words. Later in Genesis, Egyptian words are introduced. Solomon's writing contains Indian and Assyrian words. Then, during the period of the kings, there is a return of Assyrian and Babylonian terms. Daniel, Ezra, Nehemiah, Esther and Chronicles all contain a number of Persian words used for the first time in the Bible. There is strong evidence that during the time of Jeremiah and the exile, Aramaic was the common language of Western Asia and the business language of the Jews.

This would explain the otherwise strange fact that one verse in Jeremiah and half of Ezra and Daniel are written in Aramaic and not in Hebrew. So, all these books reflect the ruling nation of the day and the area of the world in which the story of the Jews is set.

Very significantly Wilson showed that Greek words are virtually absent in the Old Testament because by the close of the Old Testament (around 400 B.C.) Greek power was not yet evident. If, as the higher critics demand, much of the Old Testament was written as late as the second century B.C. — and many claim Daniel was written in Palestine in 164 B.C. — where are all the Greek words? Interestingly there are references to Greek musical instruments, but that is because, as we now know, Nebuchadnezzar employed Greek mercenaries in his army.

Some critics also claim that parts of the Pentateuch (Genesis to Deuteronomy), and especially the priestly laws in Leviticus, were not written by Moses fifteen hundred years before Christ, but by Ezra and his editors between 500 and 300 B.C. This was right in the middle of the Persian period and naturally the book of Ezra abounds with Persian words. But there is not one Persian word in those so-called 'priestly documents' in Leviticus. Ezra must have been a quite remarkable forger if he really was writing Leviticus between 500 and 300 B.C.! More likely, the higher critics are wrong.

Dick Wilson maintains that each narrative and section of the Old Testament reveals the customs of that particular time which would have been unknown to writers a few centuries later. Among the many examples he gives is the fact that the reference to the horse appears first in the story of Joseph at the very time we know the horse was being introduced into Western Asia and Egypt. On the other hand, asks Wilson, if so much of the Old Testament was supposed to have been written late in the Greek period, why is there not one reference to the elephant which was, by the time of the Greek power, important for both work and war?

It seems that the very least we must claim for these deceivers, who were supposed to have written books of the Bible and then claimed a great age for them, is that the brilliance of their scholarship, their knowledge of archaeology, and their literary ability, demanded divine aid not far different from an evangelical view of verbal inspiration!

Critics have concluded that the understanding of God's character which is found in the earlier parts of the Old Testament — as

Creator, preserver, guide, Judge, Saviour and sanctifier — is so far in advance of the beliefs of surrounding nations that the records must have a very late date for their origin. Of course it is true that the Jewish ideas about God, man and salvation are nowhere paralleled in the surrounding nations; but it is hardly believable that serious men should assume that some books are of a late date simply because they express ideas about God and resurrection that are too far in advance of their times. Did Jewish views of the resurrection have to wait until the Persians taught the concept to them? Who taught whom? To make this an argument for dating would be to prove that every teacher was born after his students and learnt his subject from his students!

Grammar

Perhaps the very word frightens us away from this section! How can we compete when great Hebrew scholars claim certain terms prove a late date for, say, the book of Ecclesiastes? Professor Delitzsch was probably the greatest Hebrew scholar in the last century, and although he died in 1890 he was one of the founders of modern Bible criticism. Delitzsch claimed that certain forms in words in Ecclesiastes, like *ûth*, *ôn*, and *ân*, were proof 'beyond all doubt' that this book was not written by Solomon or anyone else near his time, but during the days of Ezra/Nehemiah at the earliest. Cornell, in his *Introduction to the Canonical Books of the Old Testament* (p. 449), claims this to be 'absolutely convincing and irrefutable'. Do we surrender in the face of such scholarly assurances?

Wilson had read and studied more widely than Delitzsch and could assure us that this great master was very mistaken. Wilson put forward sixty-seven uses of *ûth* from eight sources between 2,000 and 625 B.C. and claimed that this form is found in every book of the Old Testament except Song of Solomon, Ruth and Lamentations — many of them in passages that even the critics themselves insist are early in date! He dealt similarly with *ôn* and *ân*. We do not have to understand the issues to appreciate the result. True scholarship will always find the claims of the Bible to be reliable. If the critics are proved to be in error so often, have we any obligation to trust them anywhere?

The plain man, untrained in languages and biblical criticism, is often beaten into submission by the impressive arguments about grammar and syntax proving this date or that. But we have no need to submit, because we can trust confidently in the brilliant and careful scholarship of a man like Professor Dick Wilson, who once commented, 'These forms and constructions are irrelevant as evidence of the time at which a document was written.' We are quite right to accept his word for it and not be troubled by such arguments again.

Wilson's conclusions

It is impossible to do justice to the clear arguments of Professor Wilson. His brilliance was unequalled and we are fully justified in accepting his conclusions even when we cannot follow all his arguments; after all, the critics have relied upon such submission to their views for more than a century. Wilson used to complain at what he called the 'inquisitorial' methods of the Old Testament critics; that is, they would assume the Bible to be untrustworthy and misleading, and all evidence challenging this assumption was scorned. This unjustified assumption is still with us. Many critics have ceased to bother whether or not the Bible stories are reliable; they simply assume they are not and then tell us why, nevertheless, we can trust the authority of Scripture! That is a position we would never allow in any other literature; reliability in matters of history are a clear indicator to reliability in matters of theology.

Wilson claimed that the Old Testament has a right to be accepted 'until it shall have been proved false', and proof, the professor sternly demanded, is not the same as the 'opinions of men of our generation'. For too long Christians have been afraid to trust the very words of Scripture in case they find themselves ridiculed by clever minds. Before he died in 1936, Professor Wilson had shown that these minds are not always clever, scholarly, or even honest.

We have already noted that the result of his scientific approach to the Old Testament led Wilson to believe that 'No man knows enough to assail the truthfulness of the Old Testament.' He offered the fruit of his lifetime of painstaking study with the bold assertion: 'We are scientifically certain that we have substantially the same text that was in the possession of Christ and the apostles and, so far as anybody knows, the same as that written by the original composers of the Old Testament documents' (*A Scientific Investigation of the Old Testament*, p.8).

Sir William Mitchell Ramsay
(Reproduced by courtesy of Manchester University Press)

The New Testament:
Sir William Mitchell Ramsay, D.C.L., Litt D., LL.D., D.D.

William Ramsay was born in Glasgow, Scotland, in 1851. By his death in 1939 he had become the foremost authority of his day on the history of Asia Minor and a leading scholar in the study of the New Testament. From the post of Professor of Classical Art and Architecture at Oxford, he was appointed Regius Professor of Humanity (the Latin Professorship) at Aberdeen. Knighted in 1906 to mark his distinguished service to the world of scholarship, Ramsay also gained three honorary fellowships from Oxford colleges, nine honorary doctorates from British, Continental and North American universities and became an honorary member of almost every association devoted to archaeology and historical research. He was one of the original members of the British Academy, was awarded the Gold Medal of Pope Leo XIII in 1893 and the Victorian Medal of the Royal Geographical Society in 1906. So many books and articles came from the pen of Sir William Ramsay that it is difficult to obtain a complete list.

Ramsay, unlike Wilson, never claimed to be an evangelical Christian and never committed himself to a view of Bible inerrancy.

In fact, when he began his research he had no interest in proving the accuracy of the New Testament. In 1868 Ramsay had earned the first three prizes in Greek and Latin from his class at the University of Aberdeen and by 1872 he won a five-year scholarship at Oxford. He soon became a keen follower of the professors at Tübingen and Göttingen, fell under the domination of Baur and 'worshipped Wellhausen' (see chapter 1). Admitting all this, Ramsay agreed that he 'dutifully accepted the current opinion that the Acts of the Apostles was written during the second half of the second century by an author who wished to influence the minds of people in his own time by a highly wrought and imaginative description of the early church'. Like Tübingen scholars, he considered that the author of Acts wrote somewhere between the years A.D. 160-180, cared nothing for facts of history, or geography, and aimed only to influence the minds of his readers by imaginative stories of his heroes, especially Peter and Paul (*The Bearing of Recent Discovery on the Trustworthiness of the New Testament,* pp. 16, 37-38.)

When William Ramsay first went to Asia Minor, many of the cities mentioned in Acts had no known location and almost nothing was known of their detailed history or politics. The Acts of the Apostles was our only record and Ramsay fully expected his own research to prove the author of Acts hopelessly inaccurate since no man could possibly know the details of Asia Minor more than a hundred years after the event. He devoted his life to unearthing the ancient cities and documents of Asia Minor and the facts he discovered brought about an amazing change in his thinking.

In the first place Ramsay recognized that 'No other ancient traveller has left an account of the journeys which he made across Asia Minor.' Therefore the account of Luke, if we assume the traditional view of Luke as the author of Acts, had first to be shown to be true or false. If it was proved to be the accurate narrative of an eyewitness then, for Ramsay the historian, it was the most valuable document we were ever likely to possess describing Asia Minor in the first century A.D.

Ramsay therefore set out to put the writer of Acts on trial. Remember, Ramsay was an outstanding scholar whose work has still not been surpassed, and he had no special concern to prove Luke an accurate and careful historian; in fact it would have well suited his own views to have found Luke hopelessly inaccurate. After a lifetime of study, however, this was his conclusion: 'Further study

... showed that the book could bear the most minute scrutiny as an authority for the facts of the Aegean world, and that it was written with such judgement, skill, art and perception of truth as to be a model of historical statement' (*The Bearing of Recent Discovery*, p.85).

Perhaps no finer statement was ever made by Ramsay on the trustworthiness of Luke than that found on page 89 of the same book: 'I set out to look for truth on the borderland where Greece and Asia meet, and found it there [in Acts]. You may press the words of Luke in a degree beyond any other historian's and they stand the keenest scrutiny and the hardest treatment...'

Two things particularly impressed Ramsay. In the first place, Luke was a historian not to be compared with other ancient historians and writers. They were sometimes right and accurate, and sometimes wrong and careless; Luke was always accurate and careful. Secondly, he was interested to notice that 'Scholars who aimed simply at collecting facts, and had evidently no bias either for or against him [Luke] seemed to regard him as a sufficient authority,' whereas those who had already set out to prove that the Bible is a false witness dismissed him as untrustworthy. This is a valuable warning from a scholar like Sir William Ramsay. He never found Luke to be in certain error even at one small point; there are unsolved problems, of course, but problems are not errors.

When Ramsay turned his attention to Paul's letters, most of which the critics dismissed as forgeries, he concluded that all thirteen New Testament letters that claimed to have been written by Paul were really his. Despite this, Ramsay did not accept biblical inerrancy; he was not a theologian but simply a brilliant historian and archaeologist.

Ramsay found Luke to be well acquainted with all the political arrangements in the various provinces of Asia. We shall look at just a few examples. At the time Paul was in Cyprus a proconsul was in charge and, although there had been many changes, Luke used exactly the correct title when referring to Sergius Paulus (Acts 13:7). Philippi was accurately described as a Roman colony whose officials are referred to as '*stratagoi*', or magistrates (16:38). At Thessalonica the reference to the '*politarchs*', or 'city officials'(17:6), is now well attested by inscriptions from that town. In Ephesus the 'officials of the province' are called the '*Asiarchs*' (19:31), exactly the people we now know controlled religious affairs. At Malta the *'protos'* (28:7) is the 'chief official'. Small things? Perhaps, but these are facts that would never be known to later generations and therefore constitute clear evidence that Luke was an eyewitness of all that he recorded.

Iconium and the cities of Lycaonia

It was a seemingly insignificant statement in Acts 14:6 that first caused William Ramsay to suspect that Luke was deserving of more honour as a historian than had generally been given to him. The verse describes what happened when Paul and Barnabas were forced to leave the city of Iconium on account of a plot by the Jews: 'They ... fled to the Lycaonian cities of Lystra and Derbe and to the surrounding country.' It had long been believed by the critics that the city of Iconium was in fact the chief city of the Roman province of Lycaonia and therefore the statement that Paul and Barnabas fled from Iconium 'to the cities of Lycaonia' was simply nonsense. It was rather like saying a man escaped from London to England; we would rightly assume that anyone making this statement had little knowledge of geography.

In the fourth chapter of *The Bearing of Recent Discovery*, Ramsay produced a mass of detailed evidence to show that Luke was, in fact, quite right. Iconium, at the time of Paul's journeys, was a city of Phrygia, and not Lycaonia. In fact the citizens of Iconium were of altogether different stock and did not even speak the Lycaonian language — a fact that obviously impressed itself upon Paul (Acts 14:11). Not until A.D. 372 was the province of Lycaonia reformed by the Emperor Valens and Iconium made its capital city. Modern scholars had never gone further back than A.D.372 and had therefore ignored Luke's evidence, which was correct all the time. This fact is now universally accepted.

Two examples of Ramsay's evidence will have to be sufficient. In A.D.163 the Christian leader Justin, together with several other Christians, was put on trial in Rome. One of these Christians was a slave named Hierax who, when asked who his parents were, replied, 'My earthly parents are dead, and I have been brought here [as a slave] torn away from Iconium of Phrygia.' Even Pliny, the Roman governor of Bithynia early in the second century A.D., referred to Iconium as one of the ancient and famous cities of Phrygia.

Every detail in the story recorded by Luke in Acts 14 was found by Ramsay to be so accurate that he reversed his judgement on Luke as a historian. He was prepared to trust Luke from now on because 'No writer is correct by mere chance, or accurate sporadically. He is accurate by virtue of a certain habit of mind.' After all, Luke had been condemned as unreliable everywhere because of this supposed blunder in Acts 14:6; when that 'blunder' was shown to be accurate historical reporting, the same reasoning must allow him to be trusted elsewhere! That is exactly what Ramsay found him to be. Both in his Gospel and the record of the infant church in Acts, when Luke writes of cities or slaves, languages or customs, prophets or poets, travel or trials, government officers or religious leaders, merchants or magicians, not only is Luke's variety remarkable, but his accuracy is without equal.

The census in Palestine

There is a passage in Luke's Gospel that for many years appeared to be a clear example of the author's historical ignorance. The 'experts' dismissed it, and those who believed in the inerrancy of Scripture found it almost impossible to defend because there were so few facts available. The passage in question is Luke 2:1-4: 'In those days Caesar Augustus issued a decree that a census should be taken of the entire Roman world. This was the first census that took place while Quirinius was governor of Syria. And everyone went to his own town to register. So Joseph and Mary also went up from the town of Nazareth in Galilee to Judea, to Bethlehem the town of David...' The list of criticisms against it ran like this:

1. The emperor never issued any decree ordering a census.
2. Never, under the Roman emperors, was any regular census ordered.
3. Where a casual census was ordered only the husband was required to register; the wife did not have to accompany him.
4. On such occasions the husband was not required to return to his place of birth in order to register.
5. Quirinius was not governor of Syria until A.D.5-6, that is, nine years after the death of Herod in 4 B.C., in whose reign our Lord was born. Both Tertullian, an early Christian leader born around the year

A.D.155, and Josephus, the Jewish historian born in A.D. 37, claim that Sentius was governor in Syria and took the census when Jesus was born.

6. Quirinius actually called a census in A.D. 6 and Luke must have mistakenly placed it during the reign of Herod.

7. The story of Joseph and Mary at Bethlehem was therefore entirely false as were all the details surrounding it.

These were the 'certain results of critical scholarship' a hundred years ago. The 'experts' knew the 'facts' and there was nothing more to be said.

(A note should be added here regarding the date of Christ's birth. This is not Ramsay's comment, but will be helpful since the reference to the death of Herod in 4 B.C. may seem a little confusing in the light of Matthew 2:19 that Mary and Joseph returned from Egypt to Nazareth 'after Herod died'! The fact is that when our present dating system was fixed by a monk in the year A.D. 533, he made a few mistakes in his calculations! We now know that Herod died in what would be 4 B.C. and, if we allow for a period of up to two years from Christ's birth to his return to Nazareth, the date of his birth must therefore have been around 6 B.C.)

We now turn to Sir William Ramsay's answer to these accusations.

1. When Egypt came under the authority of Rome in 30 B.C., the Roman emperor, Augustus, left undisturbed the Egyptian system of an annual census. So it is untrue to claim that no emperor ever ordered a census. In addition to this, the letters of Pliny, a Roman governor of Bithynia, reveal quite clearly that a regular census was taken in the Roman Empire. So accurate was this system that when the authorities were suspicious of a man who claimed to be 150 years old, the emperor himself ordered a check of past enrolments to test the man's claim!

2. There is definite evidence of enrolments around the years 28 and 8 B.C. and A.D.14, 34, 48, 62 and 76. In other words, it would appear that the emperor ordered an empire-wide census approximately once every fourteen years. Ramsay has offered a great deal of undeniable evidence for this regular census system of the Romans.

3 and 4. It is undoubtedly true that the census taken by the Romans in Egypt in A.D.104 involved the return of all persons 'to their home to enrol themselves'; this was the actual wording of the census. Ramsay has shown this was 'the customary Roman method of making the census'.

These first four points are now generally admitted and so, very reluctantly, the critics have to admit that Luke could have been recording historical facts. But remember, for many years hardly anyone dared to suggest that Luke was right because there seemed to be no evidence to support him. But what of the problem concerning Quirinius?

5 and 6. We know for a certainty that Quirinius was governor of Syria in A.D.6 and that he organized a census during this period of his office. But Luke himself knew all about this, and he refers to it in Acts 5:37. It is therefore very unlikely that he would mistakenly place this governorship of A.D. 6 back in 4 B.C. Ramsay needed to show that Quirinius held office in Syria within a year either way of 4 B.C.

(We should note that more recently it has been suggested that Luke 2:2 could be translated: 'This census was before the one made when Quirinius was governor of Syria.' This is perfectly acceptable as an alternative translation, and if it is right then we do not need to find Quirinius in Syria in 4 B.C. However, since Ramsay has found evidence of this, we have no need to fall back on the alternative translation.)

To return to Ramsay's evidence: we know that Quirinius was a consul in Rome in 12 B.C. but this, Ramsay maintained, was intended to prepare him to take command of a large army to fight the emperor's war in Syria shortly after this date. Ramsay discovered an inscription in Antioch, a leading military stronghold in Syria, that clearly revealed Quirinius was the chief magistrate of the city in 8 B.C. But, and this is important to note, according to the inscription Quirinius' office was an honorary position and a deputy actually carried out the duties. The reason for this arrangement was that Quirinius was fighting the emperor's war in Syria. This war lasted from 10 to 8 B.C. and the final resettlement of Syria would possibly require another two years. Clearly then Quirinius could have held the chief post of the Roman legions fighting in Syria during the last years of the reign of King Herod in Palestine.

However, Tertullian, as we have seen, tells us that Sentius Saturninus was governor of Syria at the time of Jesus' birth and it was he who ordered the census. Josephus gives the date of 8-6 B.C. for this census. So at least there is now good evidence to show that there was a census around the time of our Lord's birth. A full census, requiring people to travel long distances, could take a few years to complete. Ramsay suggests that Quirinius was military governor and Sentius was administrative governor for a short period together. Sentius may have ordered the census and Quirinius, possibly staying on after Sentius had left, actually carried out the command in 6 or 4 B.C. We know that Quirinius had moved to Asia as proconsul by 3 B.C.

There is still a degree of uncertainty in this whole subject, not because Luke's account has been shown to be wrong, but because we do not have sufficient evidence to show every part of it to be right. However, all that Ramsay discovered — and there is little more since then — demonstrates that Luke's account has the right to be accepted as trustworthy.

Many of Sir William Ramsay's arguments are long and detailed and it would be tedious to reproduce all the evidence here, but these two examples illustrate his general conclusion that the writer of Acts 'has now been found to show excellent knowledge and the minute accuracy which comes from the faithful report of an eyewitness and participator in the action'. The years of patient and careful research and the thousands of pages that William Ramsay devoted to Luke's Gospel and Acts all show that the customs and language, the synagogues, trials, councils, magicians, in fact everything mentioned, reveal a detailed knowledge that could only be written down by an eye-witness of the events.

Conclusion

In this chapter I have taken the work of two outstanding scholars and, by a few illustrations from their mass of published material, have shown how consistently sound scholarship defeats the criticisms of the Bible. These were men whose ability demands careful attention and whose conclusions have not, in general, become outdated with the passing years. But these two men are only typical of hundreds of others who have shown that the more we compare the Bible records with inscriptions and manuscripts discovered from the past, the more it is found to be accurate in every detail. Nowhere has the Bible been proved in certain error at any point. If Wilson and Ramsay have shown how accurate the Bible is proved to be in so many areas where once it was fiercely attacked, then we surely have the right to trust it everywhere. Where there are still problems unsolved, it is perfectly reasonable to accept the Bible's account and wait in the certain knowledge that eventually scholarship will come to the same conclusion. It always has.

Unfortunately it has become commonplace for modern critics of the Bible simply to assume the Scriptures are full of historical blunders. Even more unfortunately some evangelicals are now making the same assumption. One such has written, 'There may be a stage at which the difficulties involved in explaining away an apparent historical error are greater than those caused by accepting the existence of the error... One may ask whether there is a stage when the number of alleged historical difficulties for which there is yet no solution must lead the conservative scholar to conclude that the absolute historical reliability of the New Testament is a mirage' (Howard Marshall, *New Testament Interpretation,* 1977).

A statement like this entirely ignores the implications of the work of men like Wilson and Ramsay. Interestingly many New Testament scholars ignore the work of Ramsay altogether. This is a point that did not escape the attention of Professor F. F. Bruce, who commented: 'I am repeatedly amazed by modern writers who deal with areas of New Testament scholarship to which Ramsay made contributions of peculiar value, with hardly so much as a hint that such a person ever lived.'

Of course there are still unsettled historical problems in the Bible, but wherever it can be tested, the Bible is proved true. Time will no doubt resolve those problems that remain, and we have no need to give in to the tyranny of unbelieving critics any more than we surrender to the arguments of those who present their reasons why they do not believe in the existence of God. Besides, many would deny the existence of 'apparent historical errors' that present insurmountable difficulties; and the number of 'alleged historical difficulties' is certainly not so great that we need to doubt 'the absolute historical reliability' of the Bible.

Professor Robert Dick Wilson claimed to give his students 'such an intelligent faith in the Old Testament Scriptures that they will never doubt them as long as they live'. Sir William Mitchell Ramsay dared to maintain that 'Christianity did not originate in a lie, and we can and ought to demonstrate this, as well as to believe it.' He is no fool who agrees with men of the intellectual calibre of Wilson and Ramsay.

10.
Why only thirty-nine books in the Old Testament?

Our Bible contains sixty-six books written over a period of fifteen hundred years by about forty different men, all of whom taught the same central message and in no way contradicted those who came after them or before them. These facts alone, which we looked at in chapter 8, make the Bible unique. The question we are faced with now is simply this: 'Why are there just sixty-six books in our Bible?' Why no more or less? Who decided that these were sufficient and for what reasons? Was it a meeting of Jewish rabbis or church bishops? Was there ever any doubt about which books should be included or excluded? It may be comforting to imagine that the Bible fell out of heaven all neatly printed and packaged, but it certainly did not happen that way.

The issue of which books should be in our Bible is known as the 'canon' of Scripture. 'Canon' is a Greek word for a reed, which was used as a rule or measuring line. Paul uses the word in Galatians 6:16 where he speaks of those who 'follow this rule'. The word 'canon' was first used in the fourth century A.D. to refer to the collection of Bible books. Our subject in this chapter is why we have just thirty-nine books in the Old Testament canon.

Long before the birth of Christ the canon of the Old Testament had been settled, and our Old Testament was the Bible of Christ and his disciples. The Jews divided the Old Testament in a different way from how we do today. They divided their Bible into three sections: the Law, the Prophets and the Writings. Although they have not always agreed which books belong to which sections, the following list represents the present-day position:

The Law contains the five books of Moses: Genesis to Deuteronomy.

The Prophets include the earlier prophets: Joshua, Judges,

Samuel and Kings, and the later prophets Isaiah, Jeremiah, Ezekiel and Hosea to Malachi.

The Writings consist of Psalms, Proverbs, Job, Song of Solomon, Ruth, Lamentations, Ecclesiastes, Esther, Daniel, Ezra, Nehemiah and Chronicles.

This may seem a rather strange division for the Christian. We must also remember that the Jews frequently combined two books into one; for example, the two books of Samuel, Kings and Chronicles, each became one book, and Ezra and Nehemiah were combined as one. For this reason the list of books given by the Jewish historian Josephus, around A.D. 70, numbers only twenty-two, although these twenty-two contain all our thirty-nine. In fact, to confuse the situation further, Josephus listed five books under the Law, thirteen under the Prophets and four under the Writings! But however the number and order of books varied, long before Christ the Old Testament contained all the books now in our Old Testament, and no more. This was not because the Jews had no choice about it. There were many interesting books that were not included, like those which make up the Apocrypha, which we shall consider later in this chapter. How did our Bible books of the Old Testament come to be so clearly accepted as the only books?

The evidence of the Old Testament

The most important answer to our question must be found in what the Old Testament says about itself. If we have to rely upon what men, or councils of men, have said about it then we are on dangerous ground, because men make mistakes, whereas God's Word does not.

Moses is always seen as the mouthpiece and scribe of God

The first five books of the Bible (the 'Pentateuch' as they are called) were written by Moses, and all through the Old Testament there is agreement on this point. Frequently we find Moses himself writing in a book the laws and activities of Israel. If you read Exodus 24:4; 34:27-28; Numbers 33:2 and Deuteronomy 31:9,22,24 you will notice that Moses recorded the laws, the history and even the geography of Israel's wilderness wandering. Joshua took over from

Moses as leader of Israel and he was careful to read all the books of Moses to the people (Joshua 8:31-35). After Joshua came the sad years of Israel's disobedience during the period of the judges, but even here there are references to the commandments of Moses (e.g. Judges 3:4).

The same 'Law of Moses' (always understood as those first five books in our Bible) was handed down through the line of the Kings of Judah. David gave it to his son Solomon (1 Kings 2:3). Amaziah reacted to the children of his father's murderers 'in accordance with what is written in the Book of the Law of Moses' (2 Kings 14:6). The accounts of the reigns of Hezekiah (2 Kings 18:6), Manasseh (2 Kings 21:8), Josiah (2 Kings 23:25), Jehoshaphat (2 Chronicles 17:9), Jehoiada (2 Chronicles 23:18) and Amaziah (2 Chronicles 25:4) all contain references to the 'Law of the Lord' or 'the Law of Moses', which was understood to be the same thing.

After the kings came the exile in Babylon, and the prophets of the exile continued to remind the people of the law of Moses (see Ezekiel 7:26; Daniel 9:11,13). When the people returned from exile we find ten references in Ezra and Nehemiah to the use they made of the law of Moses (e.g. Ezra 6:18; Nehemiah 8:1).

References to God's law in the book of Psalms are so numerous that the reader can find them at a casual glance. Psalm 119 is the greatest example of this, where only five of the 176 verses do not contain a direct reference to the law. The prophets Isaiah (8:20) and Jeremiah (8:8) both refer to the law. Among the other prophets, Hosea, Amos, Micah, Zephaniah, Haggai and Zechariah all refer to the law, and Malachi, the last book of the Old Testament, urged the nation, on behalf of God: 'Remember the law of my servant Moses, the decrees and laws I gave him at Horeb [Sinai] for all Israel' (Malachi 4:4).

This brief outline shows that the Jews, throughout their history, always accepted the books of Moses as the law of God.

Moses expected his books to be copied and kept

Moses spoke of the time, many centuries away, when Israel would choose a king to rule over them. One of the first acts that the new king should carry out was described in this way: 'When he takes the throne of his kingdom, he is to write for himself on a scroll a copy of this law, taken from that of the priests, who are Levites. It is to be

'He is to read this law all the days of his life'

with him, and he is to read it all the days of his life so that he may learn to revere the Lord his God and follow carefully all the words of this law and these decrees...' (Deuteronomy 17:18-19). Moses fully expected his words to form part of Israel's religious life for ever, and because of this he not only wrote a book of the law (Exodus 24:4), but read it to the people (Exodus 24:7) and placed a copy for safe-keeping beside the ark of the covenant (Deuteronomy 31:24-26).

Moses expected others to follow him with God's words

We must not think that Moses considered God's revelation to men would come to an end when he himself died. God had already told him, 'I will raise up for them a prophet like you from among their brothers; I will put my words in his mouth, and he will tell them everything I command him' (Deuteronomy 18:18). Moses went on to warn the people against false prophets (vv. 20-22).

The prophets witnessed to the authority of each other

There was a long tradition of writing among the prophets of Israel and we have evidence of some of them being commanded to write down their message (e.g. Jeremiah 30:2; Habakkuk 2:2). But what is more important is the fact that many of the prophets referred to each other's ministry and reminded the people that it was a word from God. Look at the following examples.

Jeremiah 28:8 speaks approvingly of the authority of 'the prophets who preceded you and me', and Jeremiah 26:18 reminds the people of a verse found in Micah 3:12. Micah was a prophet who began his ministry 120 years before Jeremiah.

Ezekiel 38:17 refers to the prophecies of Isaiah concerning the enemies of Israel. Isaiah was prophesying some two hundred years before Ezekiel.

Daniel 9:2 reveals that the prophet Daniel had been reading from Jeremiah 25:11-12.

Zechariah 1:4-6 contains a reference to Isaiah 1:16; 31:6 and also to passages in Jeremiah and Ezekiel. What is particularly important about this passage in Zechariah is the comment by the prophet that although those who prophesied to 'your forefathers' have all died (v. 5), yet the words of God through the prophets have outlived both prophets and fathers (v. 6). We have here a clear witness to the continuing value and authority of prophecy.

The evidence of the New Testament

From what we have already seen, the test for an Old Testament Bible book was that it came from Moses or the prophets. But that leaves us with large parts of the Old Testament that would appear to fall outside this definition. However, if this is a problem to us, it certainly was no problem to our Lord or the Jews of his day. Christ referred to the whole of the Old Testament as 'Moses and the Prophets'. It is true that in Luke 24:44 our Lord adds to this expression the words 'and the Psalms', but this was simply to reinforce his teaching to the unbelieving disciples.

In Matthew 13:35 Christ quoted from Psalm 78:2 and said that it came from 'the prophet'; this was not a mistake and no Jew would ever have suggested it was. In Luke 11:50-51, Christ included among the lists of prophets. Abel (found in Genesis 4) and Zechariah (found in 2 Chronicles 24, and not the same man as the prophet whose book appears towards the end of the Old Testament). We know that a large part of the Old Testament was written by the prophets. A prophet did not simply foretell the future, but more especially he gave out God's Word, and therefore spoke as the voice of God. Under this definition not only Moses, but David and Solomon, Ezra and Nehemiah and others were also prophets. Even those few books whose authors we cannot be sure of, like Judges and Ruth, Job and Chronicles, were apparently accepted by our Lord and the Jews as coming from the hand of the prophets.

When our Lord claimed that not the smallest letter or stroke of the Law would pass away until heaven and earth passed away (Matthew 5:18) no one among his listeners would understand that he meant anything other than the whole of the Old Testament as we know it. We have already seen in chapter 5 that the New Testament writers accepted the authority of the Old Testament without question and without addition, and they too considered it to be God speaking 'to our forefathers through the prophets' (Hebrews 1:1). The fact that they refer to or quote from all but a handful of Old Testament books shows that the New Testament writers had no difficulty in accepting the Old Testament canon.

The evidence outside the Bible

The Dead Sea Scrolls

Some of our most important evidence comes from the Dead Sea Scrolls. We shall discuss the great value of these recent discoveries in chapter 12, but here it is sufficient to say that these scrolls, found in caves around the Dead Sea, belonged to a Jewish community that lived in this area between 130 B.C. and A.D. 68. This means that those Dead Sea Scrolls which contain Old Testament books or comment on them are the oldest copies of the text of the Old Testament and commentaries on it that we possess.

What is important for us here is the fact that all we have just said regarding the attitude of our Lord and the disciples towards the Old Testament is found in these Dead Sea Scrolls. *The Manual of*

Discipline, the book that governed the life of the community, introduces a quotation from Isaiah with the words 'It is written', and only quotations from books of the Old Testament are introduced in this way. Again 'the Law and the Prophets' is an expression used as a summary of the whole of the Old Testament.

Josephus

Josephus was the Jewish historian who lived between A.D. 37-100. In one of his works, *Against Apion* (Book 1, chapter 8,) he makes plain what the attitude of the Jews was to the Scriptures: 'For we have not an innumerable multitude of books among us, disagreeing from and contradicting one another (as the Greeks have) but only twenty-two books, which contain the records of all the past time; which are justly believed to be divine, and of them five belong to Moses ... but as to the time from the death of Moses till the reign of Artaxerxes King of Persia ... the prophets, who were after Moses, wrote down what was done in their time in thirteen books. The remaining four books contain hymns to God and precepts for the conduct of human life.' In fact the twelve prophets at the end of our Old Testament were put together as one under the title 'The Book of the Twelve'.

Josephus went on to admit that other books had been written but they had not been accepted as equal in authority with the prophets, 'because there has not been an exact succession of prophets since that time'. Josephus then contrasted the Jewish attitude towards the Old Testament with that of the Greeks to their own religious literature. Unlike the Greek, he claimed, the Jew has never been so bold 'as either to add anything to them, to take anything from them, or to make any change in them'. For Josephus and the Jews of this time, the Old Testament came from God through Moses and the prophets and when the succession, or line, of the prophets came to an end with Haggai, Zechariah and Malachi, so the Old Testament canon closed.

The Talmud

The Jewish *Talmud* is a collection of commentaries and teaching by the rabbis (teachers), compiled during the four hundred years after the death of Josephus. The *Babylonian Talmud* contains a statement that supports the view of Josephus: 'After the latter prophets, Haggai, Zechariah and Malachi, the Holy Spirit departed from Israel.' For the Jew, God's revelation through Scripture ended at Malachi. At that time the prophets, and therefore the God-breathed Word, ceased.

The early Christian church

After the apostles had all died, the post-apostolic church followed exactly the canon of the Jewish Old Testament accepted by the apostles, but the order of the books began to change. Origen, one of the early church leaders who died, probably under torture, about the year A.D. 254, listed the books of the Old Testament and agreed with Josephus, except that Origen accidentally omitted the twelve prophets at the close of the Testament! It is clear that this was an oversight because, having agreed there are twenty-two books, he then lists only twenty-one, needing the 'Book of the Twelve' to complete his figure.

The Old Testament canon is complete

The Old Testament Scriptures were written by Moses and the prophets; nothing more was to be added. This was the view of the writers themselves, of our Lord and his apostles, and of the Jewish leaders and historians from the close of the Old Testament period, around 400 B.C.

The Old Testament was not, as some suggest, accepted as Scripture over a long and slow process of time. Each part was admitted into the canon almost at once, and concerning the limit of that canon there has never been any serious debate until critics of a modern age looked for some further attacks to make upon the inspiration and authority of Scripture. The single exception to this is the Apocrypha, which we shall come to in a moment. Therefore we must insist that it was not a council of Jewish rabbis or Christian bishops, but the Scripture itself that determined and fixed the limit of the canon of the Old Testament. The Jewish Council of Jamnia, held shortly after the destruction of Jerusalem by the Roman armies in A.D.70, merely confirmed the books that were already widely accepted as canonical.

Where does the Apocrypha fit in?

Toby, Judith and Susan are old English Christian names that may reveal the influence the Apocrypha once had upon English thought. Tobit and Judith are books within the Apocrypha, and in the story of Daniel the prophet saves Susanna!

When we turn in our Bibles from the prophecy of Malachi to the Gospel of Matthew we have turned over four hundred years of history. These four hundred years were very important in the history of the Jewish nation; they were full of battles and suffering, but the Bible is silent about them. However, many Jews were busy writing, and fourteen books were written during these four hundred years. Some put the number at fifteen because the book Baruch is sometimes divided into two. These fourteen books are called the Apocrypha, a Greek adjective meaning 'hidden'; they are an important collection of Jewish religious books from the period between the Old and New Testaments.

The Apocrypha is a strange mixture of legend and history, fact and fantasy. Sometimes its prayers and statements climb to a high point of spiritual experience, whilst elsewhere it is childish nonsense. However, it is a useful collection of books to help us understand the hopes of the Jews for the coming of the Messiah. Some of the books that make up the Apocrypha are concerned with stories already found in the Bible. For example, 1 and 2 Esdras deal with the events of rebuilding the city after the exile, recorded in Ezra and Nehemiah in our Bible. The Rest of Esther retells the Bible story of Esther, whilst Tobit and Judith are accounts of life after the destruction of Jerusalem by Nebuchadnezzar; and The Song of the Three Holy Children is concerned with the three friends thrown into the furnace by Nebuchadnezzar. The History of Susanna and Bel and the Dragon are both stories of Daniel. Finally the two books of Maccabees record some of the Maccabean wars before the birth of Christ. During these wars many of the vigorously nationalistic Jews fought hard for their independence against the Syrians and the Romans.

The fourteen books of the Apocrypha have never been accepted by Protestant Christians as part of the Bible. In 1643 a preacher before the Commonwealth Parliament in London denounced 'that wretched Apocrypha'; though others have been more lenient towards it whilst never accepting its authority, and even John Bunyan spoke of the benefit he had gained by reading from Ecclesiasticus.

On the other hand, the Roman Catholic Church since the Council of Trent in 1546 has officially attibuted to them the same authority and inspiration as to Scripture itself. The church of Rome was itself divided on the issue for a long time. In A.D. 405 Pope Innocent I endorsed the Apocrypha, but in A.D. 600 another pope excluded it, as Jerome had done before him and so had Cardinal Ximenes early in the sixteenth century. Today the Roman Catholic Church stands alone in officially accepting the Apocrypha, with the exception of the two books of Esdras and the Prayer of Manasses, as part of the inspired revelation from God. At the Council of Trent in April 1546 a curse was placed upon all who reject the Apocrypha as part of Scripture.

Lacking the strong central authority of the church of Rome, the Russian and Greek Orthodox churches are less decided in their attitude towards the Apocrypha. Whilst sometimes making a distinction between the Apocrypha and Scripture, in practice they treat them as equal, and most Orthodox priests will insist that the Apocrypha is part of their Bible even though there are few official statements to this effect.

The important question for us is this: should the Apocrypha be accepted as part of the inspired Scriptures or not? Because it was translated into Greek in the third century B.C. along with the Old Testament Scriptures, some of the early church leaders referred to the Apocrypha in much the same way that they quoted from the Old Testament itself. On the other hand, many of the leaders, like Melito of Sardis, Origen in the third century, Athanasius, the great theologian who contended for the full deity of Christ, Cyril of Jerusalem and John of Damascus all rejected the Apocrypha as being inferior to the Scriptures. However, there were sufficient leaders in its favour, including the influential Augustine of Hippo, for many in the church, both in the east and in the west, to accept the Apocrypha as Scripture right up until the time of the Reformation in the sixteenth century. But there was little certainty about it, and much confusion. The reasons for rejecting the Apocrypha are simple and many.

1. Neither our Lord nor any New Testament writer ever quoted from the Apocrypha, although, as we have seen in chapters 4 and 5, they were constantly quoting from the Old Testament. It was not that they avoided reference to other writings, because Jude 14-15 refers

to the book of Enoch, written during the time of the Apocrypha, and Paul quotes from Greek poets (Acts 17:28; 1 Corinthians 15:33; Titus 1:12). Having said this, there may be evidence that they were not unacquainted with the Apocrypha since there are a number of expressions in the New Testament that are found there. Here are a few examples: 'I gathered you together as a hen gathereth her chickens under her wings' (2 Esdras 1:30, compare Matthew 23:37). 'The innumerable multitude of angels' (2 Esdras 6:3, compare Hebrews 12:22). 'There was a voice that spake, and the sound of it was like the sound of many waters' (2 Esdras 6:17, compare Revelation 1:15). Some of these may be coincidence, but there is no reason to suppose that New Testament writers, familiar with the language of the Apocrypha, did not employ it to their own end. It was no sin to read the Apocrypha! But significantly they never once hinted that that was their source.

2. Josephus and the *Talmud* are quite clear that the books of the Apocrypha form no part of the Old Testament. They were never part of the Jewish Scriptures.

3. The community who copied out the Dead Sea Scrolls never refer to these books with the special phrases, 'It is written', or 'God says', and therefore clearly did not accept them as part of the Old Testament Scriptures.

4. Philo, a Jew writing from Alexandria in A.D. 40, quotes from, or refers to, all but five Old Testament books, but the Apocrypha is never mentioned or quoted. Similarly the Jewish Council of Jamnia, three decades after Philo, rejected the Apocrypha.

5. None of the books of the Apocrypha ever claims inspiration or a divine origin. They never claim, 'Hear the word of the Lord.' It would almost seem that the writers were careful to avoid their work being confused with Scripture. In fact the first book of Maccabees on three occasions states that a prophet was no longer available in Israel. In 1 Maccabees 9:27 the writer speaks of the terrible sufferings of the Maccabean wars and claims, 'So there was a great affliction in Israel, unlike anything since the time a prophet had ceased to be seen among them' (see also 1 Maccabees 4:46; 14:41).

6. Some parts of the Apocrypha contain historical errors and even contradict the teaching of the Old Testament as, for example, when the Prayer of Manasseh includes the statement: 'Thou therefore, Oh Lord, that art the God of the just, has not appointed

repentance to the just, to Abraham and Isaac and Jacob, which have not sinned against thee…' All scholars admit the many errors in Tobit and Judith; in fact the opening verse of Judith refers to Nebuchadnezzar as king in 'Nineveh' instead of Babylon! 2 Maccabees 12:40-45 claims not only the right, but the great value, of praying for the dead, 'that they might be delivered from sin' — a thought never found in Scripture and clearly contrary to the teaching of both the Old and New Testaments. Since there is not one verse in the whole Bible that gives us authority to pray for the dead or to believe in purgatory, it was chiefly to include this verse that the Roman church added the Apocrypha to the Bible. Though from a historical point of view the two books of the Maccabees are of some value, most of the stories in the Apocrypha are clearly fables with little historical base.

7. In A.D. 170 Melito, the leader of the church at Sardis, travelled to Jerusalem to assure himself of the exact limit of the Jewish Scriptures. He came back with a list exactly like our Old Testament, with the exception of Esther, which he seems to have omitted in error. Most of the church leaders agree with this for the first four centuries of the Christian church. Augustine, as we have seen, is an important exception, together with the two councils he led (Hippo in A.D. 393 and Carthage in A.D. 397). But even he admitted the Jews did not accept the Apocrypha as part of the canon of the Old Testament.

8. There is only little of spiritual value to be found in the Apocrypha and nothing that is not exceeded in the Old Testament. It is therefore surprising that any Christians should consider reading it as a serious aid to devotion. The evangelical church, since the Reformation, has never doubted that the Apocrypha is not part of the inspired Scripture, and with this all the evidence agrees.

11.
Why only twenty-seven books in the New Testament?

Almost as soon as the New Testament letters were written, other people began to write gospels and letters as well, and sometimes they tried to claim that these gospels and letters were really written by the apostles; these are called *pseudepigrapha*, meaning 'false writing'. Some of the books of the Apocrypha were pseudepigraphal, and so the early church was faced with false writers just as the Jews were. We have seen that none of the false books found its way into the Old Testament, but can we be just as sure that none found its way into the New Testament?

Some people claim that it was the church that decided which books should be in the canon of the New Testament and therefore the church made the Bible. This is the position taken by the Roman Catholic Church. Others go so far as to believe that it was little more than an accident which books finally formed our New Testament; they believe that almost any of the books being written in those early days could have ended up in the Bible. Because of this they find the evangelical doctrine of Bible inerrancy very strange.

In answer to these views we may say at once that it is hard to understand how anyone could read the facts of the first two hundred years of the Christian church without realizing that the early Christians were by no means as confused on this issue as we are led to believe; indeed they had clear principles to guide them in knowing which books were divinely inspired. Our New Testament was certainly no accident, nor was it decided by the church.

The witness of the New Testament itself

We have already seen in chapter 6 that the New Testament writers had no doubt about their own inspiration by God. More than this, they expected their letters to be read and exchanged among the churches (see for example Colossians 4:16; 1 Thessalonians 5:27; Revelation 1:19). The New Testament writers knew they were writing Scripture. The pseudepigraphal writers never spoke with the same authority and they therefore betrayed their position. Our chief reason for accepting a book as rightly belonging to the New Testament is that it speaks with an authority and accuracy that are completely unknown in other writings. In the majority of instances, the early Christians had little difficulty in recognizing this, as we shall see.

The writers of the New Testament were apostolic

We saw in the last chapter that the great principle which governed the Old Testament was that books had to be written down by Moses or one of the prophets; this was the Jewish test for the canon of the Old Testament. Similarly it was the apostles of Christ who were responsible for the New Testament.

If we accept this word 'apostle' to refer just to the thirteen apostles (this includes Paul) then we have covered the authorship of every New Testament book with the exception of the Gospels of Mark and Luke, the book of Acts and the letters of James, Jude and possibly Hebrews. Of course, New Testament critics frequently deny the authorship of Peter and Paul even when a book claims to come from the pen of one of them! We looked at this kind of approach in chapter 1 and will not bother to return to it here.

Neither Mark nor Luke (who also wrote Acts) were officially apostles of our Lord. Two of the early church leaders, Papias and Tertullian, both of whom lived in the middle of the second century A.D., claimed that Mark wrote his Gospel in partnership with the apostle Peter. Papias says, 'Mark, having become Peter's interpreter, wrote accurately all that he remembered... So Mark committed no error as he wrote down some particulars just as he recalled them to mind.' Tertullian was even more clear in his statement: 'That which Mark had published may be affirmed to be Peter's whose interpreter Mark was.'

Similarly, Tertullian claimed: 'Even Luke's form of the Gospel men usually ascribe to Paul.' We know that Luke was the close companion of Paul and the author of Acts. Another church leader,

Irenaeus, writing around A. D. 180, could say that Luke was 'always attached to and inseparable from Paul ... and with him performed the work of an evangelist and was entrusted to hand down to us a Gospel'. Origen, writing from Alexandria in Egypt around A. D. 230, referred to Luke's Gospel as 'composed for Gentile converts ... the Gospel commended by Paul'.

These men reflected the view of the early church that Mark's Gospel carried Peter's authority and Luke's Gospel and the Acts carried that of Paul, and for this reason they were unquestionably part of the canon of the New Testament. Mark and Luke were, in a way, scribes for the apostles and this is not unusual in the New Testament. Romans 16:22 and 1 Peter 5:12 both show that Paul and Peter used others to write down their letters for them. Mark and Luke were obviously more than merely scribes, but they carried out their work with the authority of the apostles and, as we have seen, this was recognized by the churches.

What can we say about James and Jude? Who were they? James could not have been the brother of John, since he was killed by Herod in A.D. 44, as recorded in Acts 12, and it is very unlikely that the letter was written before that date. The usual view has always been that both James and Jude were brothers of our Lord himself (see Matthew 13:55). There are good reasons for accepting this position and although it has been denied by some, the available evidence points strongly to this claim. But of course, even such a close relationship to our Lord does not make them members of the Twelve.

However, in Acts 1:21-22 the disciples looked for an apostle to replace Judas from among 'men who have been with us the whole time the Lord Jesus went in and out among us, beginning from John's baptism to the time when Jesus was taken up from us. For one of these must become a witness with us of his resurrection.' James and Jude certainly fulfilled this qualification even though they were not actually 'apostles'. Although they did not at first believe in Christ (John 7:5), it is evident that they watched his movements carefully and by Pentecost were among the rest of the disciples (Acts 1:14).

James was a highly respected leader of the church in Jerusalem (see Acts 15:13 and 21:18) and Paul linked him closely with the apostles in Galatians 1:19: 'I saw none of the other apostles — only James, the Lord's brother'. The leaders in the early church appear to refer to both James and Jude as apostles, and though strictly incorrect in doing so, Tertullian has no hesitation in referring to the epistle of Jude, who calls himself 'a servant of Jesus Christ and a brother of James', as coming from 'Jude the apostle'.

The question of who wrote the letter to the Hebrews has been discussed for the last nineteen hundred years. If it was written by Paul it is unusual in that it does not claim to be his and no fewer than eight alternative names have been offered! However, there is no compelling reason why we may not accept Paul's authorship of Hebrews, and Clement of Rome, writing before the end of the first century, concluded: 'The epistle to the Hebrews is Paul's.' Origen, writing from Alexandria about A.D. 230, considered the thoughts and language to be very like those of Paul and concluded: 'If any church holds that this epistle is by Paul, let it be commended for this. For not without reason have the ancients handed it down as Paul's. But who wrote the epistle, in truth God knows.' Notice that the idea of Paul being author was of such long standing that Origen, writing in the middle of the third century, could refer to it as the view of the 'ancients'. It is true that although Hebrews was accepted as part of Scripture the possibility of Paul as author was doubted by some in the west, whilst almost all the eastern churches accepted Paul as the author. However, it was because the early church leaders had little doubt that Paul was the author of Hebrews that the book was so easily accepted as part of the New Testament canon.

We have therefore seen that the principle for a book forming part of the New Testament canon was that the writer had to be an apostle, or writing under the direction of an apostle, or had to be an eyewitness and companion of our Lord in the sense of Acts 1:21-22. All the twenty-seven books of our New Testament meet this requirement and not one of the false writings does.

The false writings were quickly rejected by the early church

We have already made reference to the New Testament *pseude-pigrapha* or false writings; these are sometimes referred to as the 'New Testament Apocrypha'. There is quite a lot of this material, and around forty gospels are available either complete or in fragments. In addition there are many letters claiming to come from the apostles. In a strange way all this material is really very useful because it helps us to see how certain it is that our New Testament canon is the correct one.

In the first place, this large amount of alternative material, some of which was admittedly written at a late date, underlines the widespread agreement among the early Christians as to what should be left out of the New Testament. It is not really amazing that with so much material available these early Christians had little doubt which books were inspired by God. They had only to apply the test of the witness of the books themselves and the need for apostolic authorship, and the issue was clear.

Secondly, the fact that so much of this false writing pretended to come from the apostles shows that the test of apostolic authorship was considered essential to qualify for recognition as part of Scripture. In 1740 the Italian scholar Muratori published a document he had discovered in a library in Milan. It had been written some time before the middle of the second century A.D. and contained our oldest known list of New Testament books. Not all our New Testament books are found in this list but no books occur that ought not to be there. A reference is made to the Apocalypse of Peter with a note that it is not generally accepted: 'Some of our body will not have [it] read in the church.' This *Muratorian Canon*, as it is now called, contains also a list of heretical books not to be used; it refers to Paul's epistles to the Laodiceans and to the Alexandrians as forgeries (these two letters have not survived) and comments: 'Gall ought not to be mixed with honey.'

Thirdly, the early church leaders held clear and strict views regarding these false writings. Tertullian tells us of a leader in an Asian church being severely disciplined when he admitted writing the Acts of Paul, and he had only done so, he claimed, because he admired Paul so much. That list in the *Muratorian Canon,* warning against dangerous books, is also evidence of the strong stand taken by the early church leaders.

Fourth, the contents of these false gospels and letters are in such obvious contrast to the New Testament Gospels and letters that we have little difficulty in realizing why the early church leaders rejected them. There is a false Gospel of Matthew that includes two cruel stories of Jesus as a boy, cursing another child for interfering with his game, and in both cases the child died. Another story of the boy Jesus has him turning clay sparrows into living birds. A Gospel of Thomas retells these stories with differences and Jesus is said to have killed a Pharisee who spoiled his game. There are letters pretending to have been written by Herod, Pilate, Joseph of Arimathea, the woman healed of an issue of blood (Matthew 9:20-22), and even by Jesus himself. Many of the details in them are hopelessly inaccurate, as for example when the forger of the Letter of Herod obviously forgot that the Herod of the time of our Lord's birth was not the same man as the Herod of his trial and crucifixion!

These are typical of the fanciful stories and errors contained in the false writings; they are very different from the convincing reality of the true stories. Among other false writings are the Preaching of Peter, the Acts of Peter, the Apocalypse of Peter and the Gospel of Peter; they are all so different from the true letters of Peter that the early church leaders had no hesitation in rejecting them.

To be fair, not all the non-apostolic letters written during the first and second centuries and circulating among the churches were *pseudepigrapha*. Some made no false claims and were good and helpful teaching documents, like the Epistle of Barnabas, the Shepherd of Hermas and the *Didache*. However, the early church leaders never allowed even these to be placed on the same level as our New Testament canonical books. The Muratorian text, for example, acknowledged that the Shepherd of Hermas could be read with benefit, but it must not be read alongside the apostles or prophets. The fact that a letter or book was read among the early churches is no more an indication that it was necessarily given divine authority than would be the case in our churches today.

The witness of the early church leaders

We have insisted already that for both the Old Testament and the New Testament it was not the church that made or decided upon the books that would form the Bible; the church merely recognized the inspiration and authority that were already there. This is seen very clearly when we compare what the early leaders said about themselves and their own writings with what they said about the New Testament books and those who wrote them.

What the leaders said about themselves

Ignatius was the leader in the church at Antioch around the year A.D. 112, not long after the death of the apostle John. He contrasted himself with Peter and Paul saying, 'I do not, as Peter and Paul, issue commandments unto you. They were apostles; I am but a condemned man.'

Polycarp was leader of the church at Smyrna and possibly the most influential church leader in Asia. He tells us that he was a Christian by the year A.D. 70 and had actually sat under the teaching of the apostles. Before his martyrdom in A.D.156 he referred to himself in this way: 'For neither am I, nor is any other like me, able to follow the wisdom of the blessed and glorious Paul.' Ignatius and Polycarp are typical of the attitude of almost all the early church fathers; even the heretics preferred to quote the apostles rather than themselves. These early leaders wrote many letters, some of which we still possess, but they never claimed the same inerrancy and authority for themselves that they gave to the New Testament books.

What the leaders said about the apostles

Polycarp was sure that the apostles wrote with the same authority as the Old Testament prophets: 'Let us therefore so serve him with fear and all reverence as he himself gave commandment and the apostles who preached the gospel to us, and the prophets who proclaimed beforehand the coming of our Lord.'

Origen, writing from Alexandria about A.D. 230, was a well-informed leader who knew what the churches everywhere believed. He reflected that belief when he wrote, 'The records of the Gospels [he was referring to our four] are oracles of the Lord, pure oracles as silver purified seven times in the fire... They [the Scriptures] breathe the Spirit of fulness and there is nothing, whether in the Law or in the Prophets, in the Evangelists [the Gospels] or in the Apostles, which does not descend from the fulness of the Divine Majesty.' Origen's New Testament contained all our twenty-seven books when he wrote this.

Clement of Alexandria was Origen's teacher and he once declared, 'There is no discord between the law and the gospel, but harmony, for they both proceed from the same author.'

Tertullian wrote at length about the apostles' authority and one brief quotation must be sufficient: 'In the Lord's apostles we possess our authority, for even they did not of themselves choose to introduce anything, but faithfully delivered to the nations the doctrine which they have received from Christ.'

How the New Testament books were accepted

The first official list of New Testament books is found in the *Muratorian Canon,* compiled somewhere during the second century. The document Muratori discovered had apparently been damaged because Luke's Gospel, which commences the list of accepted books, is referred to as the third Gospel. Hebrews, James, 1 and 2 Peter and 1 John are also missing, but since 1 Peter and 1 John were never doubted as canonical among the churches, these also may be missing through damage.

However, it would be inaccurate to assume that the mid-second century was when the New Testament was formed. Although earlier writers do not give us an official list of books, it is quite clear that they knew which books belonged to the New Testament. Clement of Rome wrote a letter to Corinth about A.D. 95, and we could hardly expect anything much earlier than this. He quoted from Isaiah adding, 'And another Scripture however says, "I did not come to call the righteous but sinners."' This quotation comes from Matthew 9:13 and Clement called it Scripture. Similarly, Polycarp referred to the 'sacred books' and then continued: 'as it is said in these Scriptures', concluding with a quotation from Ephesians 4:26. Polycarp, remember, became a Christian in A.D. 70. The writings of Clement of Rome and Polycarp are full of quotations from the New Testament, and between them most books are covered and they may well have possessed even those they did not refer to.

We should for ever reject the strange idea that for two or three hundred years after the death of Christ there was no suggestion of a New Testament to complete the Old Testament. On the contrary, within twenty years of the death of the apostle John we have much evidence of large parts of the New Testament, especially the Gospels, being circulated and eagerly read by the young churches and, what is just as important, they were accepted as having an authority equal to that of the Old Testament. Throughout these early years of the church, leaders and teachers were quoting New Testament books, and no other writings, as Scripture to prove their doctrine.

There was no book that was once generally accepted as Scripture and then thrown out, although it is true that some of our New Testament books, particularly James, 2 and 3 John and 2 Peter, took a little longer to be accepted by some parts of the Christian church.

Revelation took longer to be accepted among the eastern churches, but this was for theological reasons; and similarly Hebrews took longer to be accepted in the west.

We cannot possibly look at what all the early writers say but we can glance at a few to see the progress of our New Testament.

From the apostles to A.D. 170

We have already seen that Clement of Rome and Polycarp lived during the lifetime of the apostles and both often referred in their letters to New Testament books. Clement, who was leader in the church of Rome before the close of the first century, quoted, for example, from Psalm 118:18 and Hebrews 12:6 and described both as the 'Holy Word'. In the letter of Polycarp to the church at Philippi, some scholars have found fifty clear quotations from sixteen New Testament books, including Matthew, Luke, Acts, and Romans, and allusions to five more. He refers to them all as 'the Scriptures'.

Ignatius was leader at Antioch and wrote around A.D. 112. His writing contains many clear references to New Testament books and some scholars claim that he must have known almost the whole of our New Testament.

Justin Martyr, who was killed for his faith in A.D.165, referred to the four Gospels, Paul's letters (including Hebrews) and Revelation. He wrote a long letter to a Jew named Trypho, and quoted extensively from the Old Testament to prove to Trypho that Jesus was the Christ; he gave equal authority to the writings of the apostles as he did to the Old Testament.

From A.D. 170 to 300

Irenaeus wrote against heretics about A.D.180 and he quoted from the whole of our New Testament with the exception of Philemon, 3 John and possibly also James, 2 Peter and Hebrews, though of course this does not mean he did not know of them, or did not accept them. Irenaeus made it clear that he considered God the author of both the Old and New Testaments.

Tertullian, in North Africa, referred to all except James, 2 and 3 John and 2 Peter, and wrote that the church 'unites the law and the prophets in a volume with the writings of evangelists and apostles'.

The *Muratorian Canon*, as we have seen, omits Peter, Hebrews,

James and 1 John but the copy is of poor quality and perhaps part is missing since 1 Peter and 1 John were accepted without question in all the churches. Origen listed all twenty-seven books but admitted some had doubts about Hebrews, James, 2 and 3 John, Jude and 2 Peter. However, Origen did not share these doubts.

From A.D. 300

Eusebius was the first church historian and was leader in the church at Caesarea from A.D. 313. He claimed that he had enquired into the attitude of all the churches and he found that twenty-two books were accepted without question. James, 2 Peter, 2 and 3 John and Jude were doubted by some but, said Eusebius, they were generally received.

Athanasius stood against the heretic Arius who denied that Christ was truly God, and by A.D. 367 he listed the New Testament exactly as we have it today, with the only exception that Hebrews comes before 1 Timothy, a strong indication that Athanasius believed Hebrews belonged to Paul.

At the Council of Carthage in A.D. 397 all the New Testament books were placed in our present order. But, remember, this council did not decide upon the New Testament; it simply recognized what had been accepted by the church with a growing conviction over the previous three hundred years. It has been claimed that writers quoted so much from the New Testament that by the seventh century we could reproduce almost the whole of the New Testament from these writings. Perhaps this is a slightly extravagant claim, but it makes an important point.

Conclusion

The picture is therefore much clearer than many would have us believe. Our acceptance of the canon of the New Testament does not depend upon the decision of the church or a council of bishops; it does not therefore depend upon the judgements of men. Scripture is its own witness and the early church leaders generally recognized this. Certainly there were no great conflicts among the early churches concerning the canon of Scripture; and when the heretics, like Marcion in the late second and early third centuries, began to cut out from the canon books that did not suit their theology, the church leaders vigorously opposed them. In addition, all the evidence reveals that the early church leaders were far from gullible in their acceptance of Scripture. With so much material available, they were not quick to accept just anything claiming to come from the pen of an apostle. On the contrary, they were cautious and looked for the force of truth before they recognized the authority of a particular book. They were particularly cautious to ensure the all-important apostolic authorship or influence upon any writing claiming to be Scripture — a point that modern scholars would do well to recognize.

If the early church leaders were concerned to know the identity of the writers of Scripture, they were equally concerned to recognize its divine origin. The New Testament is its own witness, not simply by its content, but by its claim; the pseudepigraphal writings cannot be compared to it. Not all the other writings were foolish; as we have seen, some were good and helpful letters, but they made no claim to inspiration as the New Testament does, and they were not written by apostles or with their authority, as the New Testament was. Our final appeal is not to man, not even to the early church leaders, but to God, who by his Holy Spirit has put his seal upon the New Testament. By their spiritual content and by the claim of their human writers, the twenty-seven books of our New Testament form part of the 'God-breathed' Scripture.

12.
How the Bible came to us

When we talk about the Bible as the 'God-breathed' Word, we are not referring to any modern-day translation, but to the words originally penned by the human writers under the infallible guidance of the Holy Spirit. How did the Scriptures come to us down the many centuries between then and now?

The Old Testament was written in Hebrew, with the exception of a few small portions which were written in Aramaic. Hebrew was the language of the Jews and here is an example from Isaiah 7:14. Hebrew is read from right to left.

לָכֵן יִתֵּן אֲדֹנָי הוּא לָכֶם אוֹת הִנֵּה הָעַלְמָה הָרָה וְיֹלֶדֶת בֵּן וְקָרֵאת שְׁמוֹ עִמָּנוּ אֵל:

Over the centuries, from the time Moses first wrote the Pentateuch, the shape of the Hebrew letters has changed considerably. Those illustrated here are the letters that have been used since about A.D.100.

Those tiny dots and dashes within and under the letters are a mixture of vowel signs to aid pronunciation (they are known as vowel 'points') and punctuation. Until about 600 years after the birth of Christ, Hebrew was never written with vowel points and the Jews knew how to pronounce the words only by the way they learned them in the school or synagogue. The Jewish Masoretes (the name comes from the Hebrew for 'tradition') gradually introduced the vowel points, and the work was completed by the tenth century A.D. Before then, Hebrew writing was unpointed and unpunctuated, with no space between the words either! Isaiah 7:14 in English and without vowels, punctuation or spacing would look like this:

THRFRTHLRDHMSLFWLLGVYSGNTHVRGNWLLBWTHCHLD
NDWLLGVBRTHTSNNDWLLCLLHMMMNL

The New Testament, on the other hand, was originally written in Greek which, during the first few centuries of the Christian church, was the most widely spoken language and could rightly be called the language of the ordinary people. Here is Isaiah 7:14 (taken from Matthew 1:23) in Greek. Greek is read from left to right.

Ἰδού, ἡ παρθένος ἐν γαστρὶ ἕξει, καὶ τέξεται υἱόν, καὶ καλέσουσι τὸ ὄνομα αὐτοῦ Ἐμμανουήλ·

Where are the originals?

At first it may come as a shock to learn that although we believe the Bible is without error 'as originally given' we then have to admit that we do not possess any of the original writings today. In other words, nowhere do we have an example of the handwriting of Moses, or Isaiah, or Paul, or Peter, or anyone else who originally wrote the Bible. These are known as the 'autographs', the author's own writing. All that we have are copies of copies of copies, sometimes many times over. These handwritten copies are known as 'manuscripts' from the Latin *manu scriptum* meaning 'written by hand'; the word is often abbreviated to MS with the plural MSS.

These handwritten copies were, of course, necessary because printing was not available until the fifteen century. The Hebrew Old Testament was first printed in 1488 and the New Testament in Greek not until 1516. Before this, every copy of the original text, and every translation into another language, had to be written out by hand. The critic of the Bible assumes that this is exactly where all the mistakes came in. Perhaps it was originally free from error, but as the centuries went by and more and more copies were made, so more and more mistakes entered the text and by now it is quite impossible to claim that we have the words of Moses or Paul. That argument of the critic may sound convincing but here are a few facts to consider.

First, it is very strange that the same argument is rarely raised against the works of other writers of the ancient world. Take the Greek philosopher Plato, for example. He died 350 years before Christ was born, but hundreds of students study the philosophy of Plato and few suggest that the words of his *Republic* may not be his words after all; at least no one made this suggestion to me when I had to study it. As a matter of fact I was not even told that for his work I was relying upon manuscripts copied thirteen hundred years after his death. Similarly the Roman poet Gaius Catallus lived half a century before the birth of Christ and the earliest manuscript of his work is dated sixteen hundred years after his 'autograph' copies. We are taught that Julius Caesar was assassinated on the 'Ides of March', that is, on 13 March 44 B.C. How do we know this? Because Shakespeare retells the story and he apparently gathered his information from the first century A.D. Greek historian Plutarch. In other words, we believe a two-thousand-year-old story about a Roman, because four hundred years ago an English poet wrote a play loosely based upon a Greek biography written by a man born ninety years after Caesar is said to have died! Compare that with the resurrection appearances!

Similarly, for our knowledge of the Roman emperors from Augustus to Nero we lean heavily upon the works of the Roman historian Cornelius Tacitus, who was born around A.D. 55. However, we have only ten manuscripts of his work, and the earliest is dated A.D. 900. By contrast we can compile our New Testament from Greek texts copied well before the close of the fourth century A.D. Two thousand years after his death, the story of the Greek general Alexander the Great was known in twenty languages from Britain to China; yet historians cannot rely upon any of the records of his life, not even that of his official biographer Callisthenes; within a few years of his death a mass of forgeries and legends had grown up.

The second fact to consider in the argument against the existence of errors in the transmission of the text of the Bible is that it would be a strange sort of God who gave an infallible Scripture to the original writers and then left copyists to so confuse the revelation that it became quite unintelligible.

Third, there is a very good reason why God allowed all the original manuscripts to be destroyed. Some parts of the professing Christian church have always been eager to honour relics of the past in a way that soon becomes idolatrous worship. Through the centuries people have worshipped bones, clothes, blood and even pieces of hair that are supposed to have come from the disciples or other Christians — or even from Christ himself. They still do so in some parts of the world. It requires little imagination to see what would have happened to the actual written words by Moses or Paul. We are never to worship a book, not even the Bible.

Fourth, in a court of law a copy of an original is acceptable as evidence providing it can be demonstrated that it is an exact representation of the original.

But there are much greater reasons than all this why we may be sure that we have an accurate Bible.

How careful were the copyists?

We have already noted how the Jewish Masoretes added the vowel points to the Hebrew consonants, so that future generations would be in no doubt as to exactly what the words meant and how they were to be pronounced. They continued their work into the tenth century. The word 'Masorete' means 'tradition', because they were not inventors, but were looking for what tradition had always accepted and they were very careful not to alter the text of Scripture. The Masoretes had no difficulty in finding the correct text of the Old Testament because they built upon work already completed between A.D. 90 and 100 at a Jewish council at Jamnia, near the modern Tel-Aviv. The Council of Jamnia agreed upon both the books and the actual text of the Old Testament. As we saw in chapter 10, this council did not decide upon the content of the Old Testament, they simply recognized what was already accepted among the Jews.

The care and scholarship of both the Council of Jamnia and the Masoretes, together with the large amount of material available to them, means that we can place infinitely more confidence in our Old Testament text than in the possibility of *Hamlet* really being the work of Shakespeare or the *Republic* that of Plato.

When the Masoretes had invented the dots and dashes of the Hebrew vowels, they had not finished. Their next task was to set down detailed rules to govern the copying of the Scriptures. To listen to many people talk, you would gain the impression that the scribes who copied out the Old Testament Scriptures carried on their work at odd moments, with only half a mind on their task, and with as little care as a child copying out a shopping list. When next someone talks of the 'thousands' of mistakes that must have crept in from copy to copy, remember the almost unbelievable regulations of the Masoretes.

The size of the pages, or scrolls, to be used was carefully recorded; the size of columns, spaces between words and letters, even the colour of the ink to be used and the clothing to be worn by the scribe were all given in great detail. The Masoretes counted the number of words and letters of each book of the Old Testament, and fixed the middle letter of each line and each book. In fact, as one scholar has commented: 'Everything countable seems to be counted'! The scribe would have to submit his manuscript for checking and if it was in error at any point then it was ordered to be destroyed; he must then start all over again! Occasionally the scribe might think that he had found an error in the copy before him, but even then he was not allowed to make any alteration. Instead he would write the Hebrew word *Kethib* ('it is written') above the suspect word and add his suggested correction in the margin under the word *Kere* 'it should be read'). The Masoretes actually collected the variant readings they discovered in the Old Testament, most of which were minor points, and they amounted to about 1,200, that is, less than one for each page of the Hebrew Old Testament.

There is a good reason why very few really old manuscripts are in existence today. When one copy had been carefully checked, and found to be accurate in every detail, the older copy from which it was taken would be destroyed if it was found to be damaged or fragile with age. This was done with the very purpose of preventing a poor quality copy from being used again. In a copy torn with age, a reader might be tempted to add his own words to the parts that were missing or were too faded to be read.

This detailed care by the Jewish scribes should give every impartial reader of the Bible confidence that what he has before him is as God first gave it. Admittedly there are a few small mistakes that, in spite of such care, did find their way into the text. We shall look at some of these in chapter 17.

The situation with the New Testament is considerably different. Although we may assume that many of the early Christians copied the New Testament books with great care, it is also true that some did not. Often it was not their fault. There was a great demand for the New Testament and copies were needed urgently to instruct young churches; without printing presses, which were not available in Europe until the middle of the fifteenth century, every copy had to be produced by hand. Often Christians carried on this work with constant interruptions during the years of severe persecution. In the year A.D. 303 the Roman Emperor Diocletian ordered all the sacred books of the Christians to be burned and so the New Testament must have become scarce and in great demand. However, there are two facts that re-establish our confidence in the accuracy of our New Testament text.

First, the copies that we do possess are close in time to the original manuscripts and therefore are more likely to be accurate. Secondly, we have literally thousands of portions of New Testament texts and so, by comparing them, it is much easier to discover the original text. Suppose five children were asked to copy a sentence from the school wallboard, and only two produced identical copies. If we did not know the original sentence we might not be sure whether the two were right, or whether they made the same mistakes by coincidence. But if 500 copied the sentence and 200 were identical, we should be fairly certain that they represented the original exactly. It is something like this with the large number of New Testament texts available to us. Some time after A.D. 325, the Emperor Constantine, having professed to be a Christian, ordered copies of the New Testament to be produced, and we may assume that greater care was now taken in their production.

One thing we can be absolutely certain about in the New Testament is the fact that not one Christian doctrine is based upon a verse that has conflicting texts behind it. It is often wrongly assumed that the New Testament is one mass of contradictory readings and that to talk of an errorless text is nonsense in the light of this. Some scholars toss about frightening figures of up to a quarter of a million 'textual variants' in the New Testament. This is very misleading, even to the point of dishonesty. The fact is that one small difference in the spelling of a word may be copied into, say, 500 other texts; this is counted as five hundred 'textual variants', whereas it is only one variation copied faithfully 500 times! Many of the variants are at this level of spelling differences, and when you consider that in his English translation of the New Testament in 1526 William Tyndale managed to spell the word 'it' three different ways in Matthew 5:34-35 and seven different ways throughout the New Testament, it is hardly suprising that fifteen hundred years earlier copyists also had problems with spelling!

Dr Hort, though not an evangelical Christian, was a great scholar of the late nineteenth and early twentieth centuries and together with Dr Westcott he compiled what he believed to be the correct text of the New Testament. In doing so he researched every known text available and concluded that the amount of the New Testament where there is any significant variation in the various sources 'can hardly form more than a thousandth part of the entire text' (*The New Testament in the Original Greek,* p.2). We must never accept that even the 'thousandth part of the entire text' is unimportant, but this figure is reassuring. However, our belief in an errorless Bible demands that we treat every possible discrepancy with seriousness.

Where did the chapters and verses come from?

When we read our Bible we ought to be aware that the chapter and verse divisions of both the Old and New Testaments are not part of the original Scripture. Isaiah and Paul were no more concerned to divide their letters into chapters and verses than we are when we write a letter to a friend. Therefore some of these divisions in our Bibles can be misleading and occasionally they break into the writer's argument quite unnaturally. But where did these divisions come from?

The earliest existing copies of the Hebrew Old Testament that we possess are manuscripts of the prophet Isaiah and these copies are dated about 150 B.C. They contain an old system of indicating paragraph divisions by the use of Hebrew letters; however, these divisions are not the same as we find in our Bible today. Strangely, the verse divisions of the Old Testament appear to be older than the chapter divisions. Although there was no fixed system for a long time, the present verse division of the Old Testament was established by the Masoretes about A.D. 900. Chapter divisions of the Old Testament do not appear to have been used before the thirteenth century A.D. Cardinal Hugo de Sancto Caro added them between 1244 and 1248 when he was preparing a concordance of the whole Bible. They were introduced by Stephen Langton into the Latin Old Testament and into the Hebrew Bible by Rabbi Salomon Ben Ishmael about A.D. 1330.

The situation is much clearer with regard to the New Testament. The chapter divisions of the New Testament were added by Cardinal Hugo de Sancto Caro and the verse divisions were introduced by Robert Estienne, whom we shall meet again later, into his 1551 edition of the Greek New Testament. They were first used in an English translation of the New Testament by Whittingham in 1557, and all our translations since then have followed the same pattern of chapter and verse divisions. The first complete Bible to contain our present chapter and verse divisions for both the Old and New Testaments was the Geneva Bible published in 1560.

The Old Testament manuscripts

Moses did not invent writing. Examples exist of writing from between two and three thousand years before the birth of Christ. At first all state documents were chipped onto stone or pressed into clay tablets which were then baked hard in the sun. Either way this was a slow process, and the documents were large and heavy to store in a library! Leather, from the skins of sheep, goats or cattle, was lighter, very strong and long-lasting; and it was pliable so that it could be rolled into a scroll. It soon became a rule that all copies of the Jewish Law should be written on leather. Vellum was often used; this is a high quality leather made from calf-skin, although the young of sheep, goats or deer were also used to produce vellum. Almost certainly the scrolls referred to in Psalm 40:7; Jeremiah 36:23 and Ezekiel 2:9 were made of animal skins.

However, a more generally used, and cheaper, form of writing material was papyrus. This was made from the inner bark of the papyrus plant that grew plentifully along the banks of the Nile river. Another name for papyrus was *biblos* and a *biblion* was a roll of *biblos*; hence our word 'Bible'. Papyrus was the nearest material to our paper and it was easy to write on, easy to roll (one scroll reached 133 feet in length, but generally thirty-five feet was a maximum) and cheap to produce. The disadvantage was that it was not so strong or long-lasting as leather or vellum, and bright sunshine, a damp cave or nesting rodents would soon destroy it.

The Old Testament manuscripts are far more simple to list than those of the New Testament since there are fewer of them.

Hebrew scrolls

We have already seen in this chapter that the Hebrew text of our Old Testament achieved its final form around A.D. 100 at the Council of Jamnia and that the Masoretes of the seventh century added the vowel points. If the Masoretes possessed much older copies of the Old Testament they destroyed them as soon as the new and highly accurate copies were made, to avoid old and damaged copies influencing future scribes. Until 1946 — and the importance of this year will be seen shortly — we had to admit that our oldest Hebrew manuscripts went back only to the ninth century A.D., although they obviously reflected accurately the text available during the time of our Lord. In 1939 Sir Frederick Kenyon, at one time Director of the British Museum, commented rather hopelessly: 'There is, indeed, no probability that we shall ever find manuscripts of the Hebrew text going back to a period before the formation of the text which we know as Masoretic.' How wrong he was we shall see later.

There is, however, one Hebrew text that does not come from the 'family' of texts used by either the Masoretes or the Council of Jamnia. It is known as the *Samaritan Pentateuch*, and was discovered in 1616; the oldest copy we possess goes back to the tenth century A.D. For historical reasons that we need not trouble with here, the Jews and Samaritans lived as bitterly opposed neighbours from at least the division of the kingdom under Rehoboam in the tenth century B.C. The Samaritans worshipped separately and made their own copies of the first five books of the Bible; they were not interested in the rest, since it was concerned with the history of the Jewish kingdoms. This copy of the *Samaritan Pentateuch*, which is written in Hebrew, has been deliberately altered in places to suit Samaritan ways of worship and customs; these changes amount to about 6,000 differences from the Hebrew Pentateuch, though most of these are matters of grammar or spelling. The value of this text is that it is quite independent of the Masoretic Text and obviously came from a different 'family' of manuscripts. Of course, it agrees exactly with the Masoretic Text in the overwhelming proportion of the work and scholars only allow around thirty-five occasions where the Samaritan Text is equal to, or to be preferred to, the Masoretic Text. We may safely conclude that the Samaritan Text confirms the accuracy of the Masoretic Text.

Versions of the Old Testament

By the word 'versions' we mean translations of the Old Testament into other languages. We must never forget that they are translations, and it is always possible that a translator made a mistake. But the value of the versions is that we can often discover exactly what text they were using as a basis for the translation. For example, I may ask three of my friends in France to give me an English translation of a particular event that was reported in the French press. Two of my friends may translate the article from *Le Monde* and the third may take his article from *Le Figaro*; it will be obvious to me that two used the same source, even though their translations will vary a little here and there. Now if three or four friends translated the article from *Le Monde*, it would be quite easy for me to discover the exact French words that occurred in the original article even though there were minor variations in each version.

The most important version of the Old Testament is the Septuagint. The Septuagint is a Greek translation of the Hebrew Old Testament produced in Egypt! As the Greek language became more and more the common tongue, and Jews spread all over the known world, there was a great need for the Old Testament to be translated into Greek. Some time during the reign of the Egyptian king Ptolemy Philadelphus (285-246 B.C.), the king asked for copies of the Jewish Scriptures to be sent to Alexandria, accompanied by scholars who could translate them, so that he could add these writings to his magnificent library. The Jewish leaders in Jerusalem obliged, and despatched a copy of the Scriptures, written in letters of gold, it is claimed, together with seventy-two learned men to do the work of translation. The result was known as the Septuagint from the Latin word for seventy. For this reason it is frequently identified simply by the Roman numeral LXX.

The original translators probably limited themselves to the Pentateuch, but it is fairly certain that the whole Old Testament was complete by the middle of the second century B.C. The Septuagint at once became the Bible of the Greek-speaking synagogues and, what is even more important for us, it was the version used by the early Christians. Many of the New Testament quotations taken from the Old Testament are based upon the Septuagint.

Of significant interest to us is the fact that the Septuagint is based upon a Hebrew text in existence at least eight hundred years before the Masoretic Text was established, and it appears to be a text from a different 'family'. There are numerous portions of the Septuagint available to scholars today; though sometimes they are little more than fragments. *Codex Vaticanus* includes what is probably our best copy of the Septuagint.

The Septuagint is not the only version available to us. There is a Syriac version known as the *Peshitta*, or 'Simple' version; this also

includes the New Testament. It was completed at the very latest by
the end of the third century A.D. and one copy available bears the
date A.D. 464. This is the oldest copy of the whole Bible, in any
language, for which the date is certainly known. Unfortunately the
Peshitta is often more of a paraphrase than a translation and it does
not really help our search for an accurate text.

A number of Coptic versions were produced around the second
and third centuries A.D. Coptic was the language spoken in Egypt
by the end of the first century A.D. Once again both Old and New
Testaments are translated, but since the Old Testament was evidently based upon the Septuagint, the Coptic versions are of no help
in finding the Hebrew text. There are also versions from such areas
as Ethiopia, Armenia, Georgia (in the Caucasus) and Slavonia, but
they are all based upon the Septuagint.

The only other versions to note are those of the Latin translations
and particularly the work of Eusebius Hieronymus, or Jerome as we
more commonly know him, in the years between A.D. 390 and 404.
Jerome had no doubt in his mind that the Hebrew text was more
reliable than the Septuagint and his Old Testament in Latin clearly
shows that he had access to the Hebrew texts which would be used
by the Masoretes two centuries later. His translation is known as the
Vulgate because it was written in the common (vulgar) tongue. This
became the standard text for many centuries, and our earliest
English versions up to the time of John Wycliffe in the fourteenth
century were translated from the Vulgate.

What conclusions can we draw so far?

There can be little doubt that the Masoretic Text reflects the oldest
and most accurate text that formed the Jewish Old Testament. The
only real challenge to this statement comes from the Septuagint but
it is significant that two outstanding Hebrew scholars of their day,
Origen in the early years of the third century and Jerome late in the
fourth century, both rejected the Septuagint in preference for the
Hebrew text that clearly formed the basis for the Masoretes' work.
All our Bible translators from the Authorized Version up to the
present time have followed Origen and Jerome in this judgement.
However, there are some places where the Masoretic Text is not
easy to understand and other places where it is obviously wrong;
here the Septuagint comes to our aid and it is therefore a valuable

tool in helping to correct the occasional problems of the Hebrew text. If you look back to that example at the beginning of this chapter, you will see how difficult it can be to translate a row of consonants without punctuation or spacing. The Septuagint can guide our translators where the Hebrew text is particularly hard; nowhere has it been more useful than in the book of Job.

As an example of the differences, and the way some of our modern translators have used the Septuagint, we may turn to Genesis 4:8: 'Now Cain said to his brother Abel, "Let's go out to the field."' The Masoretic Text simply reads: 'And Cain said to his brother Abel.' Apparently something is missing, and some translations render it: 'And Cain told Abel his brother' (NASB) and refer it back to the previous verse. The Greek translation obviously used a text that included the words: 'Let's go out into the field,' unless the translators added the words to make sense, but this is not likely.

We have said that the Septuagint was the version of the Old Testament most commonly used by the Christians in the first century. Sometimes this put them at variance with the exact wording of the Masoretic Text. We discussed this in detail in chapter 5 but one example is found in Acts 15:16-18 where there is a difference between James' quotation of Amos 9:11-12 and what we actually find in our Old Testament. James was using the Septuagint whereas our Old Testament translation is based on the Masoretic Text. However, this need not alarm us because it is clear that James was using the passage correctly and the Septuagint was not at variance with the Masoretic Text in its meaning.

It is therefore clear that the New Testament writers often used the Septuagint in preference to the Hebrew text. We must not forget, either, that the areas of conflict between the versions and the Masoretic Text form only a tiny fraction of the whole of the Old Testament. A good way of testing this statement is to take a reference copy of a modern translation and look at the bottom of the page, or the margin, where alternative readings are given; these will give you some idea of the fact that there are very few areas where a difficulty of any sort occurs; and those are nearly all concerned with isolated words or the occasional short phrase.

But for years a problem lay in the fact that our oldest existing Hebrew manuscript of the Old Testament was dated somewhere around the ninth century A.D. and, so claimed the critics, that left a long time for thousands of errors to have crept in since the original

manuscripts were written. There seemed no firm answer to this and
Kenyon's hopeless conclusion that 'there is no probability' that we
would ever find Hebrew manuscripts older than the Masoretic Texts
appeared to be a sad statement of fact. Then, as the dust of the
Second World War began to settle, a most incredible discovery was
made.

The Dead Sea Scrolls

Some time during the summer of 1945, a Bedouin shepherd boy was
searching for a lost goat between Bethlehem and the Dead Sea.
Slipping into the shade of a large rock, he rested himself for a while
and idly tossed a stone into the narrow opening of one of many caves
scattered about the barren wilderness of the Dead Sea. Suddenly the
boy sat upright and began to throw more stones into the cave, for
what he heard was not the thud he had expected, but a hollow ring
of pottery. That discovery laid bare some of the most amazing finds
ever made by archaeologists. Over the next few years thousands of
scrolls, in various stages of decay and preservation, were discovered, all carefully wrapped and stored in pottery jars.

The area in which they were found is known as Wadi Qumran,
and between them eleven caves produced 40,000 manuscript fragments. These represented 500 separate scrolls, a few of which were
almost perfect and untouched. 100 of these scrolls were parts of the
Bible and altogether every Old Testament book except Esther is
represented in the Qumran, or Dead Sea Scrolls. All this material is
dated over a hundred years before Christ, which means that we now
have Hebrew manuscripts almost 1,000 years older than the existing
copies of the Masoretic Texts!

At another site, a few miles distant, at Wadi Murrabba't, a
garrison of Jewish rebels had been stationed before they were finally
crushed by the Roman troops in A.D. 135. There were military
despatches, personal letters and also parts of the Old Testament.
Some of these manuscripts had been deliberately torn up, either by
the escaping rebels or by the victorious Romans, and others had been
used by rats, mice and birds for nesting materials! But here were
Hebrew texts of the Old Testament, from the same family as the
Masoretic Text, but going back to the second century A.D.

In the Qumran caves a complete scroll of Isaiah was found. This
scroll was written between 175 and 150 B.C., but the prophet was

The Qumran Caves, where the Dead Sea Scrolls were found
(Reproduced by courtesy of Barnaby's Picture library).

A section of the Isaiah scroll (Hebrew text) from Cave 1 at Qumran
(Reproduced by courtesy of the Israel Information Office).

writing just over 700 years before Christ, so the gap between the original manuscript (734 B.C.) and our now earliest existing copy of it (about 150 B.C.) has narrowed to 600 years. That may still seem a long time, but remember, previously our earliest existing copy was a Masoretic Text of A.D. 900. So the gap has been closed by 1,000 years.

What is particularly important is the fact that the Qumran copy of Isaiah is remarkably in line with the earliest Masoretic Text. Of course there are differences but they are few and most are insignificant. In fact some scholars will only allow four occasions where the Qumran scroll of Isaiah is different from and better than the Masoretic Text. Often these differences actually help us to arrive at an even more accurate text for Isaiah. The differences are mostly confined to words or even letters. Here is just one typical example. The Masoretic Text for Isaiah 40:12 reads, 'Who has measured the waters [Hebrew *Mayim*] in the hollow of his hand?,' whereas the Qumran text reads, 'Who has measured the waters of the sea [Hebrew *Mê yam*] in the hollow of his hand?'

One Qumran scroll of Isaiah was discovered just in time for the team working on the Revised Standard Version in 1952 to make use of it. From the entire scroll the translation team adopted only thirteen readings from the Qumran scroll in preference to the Masoretic Text. One of the leading team members later regretted the adoption of some of these thirteen.

The New International Version lists no more than sixteen occasions in Isaiah where it sees any need even to note that the Dead Sea Scroll and the Masoretic Text differ; on eleven of these occasions the Qumran text is preferred, but sometimes only because the Masoretic word is unclear. Here are the first few such notes; the rest are similar in importance: in 7:14 Qumran has 'and he' or 'and they' instead of the Masoretic 'and'. In 14:4 the translators adopt the Qumran 'fury' because the meaning of the Masoretic word is unclear. 15:9 is a matter of spelling a name either *Dimon* (Masoretic Text) or *Dibon* (Qumran). In 19:18 most Masoretic Texts have 'City of Destruction' whereas Qumran has 'City of the Sun'. Some of the Qumran scrolls of Old Testament books are closer to the Septuagint than to the Masoretic Text, but even then the similarities are remarkable and differences are chiefly of the order noted above — occasional words and spelling.

Sir Frederick Kenyon's fear that we should never find manuscripts of the Hebrew Old Testament going back before the Masoretic Texts is now out of date. We have gone back 700 years before the Masoretes did their work and 1,000 years before the earliest existing copy of their work. We may reasonably claim that if that 1,000 years showed such detailed accuracy and care in copying the manuscripts, then we must allow the same accuracy for the previous 600 years from Isaiah's 'autograph' to the Qumran copy. Professor F. F. Bruce concluded: 'The new evidence [from the Qumran scrolls] confirms what we had already good reason to believe — that the Jewish scribes of the early Christian centuries copied and recopied the text of the Hebrew Bible with the utmost fidelity' (*Second Thoughts on the Dead Sea Scrolls*, p.62).

A word of warning: the University of Israel that houses the Dead Sea Scrolls has recently declared 'open house' to all scholars who seriously wish to study the thousands of texts that remain to be translated. There will be a rush of applications and over the next few years we shall see the results of some of their work. In order to gain prominence, some scholars will hurry into print before conclusions have been properly tested. Beware of the extravagant claims that will come from some sections of the popular press.

The New Testament manuscripts

Before we look at the vast quantity of material available to us today to discover an accurate New Testament Greek text, there is a question we should settle at once. So often we hear people say, 'Well, of course, the Gospels and Acts were not written until so long after the events that we must admit they are only vague and twisted recollections of what actually happened.' This, in a very simple form, was the teaching of the theologians at the University of Tübingen in Germany in the latter part of the nineteenth century and the early part of this century. It was certainly the view of the German theologian Rudolf Bultmann and the Swiss theologian Karl Barth, who claimed the New Testament was written long after the close of the first century and was the product of the wishful imagination of the second or third-century church.

How old is the New Testament?

The dating of the books of the New Testament has been debated and discussed for a long time, but there is really little doubt that the books were written by the authors named in them and that therefore the New Testament was completed in the lifetime of the apostles. In 1972 one scholar suggested that if we could prove that the New Testament was complete before A.D. 70, 'All contemporary Barthian and Bultmanian views of the New Testament's formation will come crashing down in one inglorious heap.' Or, as one writer put it in *Time Magazine*, 'They can make a bonfire of seventy tons of indigestible German scholarship.' Well, can we build that bonfire?

Evangelical scholars have consistently argued that the New Testament was complete certainly before the end of the first century. For example, Dr Donald Guthrie of London published a masterful *New Testament Introduction* in 1965, in which he carefully studied every argument of the critics and showed the evangelical position to be in harmony with all the known facts. It may not be claiming too much to say that Dr Guthrie has written the last word on this subject, for his work is so full of detailed and careful arguments that very little more can be added. We will nevertheless allow someone very different from Dr Guthrie to have the last word on this point!

Perhaps we need not look at any evidence beyond that of the very liberal New Testament scholar John A. T. Robinson. Certainly no evangelical, and with no particular reason to defend the New Testament, John Robinson published a book in the 1970s called *Redating the New Testament*. In this book he dismissed what he called the 'tyranny of unexamined assumptions' of the modern disciples of the Tübingen school, defended the authorship of all the New Testament letters, claimed that 'There is virtually no one who denies the genuineness of Philemon,' and that Acts was finished by A.D. 62 and the letter of James as early as A.D. 48, and concluded that the whole of the New Testament was complete before the Romans destroyed Jerusalem in A.D. 70. These are the sort of conclusions that evangelical Christians have held for centuries and it is encouraging to find, occasionally, a liberal theologian catching up at last! However, Robinson warned that he wanted to claim nothing 'fixed or final' about the results and admitted that what

ended as a serious study began as a 'theological joke' to see whether
the whole New Testament could be dated before A.D. 70. This
eminent New Testament scholar died before he had time to change
his mind on these conclusions.

Material for our New Testament texts

The amount of material available for discovering our New Testament Greek text is enormous. It needs to be, because, as we have
already noted, many of the manuscripts of the New Testament were
copied in a hurry and mistakes crept in easily; others may have been
deliberately altered to suit the false doctrines of those copying them.
But before we find out how much is available and how reliable it all
is, we must discover the type of material that exists today.

Just as the Masoretic Text, compiled in the seventh century A.D.,
formed the basic text for our Hebrew Old Testament, so the *Textus
Receptus* (or Received Text), compiled in the sixteenth century
A.D., for many years formed the basic text for our Greek New
Testament. The Textus Receptus came about in the following way.

There was very little Greek scholarship in western Europe before
A.D. 1453; in that year Constantinople fell to the armies of Islam,
and Christian scholars fled to the west with priceless Greek manuscripts. During the next century many editions of the Greek New
Testament were produced. Before this time the only Bible allowed
was the Latin translation of Jerome, the Vulgate, the New Testament of which was completed some time after A.D. 382. But even
Jerome used mainly Latin texts for his work and only a few Greek
manuscripts.

In 1516 a Dutchman, Desiderius Erasmus, one of the greatest
Greek scholars of the sixteenth century, published a Greek New
Testament based upon five Greek manuscripts. This was followed
by many other editions, all using Erasmus as a basis, but with access
to other Greek manuscripts. It was an edition printed by Robert
Estienne (often incorrectly referred to as Stephens) of Paris in 1550,
that became known as the Received Text. This formed the basis for
our first printed English New Testament by William Tyndale in
1526, and of the Authorized, or King James, Version in English
translated in 1611. Estienne used Erasmus' work, that of Cardinal
Ximenes, and about sixteen Greek manuscripts.

Greek texts

Since the time of Erasmus and Estienne literally thousands of Greek manuscripts, some of them only fragments, have been discovered and these have all added to our production of an accurate New Testament text. Much of our New Testament was copied on to papyrus scrolls, just as much of the Old Testament was. Fragments of these remain and two of the most important are the *Chester Beatty Papyri,* which in addition to the Old Testament contain most of the New Testament and are dated in the third century A.D. or earlier, and the *John Rylands Papyrus,* which contains only five verses of John 18 and may have been written only thirty years after John wrote his Gospel.

There are some 5,000 or more Greek texts available to textual scholars today, although, as we have seen, some are mere fragments whilst a few are nearly complete New Testaments. Rarely was the entire New Testament contained in one book because it would be far too bulky and for this reason we hardly expect to find more than portions of it in one volume. Most of the Greek texts are in a form of joined handwriting that is known as 'cursive' or 'minuscule' because they were small and took up less room. These are generally dated from the ninth to the fifteenth centuries A.D. One, known as 'the Queen of the Cursives' is very similar to the *Codex Vaticanus* mentioned below. Less than 400 of the available texts are in the 'uncial' form, a word meaning that they were written with letters similar to our capitals. The uncials are dated earlier than the cursives.

Most of our Greek manuscripts are in the form of books or codices, a word which comes from the Latin word *'caudex',* a tablet, or book. These were often made out of papyrus or vellum. Of the many codices available we shall mention just five of the most valuable. These are all in the uncial form of writing.

Codex Sinaiticus was discovered in 1859 at a monastery on Mount Sinai. It contains part of the Old Testament and the entire New Testament. It is in excellent condition, and is dated around the middle of the fourth century A.D. It comes from Alexandria and is now in the British Library.

Codex Vaticanus has been in the Vatican since 1481 but even Erasmus was not allowed to use it. It also comes from Alexandria

Folio from *Codex Sinaiticus*
(Reproduced by courtesy of the British Library)

and contains both the Old Testament and the New in Greek, though the beginning and the end are missing. But *Vaticanus* may be even older than *Sinaiticus*, and is considered by many scholars to be the best Greek text we have of the New Testament.

Codex Alexandrinus was presented to King Charles I of England by the Patriarch of Alexandria in 1627. Written somewhere between A.D. 350 and 450, the New Testament is not complete. Like *Sinaiticus*, this is in the British Library.

Codex Ephraemi is a fifth-century manuscript containing the entire New Testament with the exception of 2 Thessalonians and 2 John. First published in 1845, it is called a *'palimpsest'*, which is a Greek word meaning 'rescraped', because someone tried to rub out the original text and write over the top of it! Fortunately it is possible to discover that original, which is the New Testament text. The text is similar to *Codex Vaticanus*. *Ephraemi* is in the National Library of Paris.

Codex Bezae was given to the University of Cambridge in 1581. It contains only the Gospels and Acts and part of 3 John and is clearly not very reliable in its text.

Lectionaries

Over two thousand lectionaries are available to us today. These were selected passages of Scripture used in worship and their value is that they reveal the care with which they were copied; they can tell us what Greek text is being used, but they are not as old as the uncials.

The versions

Just as we noted the versions, or translations, of the Old Testament so we have the same for the New Testament. The first evidence of a need to put the Greek text into another language comes from Africa as early as A.D. 180.

Unfortunately the versions are often translations from the Latin, and this does not help us to discover the Greek text. There are many of these old Latin translations. But a Syriac translation known as *Tatian's Diatessaron* is interesting since it probably represents the text used by the eastern church and is dated around A.D. 170. However, we cannot be sure whether it is based upon a Greek text or not. In addition we have versions in Egyptian, Armenian, Georgian,

Gothic, Ethiopian, Arabic and Syriac. However, no great value can be placed upon some of these versions in our attempts to discover the best Greek text. One of the most famous versions is the Latin Vulgate of Jerome in the fourth century.

The early church leaders

Many of the early Church Fathers quote the New Testament in their writings and from their quotations we can often discover what text they were using. Of course we must always bear in mind that these writers often quoted from memory or deliberately paraphrased a quotation. When they do this, we would not expect their quotations to agree, word for word, with the Greek text. From Clement of Rome in A.D. 96 to Tertullian in A.D. 208 the church leaders were quoting the apostles, claiming authority for their words and challenging heretics with their words. Therefore they must have held accurate and authentic copies, even if not the autographs themselves.

As we noted at the end of chapter 11, there are so many quotations from the New Testament Scriptures in the writings of the early church leaders that one scholar has claimed we could reconstruct almost the whole New Testament if we had these writings alone.

How much material is available for our New Testament text?

From all that has been said, we can see that the modern scholar has an immense amount of material available to help him discover the best Greek text. There are more than 5,000 Greek manuscripts, ranging from fragments of a few verses or even lines, to the complete New Testament of *Codex Sinaiticus*; this number includes 170 papyrus fragments, nearly 2,500 minuscules and almost 300 uncials. In addition there are thousands of versions and hundreds of quotations from early church leaders. In all, it has been estimated that we have around 20,000 sources to help us piece together our New Testament.

However, it would be quite wrong to believe that this large quantity of material is a mass of confused and conflicting texts. The exact opposite is the case. In fact, by far the largest proportion of the New Testament finds full agreement in all the major sources and nowhere does a Christian doctrine depend upon an uncertain passage.

However, there are differences, and where reliable texts differ from each other the scholar has to discover which text is most likely to reflect the original. Once again, a glance down the margin or at the foot of the page of a modern translation will show how comparatively few are the places where there is any significant doubt at all.

Finding the best text

It is pious dreaming to imagine that all our New Testament translations are based upon a single, undisputed Greek text that exactly and in every detail corresponds to the very words penned by the apostolic writers of the New Testament. As we noted earlier in this chapter, we have no manuscripts actually written by Paul himself (the 'autographs') but only copies. In fact we have some 20,000 different sources to help us, and at times confuse us, in our search for an accurate text for the New Testament. Sorting out all this is called 'textual criticism'. It is like putting together a 200-piece jigsaw from a box of 20,000 assorted bits, thousands of which are duplicates and hundreds of which have been very slightly altered in shape or colour. It takes time and patience — but it can be done.

Because there is so much material available and because there are differences between them, it is the task of the expert, the textual critic, to discover the best text. In 1796 J. J. Griesbach classified the available New Testament documents into three families, and this is generally considered an accurate division today. First, those that reflect a western origin with Rome as the centre. Second, those that reflect an eastern source, with Alexandria as the centre. Third, those that come from the Byzantine Empire, the eastern part of the Roman Empire, which was based upon Constantinople and lasted from the fourth century and continued with steadily declining power until 1453 when the Turks captured that city. It is the task of the textual critic to compare these various families or groups of texts in order to discover the best reading wherever there may be a difference among available texts. In order to simplify the problem we can divide these textual critics into three groups.

Those who prefer the Received Text

Some believe that since God gave a verbally infallible Scripture, he must have protected a pure Greek text upon which the church could

later base her translations. There is no biblical argument in favour
of this view and therefore we should beware of making it a rigid
matter of essential belief or a test of whether or not we can have
fellowship with another Christian. On the other hand, it would seem
a fairly reasonable and logical point of view.

The text that these Christians believe to be divinely protected is
the Received Text of Estienne of 1550, the *Textus Receptus*.
Estienne's text of 1550 is really based upon Erasmus' work of 1516.
Bishop Ellicott, the chairman of the committee that produced the
Greek text for the Revised Version, could remark: 'The manuscripts
which Erasmus used [the uncials] differ, for the most part, only in
small and insignificant details from the great bulk of the cursive
manuscripts [like *Vaticanus* and *Sinaiticus*]. The general character
of their text is the same.' Ellicott goes on to tell us that the ancestors
of the texts used for the Received Text must go back as far as,
possibly much further than, any of our existing texts. This is a good
recommendation and we should treat the Received Text with great
respect. The Received Text comes from the Byzantine family and is
sometimes referred to as the Majority Text because by far the largest
number of our available Greek manuscripts come from this family.
In fact more than eighty per cent of our Greek texts belong to this
family. However, their value is not decided merely by playing the
numbers game since many of them are copies of each other.

There are some difficulties in accepting this text as the only text
from which we should work. In the first place Estienne's text of
1550 was not the only text to be called the Received Text. In fact it
was a text of two Dutch brothers by the name of Elzevir that first
called itself *Textum Receptum*, but this edition was not published
until 1633 and therefore was too late for the translators of the
Authorized Version who had completed their work by 1611. There
were many New Testament Greek texts produced between 1516 and
1524, all with minor differences and each using more Greek
manuscripts than the one before it. Any one of them could have been
chosen as the Received Text. Besides this, in places (for example,
Acts 8:37; 1 John 5:7-8; Revelation 22:16-21) the text produced by
Erasmus does not follow the majority Byzantine Text, but the Latin
Vulgate.

The second problem is that, whether we like it or not, we still
have thousands of fragments of the New Testament that have come

ΕΠΙΣΤΟΛΗ ΙΩΑΝΝΟΥ ΚΑ-
ΘΟΛΙΚΗ ΠΡΩΤΗ.

Η Ν ἀπ᾽ ἀρχῆς, ὃ ἀκηκόαμεν, ὃ ἑωράκαμεν τοῖς ὀφθαλμοῖς ἡμῶν, ὃ ἐθεα-
σάμεθα, κὴ αἱ χεῖρες ἡμῶν ἐψηλάφη-
σαν περὶ τῦ λόγου τῆς ζωῆς, (κὴ ἡ ζωὴ
ἐφανερώθη· καὶ ἑωράκαμεν, κὴ μαρ-
τυροῦμεν, καὶ ἀπαγγέλλομεν ὑμῖν τὴν
ζωὴν τὴν αἰώνιον, ἥτις ἦν πρὸς τὸν

Β πατέρα, κὴ ἐφανερώθη ἡμῖν·) ὃ ἑωράκαμεν καὶ ἀκηκόαμεν,
ἀπαγγέλλομεν ὑμῖν, ἵνα ὰ ὑμεῖς κοινωνίαν ἔχητε μεθ᾽ ἡμῶν,
καὶ ἡ κοινωνία ἡ ἡμετέρα μετὰ τῦ πατρὸς κὴ μετὰ τῦ ἱοῦ αὐτῦ
Ἰησοῦ Χριστοῦ. καὶ ταῦτα γράφομεν ὑμῖν, ἵνα ἡ χαρὰ ἡμῶν
ᾖ πεπληρωμένη. Καὶ αὕτη ἔστιν ἡ ἐπαγγελία ἣν ἀκηκόαμεν
ἀπ᾽ αὐτῦ, κὴ ἀναγγέλλομεν ὑμῖν, ὅτι ὁ Θεὸς φῶς ἔστι, ὰ σκο-

Γ τία ἐν αὐτῷ ἐκ ἔστιν οὐδεμία. Ἐὰν εἴπωμεν ὅτι κοινωνίαν ἔχομεν μετ᾽ αὐτοῦ, καὶ ἐν τῷ σκότει περιπατῶμεν, ψευδόμεθα,
κὴ οὐ ποιοῦμεν τὴν ἀλήθειαν· ἐὰν δὲ ἐν τῷ φωτὶ περιπατῶμεν,
ὡς αὐτός ἔστιν ἐν τῷ φωτί, κοινωνίαν ἔχομεν μετ᾽ ἀλλήλων, κὴ
τὸ αἷμα Ἰησοῦ Χριστοῦ τῦ ἱοῦ αὐτῦ καθαρίζει ἡμᾶς ἀπὸ πά-

Δ σης ἁμαρτίας. ἐὰν εἴπωμεν ὅτι ἁμαρτίαν ἐκ ἔχομεν, ἑαυτοὺς
πλανῶμεν, καὶ ἡ ἀλήθεια ἐκ ἔστιν ἐν ἡμῖν· ἐὰν ὁμολογῶμεν τὰς
ἁμαρτίας ἡμῶν, πιστός ἔστι ὰ δίκαιος ἵνα ἀφῇ ἡμῖν τὰς ἁμαρτίας, ὰ καθαρίσῃ ἡμᾶς ἀπὸ πάσης ἀδικίας· ἐὰν εἴπωμεν ὅτι
οὐχ ἡμαρτήκαμεν, ψεύστην ποιοῦμεν αὐτόν, καὶ ὁ λόγος αὐ-

β τῦ ἐκ ἔστιν ἐν ἡμῖν. Τεκνία μου, ταῦτα γράφω ὑμῖν,
ἵνα μὴ ἁμάρτητε· κὴ ἐάν τις ἁμάρτῃ, παράκλητον ἔχομεν πρὸς
τὸν πατέρα, Ἰησοῦν Χριστὸν δίκαιον· καὶ αὐτὸς ἱλασμός ἔστι

The opening page of John's First Epistle from the Greek Text of Robert
Estienne (Reproduced by courtesy of the Bible Society).

to light since 1550; what are we to do with them? To ignore them all would seem an unscholarly and unreasonable thing to do; to claim that they have been preserved for so long because they were unreliable and therefore unused is an argument that could dispense with all the Dead Sea Scrolls as well! Surely no one would claim that God preserved these other texts in order to test our faith in the Received Text!

Thirdly, there are some very definite weaknesses in Estienne's text. When Erasmus' Greek texts ended at Revelation 22:16 he simply retranslated Jerome's Latin Vulgate back to Greek! Dr E. F. Hills, who is a very strong supporter of the Received Text in the United States of America, admits here that 'It is the text which should be followed almost always' (*The King James Version Defended*, p.35). Similarly, referring to 1 John 5:7, a verse which has no genuine Greek manuscript support, Dr Hills concludes that 'On believing principles [it] must also be regarded as possibly genuine' (*Believing Bible Study*, p.189). But phrases like 'almost always' and 'possibly genuine' bring us no nearer to certainty.

On this verse in 1 John 5:7, Martin Luther was so certain that it should not be part of the New Testament that he offered 200 florins to anyone who could produce just one Greek text with it in; though he added, with his florins in mind: 'God alone knows where I will find them'! Erasmus found this verse in no Greek text and therefore left it out of his Greek New Testament but offered to include it if someone could produce a Greek manuscript containing the verse. The earliest Greek manuscript containing 1 John 5:7 is dated in the sixteenth century — quite possibly produced by some monk for the occasion!

The text of Westcott and Hort

In 1881 two New Testament scholars called Westcott and Hort put forward a text based almost entirely upon *Codex Sinaiticus* and *Codex Vaticanus*. They assumed that because these two texts were very old they should have precedence over everything else, including the Received Text. This theory was almost worshipped for a long time and few dared to disagree with it for fear of not being considered scholarly. It was very ably attacked by Dean Burgon, but he was almost alone. Westcott and Hort were quite wrong to disregard the Received Text to the extent they did, for although these two texts are very old there are also some very strong arguments in favour of the Received Text.

However, to accuse *Sinaiticus* and *Vaticanus* of coming from the pen of scribes seeking to deny the full deity of Christ is really unfair and, even if it is so, those scribes made a strange blunder at John 1:18. Here *Sinaiticus* and *Vaticanus* both speak of Christ as 'the only begotten God', whereas the Received Text has merely 'the only begotten Son'. The difference is between *Theos* and *Uios* in the Greek; an illustration of how possible it is for a scribe to make a slight, but significant, mistake.

Those who favour an 'eclectic' text.

For centuries the church of Rome would only allow the Latin Vulgate to be used and was convinced that it was the only reliable and accurate text. Strictly this is still the position of the Roman Church, and any translation has to be based upon the Latin Vulgate. We should be cautious about giving any one text an infallibility above all others. More texts are available to us today than were available even to Westcott and Hort.

Many Christians prefer to avoid the rigid boundaries of accepting only the Received Text or that of Westcott and Hort, and steer a middle course following many evangelical scholars both of the past and the present. Godly textual scholarship is not to be opposed in its attempt to find a pure text. William Cunningham once wrote, 'Most of those who have examined this subject with attention have been of the opinion that, upon the whole, Griesbach's text (a text which uses all the available material) is more pure and correct, approaches nearer to the original text of the inspired authors than the *Textus Receptus*, and I am disposed to think that this opinion is correct' (*Theological Lectures*, 1878, p.549). The text resulting from the evaluation of everything that is available is called an 'eclectic' text, that is, using all sources. A preference for the Received Text would therefore not exclude us from using the evidence of other, equally valuable, texts.

Two working examples

Mark 16:9-20 has been challenged as to whether it rightly belongs to Mark's Gospel, and this is why most modern translations of the

New Testament indicate that there is some doubt about the passage. The evidence, briefly stated, is that these twelve verses are not found in our two oldest Greek manuscripts, *Codex Sinaiticus* and *Codex Vaticanus* (the first could not have been written before A.D. 340, though *Vaticanus* may be a little earlier). In addition, a few other old manuscripts written in non-Greek languages, known as the versions, leave out these verses. On the other hand, the verses are included in all the other Greek manuscripts, in all the early Latin manuscripts except one, and are quoted as Scripture by many early church leaders who lived even before *Sinaiticus* and *Vaticanus* were written: men like Justin Martyr, Tatian, Irenaeus and Hippolytus. The evidence in favour of keeping Mark 16:9-20 where it is, at the end of Mark's Gospel, is very strong. One thing is certain: it is not a matter of indifference whether or not these verses are part of Scripture; it is essential that we have good reasons either to keep them in or to throw them out.

In the New International Version part of 1 Timothy 3:16 reads: 'Beyond all question, the mystery of godliness is great: He appeared in a body...' A footnote adds, 'Some manuscripts read God' in place of 'he'. What our translators do not tell us is that some other manuscripts read 'who' and some read 'which'! The facts are that 300 Greek manuscripts read 'God', six read 'who', two read 'he' and one reads 'which'. The NIV has 'he' because the translators believe that *Codex Sinaiticus* and the other manuscripts and versions where this word is found have the best reading at this point. However, the fact that some later editions of *Sinaiticus* have the word 'God', as do ninety-seven per cent of Greek manuscripts and a number of versions, means that there is something to be said on both sides. Why the difference? Since the words 'who', 'he' and 'which' are quite similar in the Greek a scribe might well have confused them; of these three the most likely is 'he'. On the other hand, 'God' is a very distinct word and likely, therefore, to be the original. But some think the scribe may have allowed his eye to wander to the verse he had just written (v. 15), where the word 'God' appears twice, and he mistakenly copied it in at verse 16 also. Alternatively a helpful scribe might even have changed 'he' to 'God' to make it clear who 'he' is!

A judgement has to be made on which evidence we believe is best, but most of us do not have the skill for this and have to rely on our translators. Fortunately not many passages are up for discussion in this way, as we have already noted; and even this one in 1 Timothy

3:16 does not affect our theology. If the word is 'God' then clearly we have evidence that Christ who 'appeared in a body' was God. If the word is 'he' then it can only refer to the 'living God' who is referred to in the previous verse and who we are now told 'appeared in a body'. If there was a helpful scribe trying to make it clear that 'he' refers to God, he need not have bothered since there is no other way to understand the passage!

This little exercise is what is meant by 'textual criticism'.

Conclusion

We may conclude with the assurance that although textual criticism and the assessment of the material available are complex and highly academic tasks, all but a tiny fraction of the New Testament is unquestioned on any ground, and no doctrine or historical fact hangs upon a disputed passage. It is not generally appreciated that virtually all the main doctrinal passages of the New Testament are entirely free from any textual problem.

The New Testament is unique for the amount of ancient material available and no one can doubt that in all but a few areas we can be certain of the words of the original text. However, we must not underestimate the significant problem of any passage in which equally valuable manuscripts differ. The doctrine of verbal inspiration can never allow us to call any difference 'insignificant', even if it is only a dispute over 'your' or 'our', 'of' or 'from'. But what is equally true is that we may safely turn to our Greek New Testament and be sure that it reflects accurately in verbal form the mind of God. Where there are difficulties we must with honesty admit our limited knowledge at that point. The problems of textual criticism need never cause us to turn aside from a belief in verbal and plenary inspiration.

Sir Frederick Kenyon, Director of the British Museum for twenty-one years, expressed his own confidence in our Bible text like this: 'The Christian can take the whole Bible in his hand and say without fear or hesitation that he holds in it the true word of God, handed down without essential loss from generation to generation throughout the centuries' (*Our Bible and the Ancient Manuscripts*, p.55). All the evidence that has come to light since Sir Frederick Kenyon wrote that only reinforces the claim.

13.
The story of our English Bible

This chapter follows the story of our English Bible. It is not intended as a discussion in detail of the merits and demerits of the various translations, because that would require a book in itself; neither is it complete because the total number of translations or revisions of the Bible into English over the past six hundred years is enormous.

As the Christian gospel spread across the Roman world, so the Bible spread with it. At first, the Bible that was common in western Europe was the translation of Jerome completed by the year A.D. 405. Jerome's translation was in Latin, because that was the language used in Europe for official business and also in the church. Jerome's translation was known as the Vulgate, a word taken from the Latin for 'common' or 'popular'. The Latin Vulgate was faithfully copied all over the Roman Empire.

The Anglo-Saxons and their Bible

A Bible in Latin was of little use to English-speaking people, and for many centuries the ways in which Bible stories were communicated to the ordinary people were through the preaching of travelling friars and the decoration of churches by wall paintings, carvings and later by stained-glass windows. The church services were largely unintelligible since they were all in Latin, but the elaborate ceremonies and ornate dress of the priests were all intended to teach the people.

The people also learnt poems and songs which they used at their gatherings. One of the most gifted poets was a labourer called Caedmon who eventually joined the monastery at Whitby in Yorkshire because of his gift of turning Bible stories into simple poems and songs for the people.

The language which was spoken by the Anglo-Saxon people of Britain before the Norman conquest of 1066 is known as Old English. It was so different from our modern English that it is virtually another language. A poem recounting the story of the Exodus from Egypt closes with the words: 'It is the eternal God of Abraham, creation's Lord, who this camp protects, valiant and powerful with a mighty hand.' In the Old English version it appears as: 'This is se ecea Abrahames god, frumsceafta frea, se thas fyrd wereth modig and maegenrof mif thaere miclan hand.'

At first there was little obvious reason to translate the Bible into English. The common people could not read and the priests were supposed to be able to understand their Latin Bible. However, it is believed that Aldhelm, the first Bishop of Sherborne in Dorset, was the first to begin some translation about the year 700; he began with the Psalms. Bede, a monk at Jarrow and our first writer of English church history, also translated parts of the New Testament; unfortunately none of his translation work has survived. He urged that the less able priests should be taught the Apostles' Creed and the Lord's Prayer in English. Less than eight hundred years later men and women were burnt at the stake in England for this very 'crime'!

Alfred the Great should not only be remembered for burning the cakes, building a navy and beating the Danes; he was a just and educated king whose Christian faith was real. How much translation Alfred undertook himself and how much his scholars did for him is uncertain, but in addition to the translation of many good books into English, he had the Ten Commandments and other parts of Exodus and Acts translated. He is said to have been engaged in a translation of the Psalms when he died in 901.

The Wessex Gospels are the first example we possess of a translation of the Gospels into Old English, and they are dated some time after the death of Alfred in the tenth century. Later in that century an abbot at Eynsham in Oxfordshire made a translation of the first seven books of the Old Testament. Whilst the Latin translation continued to circulate, sometimes a helpful monk would add an English translation to it. The Lindisfarne Gospels are perhaps the most famous example of this. They were originally copied towards the end of the seventh century and 250 years later an obliging priest named Aldred added a literal English translation in the Northumbrian dialect between the lines.

1066 — a blow to the Bible

The conquest by William of Normandy changed the English language and culture. The new lords were Norman French and within a short time the old Wessex Gospels would have been virtually unintelligible even to the ordinary people; a new way of speaking, Middle English, took over.

Translations of parts of the Bible into an anglicized French were of little value and, with the ever-increasing authority of the pope as the absentee landlord at Rome, Bible translation took a step backwards. Until the middle of the fourteenth century it seemed never to occur to anyone that a whole Bible in the language of the people might be a good thing. Occasionally parts of the Bible were translated by individuals, and Richard Rolle, a godly hermit of Hampole near Doncaster, translated the Psalms into prose. But such translations were chiefly for the benefit of the priests, monks and nuns, and all were from the Latin Vulgate.

John Wycliffe — a translation

At the beginning of the thirteenth century King John of England was tired of Pope Innocent III, and the feeling was mutual. In order to bring the king to heel, the pope ordered the church to take industrial action by refusing all marriages, baptisms and burials. Bowing to this pressure, King John signed away his crown and kingdom to the pope and the knights responded by forcing the king to sign the Magna Carta in 1215, a people's charter of rights. The knights and barons were determined not to let the king or the pope have unrestricted power in England.

John Wycliffe was born into a nation of intrigue and strife in the year 1324. In 1348 the plague killed a third of the population of Europe, and 200 a day were dying in London alone. Not surprisingly Wycliffe's first tract, in 1356, was called *The Last Age of the Church*. Four years later he began his attack against the wandering friars who robbed and deceived the people. He also defended the right of the king to rule in England. This theologian from Oxford became popular among the nobility, and the powerful John of Gaunt, Duke of Lancaster, became his patron.

In his writings, Wycliffe frequently quoted from Scripture and clearly he had access to a Latin Bible. He wrote against the abuses and errors of the church of Rome and survived every attempt to silence him. Looking at the nation he concluded: 'The chief cause, beyond doubt, of the existing state of things, is our lack of faith in Holy Scripture... It is his pleasure that the books of the Old and New Law should be read and studied.' For this, the people must have the Bible in English. Wycliffe set out his threefold purpose in translating the Bible: first, to test and correct the doctrine of the church; second, to anchor men's experiences in the truth; and third, to lead men and women to Christ. Aided by Nicholas of Hereford and John Purvey, Wycliffe completed his translation of the Bible from the Latin Vulgate before his death in 1384.

Here is Hebrews 1:1 in Wycliffe's translation: 'Manyfold and many maners sum tyme God spekinge to fadris in prophetis, at the laste in thes daies spak to us in the sone: whom he ordeynede eyr of alle thingis, by whom he made and the worldis. The which whanne he is the schynynge of glorie and figure of his substaunce, and berynge alle thingis bi word of his vertu, makyng purgacioun of synnes, sittith on the righthalf of mageste in high thingis; so moche maad betere than aungelis, by how moche he hath inherited a more different name bifore hem.'

This first edition was a literal word-for-word translation from the Latin; but subsequent revisions showed greater concern to be read easily and reflect English idioms.

John Wycliffe sent out his 'Poor Preachers', or Lollards as they were known, throughout England and Wales, each with a copy of the Bible in his hand. For the first time in thirteen centuries the Englishman had the Bible in his own tongue. Without the printing press, every copy was handwritten.

The church responded in alarm, and in 1394 a bill was presented to Parliament forbidding anyone to read the Bible in English without a bishop's licence. 'What!' exploded John of Gaunt in 1390 when the House of Lords was presented with a motion to burn all Wycliffe's Bibles, 'Are we the very dregs of humanity that we cannot possess the laws of our religion in our own tongue?' The effect of the Bible was to bring both revival and reformation into the nation, and the later revision of Wycliffe's Bible by John Purvey enjoyed great popularity throughout the fifteenth century. However, the law was applied so vigorously that by the early sixteenth century Wycliffe's Bible was scarce.

Wycliffe's Bible
(Reproduced by courtesy of the Dean and Chapter of
Hereford Cathedral)

Wycliffe's principles of translation

John Purvey, in a tract called the *General Prologue*, published about 1395, set out the principles of translation which Wycliffe and his team had adopted. Bearing in mind that they had no one to model themselves on, their principles are remarkably modern.

The first need was *to find the best Latin text and then to understand it.* First the translator must 'with divers fellows and helpers, gather many old Bibles, and other doctors, and common glosses, and to make one Latin Bible some deal true; and then to study it anew, the text with the gloss, and other doctors, as he might get, and specially Lyra on the Old Testament, that helped full much in this work; the third time to counsel with old grammarians and old divines, of hard words and hard sentence, how they might best be understood and translated; the fourth time to translate as clearly as he could to the sentence, and to have many good fellows and cunning at the correcting of the translation.'

Then follows *the method of translating:* 'First, it is to be known that the best translating out of Latin into English is to translate after the sentence and not only after the words, so that the sentence be as open, or opener, in English as in Latin, and go not far from the letter; and if the letter may not be followed in the translating, let the sentence ever be whole and open, for the words ought to serve to the intent and sentence, or else the words be superfluous or false… And whether I have translated as openly or openlier in English as in Latin, let wise men deem, that know well both languages, and know well the sentence of Holy Scripture.'

Finally, *the life of the translator himself* came under scrutiny: 'A translator hath great need to study well the sense both before and after, and then also he hath need to live a clean life and be full devout in prayers, and have not his wit occupied about worldly things, that the Holy Spirit, author of all wisdom and knowledge and truth, dress him for his work and suffer him not to err. By this manner, with good living and great travail, men can come to true and clear translating, and true understanding of Holy Writ, seem it never so hard at the beginning. God grant to us all grace to know well and to keep well Holy Writ, and to suffer joyfully some pain for it at the last.'

William Tyndale and the first printed Bible — a translation

William Caxton set up his printing press, close by Westminster
Abbey, in 1476. The first paper-mill was established in England in
1490, a century after Wycliffe's Bible was painstakingly copied and
recopied by hand and, by a neat coincidence, within a year or two of
the birth of William Tyndale.

Tyndale, a graduate of Oxford and then Cambridge, trained for
the priesthood, came to a living faith in Christ, and early decided to
give the Englishman a translation he could easily read. At Cambridge he studied the Greek texts of Erasmus, first published in 1516
(see chapter 12), and when Tyndale arrived at Little Sodbury Manor
in Gloucestershire in 1521 to tutor the two children of Sir John and
Lady Walsh, he was already preparing the first drafts of his New
Testament translation. It was here, in debate with a priest who was
visiting the manor and who maintained we would be better without
God's laws than the pope's, that Tyndale 'went public' with his life
ambition: 'I defy the pope and all his laws; if God spare my life, ere
many years I will cause a boy that driveth a plough shall know more
of the Scripture than thou dost.'

Since there was no place in England for a Bible-translating
priest, Tyndale slipped across to the continent and in 1525 his New
Testament started to come off the press of Peter Quentel in Cologne.
The work was discovered after a few sheets had been printed and
Tyndale and his colleague fled to Worms where, after a hasty
revision of the text, the New Testament was printed in 1526 and
copies of the contraband book landed in England the same year.

Naturally the bishops hated this New Testament. Tunstall of
London ordered it to be burnt and wrote to his archdeacons on 24
October 1526 complaining of the 'holy gospel of God' in the
common tongue which was intermingled with 'certain articles of
heretical depravity and pernicious erroneous opinions, pestilent,
scandalous, and seductive of simple minds ... of which translation
many books, containing the pestilent and pernicious poison in the
vulgar [common] tongue, have been dispersed in great numbers
throughout our diocese; which truly, unless it be speedily foreseen
will without doubt infect and contaminate the flock committed to us,
with the pestilent poison and the deadly disease of heretical depravity'. At this point the bishop seems to have exhausted his store of

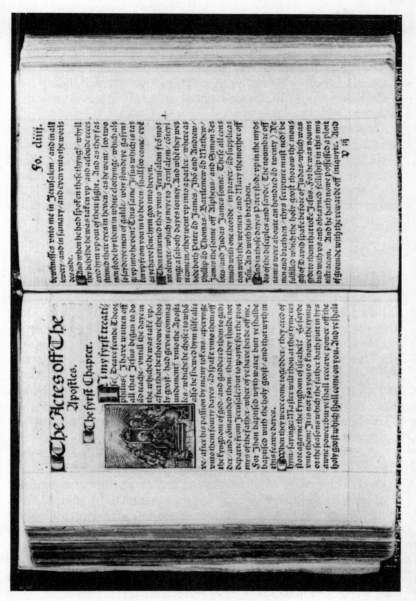

The opening page of Acts from the only complete copy of Tyndale's 1526 New Testament known to exist (Reproduced by courtesy of the Bristol Baptist College)

expletives; but such language was calculated to make the most lazy
archdeacon wake up and take action! Within thirty days all copies
must be called in, upon pain of excommunication and the charge of
heresy. The following day the bishop marshalled the London
booksellers before him in a private chapel and warned them, in no
uncertain terms, of the consequences of handling Lutheran books,
whether in Latin or English.

Not only were the booksellers and traders warned, but soon
severe punishment was given to those who were discovered with a
New Testament in their possession. An old labourer by the name of
Harding was found reading his New Testament by a wood; his house
was plundered, and under the floorboards more copies of the
offensive book were discovered. Harding was hurried to prison and
finally burnt at the stake.

Tyndale's preface

Tyndale's preface to the reader in his New Testament is worthy of
notice: 'Give diligence dear Reder (I exhorte the) that thou come
with a pure mynde and as the Scripture sayth with a syngle eye unto
the wordes of health and of eternal lyfe: by the which (if we repent
and beleve them) we are borne a newe created a fresshe and enjoye
the frutes off the bloud of Christ.' Tyndale urged his readers to
notice the plain and clear parts of Scripture and to be careful in hard
places not to add anything contrary to that which is plain. Notice
also, he continued, the difference between the law and the gospel:
'The one axeth [asks] and requyreth, the wother perdoneth and
forgeveth.'

After briefly urging his readers to repent and believe the gospel,
Tyndale turned his attention to 'them that are learned in Christianity'. If his language offends them he requests pardon, but reminds
them that he had no one to copy and no one from the past to help him
with his English. It was therefore open to future revision: 'Count it
as a thynge not havynge his full shape.'

Such a revision the translator promised to undertake as soon as
possible, and over the next ten years, as an outlaw hunted at times
by as many as five government agents, Tyndale slipped from city to
city as he continued his work of translation and revision.

Tyndale's language

Tyndale provided the nation with an English New Testament, and later also with parts of the Old Testament, that spoke to the heart of the ordinary man. His style was rich in variety and many of his phrases have remained part of our English heritage:

'Borne the burden and heat of the day' (Matthew 20:12).
'Take thine ease, eat, drink and be merry' (Luke 12:19).
'For in him we live, and move and have our being' (Acts 17:28).

Besides his native English, Tyndale was a master of six languages, including Greek and Hebrew. A complete Hebrew Old Testament had been printed in Italy in 1488. His translation was remarkable for a man working often alone and as a fugitive. Bishop Westcott, a highly skilled textual critic of the nineteenth century, claimed: 'He deals with the text as one who passed a scholar's judgement upon every fragment of the work, unbiased by any predecessor.'

Among the list of helps that the translator tells us he possessed, he had read the German translation by Martin Luther that arrived in England in September 1522; it is clear that he did not have access to a copy of Wycliffe's outlawed Bible. Here is a familiar passage from Tyndale's New Testament of 1526, and because it is one of his most beautiful translations, it is worth quoting in full. It is 1 Corinthians 13.

Though I speake with the tonges of men and angels, and yet had no love, I were even as soundynge brasse: and as a tynklynge Cynball. And though I could prophesy, and vnderstode all secretes, and all knowledge: yee, if I had all fayth so that I coulde move mountayns oute of there places, and yet had no love, I were nothynge. And though I bestowed all my goddes to fede the poore, and though I gave my body even that I burned, and yet have no love, it profeteth me nothynge.

Love suffreth longe, and is corteous. Love envieth nott. Love doth nott frawardly, swelleth not, dealeth not dishonestly, seketh nott her awne, is not provoked to ange, thynketh not evyll reioyseth not in iniquitie: but reioyseth in the trueth, suffreth all thynge, beleveth all thynges hopeth all thynges, endureth in all thynges. Though that prophesyinge fayle, other tonges shall cease, or knowledge vanysshe awaye: yet love falleth never awaye.

For oure knowledge is vnparfet, and oure prophesyinge is vnperfet: but when thatt which is parfet is come: then that which is vnparfet shall be done awaye. When I was a chylde, I spake as a chylde, I vnderstode as a child, I ymmagened as a chylde: but as sone as I was a man I put awaye all childesshnes. Nowe we se in a glasse even in a darke speakynge: but then shall we se face to face. Nowe I knowe vnparfectly: but then shall I knowe even as I am knowen. Nowe abideth fayth, hope, and love, even these thre: but the chefe of these is love.

One thing will be clear from reading this, and that is that the Authorized Version of 1611 was heavily dependent upon Tyndale. In fact ninety per cent of it was copied almost straight from Tyndale's revision of 1534. The year following this revision, Tyndale was betrayed, taken to the Castle of Vilvorde and in October 1536 he was strangled and burnt at the stake. History records that he died with the prayer: 'Lord, open the King of England's eyes.'

In that same year two Bibles were circulating in England: one came from the pen of Myles Coverdale and the other, called Matthew's Bible, from that of John Rogers, the converted chaplain of the English House in Antwerp where Tyndale stayed before his betrayal and arrest. Both Bibles were dedicated to His Majesty and awaited his royal consent. Both contained Tyndale's New Testament virtually unaltered, and were heavily dependent upon his translation of the Pentateuch and parts of the rest of the Old Testament. Henry VIII ran his eyes over Coverdale's Bible. Tyndale's name did not appear, and the bishops assured him they could find no errors. 'Then if there be no heresies,' roared Henry, 'in God's name, let it go abroad among the people.'

The following year His Majesty authorized a small phrase of immense significance to be added to the foot of the title page of Matthew's Bible: 'Set forth with the kinges most gracyous lycense.' On 5 September 1538 Henry ordered every church in England to display 'one book of the whole Bible of the largest volume in

English', the cost to be borne equally by the parson and the parishioners. Among other injunctions the people were urged to learn the Lord's Prayer, the Creed and the Ten Commandments in English, the very crime for which a woman and six labourers had been burnt at Coventry in 1519.

In the year of Tyndale's death Bishop Fox of Hereford declared in convocation: 'The lay people do now know the Holy Scripture better than many of us.' By 1539 the king had received so many complaints that the people gathering around the chained Bible were reading it loudly, even during the celebration of mass, that he ordered them to refrain from reading the Bible during divine services! On 14 November 1539 the king sent to all 'printers and sellers of books' a royal encouragement for the 'free and liberal use of the Bible in our own maternal English tongue'. As if to anticipate the king, Robert Redman was printing Tyndale's translation in 1538, and his print shop was next door to St Dunstan's where the great Reformer once preached.

The Bible and the Reformation

The translations of Myles Coverdale (Coverdale's Bible) and John Rogers (which was known as Matthew's Bible) were circulating freely and with the king's permission by the start of the new decade in 1540. Coverdale, on his own admission, had little knowledge of Hebrew or Greek and relied heavily upon Tyndale's work, which for obvious reasons he did not dare admit; he translated much of the Old Testament from the German and Latin. It was, in fact, Coverdale's translation of the Psalms that entered the *Book of Common Prayer* in 1539 and stayed there even when the rest was updated. The version of John Rogers, which the king liked sufficiently to give it his royal licence, was a mixture of the work of Tyndale, Coverdale and Rogers. Rogers used the pen name of Thomas Matthew but at the end of Malachi the initials 'W.T.' appear, which may have been left in by oversight, or to deliberately indicate that the hand of the great Reformer and translator was behind the Old Testament.

With Bibles now circulating freely, Coverdale was given the task of revising Matthew's Bible, so that a single recognized edition could fulfil the royal command of 1538 that by a certain day a copy of the Bible should be placed in every parish church in the land under

penalty of a fine of four times the cost of the Bible for every month
of delay! This was the Great Bible of 1539, which, like its predecessors, was heavily dependent upon Tyndale.

Henry VIII died in 1547 and in the closing years of his life he
turned against the movement for reform, ordering that the possession of translations by Tyndale or Coverdale should be punish-
able by death. The Great Bible, however, containing the work of
these two translators, remained in every parish church!

During the brief reign of Edward VI, a number of attempts were
made to offer alternative translations but they each came to nothing
and the Great Bible held its ground. The reaction under Mary in
1553, during which poor John Rogers, along with many others, was
executed, actually had little or no impact upon the Great Bible, and
by the accession of Elizabeth I in 1558 only age had made inroads
on the copies of the Bible in each parish church.

The persecution under Mary had driven many good men abroad
and some of them met in Geneva, the city of the Reformers which,
in the view of John Knox of Scotland, was 'the most perfect school
of Christ' since the days of the apostles. Some of the English exiles
set to work on a new translation using some of the help given by the
great scholar Theodore Beza. William Whittingham led the team
and a year before Mary died they produced their New Testament. By
1560 the Old Testament was complete, and the Geneva Bible was
born.

The Geneva Bible took Tyndale as its basis and revised it with
the aid of Beza's Latin version and the latest Greek text of Robert
Estienne in 1550. Perhaps one of the most notable features of the
Geneva Bible, which shouldered its way into first place for the next
half-century, was the notes that accompanied it. These notes reflected the strongly Reformed theology of John Calvin's Geneva
and played a large part in moulding the minds of its readers. The
Geneva Bible was the Bible of the later Reformers, the Puritans, the
Pilgrim Fathers who sailed to America in the Mayflower in 1620,
and even of Shakespeare. Its immense popularity is seen in the fact
that it was still being printed in 1644, thirty-three years after the first
edition of the Authorized Version. The Soldier's Pocket Bible that
Oliver Cromwell issued to his army in 1643 contained extracts from
the Geneva Bible.

The Geneva Bible was the first English translation to use verse
divisions, as we saw in chapter 12, and the first to use italics for

words that have been added to the text to make clear the meaning. It is sometimes referred to as the Breeches Bible because Genesis 3:21 is rendered: 'The Lord God made breeches of skin for Adam and his wife.' It was, however, an excellent revision for both accuracy and readability.

Meanwhile the bishops were busy with their own Bible, which, not surprisingly, was called the Bishops' Bible and was ready by 1568. Although it was a good revision of the Great Bible, it had already been outclassed by the greater ability of the translators of the Geneva Bible and could never catch up.

The Authorized Version — a revision

When James I succeeded Elizabeth in 1603 he called a conference of leading churchmen and theologians at Hampton Court Palace to discuss 'things pretended to be amiss in the church'. The only result of this meeting worthy of note was the resolution 'That a translation be made of the whole Bible, as consonant as can be to the original Hebrew and Greek; and this to be set out and pointed [punctuated], without any marginal notes, and only to be used in all churches of England in time of divine service.'

This was the birth of the Authorized, or King James Version. In fact it was no more King James' than Coverdale's Bible was King Henry's, and it was never formally authorized by Parliament. But James was glad of any opportunity to get rid of the Geneva Bible with its notes which were, to his mind, far too Protestant and Reformed; after all, he was the son of Mary, Queen of Scots!

James arranged for six groups of translators to divide the work: three on the Old Testament, one on the Apocrypha, and two on the New Testament. Forty-seven scholars were chosen for the work. The work was modelled on the Bishops' Bible and for this reason was in some respects a backward step from Geneva and those before it. The Authorized Version, which was completed in 1611, reintro-duced words that had a loaded ecclesiastical meaning in pre-Reformation days. For example, 'confess' was introduced in place of 'acknowledge', which appeared in both the Geneva Bible and in Tyndale's New Testament before it, 'charity' in place of 'love' and 'church' in place of 'congregation'. At John 10:16 the Authorized Version translators chose 'There shall be one fold and one shepherd,' which Westcott, years later, rightly called a 'disastrous' translation since it gave support to the Roman idea of one visible organized church on earth; Tyndale had rightly translated by the word 'flock'. These may be small issues today, but for the strong supporters of the Geneva Bible they were seen as a drift back to the church of Rome. In fact the translators were trying to steer a middle course, but whether or not they succeeded is a matter of opinion.

Certainly the Authorized Version was no stiff, word-by-word translation. At times it could be accused of being too free: for instance, in Romans 5:2-3 the same Greek word appears as 'rejoice', 'glory' and 'joy' within the space of two verses. It is even open to the charge of paraphrasing: for example, in Matthew 27:44 the single Greek word 'revile' is rendered 'cast the same in his teeth', and Paul's expression, 'It cannot be' in Romans 6:15, for example, is paraphrased as 'God forbid' — though we can blame Tyndale's 1526 New Testament for both these readings! In fact the Authorized Version, like all its predecessors, was heavily dependent upon Tyndale and, as we have already noted, fully ninety per cent of the Authorized Version New Testament is taken from Tyndale's 1534 revision. This is why, strictly, the Authorized Version is a revision and not a new translation.

Like every version before and after it, the Authorized Version did not lack critics, particularly from among those who were brought up on the Geneva Bible. The most vigorous critic was Dr Hugh Broughton, a recognized Hebrew and Greek scholar who was left out of the translation team possibly because of his abrasive character and because he was known to be working on his own revision of the Geneva Bible. Broughton hated the new translation and told the king so: 'The cockles of the sea shore, and the leaves of the forest, and the grains of the poppy, may as well be numbered as the gross errors of this Bible.' This charge is reminiscent of Bishop Tunstall who, within a few short months of Tyndale's New Testament arriving in this country, claimed to have found 3,000 errors within its pages. It is hard to be an unprejudiced critic when we feel threatened!

In spite of Hugh Broughton, and the strong supporters of the Geneva Bible, the Authorized or King James Version won its way into the hearts and minds of the people and remained at centre stage for the next three and a half centuries. At first the Apocrypha was bound in with it and in 1615 Archbishop Abbott forbade anyone to issue an edition without this inclusion. The Puritans objected, and the issue remained a lively one for many years; it is still possible to buy copies of the Authorized Version with the Apocrypha, but we have already seen why it should not be included (see chapter 10).

Because the English language has changed considerably since 1611 there has been a need for revision of the language of the Authorized Version over the years. In 1769 it was updated by a Dr Blayney, and the spelling of the 1611 edition would be oddly unreadable for a modern congregation. For comparison with Tyndale's 1526 translation of 1 Corinthians 13 quoted earlier in the chapter here is the same passage in the exact words and spelling of the first edition of the King James Authorized Version in 1611:

1. Though I speake with the tongues of men & of Angels, and haue not charity, I am become as sounding brasse or a tinkling cymbal.

2. And though I haue the gift of prophesie, and vnderstand all mysteries and all knowledge: and though I haue all faith, so that I could remooue mountaines, and haue no charitie, I am nothing.

3. And though I bestowe all my goods to feede the poore, and though I giue my body to bee burned, and haue not charitie, it profiteth me nothing.

4. Charitie suffereth long, and is kinde: charitie enuieth not: charitie vaunteth not it selfe, is not puffed vp,

5. Doeth not behaue it selfe vnseemly, seeketh not her owne, is not easily prouoked, thinketh no euill,

6. Reioyceth not in iniquitie, but reioyceth in the trueth:

7. Beareth all things, beleeueth all things, hopeth all things, endureth all things.

8. Charitie neuer faileth: but whether there be prophesies, they shall faile; whether there bee tongues, they shall cease; whether there bee knowledge, it shall vanish away.

9. For we know in part, and we prophesie in part.

10. But when that which is perfect is come, then that which is in part shall be done away.

11. When I was a childe, I spake as a childe, I vnderstood as a childe, I thought as a childe; but when I became a man, I put away childish things.

12. For now we see through a glasse, darkely: but then face

to face: now I know in part, but then shall I know euen as also
I am knowen.

13. And now abideth faith, hope, charitie, these three, but
the greatest of these is charitie.

A Bible for Roman Catholics — a revision

At first the church of Rome was violently opposed to any suggestion
that the people should have what John of Gaunt referred to as 'God's
laws in their own language'. The reason for this is that in the view
of Rome only the church could interpret the Word of God. However,
when that battle had been lost, it was considered wiser to approve a
translation suitable for members of the church of Rome. But Rome
was slow to move. The first version was a revision of a translation
completed around 1610 by Gregory Martin, a Roman Catholic exile
during the reign of Elizabeth and a member of the English College
at Douai, northern France. Because the New Testament was published whilst the college was still at Rheims, it is sometimes referred
to as the Rheims New Testament. This revision was completed in
1749 and is known as the Douai Bible.

The first principle was that the basic text for translating had to be
the Latin Vulgate of Jerome. This is still the first principle for any
translation by the church of Rome and therefore, strictly, Catholic
versions of the Bible are revisions rather than translations. The
translators of the Douai Bible kept Latin words and even phrases and
admitted to a word-for-word approach at times. This occasionally
led to such unhelpful renderings as 'against the Spirituals of wickedness in the celestials' (Ephesians 6:12). If a verb is not required
in the Latin (or the Greek), it is not supplied in the English either,
therefore they rendered Hebrews 13:4 as: 'Marriage honourable in
all.' The Psalms contain some quite unintelligible phrases because
here Jerome translated from the Septuagint; the Douai Psalms are
therefore a translation from a translation of a translation!

The marks of Roman theology are evident. John and Jesus both
call upon their hearers to 'do penance, for the Kingdom of heaven
is at hand'. Our Lord prays that 'this chalice' might pass from him,
and Paul and Barnabas ordain 'priests in every church'. The Douai
Bible included the Apocrypha, with the exception of the books of
Ezdras and the Prayer of Manasseh which were printed separately

at the end. The commentary that ran alongside the text helped the faithful to interpret the Bible in a Roman way.

Bishop Challoner revised the Douai Bible in the eighteenth century and this, with its considerable Authorized Version influence, lasted until the Confraternity Version in 1941. Even this was based upon the Latin Vulgate, although it was preceded by the commencement of the Westminster Version of the Sacred Scriptures in 1935 based upon the Hebrew and Greek texts.

By far the most popular English translation for Roman Catholics, partly because it is an official version, is that of Ronald A. Knox, called 'a translation from the Latin Vulgate in the light of Hebrew and Greek originals'. This was completed in 1949 but its great weakness was in being tied to a copy of the Vulgate authorized in 1592 and clearly not accurate in places.

It is not always appreciated, even by evangelicals, that the Jerusalem Bible is a Roman Catholic translation of the Bible. Published in 1966, the full version contains commentary notes to draw out Roman Catholic theology. For example, the note on Exodus 12 claims, 'The Jewish Passover becomes a rehearsal for the Christian passover, the Lamb of God, Christ, is sacrificed (the cross) and eaten (the Last Supper) ... the mystical re-enactment of this redemptive act becomes the central feature of the Christian liturgy, organized around the Mass which is at once a sacrifice and a sacrificial meal.' The notes are also clearly liberal. For example, the note on Jonah dismisses Jonah as the author and claims the book was written at a late date, concluding, 'The late date is warning enough against any interpretation of the book as history.'

The Jerusalem Bible is of little value as a translation, though it is still the most widely used for reading in Roman Catholic churches. However, Roman Catholics are now permitted to use the Revised English Bible.

Beyond the Authorized Version

The eighteenth, nineteenth and twentieth centuries saw an increasing number of new translations, revisions and paraphrases until, at the present time, there is a bewildering assortment available to the modern reader with little sign of the flow coming to an end.

Translation or paraphrase?

Throughout this survey we are drawing a distinction between translations, revisions and paraphrases. A *translation* goes back to the original Hebrew and Greek and attempts to give the meaning of the words in the nearest equivalent English words. A *revision* is based upon an existing translation and, though the revisers may consult the original Hebrew and Greek, their main aim will be to update the language of the translator and correct any errors. A revision may still be a translation. A *paraphrase* attempts to give the meaning rather than the words of the original writer; it therefore translates thoughts rather than words. A paraphrase will change words, phrases and idioms to make the text easy to understand. A paraphrase can never be described as an accurate translation, and however readable it may be, it should never be used as a serious study Bible either privately or publicly.

It is not the popularity or readability of a translation or paraphrase that matters most, but whether it is based upon the best possible original text and is an accurate translation of that text. That there is no perfect translation will soon be obvious.

Most of the attempts in the eighteenth century were revisions of the Authorized Version: Whitby in 1703; Wells in 1718-24; Mace in 1729; Whiston in 1745 and Blayney in 1769. In 1768 even John Wesley produced a revision of the Authorized Version with notes for 'plain, unlettered men who understand only their Mother Tongue'. Wesley carefully studied the Greek and made about 12,000 alterations, all of which he considered necessary.

By the nineteenth century full use was being made of the Greek manuscripts that were not available to the 1611 translators. *Codex Alexandrinus* (see chapter 12) for example, arrived in England just sixteen years too late for King James' translation teams, and many more followed. Translations and paraphrases continued: Sharpe in 1840 and 1865; Young in 1862; Conybeare and Howson in 1864; Dean Alford in 1869; J. N. Darby in 1871 and 1890; Rotherham 1872, 1897-1902; and Newberry in 1890.

The Revised Version — a revision

In 1870, the Upper House of Convocation of the Province of Canterbury agreed to a revision of the Authorized Version and a committee prepared the ground by listing a number of principles including the instruction that as few alterations as possible should be introduced into the text of the Authorized Version. In addition an eclectic text would be used (see chapter 12) and where this differed from the Authorized Version the alteration would be indicated in the margin. Scholars in the United States of America began a parallel work and it was hoped one version would result. In the event the American Standard Version, free from some of the restrictions placed upon the Revised Version committees, was published separately in 1901.

The Revised Version New Testament was ready in 1881 and the Old Testament by 1885. Sales were enormous, and so was opposition, especially by the brilliant Oxford scholar Dean Burgon. The Revised Version was largely the product of men unsympathetic to a conservative approach to Scripture and this was evident in some of the footnotes casting doubt upon portions of Scripture. Many mourned the loss of the dignified Authorized Version language and style: for example, 'the interrogation of a good conscience' is hardly a helpful translation at 1 Peter 3:21. The Revised Version achieved little advance upon the Authorized Version in the New Testament, and hence it did not remain a popular challenge for long because it was soon overshadowed by the American Revised Standard Version.

The American Revised Standard Version — a revision

This is a revision of the 1901 American Standard Version and the work began in 1937 using 'the best results of modern scholarship'. The New Testament was published in 1946 and the whole Bible in 1952. It is a great improvement upon the Revised Version in terms of style and readable English.

The language is modernized: 'saith' becomes 'says', 'sendeth' becomes 'sends' and so on. 'Thou' becomes 'you' except when God is addressed — although the revisers would have saved themselves some criticism if they had not made this exception, since their decision to make the disciples refer to Christ as 'you' during his earthly ministry is merely a subjective judgement. In fact the original Greek knows of no such 'reverent' language when addressing Deity. Quotation marks are introduced for direct speech and the printing of prophetic statements as poetry is included. For these reasons the Revised Standard Version achieved a more consistent usage in public than the Revised Version.

One of the most serious criticisms levelled against the Revised Standard Version is that it attempts to downgrade the full deity of Christ, thus reflecting the liberal theology of the majority of its translators. In places this criticism is valid — there is no justification for 'your divine throne' in Psalm 45:6 (though the expression is correctly translated in Hebrews 1:8). More instances are cited but not always with justification. On the other hand, the translation of Titus 2:13, 'awaiting our blessed hope, the appearing of the glory of our great God and Saviour Jesus Christ', and 2 Peter 1:1, 'the righteousness of our God and Saviour Jesus Christ', unquestionably affirm the true deity of Christ, where the Authorized Version obscures it.

The Revised Standard Version has much to commend it. Of course there are some poor translations but it has the advantage of being generally more careful than the Authorized Version in translating particular words. For example, the Authorized Version obscures the difference between 'creatures' in Revelation 4 and 'beast' in Revelation 13; two entirely different Greek words are used and the Revised Standard Version makes this clear. Similarly the Authorized Version frequently translates the word *'daimonion'* as 'devil'. But the words 'demon' and 'devil' are very different; the Revised Standard Version gives the correct word at this point in Matthew 8:31; 1 Timothy 4:1 and James 2:19, for example. Because the translators used an eclectic Greek text, they were at times too ready to relegate passages like Mark 16:9-20 and John 8:1-11 to a footnote.

However, the Revised Standard Version was very popular among evangelicals until the New International Version came on the scene; but before we arrive at this there are a number of translations and paraphrases to note.

J. B. Phillips — a paraphrase

J. B. Phillips completed his paraphrase by 1957 and for a time it was very popular, even amongst evangelical Christians, who were often unaware that Phillips denied Bible inerrancy and reserved the right to 'expand or explain' the text. He did this with sometimes disastrous results, as is illustrated by the following examples. In Matthew 7:12, 'This is the law and the prophets', becomes 'This is the essence of all true religion'! In Luke 6:37, 'Forgive and ye shall be forgiven,' becomes 'Make allowances for others and people will make allowances for you.' 'When he shall appear we shall be like him' (1 John 3:2) becomes: 'If reality were to break through, we should reflect his likeness for we shall see him as he really is.' In 1 Corinthians 14:22 the whole verse is revised into what Phillips thought Paul meant to say!

The Berkeley Version — a translation

Dr Gerritt Verkuyl of Berkeley in California, with a team of seventeen scholars, completed the Berkeley Version in 1959. It is a translation, not a paraphrase, and the team were all committed to biblical inerrancy. Unfortunately it is often so full of Americanisms and common speech (colloquialisms) that it was never a serious contender. See, for example, 'The leftovers filled seven hampers' (Matthew 15:37) and 'Look here! I have gotten my dinner ready' (Matthew 22:4).

The New World Translation

The New World Translation is the Bible of the Watchtower Bible and Tract Society (Jehovah's Witnesses) and is the only translation produced by a cult. It was completed in 1960 and revised in 1961 but the names, and therefore the qualifications, of the translators were never officially revealed. Subtle changes are made to the text to agree with Watchtower doctrine, and this is seen most clearly in the attempts to avoid the deity of Christ. However, it is only in the large library edition that these changes are admitted. Here are a few examples. We would expect John 1:1 to be rendered, 'The Word was god,' by a cult that does not believe in the deity of Christ, but consider also the following passages.

'In him all the fulness of the divine quality *[theotetos]* dwells' (Colossians 2:9-10) Yet in Romans 1:20 a related word is accurately translated 'Godship'. *The Watchtower* (August 1962, p.480) admits: 'The way these words have been rendered in the New World

Translation has given rise to the charge that the New World Bible Translation Committee let their religious beliefs influence them. That charge is true, but they did not do so wrongly or unduly. The meaning that is to be given to these two Greek words depends upon what the entire Bible has to say about Jehovah God and Jesus Christ.'

Titus 2:13 is translated: 'and *of* our Saviour Christ Jesus'. There is no manuscript evidence for the genitive, 'of', and without it the deity of Christ is plainly stated. The library edition provides a lengthy statement to justify the inclusion of the genitive, offering only Moffatt and obscure German, French and Spanish translations (all by individuals) as evidence, but admitting that it is inserted to avoid attributing deity to Christ! (Appendix, p.3592).

2 Peter 1:1 is rendered: '... of our God and (the) Saviour Jesus Christ'. The library edition footnote on page 3480 admits there is no evidence for the definite article but it is inserted 'to agree with the distinction between God and Jesus in the next verse'.

Another example of interpretation rather than translation is found in the rendering of the word 'worship'. The Greek word (*proskuneo*) appears fifty-nine times in the New Testament and with two exceptions (Matthew 18:26; Acts 10:25) is used only with reference to God, Christ or the false worship of idols and demons. The New World Translation consistently uses 'obeisance' when it refers to Christ and 'worship' when it refers to God the Father or demons or idols. Such manipulation is hardly worthy of a supposed translation.

The New World library edition (Appendix, p.1450) provides 'a concordance of all the places in this translation where the name Jehovah occurs in the Christian Greek Scriptures'. This is a plain deceit. There is no word in the Greek New Testament that is the exact equivalent of Jehovah. The Greek word for 'Lord' is '*Kurios*'. The New World Translation chooses to translate *Kurios* by 'Jehovah' when it refers to the Father and by 'Lord' when it refers to Christ; that is interpretation and not translation.

The Amplified Bible — a translation

Completed in 1962, the Amplified Bible endeavoured to bring out the various shades of meaning in the Hebrew and Greek words. The

New Testament text was that of Westcott and Hort. A typical example of this amplification is found in John 1:12: 'But to as many as did receive and welcome him, he gave the authority (power, privilege, right) to become the children of God, that is, to those who believe in — adhere to, trust in and rely on — his name.' Clearly this version could never be used for public reading!

By the use of parenthesis, dashes and brackets, the committee tried to distinguish between additional meanings included in the Greek and Hebrew and comments intended to clarify the meaning. This often makes for clumsy and even ungrammatical reading. For example, Romans 8:29 reads, 'For those whom he foreknew — of whom he was aware and loved beforehand — he also destined from the beginning (foreordaining them) to be moulded into the image of his son [and share inwardly his likeness], that he might become the first born among many brethren.'

The Good News Bible — a paraphrase

The Good News Bible was published by the American Bible Society in 1976 and was subtitled 'Today's English Version'. Although it claims to be a translation, it is much closer to a paraphrase. The various editions are all adorned with simple line drawings and, enjoying greater publicity than any translation before it, Today's English Version sold by the millions of copies. It is the work basically of one man, Dr Robert Bratcher, who denied both inerrancy and infallibility and went so far as to call the evangelical position 'heresy'! From the beginning serious mistranslations marred it as a serious study Bible. Frequently, for example, the reference to the 'blood' of Christ was translated by the word 'death'. In Acts 20:28, for example, 'which he made his own through the death of his Son' should literally be 'which he bought with his own blood'; this is typical of many such instances.

It is equally serious that in Romans 4:3,5,6,9,11,22 the phrase 'God accepted him as righteous,' is repeatedly used. This misses the whole point of imputed righteousness. The Greek word used here is '*logizomai*' and nowhere can it mean 'to accept'; on the contrary the word means 'to reckon' or 'pass to someone's account', 'to impute'. It is one of Paul's favourite words and he uses it twenty-seven times.

Similarly, 'the means by which our sins are forgiven' is a

pathetically weak translation of *hilasmos* in 1 John 2:2, which is best translated by 'propitiation', and refers to the satisfaction of God's anger against sin.

The New English Bible — a translation

The New English Bible, completed in 1970, had as its aim to present the Bible in English 'which is as clear and natural for the modern reader as the subject matter will allow'. Whether or not it succeeded can be judged by a glance through Paul's two letters to Timothy, where the following words are met: interminable, patricides and matricides, felicity, specious, inculcate, precepts, atrophied, fidelity, craven, adjure, refractory, implacable, insinuate, charlatans, refuting and retribution! In addition crude colloquialisms abound: 'I sponged on no one' (2 Corinthians 11:9); 'they left me in the lurch' (2 Timothy 4:16); 'they got wind of it' (Acts 14:6); 'it touched them on the raw' (Acts 7:54); 'smashing them to bits' (Revelation 2:27); and in the Old Testament, 'David got wind of it' (1 Samuel 23:25); 'itches for your gift' (Isaiah 1:23); 'you mighty toppers' (Isaiah 5:22). T. S. Elliot once described the New English Bible as 'vulgar, trivial and pedantic'.

There are many examples that represent the doctrinal weakness of the translators. 'Every inspired Scripture has its use for...' (2 Timothy 3:16), implies that not all Scripture is inspired; in 1 John 2:2 'propitiation' becomes a meaningless 'remedy for the defilement of our sins'; and in Isaiah 9:6 the magnificent Hebrew expression, 'Mighty God' *(El Gibbor)* becomes merely 'Godlike'.

In 1989 the Revised English Bible was published as 'a fundamental revision of the New English Bible'. It was planned to be acceptable 'to all Christians' and certainly it has the support of the mainline denominations including the Baptist Union of Great Britain, the Church of England and the Roman Catholic Church. The Revised English Bible sets out to use 'clear and up-to-date but dignified language that will speak in a natural and understandable way to all'. In Paul's two letters to Timothy the revisers have cleared up some of those unfamiliar words, but they have kept 'interminable', 'patricides and matricides', 'fidelity', 'implacable', 'insinuate' and 'charlatans' and have added 'avaricious' and 'perfidious'! They have also given us 'pompous ignoramus' and the quaint

'reformation of manners'. Sadly the word 'bishop' is retained at
1 Timothy 3:2; and 2 Timothy 3:16 reads, 'All inspired Scripture has
its use...' which is incredibly weak and misleading.

New American Standard Bible — a translation

'On July 31st 1970 the New American Standard Bible was completed after 9 years and 7 months of intensive work by 58 consecrated and dedicated scholars' — so reads the cover blurb of this
translation published by the Lockman Foundation of California. It
is an evangelical translation. The Greek text is based largely upon
the Nestle Greek New Testament, which is an eclectic text, and this
makes it more acceptable among evangelicals than those based
solely upon Westcott and Hort.

Punctuation and paragraphs have been changed to clarify the
meaning of the passage. Personal pronouns commence with a
capital when referring to the Deity, and the second singular ('thou',
'thy' and 'thee') are retained when the Deity is addressed. On this
latter point the New American Standard Bible follows the Revised
Standard Version in using 'you' to refer to Christ prior to his
ascension; this is an unwise approach for it necessitates a decision
when and where the speaker knew he was addressing Christ as God.
However, there is a dignity in style and language that commends this
version to public use.

The Living Bible — a paraphrase

Kenneth Taylor produced this paraphrase, completing the New
Testament in 1962 and the Old Testament in 1971. The language is
racy, down to earth and at times coarse — it may seriously be
questioned whether this is what is required even in a paraphrase. A
few examples will illustrate this: Romans 9:21 is rendered, 'one jar
beautiful, to be used for holding flowers, and another to throw
garbage into'; and Romans 14:7: 'We are not our own bosses';
whilst in 1 Samuel 24:3 we have the plainly ridiculous statement that
Saul 'went into a cave to go to the bathroom'.

There is too much of Taylor's interpretation in his paraphrase:
for example, at Genesis 37:6,9 we read, '"Listen to this", he *proudly*

announced...' and '"Listen to my latest dream" he *boasted.*' This is an addition to Scripture. The words 'proudly' and 'boasted' appear nowhere in the Hebrew text; this may be what Taylor thinks of Joseph — and he may be right — but nowhere does God's Word say so.

More serious is Taylor's ability to obscure the true meaning of a verse. There can be no defence for such a weakness, for the only justification for a paraphrase is its ability to make the text clear. The following examples are but a few of many:

'God's powerful method of bringing all who believe to heaven' (Romans 1:16). But the gospel is not God's method, powerful or otherwise; it is the power of God itself.

'God treats everyone the same' (Romans 2:11). God certainly does not! The word means 'partiality' and Paul, far from suggesting that God treats everyone the same, states that in God's dealings with man he is not influenced by circumstances or traditions.

'He used Christ's blood and our faith as the means of saving us from his wrath' (Romans 3:25). This is not even evangelical doctrine! Our faith is not additional to the blood of Christ; it is faith *in* the blood of Christ that saves us.

'And we know that all that happens to us is working for our good if we love God and are fitting into his plans' (Romans 8:28). 'Fitting into his plans' is a strange way even to paraphrase 'called according to his purpose'; besides, Paul does not write '*our* good', but '*the* good' — which is explained in the next verse as being conformed to the likeness of his Son. Sadly, Taylor has mutilated the whole verse.

The Living Bible is very popular, and certainly reads easily; however, accuracy is a more important requirement for any Bible translation or paraphrase, and Christians who wish to know what God says in his Word are advised to stay clear of this particular paraphrase.

The New International Version — a translation

Since its completion in 1978 the New International Version has rapidly become the translation used by a significant number of evangelicals. Translated by an international team, mainly North American, of 100 scholars who hold 'a high view of Scripture as set forth in the Westminster Confession of Faith, the Belgic Confession, and the Statement of Faith of the National Association of Evangelicals', the New International Version cannot fairly be accused of deliberately twisting Christian doctrine.

Based upon an eclectic text, it will never be accepted by those who favour the Received Text only. It can be fairly criticized for its inconsistency in the footnotes that refer to 'other ancient authorities'. For example, at John 5:3-4 these disputed verses, which have some good manuscript backing, are relegated to the footnote with the comment that 'some less important manuscripts' also add verse 4, whereas at Acts 8:37, where the textual evidence of this verse is very sparse (even the Received Text omits it) we are simply informed that 'some late manuscripts' add verse 37.

The second person singular ('thee' and 'thou') is omitted altogether, as are capital letters for pronouns relating to Deity ('his', 'him' etc.); this is a wise move. Modern language has been used in a dignified way; for example, the mysterious 'jot and tittle' of Matthew 5:18 becomes 'not the smallest letter, not the least stroke of a pen'. There are many occasions of helpful translations making clear a hard passage, for example John 1:13 becomes: 'children born not of natural descent, nor of human decision or a husband's will, but born of God'.

Of course there are inconsistences and blemishes but there are some strikingly good translations. 'Guests of the bridegroom' is a great improvement upon 'children of the bridechamber' (Matthew 9:15), and 'Prepare your minds for action' is an excellent approach to 1 Peter 1:13. Some of the harder parts of the New Testament are rendered with clarity and accuracy. The New International Version is one of very few translations to escape bondage to the inaccurate 'inspiration' of 2 Timothy 3:16 and declare, 'All Scripture is God-breathed.' Similarly 2 Peter 1:21 brings out the full force of the Greek word by saying, 'Men spoke from God as they were carried along by the Holy Spirit.'

The New King James Version — a revision

In 1982 a revision of the Authorized Version, based solely upon the Received Text, was completed and published by Thomas Nelson as the Revised Authorized Version. The same revision, with a few spelling adjustments, is now known as the New King James Version.

This is not a new translation but a revision, and therefore ideally suited to those who love the Authorized Version, or by conviction prefer the Received Text to any other, and yet who need a language update. This approach has at times limited the freedom of the revisers: for example, they have retained the old-fashioned and inaccurate 'inspiration' at 2 Timothy 3:16 instead of 'God-breathed', and 1 John 5:7 is retained in spite of the overwhelming textual evidence against it. However, in places the New King James Version allows itself the freedom of improving on the Authorized Version, so that Paul's 'God forbid' becomes 'Certainly not' and at Matthew 27:44, 'cast the same in his teeth' becomes simply 'reviled him with the same thing'. In 2 Peter 1:1 the New King James Version follows other modern translations by making clear, as the Greek does, that Christ is both God and Saviour; this is a decided improvement on the Authorized Version. So is the 'one flock' of John 10:16 instead of the 'one fold' of the Authorized Version.

The New King James Version rejects the principle of 'dynamic equivalence', according to which a modern idiom is chosen in place of one of Bible times; and opts for 'complete equivalence' instead; this is good, and an improvement even on the Authorized Version. Generally the translators have fulfilled their commitment in the production of a carefully accurate translation of their Greek text.

The use of the second person singular to refer to Deity is dropped. But this wise decision seems to cut across the use of capital letters to refer to Christ throughout, which makes for a clumsy appearance with a liberal use of 'You', 'Him', 'He', 'Who', and even 'Man'. This is not just a matter of preference because the system forces the translators to decide when and where the reference is to a person of the Godhead; this presents problems in the Old Testament prophetic references to Christ, and in the New Testament prior to the ascension of Christ. Even more debatable is the decision to place the words of Christ in red — a habit that serves little purpose and brings with it the danger of suggesting unintentionally that the actual words of Christ are more important than the rest of Scripture — fortunately non-red-letter editions are now available. The footnotes reveal references to alternative readings from the Nestle's Greek Text, the 'NU-Text', which is not wholly tied to the Received Text.

Selecting a Bible version

Where Bible translation will go from here is anyone's guess! Faced with a bewildering selection of translations, paraphrases and revisions, the average Christian is ill-equipped to make an informed judgement between them. Generally Christians use the one their church or spiritual adviser recommends — and the recommendations are not always helpful — or the one they grew up with. But there are an increasing number of Christians today who grew up with nothing. Some simply follow the trend by purchasing the one that sells best (the popularity test), others decide according to the quality of the cover or art-work inside (the picture test), whilst others go for the punchy, modern language used (the prose test), and some are merely influenced by a cheap edition (the price test)! The choice of translations creates confusion especially among new readers of the Bible, and it makes it almost impossible for some congregations to read together aloud in worship. Sadly also, the choice of translation or paraphrase often becomes a test of orthodoxy and therefore of fellowship.

In the attempt to persuade a generation of non-readers to read the Bible there is a danger of being more concerned with those who read it than those who wrote it. To a point it is true that the Bible, written long ago in cultures very different from our own, requires some understanding of its context. That is where the sermon and Bible study helps should assist us. But the claim that the Bible has a different 'voltage' from today and therefore requires a 'transformer' has led some to conclude that communicating the message is more important than accuracy of translation. This is a false distinction and must be resisted. The translator must never forget that he is responsible for the text of Scripture, not its meaning. To translate the 'Sabbath day's journey' (Acts 1:12) by 'about a kilometre' (Good News Bible), or 'the half mile' (Living Bible), is to reduce the Bible to a flat, colourless and cultureless technical handbook; it may also obscure a very important point of application. The New International Version is wise to give us a footnote that informs the reader of the modern equivalent. It is becoming popular to produce Bible translations for small specialist groups: children, teenagers, students, women, the handicapped, immigrants, prisoners, the sick, members of the armed forces — we even have audio Scriptures.

No translation can translate exactly word for word without it becoming meaningless and unreadable. Dr Fisher, in *The New Testament Student and Bible Translation* , provides an example of a literal translation of Genesis 33:14: 'As for me, let me lead my gentleness to the foot of the business which is to my face and to the foot of the children that I shall come to my lord to Seir.' Similarly Genesis 34:26 literally speaks of the 'mouth of the sword', but the 'edge of the sword' is more sensible. A good translation will stay as close as possible to the words of the original and will avoid interpreting or explaining a difficult passage. The translator translates; the expositor explains. However, the translator must be aware when a word in the original has a different meaning depending upon the context in which it is used.

In an excellent article in the Spring 1992 issue of *Foundations*, the theological journal of the British Evangelical Council, Robert Sheehan looked at the different approaches to Bible translation and argued the case for what he called 'principled progressives'. His starting-point is that when God revealed his words to men, he did so through writers who used the common language of the people among whom they lived. The New Testament, for example, is written not in classical Attic Greek, but in the Koine Greek — the language of the people. Therefore translation must be in the language of today and not of yesterday. However, this does not mean that we convert chariots into tanks and bows into machine guns! We must translate what Isaiah or Paul said then, not how they would have said it now. A translation must be careful in at least five areas.

1. The Hebrew, Aramaic and Greek of the original text must be turned into an English that follows normal rules of grammar. There are, for example, Greek words that can be left untranslated; the Authorized Version does this many times.

2. A literal word-for-word translation should be used wherever possible. This ensures accuracy to the original, but it must allow for the fact that one Hebrew or Greek word may have many different meanings.

3. Technical words, like propitiation, atonement and justification must be kept.

4. Modern English usage replaces the second person singular. The argument in favour of 'thee' and 'thou' as a reverent or respectful way of addressing Deity is not a biblical argument; neither the Hebrew nor the Greek makes such a distinction. In the

New Testament even the devil is addressed in the second person singular, 'thou'!

5. Cultural references should be retained wherever possible. In other words, there is little point in putting modern equivalents in place of shekels and denarii since money values change rapidly — though there is a case for weights and measures to be updated, or at least for a simple conversion table to be included in all modern Bibles.

Sooner or later we must come to an end of translations into English. Ideally a translation that shows the careful accuracy of the New King James Version together with the freedom to consult a wider text-choice and the abandoning of capitals for the Deity, as is found in the New International Version, would provide an excellent Bible for evangelical Christians. But that may be a dream too unreal to hope for its fulfilment.

14.
How we should understand the Bible

The Bible is a box of treasure. It is full of things of great value but it requires a key to unlock it. The key to unlock the Bible is within the reach of everyone and not just a special group of people with expert training, although training and experience certainly help us to use the key with greater ease and accuracy. This key is knowing the principles of interpreting the Bible, or hermeneutics. 'Hermeneutics' comes from a Greek word meaning 'interpreter'.

Many people forget that the Bible, like any other book, must be understood according to certain rules; most of these rules we are using every day when we read books, or letters, or even a newspaper. When a friend tells us that she 'cried all night', or the radio claims that 'The whole town was angry at the news', we do not seriously imagine that our friend sobbed without interruption for eight hours, or that there was not even one person in the town who was not pleased with the news that annoyed most of the citizens. We have used the key of hermeneutics to unlock the statements made. The Bible, as a book, must be interpreted sensibly, and as God's book it must be interpreted spiritually.

There is one important reason why accurate principles of interpretation are of particular concern to the evangelical. The higher our claim for the Bible, the more careful we must be to understand it correctly. We rightly complain about the critic who denies the truth of the Bible and therefore destroys its message, but the evangelical can do exactly the same by breaking all the rules of interpretation and making the Bible say what he wants it to say. As society changes its values, or the Christian finds himself living in a different culture, it is all too easy to allow these changes to influence the way we understand the Bible. In other words, we begin to make the Bible fit into our way of thinking instead of allowing it to speak for itself.

Writing in *Hermeneutics, Authority and Canon*, Don Carson expresses his concern in this way: 'Some of us, who would never dream of formally disentangling some parts of the Bible from the rest and declaring them less authoritative than other parts, can by exegetical ingenuity get the Scriptures to say just about whatever we want — and this we thunder to the age as if it were a prophetic word, when it is little more than the message of the age bounced off Holy Scripture' (p.47). More effectively the prophet Jeremiah complains about the same thing: 'How can you say, "We are wise, for we have the law of the Lord", when actually the lying pen of the scribes has handled it falsely?' (Jeremiah 8:8).

Many of the attacks made upon the Bible by its critics are due to a misunderstanding of proper interpretation. An obvious and simple example is when people criticize the Bible for being unscientific when it speaks of the sun rising and setting (for example, in Genesis 15:12,17; 19:23). We all know that this is a convenient expression that is used the world over, and it is not intended as a scientific description of the relationship of the sun to the earth. The interpretation of Scripture is a vital subject; it is as important as the doctrine of verbal inerrancy itself. There is no value in being able to say, 'These are the words of God,' if we then proceed to interpret them in a way directly the opposite of God's intention. We are answerable to God if we abuse his Word in this way.

In the history of the Christian church there have been, sadly, too many leaders who have interpreted Scripture in a fanciful or ridiculous way and, as a result, have completely missed its clear teaching. Before the Reformation in the sixteenth century it was commonplace for interpreters of the Bible to understand it in a fourfold way (this is sometimes known as the 'four-horse chariot'): literal, or historical, which was the plain sense; allegorical, or spiritual, and therefore for many, the most important meaning; tropological, which was the moral application; and anagogical, or analogical, which was the mystical meaning, using the Bible as types and allegories. Some rode this 'chariot' recklessly and played havoc with Scripture. During the Middle Ages the Bible was used, if at all, merely to illustrate what the church believed. As Hugo St Victor expressed it, 'Learn first what you should believe and then go to the Bible to find it there.'

The sixteenth-century Reformers rejected this approach and

emphasized that the Scripture should determine what the church believes and teaches. They taught an important principle that Scripture must interpret Scripture and therefore all that we believe must conform to the teaching of the whole Bible. The Reformers looked first for the literal or historical meaning of Scripture and only for an allegorical interpretation where this was allowed by Scripture itself.

Today the approach to understanding Scripture is divided into that of the church of Rome, which insists on the church as the highest authority even above Scripture; the liberal theologian, who places reason as the final court of appeal; and the evangelical, who submits all things to the ultimate authority of the Word of God. Don Carson warns of the danger when as evangelicals we 'have hungered to be masters of the Word much more than we have hungered to be mastered by it'.

Hermeneutics is not a matter of theory; it always has a practical application. Hermeneutics is the servant of exegesis. 'Exegesis' comes from another Greek word meaning 'to explain'. The preacher and Bible teacher are exegetes because they must explain the message of the Bible and apply it to the lives of those listening. But the exegete cannot explain or apply the Scripture unless he has clear principles for interpreting or understanding it. In other words, you cannot be involved in exegesis unless you first understand hermeneutics.

Much of the Bible is plain, and anyone with a little common sense can understand it, but some of it is hard to grasp, and there is at times a fuller or deeper meaning that is not immediately obvious. Both the prophet Isaiah and our Lord reminded us that it is one thing to hear the Word of God, but quite another to understand it (Isaiah 6:9-10; Matthew 13:13-15). An Amish bishop is on record as saying, 'There are no mysteries in the Bible. God never made no mysteries. But, brethren, there are some tight points'! Hermeneutics helps us not only in the plain areas, to keep them plain, but also in those 'tight points', so that we shall not compound difficulties with our foolishness.

Perhaps the simplest way of dealing with this subject is to set out a number of basic questions that we should ask whenever we want to understand a passage, or even a single verse, of the Bible.

What kind of passage is this?

Is it history?

If a passage of Scripture is clearly historical then we must remember that its purpose is to describe things that actually happened, and the facts of the Bible are without error. Generally it is not difficult to know which passages are historical and which are not. For example, it could hardly be denied that the stories of the various kings of Israel and Judah are expected to be taken as actual accounts of their lives; if anyone wants to deny this, the responsibility is his to prove that they are not intended as true stories. On the other hand, it is equally clear that the story told by Jotham in Judges 9:8-15 is in picture language, and it would be a foolish person who criticized the Bible, or Jotham, for thinking that the trees actually held a conversation.

We should always decide on the answer to this first question before we go any further; this could save a lot of problems later. When we turn to the first chapter of Genesis, or the book of Jonah, our first question must not be, 'How can I fit this into what some modern scientists say?' but, 'Is this written as history?' The answer to that last question must be 'Yes'. The entire book of Genesis is written in the form of history. The Jews never doubted it, and neither did the Christian church until 150 years ago. We cannot pick and choose to suit our convenience. If someone says Genesis 1 and 2 are poetry or 'myth' then why not say the same about the story of Babel, or the flood, or Abraham, Isaac and Jacob, or, in the book of Exodus, the escape from Egypt, or the manna in the wilderness? No one has yet shown where in Genesis it is clearly no longer poetic and certainly historic. The simple fact is that, like the book of Jonah, it is all written as history — believe it or not.

It is not our concern here to discuss the so-called scientific problems of biblical creation, or how a man could stay alive inside a great fish; that has nothing to do with hermeneutics. The evangelical who relies upon the argument that Genesis 1 and 2 (or 3 and 4) are poetic and not historical has abandoned sound principles of interpretation in order to avoid what appears to be a scientific problem; why then does he not abandon Jonah as well — or even the resurrection of Christ?

Similarly, it is dangerous for the evangelical to doubt the

historical fact of some miracles by claiming they could be interpreted in another way. Some refer, for example, to the story of Peter
and the tax money in Matthew 17:24-27. There are similar stories,
outside the Bible, of treasure being found in fish; since we are not
actually told that Peter carried out the instruction given by Christ,
some conclude that our Lord may have been just playfully referring
to these stories and was not giving Peter a command to go fishing for
the tax money. But this is exactly the approach made by the critics
who deny the miracles just because they are miracles. In fact this
passage is written as plain history, it has generally been accepted as
plain history by the Christian church, and it really makes no sense
at all unless Peter actually went and found the tax money in a fish.
Of course it is possible that Jesus was not giving Peter a literal
command to go fishing, but such a view is not the natural or obvious
reading of the passage. We must insist upon good reasons and clear
evidence before we depart from the natural and obvious meaning,
and a few pagan or Jewish stories about treasure being found inside
fish is hardly clear evidence. This question, 'Is the passage historical?' is one of the most important questions to answer.

Is it poetry?

As we have already seen, some passages of the Bible are poetical and
we shall not therefore look for detailed accuracy in matters of fact.
If we turn to Psalm 104, Job 38, or Isaiah 40: 12-15 we have what
are clearly poetic descriptions of creation. The words and phrases
are very different from Genesis and no one could seriously suggest
that the Bible views God as riding on the clouds like a man in a
chariot (Psalm 104:3), or stopping the oceans with immense doors
(Job 38:8), or weighing the mountains in a huge pair of scales (Isaiah
40:12). This language is poetic and nothing like it is found in the
historical Genesis account.

In the sixteenth century, when Galileo discovered that the earth
revolved around the sun, he was contradicted by church leaders on
the basis that Psalm 93:1 (see also 96:10; 104:5) claimed, 'The
world is firmly established, it will not be moved'! But this was a sad
ignorance of the fact that these passages are written in poetic style
and are intended only to imply the certainty of God's plans and
God's laws both for man and his creation. We must always be ready
to recognize poetry in the Bible.

Is it prophecy?

Understanding prophecy is perhaps the most difficult part of Bible interpretation, and the moment we know that a passage is prophetic we shall be looking out for certain things. Remember, prophecy is not merely telling the future (fore-telling) but telling God's word for the day in which the prophet lived (forth-telling). Poetry played a large part in the language of the prophets and we are wise not to take all their words as having a literal fulfilment. We shall return to this later in the chapter, but there is another significant question to answer whenever we come to a passage of prophecy, and this the matter of timing: when will this prophecy be fulfilled?

Unfortunately there are at least six possibilities in answering this question whenever we come to a passage of prophecy in the Old Testament:

It may refer to what God is going to do in the prophet's own day, and no more than this.

It may refer to what God is going to do later on in the Old Testament beyond the prophet's own day. Some of Isaiah's prophecies, for example, look on to the return from exile under Cyrus, 150 years later.

The prophet may be referring to what will happen when Christ comes and brings in the 'gospel age'. This is clearly the case in Jeremiah 31:31-33 for example.

Depending upon your millennial view of the second coming of Christ, the prophecy may refer to the thousand years when he will reign in Jerusalem over a willingly submissive people. That is the pre-millennial view. Or it may refer to the golden age of gospel success just before the return of Christ in glory. That is the post-millennial view. Or it may refer to heaven. Isaiah 11 and 35 are two passages that can be understood in each of the last three ways, depending upon your view of end-time fulfilment of prophecy.

This is a difficult matter at times, but we have no alternative to working hard at the passage if we are to understand what God is saying to us today.

Closely connected with the prophetic language of Isaiah or Ezekiel in the Old Testament is the language of John's Revelation in the New Testament. This also is a form of prophecy, and

Revelation is a book full of pictures and symbols. Seven is a number of perfection, 144,000 a symbol of completeness and so on. In a book so full of pictures and symbols it is unwise to take any of the numbers as necessarily representing a fixed amount, either of people or years. Once again we cannot pick and choose; if we take almost all the numbers as symbols, it is inconsistent hermeneutics to take an occasional one literally, merely because it suits our doctrine.

A few simple rules will help us when faced with prophecy in Scripture.

1. What is the context? Who was the prophet? To whom was he speaking? What was happening in the world around him at the time?

2. What was the relevance of the prophecy to the prophet's own day? Always ask this question before you run ahead to see if there is something for our own day there as well.

3. Is there a future fulfilment, as in Isaiah 9, 53 and Micah 5? Sometimes there is both an immediate and a future fulfilment.

4. Is the prophecy of a future fulfilment conditional? Micah warned Jerusalem of a judgement that would come if the city did not repent (Jeremiah 26:17-19), and Jonah's warnings to Nineveh were conditional upon the refusal of the inhabitants to repent.

5. Is the language that of poetry or is it to be taken literally? This is often one of the hardest questions to answer and we must interpret carefully. Isaiah's picture in chapter 11 of the wolf and lamb, leopard and kid, lion and calf and the young boy refers to the benefits of Christ's gospel. But whenever you believe it will be fulfilled — during or at the end of the gospel age, or in heaven — it is surely to be seen as poetry; our task is to ask what that kind of language means in its fulfilment.

6. The most important principle of all that must govern our understanding of Old Testament prophecy is the way it is used in the New Testament. The New Testament must always be our guide in interpreting Old Testament prophecy.

It is in this way that we can understand Isaiah 9:7. The passage in Isaiah 9:2-7 is a prophecy of the coming Messiah, some 700 years before the event. From the words in verse 7 we might have expected our Lord literally to revive the monarchy in Israel and reign as king in Jerusalem; in fact this is exactly how many Jews did understand it. However, because we are able to look back at the actual fulfilment of Isaiah 9:7 we can say that those words have a spiritual fulfilment and not a literal historical fulfilment. This is a warning to be careful when we expect a literal historical fulfilment of other prophecies. Sometimes we are right to expect a literal historical fulfilment, but not always. Remember that important principle of the Reformers: the whole of Scripture must be our guide.

Another example is found in Joel 2. Our understanding of this chapter is governed by its fulfilment in Acts 2. According to Peter, Joel 2:28-32 is a prophecy of the gift of the Holy Spirit at Pentecost (compare Acts 2:14-21). This being so, the situation described in Joel 2:1-27 must be a picture of our Lord's earthly ministry, because verse 28 says, 'And afterwards...' and then follows the description Peter quoted at Pentecost. For the same reason the prophecy of Joel 3 must begin to be fulfilled at Pentecost, because Joel 3:1 says, 'In those days and at that time...' Since we are compelled by the New Testament to understand Joel 2 in a spiritual way, referring to Christ and his church, it is only consistent hermeneutics that we also interpret chapter 3 spiritually as referring to the church and the gospel age up to the Day of Judgement.

Or again, in Amos 9:11-12 we have references to God repairing and rebuilding 'David's fallen tent' so that it may possess the 'remnant of Edom and all the nations that bear my name'. What does that mean? In Acts 15:16-17 James leaves us in no doubt; he told the Council at Jerusalem that it was fulfilled when the gospel was given to the Gentiles.

These brief illustrations should help us in our interpretation of many other Old Testament prophetic passages. Remember, the New Testament must be our guide, and our understanding must be consistent with the whole Bible.

What is the context?

One of the greatest dangers when using the Bible is to take a verse or phrase or passage out of its context. No text ever gains anything from being taken out of its context. Every word of the Bible has three contexts. We may think of these as the room, the house, and the street in which the word lives.

The room — the biblical context

Always read a verse and the passage around it; take care not to be influenced too much by the chapter and verse divisions of the Bible. As we saw in chapter 12, they are not part of the God-breathed Scripture and are often artificial.

A number of questions must be asked in this room: 'To whom is the writer speaking? Christians or non-Christians? Young or old? Obedient or disobedient?' For example, the familiar verse used to encourage the unbeliever to 'open the door of his heart and let Jesus in' is found in Revelation 3:20: 'Here I am! I stand at the door and knock. If anyone hears my voice and opens the door, I will come in and eat with him, and he with me.' But the context leaves us in no doubt that it is a backsliding Christian church that is being addressed here, not the unbeliever. We must never say, 'But it is just as relevant for the unbeliever,' unless we can prove this to be so by some other Scripture. In fact it is doubtful whether God ever speaks in such pleading terms to the unbeliever. He *commands* men to repent.

Again we must ask, 'Do the verses round about help to explain this one?' If we take a phrase out of its context, Joshua 24:15 provides us with a wonderful challenge for the close of an evangelistic service: 'Choose for yourselves this day whom you will serve.' We may say, 'The choice is yours, Christ or the world.' But in fact that is not what Joshua is saying at all. He is speaking to those who have already rejected the Lord, and his challenge is this: 'Go home and choose which one of the idols of the other nations you will follow.' The fact that it is a 'good text' is no reason for us to misuse it. Always read a verse in its biblical context — the verses and chapters around it.

Choosing a 'good text' can be a great snare for evangelicals. The Christian who stumbles across John 13:27, 'What you are about to do, do quickly', should read the context before he rushes out to put into practice something he thinks Christ wants him to do; our Lord was referring to Judas's treacherous betrayal!

The house — the historical context.

When reading a passage of the Bible always ask, 'What was happening in the world around Palestine at this time?' Many of the prophecies of Isaiah or Jeremiah make little sense until we become aware of the threats being made by Assyria, Syria or Babylon. Similarly, many incidents in the Gospels, Luke 2:1-3 for example, lose much of their meaning if we do not understand that Rome was the governing nation and kept a strong army of occupation in Palestine. The 'second mile' of Matthew 5:41 is a direct reference to the right of the Roman legionary to compel an Israelite to carry his pack for one mile. Many of the psalms become more vivid when we know, for example, that David wrote them while he was an exile in the desert with King Saul hunting him to kill him. The answer to this historical question is often found in the Bible itself, so we do not require a great knowledge of ancient history, but a good Bible commentary or Bible dictionary will certainly help.

The street — the local customs of the day

This is the cultural context. So much of the Bible involves people who lived in sheep-rearing or fishing communities and it may be very hard for a businessman in a modern city to understand this way of life. Passages like Psalm 23 and John 10:1-16 become much more full of meaning when we understand the foolish and helpless nature of sheep and the caring of a good shepherd. Our Lord's parables

'Much of the Bible involves people who lived in ... sheep-rearing communities'

about separating sheep from goats, or wheat from tares, take on a greater significance when we realize how similar in appearance are eastern sheep and goats, and how hard it is to distinguish some kinds of weeds from the real crop.

A little knowledge of the seven cities referred to in Revelation 2-3 will make the message to the church in each city so much more vivid. For example, Laodicea (Revelation 3:14-22) piped its water into the city from distant hot springs and it therefore arrived lukewarm (v. 16); it was also a wealthy banking city (v. 17) and boasted an eye hospital producing a special eye ointment (vv. 17-18).

Even more important, such knowledge of local conditions can avoid misunderstandings. In chapter 6 we referred to a passage in Matthew 16 that is often misunderstood and wrongly applied. When we are aware of the custom of presenting a scribe with a key as a symbol of his office in interpreting the law, we are able to understand the whole passage correctly. In the same way, in Ruth 4:8 the short sentence, 'And he removed his sandal,' would make no sense at all if we did not know of the local custom at that time; in this case the Bible is its own interpreter and explains the custom in verse 7.

The three contexts of every Bible verse are the biblical room, the historical house and the street of local conditions. The first is essential; the other two are very helpful. But if a Christian does not have access to books that will help him to understand the house and the street, he will still be able to understand God's Word and benefit from it providing he stays in the biblical room.

What is the plain meaning?

After we have asked, 'What kind of passage is this?' and 'What is the context?' our next question is 'What is the plain meaning of this passage?' This is really an obvious question, but many Christians are so busy looking for problems or hidden meanings that they forget to ask it. Sometimes the question is put in a different way: 'What is the grammatical sense? What do the words mean?' To answer this question it is essential that you have an accurate translation in front of you and not a paraphrase. As we saw in chapter 13, a translation attempts to give us what the original author actually wrote; it translates the words. But a paraphrase attempts to give us what the original author really meant; it translates thoughts. It must be admitted that no translation is completely free from some paraphrasing; however, we must always distinguish between the translation and the paraphrase. The evangelical should never use a paraphrase for serious study because hermeneutics is concerned with accuracy.

If you do not know Hebrew or Greek, you will have to trust that the translators have given an accurate translation of the grammar into your own language. Every language has its own rules of grammar and you must interpret the Bible according to those rules. For example, many young Christians find difficulty in 1 John 3:9 because it may appear from some translations that to commit one sin means you are not a Christian. However, the New International Version helpfully translates the first part of this verse: 'No one who is born of God will continue to sin.' The Greek verb used is in what we call a 'present continuous' tense and it would be more correct to translate it: 'No one born of God goes on and on committing sin as a way of life,' but this is a paraphrase! The New American Standard Bible tries to bring out the meaning of the verb with: 'No one who is born of God practises sin.'

When faced with John 20:28, those who deny that Jesus was truly God claim that Thomas looked to Christ and said, 'My Lord,' then looked to heaven and said, 'My God'. But the plain grammatical meaning of the sentence is that Thomas addressed both statements to Christ and clearly Thomas believed Christ was God. We can only change the obvious sense if we have clear scriptural authority for doing so. Understanding the Bible requires a fair amount of common sense, as well as spiritual discernment. Does Luke 10:7 forbid door-to-door evangelism? Or does Psalm 115:16 forbid space exploration? Context and common sense should provide us with an answer. This leads us to ask a further question.

What do the words really mean?

Occasional problems arise in understanding a passage because we do not really know what a particular word means. There are seven questions we can ask about the words used in a passage.

1. What is the normal meaning of the word?

A good Bible concordance is essential for this. Sometimes knowing
the actual meaning of words can make our understanding of a
passage so much more valuable. In John 21 our Lord asked Peter
three times if he loved him. Peter was eager to express his love and
in verse 17 replied, 'Lord, you know all things; you know that I love
you.' In the Greek Peter used two different words for 'know'. The
first meant, 'You know everything perfectly because of who you
are,' while the second meant, 'You know by experience that I love
you.'

Sometimes the next six questions have to be asked in order to find
the answer to this first one. *Strong's Exhaustive Concordance of the
Bible* is an excellent, though expensive, concordance because it
provides the basic meaning of virtually every word in the Bible; one
problem for some is the fact that it is based upon the Authorized
Version of the Bible.

2. How are the words used in this passage?

Sometimes a word is used with a slightly different emphasis
according to the purpose of the speaker or writer. A good example
of this is found in our Lord's words in Luke 14:26: 'If anyone comes
to me, and does not hate his father and mother, his wife and children,
his brothers and sisters — yes, and even his own life — he cannot
be my disciple.' Can it really be that the Saviour encourages bitter
hatred among his disciples?

While it is true that the word normally carries the idea of
detesting a thing, it can also have a use that means to disregard or
overlook something in preference to something else. The same word
is used in Luke 16:13, where Christ taught that a man cannot have
two masters, not because he will have to hate or detest one, but
because he will have to disregard or overlook one. We all know that
no man can take orders from more than one employer, no tribe can
have more than one paramount chief, no country can have more than
one king, president or prime minister. So the word 'hate' has a
different emphasis here from that which we would normally give it.
This leads us to a third question about the words.

3. How are the words used elsewhere by the same writer?

In fact we have already illustrated this by the example quoted above from Luke 16:13. It is quite obvious that a man does not have to hate one man in order to obey another, but he will certainly on occasions have to disregard the one, if the commands from the two masters conflict with each other. The obvious use of the word 'hate' in Luke 16:13 has helped us to understand the same word in Luke 14:26; at times obedience to Christ will run contrary to our desire to please our family.

In the Old Testament an example is found in Isaiah 9:6. Those who deny that Christ really is God tell us that this verse only claims the Messiah to be a mighty god and that it has no reference to Jehovah God. But a little further on in the next chapter (Isaiah 10:21) exactly the same Hebrew words, *El Gibbor*, are used — and here the context shows that they can only refer to Jehovah God. It is faulty hermeneutics to assume that Isaiah has changed the meaning of a phrase from one chapter to the next. Besides, this exact phrase, *El Gibbor*, is used nowhere else in the Old Testament and therefore we can only obtain its true application from Isaiah himself — and his use in Isaiah 10:21 leaves us in no doubt.

4. How are the words used elsewhere in the Bible?

Words have slightly different meanings and a different emphasis depending upon where they are used. I may claim that my bicycle is new. To my hearer this means that I bought it brand-new from the shop and no one has yet ridden it, whereas in fact I may simply have meant that I have just sold my old bicycle and have bought this better second-hand one. We talk about a new moon when the moon is just a thin crescent shape, but we do not expect people to believe that God makes a brand-new moon every few weeks!

With the aid of a good concordance we can follow a word through the Bible and discover its slight variations in meaning. In some older translations like the Authorized Version, the Greek word 'sarx' is translated 'flesh' fairly consistently; but the word can have different meanings. The New International Version brings this out by using such words as 'flesh', 'men', 'mankind', and 'sinful nature'. You can follow this for yourself in 1 Corinthians 15:39;

'We do not expect people to believe that God makes a brand-new moon every few weeks'

1 Peter 1:24; Luke 3:6; Galatians 5:19. To force the same meaning into each passage would be unhelpful.

5. How are the words used outside the Bible?

It is not possible for most of us to do our own research here, but commentaries may help us. Sometimes a word occurs so rarely in the Bible that it is not easy at first sight to determine its exact meaning, and sometimes an exact meaning is very important. In Philippians 2:6-7 the word 'nature' or 'form' occurs. The only other place this particular word occurs in the New Testament is in Mark 16:12. Those who deny that Christ was really God claim that the word 'form' in Philippians 2:6 means only that Christ was similar to God or like God, but that he was not really God. By looking at the use of this word outside the Bible among pagan writers, two well-known Greek scholars, Vine and Strong, claim that the word means 'the nature or essence of a thing'. So we can properly understand Philippians 2:6-7 to mean that Christ always had the true and essential nature of God and that he took upon himself the true and essential nature of a servant.

6. *What does the rest of the Bible say about this subject?*

We have already seen that the context of every verse is first of all the Bible. The best commentary upon the Bible is the Bible itself. The New Testament is therefore our infallible commentary upon the Old Testament. Sometimes we may be unsure how far we can take as statements of truth the words of an unspiritual man, such as Eliphaz, who was one of Job's critics. Certainly in Job 42:7 God condemned the general criticism and arguments of Eliphaz, but Paul quoted one of his sayings, found in Job 5:13, with approval in 1 Corinthians 3:19. That is our authority for saying that where Eliphaz speaks in harmony with the rest of Scripture he may be quoted as speaking the truth, but we dare not take his words as authoritative if they find no support anywhere else in the Bible. The Bible accurately records his words, as it does some of the words of the devil, without giving authority and truth to them.

Many Christians condemn Lot for his choice of the fertile valley and his decision to settle in Sodom; they describe the sins of Sodom and conclude that Lot committed them all. But Peter calls him a 'righteous' man who was exhausted and worn out by the ungodly conduct of the men of Sodom (2 Peter 2:7-8). We must always try to find out what else the Bible teaches about the subject contained in a particular verse.

Sometimes the context of the verse does not help us. The book of Proverbs is a collection of wise sayings and quite often the surrounding verses, or even the chapter, do not say anything to help us on that subject. We must immediately ask, 'Where else does the Bible speak on this subject?' Always interpret the Bible consistently with itself. If we find one passage seemingly contradicting another, then it is our interpretation that is at fault, not the Bible.

A passage that is difficult to understand must be interpreted in the light of what is clear. Colossians 1:22-23 may seem to teach that our final security and salvation are dependent upon our ability to continue faithful. But we have only to turn to John 10:28 and Romans 8:38-39 to see how eternally secure the Christian really is. Paul is not contradicting himself in Colossians 1; he is challenging the Colossians to see whether or not they really have saving faith in Christ. This is an example of how we have allowed Scripture to govern our interpretation of Scripture.

7. What do the commentaries say?

We are not to be slaves to what other men think, but we should not be indifferent to their conclusions either. Every Christian should try to obtain a reliable evangelical commentary on the Bible. There are some excellent modern commentaries today on individual books of the Bible. It is virtually impossible to find a one-volume Bible commentary that will adequately deal with all the problem verses you need some help with. But take advice from a trusted Christian leader; don't just browse in the local Christian bookshop and pick up what looks most attractive. A commentary will not do all our work for us, but it will steer us into the right path, and help us to avoid making mistakes in our hermeneutics.

Figures of speech

When we say that the Bible is literally true we do not mean that every word has a literal interpretation. Like any other book, the Bible uses forms of speech, and recognizing these forms of speech is essential to a proper understanding of Scripture.

Simile

A simile is a vivid yet simple comparison of one thing with another. Peter uses a simile in 1 Peter 5:8: 'Your enemy the devil prowls around like a roaring lion.' The devil is not literally a lion; he is like a lion in his fierce attack upon believers.

Metaphor

A metaphor is the description of something by the use of words that do not literally apply to it. In a metaphor the words 'like' and 'as' are omitted and something is described as if it really was something else. For example, in Luke 13:32 our Lord does not say that Herod is *like* a fox but, in order to make his description stronger, he uses a metaphor and says that Herod *is* a fox. Similarly, the reference to the 'floodgates of the heavens' in Genesis 7:11 is a metaphor; it would be ridiculous to suggest Moses thought of heaven as having literal gates that could be shut and then opened to let the rain out. If you turn to Psalm 18:2 you will find five metaphors in this one verse.

Allegory

An allegory is a long metaphor in the form of a story; it describes one subject in words that more exactly belong to another. The passage we used earlier in this chapter from Judges 9:8-15 is an allegory. When we know this, we shall avoid thinking that Jotham really believed the trees talked together. When in John 10:1-16 our Lord spoke of himself in terms of the Good Shepherd, he was using an allegory. Paul used an allegory in Galatians 4:21-31 where he writes about Sarah and Hagar; in fact in verse 24 he says, 'These things may be taken figuratively,' and the Greek word he uses is the very word from which we get our word 'allegory'. We are at liberty to use Bible stores as allegories, just as Paul did, but when we do, we must beware of using them to prove a point. Allegories are only illustrations; they are not our authority. The rule for the use of illustrations applies equally to allegories. We shall deal with this important issue later in this chapter when we consider how we can use our Old Testament.

Anthropomorphism

This is a long word made up from two Greek words and it means 'to give something the characteristics of a man'. When we are speaking of spiritual things we have to use human language. We can only understand about God by using human words, and we frequently refer to God as if he had the ordinary characteristics of a man. In fact, of course, he is far greater than man. Isaiah 59:1 provides us with a good illustration of anthropomorphism: 'Surely the arm of the Lord is not too short to save, nor his ear too dull to hear.' We would be ignorant of the rules of hermeneutics if we felt that from this verse we had to believe God had a huge hand and ear! There is a similar example in James 5:4 which refers to 'the ears of the Lord Almighty'.

Hyperbole

We all use hyperbole in our everyday speech; hyperbole is a great exaggeration used to make our statement more forceful. When a child runs home and declares, 'There were millions of people at church this morning,' we do not punish him for lying because we know he is using a hyperbole. God used a hyperbole to Abraham when he promised that the Israelites would be as numerous 'as the dust of the earth' (Genesis 13:16). Similarly, in Judges 7:12 the camels of the armies of the Midianites and Amalekites 'could no more be counted than the sand on the seashore'. In Deuteronomy 1:28 the spies reported that the cities of the Amorites were large 'with walls up to the sky'. The use of hyperbole is common, especially in the Old Testament.

Another example of hyperbole is used by our Lord himself in Matthew 24:2 (and Luke 19:44). He warned that the day would come when the great stones of Herod's temple would be broken down and 'Not one stone here will be left on another.' This prophecy was fulfilled by the Roman army in A.D. 70, but anyone may go to Jerusalem today and see the Wailing Wall, which is the only remaining part of Herod's temple; to claim our Lord was in error because a few stones are still standing is to misunderstand his language. He used hyperbole to emphasize the complete and terrible destruction of the city.

Litotes

Litotes is not a well-known figure of speech, but it is well used and to recognize it can avoid misunderstanding the Bible. Litotes is a way of confirming the truth of something by denying its opposite. For example, if I am asked whether I plan to go out today, I may simply say 'yes', or I may use litotes and say, 'I certainly will not stay indoors.' I have said 'Yes', by saying 'No' to the opposite.

A useful example of how important it can be to recognize litotes is found in Revelation 3:5. Some Christians think that the expression, 'I will never erase his name from the book of life,' implies that it is possible for a Christian to lose his salvation and that God actually blots out his name from the book of life; this interpretation is very hard to accept in the light of the clear statements in John 10:28 and Romans 8:33-39, and the equally clear emphasis of the whole of the Bible that nothing can ever separate us from the love of Christ. The book of Revelation is full of figures of speech and this phrase is simply an example of litotes: God is not saying that he ever would erase our names from the book of life; in fact he is confirming the impossibility of this by saying 'No' to the opposite.

Apocalyptic language

Some of the pictures that are used in Bible books that particularly refer to the end of time, like Ezekiel, Daniel and Revelation, are strange and often hard for us to understand. This is referred to as 'apocalyptic' language. That word comes from a Greek verb meaning 'to reveal' or 'bring to light'. Actually you may think the passage does anything but reveal or bring to light! However, we often complicate these Bible pictures. Sometimes, and this is especially true in some of the visions of Daniel, the explanation is given (see Daniel 7:23; 8:19, for example). But sometimes we are left wondering. A wise principle is to accept that we do not have to understand every detail of these visions and dreams.

It is best to think of them as flash-cards that are intended to create an impression of power, or glory, or terror, or judgement; our task is to decide first what that impression is. The book of Revelation can lose much of its confusion and gain deep significance if we look at it in this way. We can often lose the overall impression because we are too busy examining the detail.

This is not to say that all the apocalyptic passages should be easy to understand; they are not! But they can still be very meaningful. When it comes to apocalyptic passages, our Amish bishop was not wholly correct: not only are there 'some tight points', but there are some mysteries also.

Understanding the parables

A parable is another figure of speech, and parables, especially those taught by our Lord, are frequently misinterpreted. The Greek word for 'parable' means 'to throw or place by the side of something'. Someone has described them as earthly stories with a heavenly meaning. Most of the prophets used parables but we shall limit our comments to those of Christ. In recent years there has been a lot of discussion about how we should interpret the parables of Christ, but let us begin with a little history!

From the early days of the Christian church there was a desire to get as much out of the parables as possible and the system of 'allegorizing' them was popular; in fact, under the influence of Greek philosophy it was not only the parables that were allegorized, but the whole Bible and especially the Old Testament. This meant, for example, reading spiritual lessons from every part of a parable. Augustine, who was bishop at Hippo in North Africa from 396 to 430, set the pace for this approach to the parables. In his interpretation of the Good Samaritan (Luke 10:30-37), the wounded man is Adam; Jerusalem is heaven; the thieves represent the devil and his agents; the priest and Levite are the Old Testament law, which cannot save; the Samaritan is Christ ,who alone can save; the inn is the church; and the innkeeper is the apostle Paul! Others added that the oil and wine represent baptism and the Lord's Supper — or was it the two coins that represent these?

This approach to the parables has continued right up to the present day, with occasional voices complaining that it is not a correct method. The problem with treating the parables like this is that no two interpreters agree on the details, and it leaves us free to read anything we wish into the parables. Our danger in interpreting parables is always one of extremes: either we can look for a significance in every detail, forgetting that, as with any story used as an illustration, there have to be details that simply help the narrative along, or we can be so general that we claim there is one lesson alone to be learnt from every parable.

Here are a few important facts to remember when we read a parable.

Parables are simple stories, but have hidden meanings

We must not forget what our Lord himself said about his parables in Mark 4:11-12, quoting from Isaiah 6: 'The secret of the kingdom of God has been given to you. But to those on the outside everything is said in parables so that "they may be ever seeing but never perceiving, and ever hearing but never understanding; otherwise they might turn and be forgiven".' Later we read, 'With many similar parables Jesus spoke the word to them, as much as they could understand. He did not say anything to them without using a parable. But when he was alone with his own disciples, he explained everything' (vv. 33-34). In other words, some things are hidden within parables that will only be plain to those with spiritual understanding. That is why our Lord expected his disciples to be able to understand the parables. This does not mean we can let our imagination run wild, which is what Augustine and many after him have done.

The context is important

To whom was Jesus speaking? Why? What was the result? Sometimes the context gives us the explanation of the parable; this is true of the parable of the seeds in Luke 8:5-15, where our Lord gave his disciples a full interpretation and at the same time left us with some important guidelines as to how parables should be understood. Sometimes the context directs our attention to the exact purpose of the parable; this happens in the parable of the Good Samaritan, which answered the question raised in Luke 10:29. In each case we can assume that our Lord has given an explanation of those parts of the parable that matter most.

Generally there is one main point to each parable

This is a wise rule to start with, even though there may be secondary lessons in a parable. Some parables are simple and require little explanation. For example, the parable of the lost sheep in Luke 15:3-7 teaches the one point that there is rejoicing in heaven over each sinner who repents (v. 7). We may also see that there is care by the shepherd who comes looking for the lost sheep, but that is a subsidiary lesson. We cannot go further, or else we might complain at his neglect of the other ninety-nine!

There are also more complex parables that are explained for us. The parable of the sower is one example of this (Mark 4). We are unwise to go beyond the interpretation our Lord himself gives and we may assume that he has given us all we need to know. There are also complex parables that are not explained. An example of this type is found in the parable of the talents in Luke 19:12-27, where we have a number of characters in the story, each of which has to be applied: the nobleman, the servants — some good and some bad — and the citizens, who were all bad. The context helps us here, since it was given just before the triumphal entry into Jerusalem.

Do not try to press every point of a parable

The great danger of the popular way of spiritualizing (or allegorizing) every part of a parable is that we are left with some parts of the parables that are highly embarrassing if we try to apply them. Our Lord used everyday and familiar situations in his parables. When he referred to slavery or a dishonest steward he was not commenting upon the morality of these situations; they were merely illustrations. Similarly our Lord does not commend the actions of an unjust judge, or compare him with God! The point of the story relates not to the judge, but to the woman who kept on and on with her request.

We have not covered all the figures of speech used in the Bible, and the whole subject is not as difficult as it may appear. Common sense solves most of our problems in interpreting figures of speech. But we must be aware of them.

Understanding the New Testament letters

There are twenty-one letters (epistles) in the New Testament, and these are possibly the most used part of our Bible. It is from these letters that we draw most of our Christian doctrine.

1. Remember they are letters

God chose this way to teach us — not Calvin's *Institutes of the Christian Religion*, but Paul's letters.

'After this letter has been read to you' (Colossians 4:16).
'Have this letter read to all the brothers' (1 Thessalonians 5:27).
'The distinguishing mark in all my letters' (2 Thessalonians 3:17).
'[Paul] writes the same way in all his letters' (2 Peter 3:16).

We need to ask, 'Who were the people he was writing to? What kind of Christians were they? Where did they live? What kind of society was it? When did he write? (You can locate most letters in the Acts of the Apostles.) Why did he write? What were the particular problems?' (See, for example, 1 Corinthians 1:11; 3:3; 5:1-2; 7:1; 11:17; 15:12; 16:1. Issues the church had written about: 1 Thessalonians 4:9; 4:13; 5:1).

Letters are always meant to be understood; go first for the obvious meaning, though there are 'some things that are hard to understand' (2 Peter 3:16). They are not books of systematic theology but personal letters, often informal, and were intended to be read at one sitting! The New Testament letters throb with life and reality. They are not the visionary meditations of a recluse; the writers were men involved with the churches every day. Study carefully those final greetings, for example in Romans 16 and Galatians 4.

2. Look for the big themes

These letters were never meant to be dissected word by word, or even sentence by sentence. What was the writer saying to his day? What has this to say to us? Was there one, or more, big issue that concerned the writer? It is the writer's theme that we must look for, not our interest, or theological hobby-horse.

What was Paul's big theme in Galatians? The true gospel contrasted with the law. But what law? The moral law (the Ten Commandments) or the ceremonial law (sacrifice and offerings)? This is a vital question to answer. The letter to Rome uses the word 'law' primarily in the sense of the moral law, whilst the letter to the Hebrews uses it with particular reference to the ceremonial law. What does Galatians refer to? What was Paul's big theme in Corinthians? Charismatic gifts? The correct ordering of worship? Or what?

3. Look for the different approaches

Just as Paul preached in different ways in Acts, so the New Testament writers wrote in different ways: Philemon is a personal letter to a friend. Romans is written to a church from a pagan background, dealing with fundamental Christian theology. Titus is written to a young pastor/preacher in Crete. Titus is teaching the theology, so Paul writes to advise on the organization of church life.

4. Grasp how radical was the early Christian ethic

The motto of the age was 'Hail profit!' — see Hebrews 10:32-34.
Not eyeservice! With all your heart! Serving the Lord! — see Colossians 3:22-23.
Suffering as a Christian — see 1 Peter 1-16
Wives and husbands — see Ephesians 5:22-33.

5. Beware of your own theological bias

It is necessary to have a theology, but be alert to the fact that this will bias you in your interpretation, sometimes unwisely.

Look at 1 Timothy 2:3-6; 4:10 Whom does Paul mean by 'all'? All kinds and types? All without exception? All without distinction? Your theological starting-point may answer the question quickly, but it would be better to begin by asking what the young Christians, just a few years old and without the benefit of Augustine, Luther, Calvin, Hodge or Warfield, would have made of it!

You may not like Romans 9:17-18, but what did it mean to Christians in a capital city of the Roman empire, in a hard and uncompromising age, and from a pagan background where the will of the gods was dominant, uncontrollable and final?

Luther had problems with James because his theological blinkers limited his understanding of James 2:24.

6. New meanings for the old

Understand how the apostles used the Old Testament. We looked at this subject in chapter 5 and shall return to it in the next section here.

Understanding the Old Testament

During the fifth century Christian writers often used that 'four-horse chariot' we referred to at the beginning of this chapter — the four ways of 'dragging' the meaning out of the Old Testament. They wrote of the literal meaning, the allegorical meaning, the moral reading and the anagogical meaning. The first looked at the Old Testament purely as history, the second to discover spiritual meanings hidden away there, the third to find lessons for the spiritual life of the Christian and the fourth to discover the mysteries of types and prophecies.

The Reformers in the sixteenth century, especially Luther and Calvin, placed the greatest emphasis upon the literal, or historical, meaning of the Old Testament but without altogether abandoning either the allegorical or spiritual meaning.

Stories as illustrations or allegories

We must always remember the difference between a verse that can be used as an illustration and one that can be used for a text — the basis upon which we can build our teaching. A preacher once took 2 Samuel 14:28 as his text and preached a sermon on backsliding: 'Absalom lived two years in Jerusalem without seeing the king's face.' It was a good sermon and a necessary subject but he chose the wrong text. Why? Because 2 Samuel 14:28 has nothing to do with backsliding and it was an abuse of Scripture to use it in this way; it is simply a statement that David had banished his son Absalom from his presence because Absalom had killed his own brother.

Taking this a step further, I once heard an excellent sermon on 2 Samuel 9 concerning David's care for Saul's surviving and disabled grandson Mephibosheth. It likened his condition to ours: he was crippled and separated from the king (the results of sin), restored to favour (salvation) and then promoted to eat at the king's table (fellowship with Jesus Christ). It was a good gospel sermon, and included the fact that Mephibosheth, even after his restoration, bore the marks of his fall, his running away! But is this really how we should use the Old Testament? Is this why God moved men of old to record those stories? This is using Old Testament stories as allegories.

The first story is not a text for a sermon on backsliding. We are perfectly entitled to use it as an illustration and may say, 'Just as Absalom spent two full years in Jerusalem and yet never came into the presence of the king, so the Christian may spend years among God's people and attending church and never come close to the presence of his Lord.' The same illustration could be used of the unbeliever as well! Remember an illustration is only a window to throw light on our subject, but a text is God's authority for our subject. Surely the story teaches us something important about the human result of sin and how it breaks relationships even within the family?

The second sermon was clever and complicated, but in no way is that what the story is about. The theology was perfect, but the hermeneutics was terrible. In presenting the story in this way we have lost one of the most beautiful stories in the Old Testament concerning true loyalty in friendship, and caring for those who have nothing to offer in return.

Some say that is an empty approach, merely discovering moral lessons in the Old Testament. But how can it be empty to learn of the disastrous effects of sin, which will point us on to Christ? How can it be empty to discover an example of true friendship in the Bible? It will not be long before we come to Christ as the greatest example of friendship.

Similarly, the story of Joseph is not in the Old Testament as a type of Christ, and the time we spend on his life trying to discover all the parallels with the life of Christ would be far better employed reading through a New Testament Gospel. Joseph teaches us scores of lessons about living a godly life in an alien culture and trusting God in both adversity and prosperity; there is a direct application from the life of Joseph to the life of any Christian. To deal with him in any other way is to miss the whole point. It would be the same if we took Job as a type of Christ: we should lose all the benefit of the story to people like ourselves.

How did the apostles read the Old Testament?

In chapter 5 we saw how the New Testament writers sometimes spoke of the Old Testament in a fuller way than may be obvious to us from a first reading of the passage. For example, Matthew 2:15 sees Hosea 11:1 fulfilled in the escape to and return from Egypt by Mary and Joseph and the infant Christ. The natural reading of Hosea is that this refers to the exodus from Egypt by the children of Israel, but Matthew sees a 'fuller fulfilment' in that passage.

Paul used Hagar and Sarah as an allegory; and that is the actual word he used in the Greek in Galatians 4:24 (see AV, NASB). He also used Adam as a type in Romans 5:14, and the rock, manna and the punishment of the people of Israel as types in 1 Corinthians 10:6,11; similarly Peter referred to the flood as an antitype of baptism in 1 Peter 3:21. The Day of Atonement is also spoken of as an illustration in Hebrews 9:9.

Does all this contradict the warnings we have given above? Do the apostles fall into the same trap of over-spiritualizing the Old Testament stories? Notice how far the apostles were prepared to go. Hagar and Sarah did, quite literally, represent the slave and the free. Adam clearly was a type of Christ since Christ gained all that Adam lost; in this way Adam represents fallen man and Christ represents redeemed man. The Day of Atonement, and for that matter all the

Old Testament ceremonies and sacrifices, had no meaning apart from Christ (see Galatians 3:24-25). Admittedly we may find the use of the rock and manna unusual, but Paul's application is perfectly correct. Twenty-eight times in the book of Psalms God is referred to as our Rock, and in Psalm 78 there is a clear link between the rock that Moses struck and 'God their Rock' (vv. 20,35). Similarly, just as they shared in spiritual food (i.e. provided by God) and yet some were punished for disobedience, so we are in the same danger at the Lord's Table. In the same way, for all their spiritual privileges, some of the Israelites died in the wilderness because of unfaithfulness; the same was happening to the Corinthians (compare 1 Corinthians 10:11 with 11:29-30).

In other words we must not go beyond the apostles in their use of the Old Testament.

A *symbol* is something that is used to represent something else. The book of Revelation is full of symbols. The 'beasts' in chapter 13 and 'Babylon' in chapter 17 are two examples among many. Similarly, Daniel and Ezekiel contain many symbols and we must be careful to avoid the temptation to interpret symbols literally. Normally a symbol does not have any reality in itself; it is merely a picture to describe something else. Once again, it is wrong to draw doctrine out of a symbol, or to use the biblical symbols as prooftexts.

The word *'type'* refers to a pattern for something else, and we have seen how the word is used in Romans 5, 1 Corinthians 10, and 1 Peter 3. The New Testament does not always use the words 'allegory', 'type' and 'antitype' in a consistent way, but some types or patterns have an inseparable connection with the thing they represent. For example, the Old Testament sacrificial system was a type of the sacrifice of Christ. We must not forget that there is only one way of salvation, whether in the Old or the New Testaments, and that is through the blood of Christ. The book of Leviticus is a book containing the details of the animal sacrifices; these were types, like signposts, pointing on to Christ and his cross. Similarly, the ark of the covenant is a type of the presence of God among his people, and the whole tabernacle, and later the temple, is a picture of God's way of salvation.

The difference between the type and the illustration or symbol is that illustrations and symbols are only pictures; in themselves they may have no importance or necessary relationship to the subject they are illustrating. On the other hand, a type has as its chief or only function the representation of that to which it points. We can illustrate the difference in this way: the Old Testament sacrifices, the ark and the tabernacle have no other purpose in history than to represent Christ, the presence of God, and God's way of salvation, and to prepare the people for these; therefore they were types. But

'The Old Testament sacrificial system was a type of the sacrifice of Christ'

when Paul uses Sarah and Hagar to illustrate a point in Galatians 4 he readily appreciates that these two women had purposes in Scripture other than merely to illustrate his point and he therefore admits in verse 24 that he is speaking allegorically.

This distinction is not always easy to follow, but it is important. Symbols, allegories and illustrations are only pictures used to describe something else; they can never be our authority for making a statement and we should therefore never use them as texts to prove our doctrine. A further example may help to make the distinction clear. We can preach from the sacrificial system and refer it directly to Christ; it becomes our authority for what we say about Christ. However, we cannot do the same with the story of Abraham and Isaac found in Genesis 22. There may be similarities between this story and God's sacrifice of his only Son, but nowhere in Scripture do we have authority for saying that this is the chief purpose, or any purpose, of that story; it is a story about the obedience of Abraham and his faith in the God who can raise the dead (see Hebrews 11:19).

What we may do, however, is use it as an illustration. But remember, an illustration is not proof, whereas a type is; an illustration can never be used as our text, whereas a type can. We must never preach about God's sacrifice of his Son from the story of Abraham and Isaac, but in talking about the sacrifice of Christ we may refer to Abraham and Isaac as an illustration.

If we accept this distinction it will help us in other parts of Scripture. For example, although our Lord refers to Jonah as an illustration of his resurrection (Matthew 12:40), we cannot refer to Jonah as a type of Christ since there are many parts of Jonah's life that bear no resemblance to our Lord's life, and even the prophet's experience in the fish has lessons to teach us quite apart from its reference to Christ. To use the story of Jonah and the fish as an illustration of Christ's resurrection is perfectly correct, but to call Jonah a type of Christ may lead us into the danger of trying to find many other comparisons; it will not be long before we are suggesting that Jonah's attempted escape from God's will is a picture of Christ in Gethsemane — and that would lead us into a completely wrong view of Gethsemane!

The danger of overlooking this important distinction between types and illustrations or symbols is also seen very clearly in the following example. There are those who believe that when Christ returns, Christians will be taken from earth to heaven ('raptured' is the word used to describe this) before a future time of terrible suffering and confusion on earth (the 'tribulation' as it is called). We are not concerned here with discussing whether this is right or wrong, but some will try to prove this by referring to Enoch. Enoch, they say, is a type of the Christian and he was taken to heaven just before the flood (Genesis 5:24). But nowhere have we any authority for saying that Enoch was a type of anything or anyone. We might just as easily, and just as incorrectly, claim that Noah was a type of the Christian and he went through the flood! Neither Enoch nor Noah are types; at the very most they may possibly be used as illustrations (as Peter used Noah in 1 Peter 3:20 and 2 Peter 2:5). But never forget, an illustration proves nothing.

In addition to looking for the plain and obvious meaning of an Old Testament story, the apostles looked for the principal lesson to be leant from instructions given in the Old Testament. In 1 Corinthians 9:9 and 1 Timothy 5:18 Paul refers to the regulations in Deuteronomy 25:4 concerning the care of the ox whilst it is treading out the corn. When Paul comments that this is not written for the sake of the animals but for us, some commentators assume Paul is denying the plain sense of an Old Testament passage. He is not doing that at all, but whilst recognizing the value of such a verse in relation to animal husbandry, the apostle is far more concerned to draw out the deeper application that if that is how much God is interested in an ox, surely he must be much more interested in our care for the servants of God. Similarly in 2 Corinthians 8:15 Paul refers to the collection of manna in the wilderness (Exodus 16:18) to demonstrate God's principle of equality among Christians.

Beware

Among those who acknowledge the Bible to be God's Word, there will always be those who in practice deny this belief by their action in mishandling Scripture. Here are a few people to be on your guard against.

The man with no problems

While the main message of the Bible is plain for even a child to understand, there are difficult passages that have puzzled commentators throughout the centuries. Beware of the man who claims to have solved all the problems. Some of the modern cults, like the Jehovah's Witnesses and the Christadelphians, think they have the final explanation for every difficult passage of prophecy in the Bible, and the Mormons claim that Paul's statement concerning baptism for the dead in 1 Corinthians 15:29, a statement that has mystified the most scholarly and spiritual commentators, is 'unambiguous' — they know exactly what it means. They don't!

There is no shame in admitting that we do not fully understand a particular passage of Scripture. Peter found some things in Paul's letters 'hard to understand' and commented that these were the very parts 'which ignorant and unstable people distort' (2 Peter 3:16). You cannot be an expert in every part of Scripture. Beware of the man with instant solutions to every problem, who is supremely self-confident in his understanding of 'the spirits in prison' (1 Peter 3:19) and the 'man of lawlessness' (2 Thessalonians 2:3). Hermeneutics requires a prayerful life, careful thought, diligent study and a humble admission that I may be wrong.

The man with a new discovery

Every so often someone 'discovers' something new in the Bible that the Christian church has apparently never seen before. Almost all the modern cults began like this: they had discovered the key to understanding the Bible. For the Jehovah's Witnesses and Christadelphians it was their special understanding of prophecy (both very different from each other though!); for the Mormons it was the so-called visions of Joseph Smith; for the Seventh Day Adventists it was the crucial importance of the Saturday Sabbath. Similarly there are many modern groups who claim to have discovered something new. In fact the Bible is quite right when it declares that 'There is nothing new under the sun' (Ecclesiastes 1:9). If you find a way of interpreting a passage that you cannot find from any commentary or Christian teacher, beware! You may be right, but it is more likely you are wrong! Almost certainly your view has been tried and rejected long before you were born.

The spiritualizer

I once knew a man who delighted to find a deep and hidden meaning in every colour referred to in the Bible. When I met him he was on a different track: he was sure that every time the donkey was mentioned in the Bible it had the same spiritual lesson for us. He had discovered the jawbone of the donkey that Samson used and Balaam's donkey and Nehemiah's donkey and, of course, the donkey that our Lord used to ride into Jerusalem; but at that time he had not yet discovered what the spiritual lesson was! This is not interpreting Scripture; it is plundering it. In the same way some have looked for a deep spiritual significance in David's five stones (1 Samuel 17:40). Perhaps, they say, they represent the first five books of the Bible and one is sufficient to deal with its critics. The trouble with this is that I am left wondering what David did with the other four — perhaps he threw them away!

Of course there is a right way to spiritualize. We must look for Christ in all the Scriptures, but not in every verse. We must read

Christ *out of* the Scriptures, but not *into* them. For example, to read the life of Joseph as a type of the life of Christ is to read him into the Scriptures, because nowhere in Scripture do we have the authority to say that Joseph is intended as a picture of Christ. But to see Christ pictured in the Old Testament sacrifices is to read him out of the Scripture because we know from the New Testament that this is exactly how we are to understand the sacrifices.

The man with dishonest conclusions

Because the evangelical believes that the Bible is God's Word without error, this does not mean that we can make a passage say whatever we want it to, and then claim God's authority for our conclusion. We must carefully apply the rules of hermeneutics and never force a verse or passage to say what we want it to say. We can fall into this temptation either to avoid the plain teaching that we do not like, or to insist on some other teaching which we do like. The authority of God's Word is what God actually said, not what we think he ought to have said.

The man with imagination and exaggeration

Perhaps one of the greatest dangers facing teachers and preachers of the Bible is that of adding to a Bible story in order to make the telling of it more effective. What we must do is to read carefully all that is said in the Bible in order to include everything that Scripture tells us. What we may also do is to add background details of geography, customs, politics and so on that set the story in its house and street context. We may even add a few suggestions of what may or may not have taken place, provided that we make it clear that we can have no certainty about these points. What we must never do is to add long imaginative events to the Bible story, weave them in so that the hearer thinks they are really part of the Bible narrative, and then proceed to apply lessons from our additions as if they had God's authority behind them. For this abuse of Scripture, however ignorantly or innocently it may be done, God will demand that we give an account to him!

Conclusion

The Bible is God's book and it has his stamp of authority across it.
His Word is authoritative — not our particular interpretation of it.
God has given us rules by which we can rightly understand his
Word; they are not hard to follow and they are within the reach of
everyone who prayerfully and carefully uses them as a key to
interpret this treasure box. Interpret the Bible sensibly and spiritu-
ally. Make it relevant, not ridiculous. Ask for the help of God's Holy
Spirit, because he is the reliable interpreter of his own book.

15.
Archaeology and the Bible

Archaeology is the science of reading history from the 'leftovers' of previous civilizations. It involves uncovering the remains of buildings and of household bits and pieces, and learning from them who the people who used them were, and when and how they lived. Archaeology has been called 'the study of durable rubbish'.

The earliest archaeologists were grave robbers who plundered the gold and silver of ancient royal tombs. In the year 530 B.C. the great Persian King Cyrus died whilst on a campaign to the east. Workmen built a magnificent tomb at Pasargadae for the great king. The massive stone-roofed tomb was approached by a platform with seven steps and above the entrance was the following message: 'O man, whoever you are and whenever you come, for I know that you will come—I am Cyrus, who gave the Persians their empire. Do not grudge me this patch of earth that covers my body.' Unfortunately somebody did just that, because in 322 B.C. when Alexander the Great climbed the steps to inspect the tomb, he discovered that the robes, cape, jewellery and scimitar of Cyrus were all gone, the stone coffin was shattered and his bones lay all over the floor. So much for the great Persian ruler! Modern archaeologists are usually more careful.

Ancient civilizations built their towns on the rubble, indeed often with the rubble, of the previous occupants. All that the earlier people left behind — their building materials, pottery, jewellery, messages, food remains, household utensils, weapons and their own bones — are covered over and therefore preserved for later generations to unearth. It is all this 'durable rubbish' that helps the archaeologist to date that part of the ancient city, often to an accuracy of within fifty years. As generation after generation built upon the rubbish of their ancestors, or of the enemy they defeated, so the town grew higher and higher. The great mountain of earth that betrays the presence of an old city is called a 'tell', an Arabic word for 'mound'. This word for mound is found in Joshua 11:3, for example, which indicates that even fifteen hundred years before Christ many cities had a long history to tell!

Megiddo is mentioned in Joshua 12:21 and in 1 Kings 9:15-19; Joshua captured it and Solomon fortified it. The tell, now called Tell el Mutesellim, is twenty-one metres high (sixty-eight feet) with the summit covering ten acres; it stands isolated and alone on the north side of the Carmel ridge, commanding the pass from the coastal plain to the valley of Esdraelon. The excavation of Megiddo began in 1903 and it reveals no fewer than twenty main occupation levels from 4,000 to 600 B.C. Stables for 450 horses, probably built in the time of King Ahab of Israel, have been discovered.

Archaeology is a fascinating science that has added immensely to our understanding of Bible times and events. We shall look at some of the conclusions of archaeology that help to show the reliability of the Bible. Although it is sometimes claimed otherwise, it is a fact that there are no archaeological results that disprove the Bible.

Archaeology is also an ongoing science of discovery; interesting finds come to light each year. Recently, archaeologists tunnelling along the western wall of the temple in Jerusalem discovered five great foundation stones that formed part of the base of the temple of Jesus' day. The largest is sixteen metres long, three and a third metres high and four metres wide, and it is estimated that it weighs some 570 tons. Such a find certainly makes what our Lord prophesied in Matthew 24:1-2 about the stones of the temple even more dramatic! Bible archaeologists are still searching for lost items of history, from the ark that Noah built to the ark of the covenant that Moses placed in the tabernacle. Exciting new finds will certainly come to light in the future. However, there is one important point about archaeology to remember.

Archaeology proves very little

The fact that modern archaeological discoveries increasingly show the Bible to be correct, even in matters of detail, presents a real danger for the evangelical. Here is an example of this danger.

The lost city of Jericho?

The story of the destruction of Jericho is described in Joshua 6. The city was plundered by Joshua many centuries before Christ and again by archaeologists in more recent years. Scholars have always been interested in the conquest of Canaan by Joshua, and various dates for it have been suggested. Obviously if we knew the exact date of the Exodus, when Moses led the children of Israel out of Egypt, we should be able to take away forty years to allow for the wilderness wandering and we would know how many years before Christ Jericho was destroyed by Joshua.

Actually 1 Kings 6:1 appears to give us a date from which to start. The verse tells us that Solomon began to build the temple in the fourth year of his reign and that this year was the 480th year 'after the Israelites had come out of Egypt'. We know that Solomon began to reign about the year 970 B.C. The fourth year would be 966 B.C. and 480 years earlier would give 1446 B.C. as the date of the Exodus. Allowing forty years for the wilderness wanderings, we are brought to the destruction of Jericho by Joshua around the year 1406 B.C.

Towards the end of the nineteenth century archaeologists began to dig up parts of ancient Egypt and some of their discoveries led critical scholars to believe that the Exodus must have taken place much later than the fifteenth century before Christ. The chief evidence was that the two cities of Pithom and Rameses referred to in Exodus 1:11 do not appear to have been built during the reign of Pharaoh Amenophas II, who was ruler of Egypt from about 1430 B.C. Various alternative dates were suggested, including one of 1290 B.C. and another as late as 1230 B.C. Whatever the new date, many scholars were satisfied that either 1 Kings 6:1 or Exodus 1:11, or both, had been proved wrong.

Then, during the 1930s, Professor John Garstang, from the University of Liverpool in England, dug up the old city of Jericho. He discovered huge walls that had obviously been broken down, and a city that had been plundered and set on fire. By the pottery and other items he found, Garstang dated the destruction of this city at around 1407 B.C. which brings us back to the traditional date! Even the critical scholars began to admit that perhaps 1 Kings 6:1 and Exodus 1:11 were correct after all and evangelical Christians were delighted.

Excavations at the site of the ancient city of Jericho
(Reproduced by courtesy of Dr George A. Turner).

However, in 1958 Dame Kathleen Kenyon, daughter of the Director of the British Museum referred to in an earlier chapter, completed her own research into Jericho and announced that Garstang's dating was all wrong. The city he had discovered was not the Jericho that Joshua destroyed, but a city on the same site which was destroyed about 1,000 years before Joshua crossed the river Jordan. In fact, Kathleen Kenyon claimed there was no large city on the site in the time of Joshua. Her conclusions are now widely accepted; even the Inter Varsity Press *Illustrated Bible Dictionary* suggests: 'It is possible that in Joshua's day (13th century B.C.) there was a small town on the east part of the mound.' Another evangelical writer claims that: 'There is enough [evidence] to show there were some people about at Jericho somewhere near the time of Joshua's attack.' All this is a far cry from the city 'with walls up to the sky' that so terrified the Israelite spies in Deuteronomy 1:28. So it would seem that 1 Kings 6:1 and Exodus 1:11 may be wrong again!

In 1978 John Bimson published a book called *Redating the Exodus and Conquest* (Sheffield Press). In it he argues for a fifteenth-century date for the Exodus and casts serious doubt upon Kenyon's conclusions. If Bimson is right then the discussion has come back again to the support of scriptural accuracy! On the other hand, Kenneth Kitchen, from the University of Liverpool, is equally sure that Rameses II was the Pharaoh at the time of the Exodus, and this would bring us again to a thirteenth-century date for the Exodus!

All this goes to show that a great danger for the evangelical is to rely upon the conclusions of archaeologists and to believe that no one can argue against their opinions. We have just seen how their claims can prove unreliable. There are three principles we must not forget as we look at the results of archaeology.

1. Archaeologists are not infallible

They discover facts but they must then interpret those facts, and that is where the mistakes come in. Suppose you are walking along a deserted road and you find some material lying in a heap. You may pick it up and examine it; you can see that it is made of cotton and that it is an article of clothing. Those are the facts; they are obvious and everyone would agree with you. But then you may wonder who owned it. Did it belong to a man or woman? How long has it been lying in the road? Is its owner alive or dead? Was he or she rich or poor? Which way was he or she travelling? Why was it left just here? And so on. The answers to these questions are your interpretation of the facts and you may get all or most of the answers wrong. Archaeologists are skilled scientists but they can still make mistakes. Garstang, Kenyon, Bimson and Kitchen cannot all be right.

2. Archaeologists can rarely account for all the facts

Those discoveries in Egypt referred to earlier do not really help anybody to be completely sure of a date for the Exodus. Archaeologists and scholars are still arguing about how to interpret the facts and no one can yet say that the facts are clearly against the traditional date. There is some evidence to suggest that there could be a great error in the dating of Egyptian history of the period of the Exodus and Conquest. Dr Donovan Courville has discussed this at length in his two-volume work, *The Exodus Problem and its Ramifications* (1971). If his suggested redating is correct then most of the problems are solved and Garstang's walls could certainly be those of the city destroyed by Joshua. But if we suppose Kathleen Kenyon was right about the Jericho that Garstang discovered, how do we answer the fact that she also claims that there was no well-fortified city on the site of Jericho in the fifteenth century before Christ?

First of all, we must remember that our record in Joshua claims to be an eyewitness account. According to Joshua 6:25 Rahab and her family were still living at the time of the record being written. Secondly, the whole story in Joshua and the faithless report forty years earlier of the spies, who spoke about those great cities with walls up to the skies, hardly describe 'a small town on the east part of the mound'.

On the other hand, assuming her dating is right, why could Kathleen Kenyon find little trace of this great city? Partly because the Israelites plundered the city of all its silver, gold, brass and iron (Joshua 6:19) and 'utterly destroyed' everything else (v. 21, NASB); it is these very items that the archaeologist looks for as traces of civilization. But another reason why Dame Kenyon found nothing of the great walls that Joshua describes is that God so destroyed them that 'the wall collapsed' (v. 20) and the Israelite soldiers had no need to rush at gaps in the wall, but 'every man charged straight in' (v. 20). If the wall that God destroyed for Joshua had been built upon the ruins of the one Garstang found, the destruction was so complete that only those original foundations remained.

There is still another reason why Kenyon would be unable to find the remains of Joshua's city. As far as this particular city is concerned Joshua placed a curse upon anyone who rebuilt it (Joshua 6:26), and the fear of this meant that the ruins of Jericho were left open to the wind, rain and sun for many centuries before Hiel, in the time of Ahab, defied the curse and paid the price for doing so (1 Kings 16:34). Those five centuries of exposure to the elements would have destroyed all the remains of the city defeated by Joshua! We are therefore not surprised that archaeologists can find little evidence of the site being occupied during these five hundred years and even less evidence of the city Joshua destroyed; for the durable rubbish to be preserved it would be essential that successive towns were built on top of it. This did not happen at Jericho.

These are biblical records that the archaeologists ought to take into account. No archaeologist can say, 'There certainly was no city with huge walls in the fifteenth century B.C. at Jericho.' The most he or she can say is, 'So far we have found no evidence of a city with huge walls in the fifteenth century B.C. at Jericho.' Archaeologists rarely have all the facts.

Our belief in the accuracy of Scripture must never depend upon archaeological conclusions. Archaeology may support biblical inerrancy, but that is not our first or most reliable argument for believing in it. The danger of trusting in archaeologists has been illustrated at Jericho. Evangelicals who made too much of Garstang's conclusions may now have lost their evidence. But what never changes is the Word of God. That is our evidence for the events of the conquest of Jericho. We must also beware of hasty and extravagant claims that are made by the press and sometimes by the archaeologists themselves. In an attempt to gain popular interest it is easy to claim too much, too soon, for too little. In an earlier chapter we warned against this danger with the Dead Sea Scrolls now that they are open for examination by any serious scholar.

3. Archaeologists are often prejudiced

Another reason why we should never rely upon archaeologists for our belief in an inerrant Bible is that they, like all of us, work with certain prejudices, the most general of which is that of all ancient documents the Bible is the least to be trusted. We saw in chapter 9 how Sir William Ramsay began his work in Asia Minor believing that Luke's Gospel and his account of the early church in Acts would be wrong at almost every point — though in his case it was actually the weight of archaeological evidence in favour of Luke that forced Ramsay to change his mind.

A seemingly trivial example is the fact that many critics believe the story of Abraham in Genesis must have been written long after the event. One reason they give is the references to camels (Genesis 12:16, for example), which are thought to have been introduced as beasts of burden not before the twelfth century B.C. Abraham is some 800 years earlier! Whilst it may be true that before the twelfth century archaeological evidence for the camel is scarce, there are some references to camels even preceding Abraham's time. However, why should the Bible not be considered the reliable historical document that provides us with evidence of camels in the time of Abraham? It is odd how when archaeologists find an ancient document that agrees with the Old Testament the headlines run something like this: 'Old Testament proved true by ancient document.' It hardly occurs to the media — or to many scholars — that a more accurate headline would be: 'Ancient document proved true by the Old Testament.' It would be wiser to test archaeological finds by the Bible rather than the Bible by archaeological finds. Having said this, we can find many examples from biblical archaeology that confirm the truth of the Bible where once the critics disputed it.

Archaeology confirms the accuracy of the Bible

We have already seen the danger of using archaeology as 'proof' of the accuracy of the Bible, but it is nevertheless a valuable tool of confirmation; again it must be stressed that nowhere does archaeology find the Bible to be in error. Here are some examples of how the findings of archaeology can confirm the accuracy of what the Bible says.

The genealogy of Ben-Hadad

In 1 Kings 15:18 we read of 'Ben-Hadad son of Tabrimmon, the son of Hezion, the king of Aram, who was ruling in Damascus'. By the time we come to the period of the Jewish kings we are not lacking letters and inscriptions from pagan kings of Syria, Assyria and Egypt that confirm the accuracy of the Old Testament history. A stele is a pillar of stone used either as a tombstone or a memorial to a military victory on which a message was chiselled or carved. In 1940 a stele of Ben-Hadad was discovered in northern Syria. According to 1 Kings 15:18 Ben-Hadad was 'the son of Tabrimmon, the son of Hezion, king of Aram (Syria), who was ruling in Damascus'. Professor Albright, a great scholar but no evangelical, claims that this is exactly the order that appears on Ben-Hadad's stele.

Ahab's use of ivory

The account of the reign of Ahab tells us that 'The palace he built was inlaid with ivory' (1 Kings 22:39). In addition to being the wife of Ahab, King of Israel, Jezebel was also a Phoenician princess, and the Phoenician craftsmen were experts in the art of carving ivory. From the time of King Solomon onwards, ivory was a symbol of wealth and when the monarchy divided both Israel and Judah squandered their riches in this way. Ruins at Samaria, where Ahab and Jezebel lived, have revealed hundreds of fragments of ivory, and larger items also, many of them intricately carved; archaeologists believe these date from the time of Ahab about 860 B.C. Among the items of tribute that the Assyrian king Sennacherib claims Hezekiah sent to him at Nineveh are 'ivory-decorated beds and ivory-decorated armchairs, elephant hide and tusks...' It was this wasteful luxury that the prophet Amos vigorously condemned in his ministry (see Amos 3:15 and 6:4). Significantly, critics once scoffed at the idea of Ahab making an ivory palace. They had assumed this meant a palace of solid ivory, whereas we now know that the custom was to overlay wood with carved ivory.

'Jehu, son of Jehoshaphat' (2 Kings 9:14)

Jehu was not of royal descent; he was a soldier who butchered his way to power. Having killed both the Kings of Israel and Judah, he doubtless felt a little uneasy about some of the enemies he had made! A strong friend and ally would be a wise policy; but where would he find one?

In 1845 a young and inexperienced archaeologist, Henry Layard, ran out of money, packed his horse and rode miserably away from the site he and his team had been digging on the banks of the River Tigris. No sooner had he left than a workman caught up with him and urged him to return to the site because a block of black polished basalt stone had been found lying in a trench. It measured two metres high and was carved with pictures and writing on all four sides. The 'Black Obelisk' (an obelisk is just a shaped block of stone, generally tapering at one end) proved to be a stone cut to commemorate the triumphs of the Assyrian king Shalmaneser III. (This is not the king referred to in 2 Kings 17, 18, who is Shalmaneser V.)

Part of the obelisk depicts rulers in national costume bringing tribute to the king. The first panel in the second line shows a kneeling figure in Israelite dress with the inscription: 'Tribute of Yaua, son of Humri: I received silver, gold, a golden bowl, a golden beaker, golden goblets, golden pitchers, lead, a royal staff, a javelin.' This is 'Jehu the son of Omri'. In fact Jehu is the fourth in line of descent from Omri, who was the founder of this dynasty (line of kings). Behind the kneeling Jehu is a line of his servants laden with the items of tribute. This is how Jehu found an ally!

But the story is not ended there, because in order to make a friend of Shalmaneser, Jehu abandoned Hazael of Damascus. Hazael is also mentioned in the obelisk, but he had resisted the Assyrian king. For this treachery Jehu and Israel paid dearly in later years, as 2 Kings 10:32 reveals.

'Sargon, king of Assyria' (Isaiah 20:1)

In the year 721 B.C. Sargon became King of Assyria; he continued the siege of Samaria begun by Shalmaneser V, and the city was destroyed (2 Kings 17:5-6). For years the critics doubted that a king by the name of Sargon ever existed because the only reference to him came in Isaiah 20:1 and it was assumed that Sargon was an invention of the prophet's fanciful imagination.

In 1843 a French archaeologist, Paul Botta, started digging at a town called Khorsabad, twenty-three kilometres (fourteen miles) to the north of Nineveh. He discovered a great palace guarded by huge winged bulls nearly five metres high. The walls were lined with great slabs of stone carved with pictures and cuneiform writing — the square script of ancient Babylon, Assyria and Persia. The

Relief portrait of the Assyrian king, Sargon II
(Reproduced by courtesy of the Trustees of the British Museum)

writing proved that Botta had discovered the palace of King Sargon.
He is now one of the best-known Assyrian kings and was one of the
most powerful rulers in the ancient world. Of the many documents
left behind by Sargon, one contains a reference to his defeat of
Samaria: 'In the first year of my reign I besieged and conquered
Samaria... I led away captive 27,290 people who lived there.' In
fact it was Sargon's predecessor Shalmaneser V, referred to in
2 Kings 17:3-4 and 2 Kings 18:9, who began the siege; however,
he died after two years and Sargon completed the work. Interestingly in 2 Kings 17:6 and 18:10, when the fall of Samaria is recorded
after the three-year siege, the name of Shalmaneser is not repeated;
it was, in fact, Sargon who finally broke the Israelite capital. We
have an incredible store of knowledge of this man, including the fact
that one of his daughters was both a priestess and a poetess!

Sennacherib's campaign against Hezekiah

Isaiah records that 'Sennacherib, king of Assyria, attacked all the
fortified cities of Judah and captured them. Then the king of Assyria

sent his field commander with a large army from Lachish to King Hezekiah at Jerusalem' (Isaiah 36:1-2).

Seventeen years after the siege of Samaria, Sennacherib, the powerful King of Assyria, sent a massive army against Jerusalem when Hezekiah rebelled against him. The details are recorded in 2 Kings 18-19; 2 Chronicles 32 and Isaiah 36-37. Sennacherib left his own account on a clay prism just thirty-seven and a half centimetres high. It was discovered in 1830 by Colonel Taylor, the British resident in Baghdad, and is therefore known as the 'Taylor Prism'.

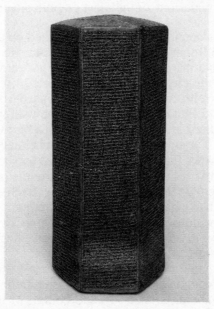

Clay prism inscribed with the details of the campaigns of Sennacherib, including his account of the siege of Jerusalem
(Reproduced by courtesy of the Trustees of the British Museum).

Sennacherib records details of his campaign against the Hebrew king. Although unable to take Jerusalem itself, he destroyed the surrounding country and spoke of shutting up Hezekiah in his royal city 'like a caged bird', adding, more for the benefit of his own conceit than for historical fact: 'The terrifying splendour of my majesty overcame Hezekiah. The warriors and select troops [Arabs and mercenaries?] he had brought in to strengthen his royal city Jerusalem did not fight.'

Sennacherib also adds that he carried off 200,150 people of all ranks from Judah and that Hezekiah sent tribute after him to his royal city in Nineveh; this is clear evidence that the Assyrian king did not enter Jerusalem to carry off plunder for himself. In fact he is careful never actually to claim that he entered Jerusalem and in the victory room in his palace at Nineveh, it is the defeat of Lachish, not Jerusalem, that illustrates his victory over the Hebrews. This all fits exactly the biblical record. The story of the defeat of Lachish was carved into stone and it occupies a room of its own in the British Museum. It provides one of the most graphic pictorial accounts of ancient warfare.

Here is an account of the battle as depicted on the stone reliefs in the 'Lachish Room'. The battle for the strategic city of Lachish begins with ranks of archers, quivers stuffed with arrows, firing over the walls into the city; some kneel, protected by the tall leather shields of the javelin throwers. Behind them are the bearded artillery men with long pointed helmets wielding their sling and carrying a spare stone in their left hand; they keep up a barrage of small but lethal missiles. The storm-troopers with flat helmets are scaling the walls, firing arrows for a protective shield as they advance. The air is thick with missiles. The siege-engines trundle up the earth and stone ramps right up to the walls of the city. Each engine encloses an archer, a man to guide the 'tank', and a 'fireman' who, with great ladles of water, douses the constantly falling fire-torches of the defenders as they try to set fire to the protective leather covering of the battering ram.

The defenders, for their part, are desperately hurling their fire-bombs and rocks upon the attackers; some are falling over the wall, victims of advancing archers. At the bottom of the panel is the gruesome scene of those who tried to escape the city and have been impaled on long stakes in the sight of the defenders. Groups of prisoners, men and women with children clinging to their dress, are led away; the spoils of war follow them on camels and in heavily laden ox-carts. The leaders of the city are spread-eagled and flayed alive, whilst others are summarily executed. King Sennacherib himself took part in this siege and he is seen receiving the defeated prisoners as he sits upon his high throne. The inscription reads: 'Sennacherib King of the world, King of Assyria, on a seat he sat and the booty of Lachish before him it passed.' The king's chariot and bodyguard are below and behind him. The king's face has been

Relief showing Sennacherib, King of Assyria, after the capture of
Lachish. The inscription is in cuneiform script
(Reproduced by courtesy of the Trustees of the British Museum).

hacked out, probably the work of a Babylonian soldier when
Nineveh itself was destroyed in 612 B.C !

The stone relief continues with the plan of the base camp in
which priests are offering sacrifices to their gods and the servants
are busy in their tents. This is the end of the Lachish sequence. But
other panels depict Assyrian cavalry, slingers and archers, and
prisoners being led away under the watchful and taunting eye of the
Assyrian guards; the prisoners are playing their lyres, which is
reminiscent of Psalm 137.

The biblical account and the Assyrian account are similar even
down to small details. The few differences may be put down to
inaccuracy on the part of the Assyrian king, or they may easily be
resolved. As an example, for many years the Bible was assumed to
be certainly in error because in 2 Kings 18:14 the record states that
Hezekiah was forced to pay 'three hundred talents of silver and
thirty talents of gold' to the Assyrian king. However, Assyrian

records showed the figures as 800 talents of silver and thirty talents of gold. The two seemed irreconcilable and, of course, it was the Bible that was thought to be wrong. More recent discoveries have revealed that although the method of calculating the weight of gold was the same for both Judea and Assyria, that for weighing silver was very different. It took exactly 800 Assyrian talents of silver to equal 300 Judean talents!

Sennacherib met a violent death in his palace at Nineveh. So says the Word of God in Isaiah 37:38 and 2 Kings 19:37, and so agrees Sennacherib's son and successor, Esarhaddon: 'My brothers forsook the gods and turned to their deeds of violence, plotting evil... To gain the kingship they slew Sennacherib their father.'

Belshazzar's feast

The book of Daniel tells how 'King Belshazzar gave a great banquet for a thousand of his nobles... That very night Belshazzar, king of the Babylonians, was slain' (Daniel 5:1,30).

At one time the critics held that Daniel was clearly in error because no king by the name of Belshazzar had ever been found in any ancient document apart from Daniel 5:1. In fact, the king at the time to which Daniel refers is named as Nabonidus in the complete lists of Babylonian kings. In 1850 a German scholar wrote that Belshazzar was simply a figment of the imagination of whoever wrote the book of Daniel.

Four years later, in 1854, Sir Henry Rawlinson was given a small clay cylinder discovered in Ur of the Chaldees; on it was an inscription by Nabonidus, King of Babylon. The inscription was a prayer for the good health and long life of the king, and for 'Belshazzar, my eldest son'! So a man named Belshazzar did live at that time. But was the king's son ever king himself? Among further inscriptions discovered he was always referred to as the 'crown prince', and still the critics assumed that the writer of Daniel had made a mistake — critics don't give up easily! But the writer did know what he was writing about; that is why Daniel was offered by Belshazzar the post of 'third highest ruler in the kingdom' (Daniel 5:7,16).

In 1876 Sir Henry discovered jars filled with over two thousand cuneiform clay tablets, the inscriptions written in the wedge-shaped characters or letters of ancient Babylon and Persia. Among them was an account by Cyrus, King of Persia, of his invasion of Babylon, in which he claimed to have taken Nabonidus prisoner but added that on a certain night 'the king died'. In fact Nabonidus lived as Cyrus' prisoner for many years and therefore the king who died must have been his son Belshazzar, acting as king and of whom the Bible claims, 'That very night Belshazzar, king of the Babylonians, was slain' (Daniel 5:30). Nabonidus spent most of his time away from Babylon in northern Arabia and during his absence his son acted as king in Babylon. For practical purposes he was acting king. However, because Belshazzar was only acting king in place of his absent father, he could only make Daniel 'third ruler in the kingdom'.

The dating of Ezekiel's prophecy

The prophecy of Ezekiel is claimed by many critics to have been written late in the third century B.C. For the Bible critic this has the advantage of placing Ezekiel long after the events prophesied in his book. Critics generally find the fulfilment of prophecy a great embarrassment because it is one of the clear evidences that the Bible is God's Word and completely reliable; they are very happy therefore if they can try to show that a prophetic book was written after the events prophesied and not before them. One reason given by the critics for the conclusion that Ezekiel was written in the third century B.C. is that the prophet dated his ministry by 'the fifth year of the exile of King Jehoiachin' (Ezekiel 1:2). This appears to be a strange way of dating when in fact Zedekiah was on the throne of Judah in the fifth year after Jehoiachin had been deported to Babylon. Presumably, so the critics say, the third-century writer pretending to be Ezekiel did not know that Jehoiachin was no longer king and that Zedekiah had replaced him!

In fact archaeology from Palestine and Babylon now proves beyond any doubt that both the Jews and the Babylonians recognized Jehoiachin as the proper and legal king, while his uncle Zedekiah was merely a puppet of the Babylonian ruler Nebuchadnezzar. Clay tablets from Babylon, and now in the British Museum, list the provisions for 'Jehoiachin, king of Judah' and for his five sons, all political prisoners in the palace at Babylon. No third-century writer, pretending to be Ezekiel, could possibly have known this detail.

Cyrus, King of Persia

'This is what Cyrus king of Persia says: "The Lord, the God of heaven, has given me all the kingdoms of the earth..."' (2 Chronicles 36:23; Ezra 1:2).

This was the Cyrus whose tomb in Pasargadae Alexander the Great found to be broken and robbed. For years it was assumed that no pagan king would have referred to the Jewish God in the terms described here. The same was said of the decree of Darius recorded in Ezra 6. When archaeologists discovered the clay 'Cylinder of Cyrus' critics were forced to change their minds. The cylinder marks the triumph of Cyrus over Babylon and part of it reads: 'I am Cyrus, king of all, the great king, the mighty king, king of Babylon, king of Sumer and Akkad, king of the four corners of the earth...'

A Greek temple in southern Turkey revealed a large stone block which was the 'deed of covenant' by the citizens of Xanthos when they planned to build an altar for their two local gods. It is 'counter-signed' by the local Persian representative who gave authority for such action. In Ezra 6:12 the God of Jerusalem is urged to protect his own people in exactly the same way that the gods at Xanthos are.

These illustrations form only a small sample of the material available to us today. Hundreds of inscriptions on monuments and tombs, and thousands of letters written on stone or clay tablets are still waiting to be translated. Archaeologists are still digging; scholars are still studying. More information will come to us as the years pass. Again and again the Bible is shown to be accurate. But the evangelical is not surprised at this.

Archaeology expands our knowledge of the Bible

Archaeology covers every period of Bible history and its greatest value is to fill in the details of everyday life in Bible times. In his excellent book *Treasures From Bible Times* Alan Millard well illustrates the value, and the limitations, of archaeology. The great-est value of archaeology is not to 'prove the Bible true', which it can never do and we do not need it to, but as an aid to our understanding of the customs and culture, the religion and ideas of the nations that significantly affected the Jews, and of Israel itself. For example, the siege at Lachish shows how archaeology can fill out our knowledge of ancient warfare. Here are some other examples of the way in which archaeology helps us to understand the Bible better.

The ages of people in Genesis

The ages recorded in the early chapters of Genesis are unacceptable to some modern critics. They do not believe that any man could live for almost 1,000 years, as did Adam (Genesis 5:5) and Methuselah (Genesis 5:27). Either the names merely represent tribes or clans, they say, or we must assume that a different time-scale was in use. But those who want us to assume that the years were really shorter periods often also require that the six days of creation should be much longer periods! Besides, if these years are really much shorter, then why was Abraham, at the age of only 100, so doubtful of the possibility of Sarah having a son? (Genesis 17:17). And how long are the seventy years of Psalm 90:10?

For many years archaeologists and scholars possessed a 'Sumerian king list', which listed the kings of Sumeria in ancient Mesopotamia, but they did not take it very seriously partly because many of the kings were given great ages. The scholars thought they were merely legendary people, invented for the sake of showing off a long history of the Sumerians. Then in 1959 one of these kings, the King of Kish, was discovered to have been a real historical person, and he was said to have reigned for 900 years!

No longer can anyone argue that Bible characters with great ages are not real people; neither can we say with certainty that their ages are not real either. We are not without a good reason for supposing that before the flood (see Genesis 6-9) people lived much longer. This would not account for the 28,000 years attributed to some of the Sumerian kings but there is evidence of an entirely different climate before the flood that was more helpful to longer living. The universal flood altered the whole climate in which man lived, and in Genesis 11 the genealogy reveals a steady reduction in the life-span. By the time that Psalm 90:10 was written God had reduced it further to seventy years. Abraham died 'at a good old age, an old man, and full of years'; he was 175 (Genesis 25:7-8). Incidentally, in Europe by the seventeenth century A.D. man had reduced his average life-span still further to fifty-three years.

Noah's ark

In 1872, George Smith, an assistant working at the British Museum, deciphered some clay tablets and found he was reading a seventh-century B.C. Babylonian story of a great flood. It is a 200-line poem about Ut-napishtim, who is ordered by his god to build an ark in order to escape the flood with which the council of gods planned to destroy the earth. Although there are many differences, and the *Gilgamesh Epic*, as it is known, speaks of many warring gods, there can be little doubt that the Babylonian story reflects the facts related in the account of the flood in Genesis 6.

From the list of Sumerian kings we have a similar story from Mesopotamia. This time the gods are concerned that man is becoming too numerous and they plan a flood to reduce the numbers. In this *Atrakhasis Epic* it is Atrakhasis whom the god Enlil orders to build a boat.

Interestingly, but not surprisingly, the story of a great flood is one of the most widely held stories in the world. The ancient literature of more than thirty nations contains flood stories, including that of Persia, Siberia, Africa, Greece, China, the Aborigines of Australia, the Maoris of New Zealand, the Eskimos of Alaska and the Red Indians of North America. The most natural explanation of these stories is the reality of the account related in Genesis 6.

A word of warning about the flood! In 1929 the renowned archaeologist Sir Leonard Woolley had his team digging in the area of the Babylonian city of Ur when his men came across three metres of clay. Within days the news flashed around the world: 'We have found the flood.' At long last, it seemed, we had firm evidence of a terrible deluge that wiped out the civilization of the area around the great river Euphrates. According to Woolley the disaster covered an area 400 miles long by 100 miles wide north-west of the Persian Gulf. Was this the biblical flood? It was even dated at 4000 B.C. The problem with Woolley's claim is that is cannot be harmonized with the claims made for the flood in the time of Noah, during which the waters rose six metres above the mountains and all life, both human and animal, was destroyed 'under the entire heavens' (Genesis 7:21-23). If Noah went through a localized flood, why was it necessary for him to take on board representatives of all the animals? Surely as the waters subsided animals from outside the flood-zone would have moved in. That Woolley found evidence of a devastating flood there is no doubt, but it was certainly not the flood of Noah's day.

Civilization in the time of Abraham

The story of Abraham begins with the account: 'Terah took his son Abram ... and his daughter-in-law Sarai ... and together they set out from Ur of the Chaldeans to go to Canaan. But when they came to Haran, they settled there' (Genesis 11:31).

Today Ur is a railway station 120 miles north of Basra in Iraq. The British Museum in London exhibits a fascinating display of items from the ancient city of Ur of the Chaldees in the time of Abraham. In 1926 Sir Leonard Woolley excavated the site of Ur, the city of Abraham's birth, and his discoveries revealed the advanced state of civilization there even centuries before Abraham. The patriarch may well have lived in a two-storey brick house with a lobby, courtyard, kitchen and toilet, bedrooms and reception rooms; Sarah could have been accustomed to wearing beautifully intricate head-dresses and jewellery. Tablets of clay and a small square-ended spatula were the paper and pencil of Abraham's day; baked hard in the sun, the completed document would last almost indefinitely. Thousands of these official records reveal a bustling city of merchants and businessmen trading across into Syria and down to the Persian Gulf; they record purchases, marriages, and all the events of the life of a busy city. There were even tablets used by teachers to help children learn to read and write — these were of immense help to the archaeologists! The priests were busy with their elaborate duties at the gigantic temple of the moon god Sin.

Obviously Abraham, thought by some to be a primitive nomadic tribesman, came from a city of culture and comforts. Cities of the same date, excavated in the same region, reveal that these people had a correct understanding of mathematics and geometry, including the theory of Pythagorus, nearly fifteen hundred years before the Greek philosopher wrote it down!

The great city of Ebla, though not mentioned in the Bible, was situated not far from Haran, the town from which Abraham was called by God into the desert. The tell of Ebla, Tell Mardikh, was positively identified in 1975 and since then valuable information has come from the clay tablets in the archive room of the royal palace. This city was flourishing in the time of Abraham, with a population at one period of more than a quarter of a million.

One interesting fact arises from all the information we gain from such cities as these. For many years critics claimed that Moses could not possibly have written the first five books of the Bible for the simple reason that writing had not been invented so early on. We now have royal libraries and archives that pre-date Abraham, not to mention Moses, by at least 500 years!

The law of Moses

'And God spoke all these words' (Exodus 20:1). So reads the verse that introduces the laws given to Moses on Mount Sinai. Hammurabi lived in Babylon at least 200 years before Moses was born in Egypt. Some of the laws of his kingdom were carefully chiselled onto a stone pillar two and a quarter metres high. These laws contain many similarities to the laws of Moses found in Exodus 21-23. There are significant differences, however, since the laws given by Moses clearly have a higher view of the value of life. There is no need to suppose, as some critics do, that Moses 'borrowed' ideas from the Hammurabi Code. Moses' laws came from God himself, and the similarities are explained by the fact that there were common concerns in the ancient world. The laws given by Moses put into writing principles that God had given his people over a long period of time. Indeed the ancient world no doubt benefited from the presence of men like Abraham and the patriarchs and the standards they set.

Child sacrifice

Deuteronomy 18:10 gives the solemn warning: 'Let no one be found among you who sacrifices his son or daughter in the fire.'

In the Syrian Room at the British Museum in London a number of small urns are on display containing the remains of children burnt in the gruesome practice of child sacrifice. Attempts to suggest that such a religious rite never existed come to nothing in the light of ample evidence that thousands of children were sacrificed, from before the time of Moses until the second century B.C. and from Syria to North Africa. It is estimated that in Carthage alone some 30,000 children were killed in this way between 400 and 200 B.C.

Ancient writers suggest that the children, normally between one and three years of age, were either drugged or had their throats slit before being offered to the gods. Vivid accounts have come down to us of the ritual which took place by moonlight and was accompanied by musicians, dancers, priests and the parents of the victim. Hideous clay masks, representing the angry demons and probably copies of those worn by the dancers, have been found near the remains of the victims. City leaders were expected to offer their sons, especially in times of national danger. Carthage, the Phoenician city in north Africa, was a centre for this terrible practice until the destruction of the city by the Romans in 146 B.C., though before this, fewer children were offered and more animals were substituted.

God condemned this foul rite among his people and ordered the death penalty for anyone found involved in it (Leviticus 20:1-5). However, both Ahaz and Manasseh burnt their children in the fire (2 Chronicles 28:3; 2 Kings 21:6). Theories about the identification of the god 'Molech' referred to in the Bible continue. Some scholars believe the word is derived from the Hebrew for 'king' *(melech)*; together with the vowels for the word 'shame', and referred to the shameful practices of the pagan nations. Others believe 'Molech' is taken from the Phoenician word for 'sacrifice' and may not refer to a god at all. The Carthaginians sacrificed their children to Ba'al Hammon, and *moloch* was the name given to the offering of the children — a practice that disgusted the Persians, Greeks and Romans as much as it does us. The prophets continually outlawed the practice in Israel (for example, Jeremiah 32:35) .

Ashurbanipal, King of Assyria

Like others before him and since, Ashurbanipal II, King of Assyria in the ninth century B.C., set out to conquer the world. As a first step his army had to secure the narrow coastal strip alongside the Mediterranean Sea — Syria and Palestine. King Omri of Israel saw the terrifying armies of Assyria and built himself the fortified city of Samaria. He might well have been afraid. Here is a vivid and blood-curdling description by Ashurbanipal himself of his occupation of Syria just north of Israel: 'I marched from the Orontes [a river in northern Syria] … I conquered the cities… I caused great slaughter, I destroyed, I demolished, I burned. I took their warriors prisoner and impaled them on stakes before their cities. I settled Assyrians in their place... I washed my weapons in the Great Sea.' This was the 'great and honourable Ashurbanipal' (or Osnapper in the Aramaic) who is referred to in Ezra 4:10; he lived 200 years before Ezra.

The palace of Susa

The book of Esther tells us that the events it recounts took place when 'King Xerxes reigned from his royal throne in the citadel of Susa' (Esther 1:2). The writer had far more important matters to write about than to give us a description of this mighty king's splendid palace. He was recording an attempted extermination of God's people. However, archaeology can fill out that verse for us.

The Persian Empire at this time stretched from India to Greece and south to Ethiopia. The great king lived in magnificent splendour and when Alexander the Great of Greece marched his victorious army into Susa about 150 years after Esther was queen there, tradition says that he carried away over 1,000 tons of gold! Here is a description of the king holding a banquet in the palace gardens; it could well describe Esther 5:4: 'The courtyard was decorated with blue and white cotton curtains, tied by cords of fine purple linen to silver rings on marble columns. Couches made of gold and silver had been placed in the courtyard, which was paved with white marble, red feldspar, shining mother-of-pearl, and blue turquoise' (*Treasures from Bible Times*, p.144)

From the excavations of other cities we know how Darius I, the father of Esther's King Xerxes, impressed his subjects with his palaces. They were magnificent buildings partly cut into the rock with a wide stone staircase leading to the entrance gate of the courtyard. Elaborate carvings decorated the walls as more stairs carried the visitor closer to the audience hall. The porch leading to the audience hall was sixty metres long with carved stone columns twenty metres high, and this is where Esther stood as she approached the king (Esther 5:1). The audience hall where the great king sat on his throne glittered with carvings and colourful paintings, tapestries and carpets. The courtiers were no less impressive, wearing their embroidered robes and dripping with jewellery. Everything was designed to display the immense wealth and power of these great despots of the ancient world.

Scenes like this are the fruit of diligent archaeology and they add
a richness to the story of Esther the queen that is overlooked in the
more important record of the book itself.

The temple courtyards

When Paul was arrested in Jerusalem, his accusers claimed, 'He has
brought Greeks into the temple area and defiled this holy place'
(Acts 21:28).

In 1871 a limestone slab was discovered in Jerusalem; it
measured fifty-seven centimetres long and eighty-five high.
Painted in red to stand out on the light limestone background was the
warning: 'No foreigner may pass the barrier and enclosure
surrounding the temple. Anyone who is caught doing so will be
himself to blame for his resulting death.' The stone originally stood
in the outer courtyard of the temple to guard the holy place against
the intrusion of any Gentile. The message was clear and even the
Roman general Titus, who later destroyed the city and went on to
become emperor in A.D. 79, acknowledged that it also applied to the
Romans themselves. Any violation would be met with instant
execution. The charge against Paul when the Jews erroneously
thought he had admitted some Greeks to the temple area brought the
city to a flash-point. Only the prompt action of the Roman duty
officer saved Paul's life.

Perhaps Paul had this very stone in mind when he wrote to the
Christians at Ephesus reminding them that 'Christ himself is our
peace, who has made the two one, and has destroyed the barrier, the
dividing wall of hostility' (Ephesians 2:14). This 'dividing wall' is
now in the museum in Istanbul in Turkey, but both Christ and Paul,
as well as all the apostles, must have looked at it often and
recognized in it the significance of their gospel.

Conclusion

We saw in chapter 9 the valuable contribution that was made to
biblical studies by the work of Robert Dick Wilson and William
Mitchell Ramsay; they were to a great extent lone voices, and the
critics found it convenient to ignore them. Since then, it has not been
so simple for those who do not believe the Bible to pretend the

evidence does not exist. Earlier this century the traveller and author P. J. Wiseman claimed that if the mass of evidence available today had been available in the nineteenth century if would have been impossible for the Higher Critics to put forward the views they did.

Some years ago, Magnus Magnusson, after a lengthy television series which put the authority of the Bible on trial under the pretence of scientific investigation, admitted: 'I'm not an archaeologist but a journalist. I'm quite sure that in ten years time much of the line which I have taken in this series would need to be rewritten.' In fact it needed to be rewritten more than ten years *before* his series! But sadly the media are frequently more interested in destructive criticism than in the truth.

Alan Millard, Professor of Hebrew and Ancient Semitic Languages at the University of Liverpool and a noted archaeologist, has more recently given his own conclusion on this subject: 'Finally, we affirm that nothing has been found which can be proved to contradict any statement of the Old Testament. Archaeological research is a welcome aid to a richer knowledge of the Bible's message.'

16.
Errors and contradictions?

'The Bible is full of errors and contradictions!' Almost every evangelical Christian has faced this challenge. Throughout this book we have made the claim that the inerrancy of Scripture is plenary (covering all its facts as well as doctrines) and verbal (including the actual words of the original manuscripts). But such a claim is not without its problems, because there are parts of the Bible that appear to contain errors and contradictions; it would be dishonest to pretend otherwise. Sometimes we can give a good answer to those who attack the Bible, but sometimes we just do not have sufficient information to solve the problem beyond doubt. When we face this situation there are a number of facts we must never forget.

Some principles to remember

Is inerrancy Bible nit-picking?

A not uncommon charge against those who believe in inerrancy is that it forces its defenders to concentrate on the detail of Scripture at the expense of its message. This, of course, is nonsense; those who believe in inerrancy are at the forefront of sharing its message. Besides, evangelicals only defend inerrancy when it is attacked. It is surely better to give a vigorous defence rather than duck the issue by mumbling about minor errors not making any difference to our full confidence in an infallible Scripture. The Swiss theologian Karl Barth once claimed that the authors of Scripture could 'be at fault in any word, and have been at fault in every word, and yet they have still spoken the Word of God in their fallible and erring human word'. Theologians may understand what that is supposed to mean, but for most of us it stands reason on its head and faith goes cross-eyed!

What about memory loss?

For some who read the Bible, it seems impossible that men could accurately record events that happened so long before; surely, the argument runs, with the passing of time they would have forgotten the details and we can therefore assume that even if the Gospel writers intended to be accurate, they must have suffered from slips of memory. We are then entertained by the imaginary example of four people reporting on the same incident who will each, unintentionally of course, contradict the others. There are two replies to this.

In chapter 6 we made the point that Christ promised that the Holy Spirit would aid the memory of the disciples and 'remind you of everything I have said to you' (John 14:26). Our first answer, therefore, is to point out that the writers of the Bible were supernaturally aided to ensure the accuracy of their work. We have covered this in detail earlier and need not repeat it here.

The second response to this assumption of memory-loss is to lament the fact that in our modern age of technology so much of our knowledge is stored in electronic files and we no longer have to exercise our memories. Like unused muscles, our memory bank has become flabby. The modern student does not know the answer, but he does know where to find the answer!

At one time memories were trained to be sharp. Xenophon, the fourth-century B.C. Greek historian, philosopher and soldier, tells of a Greek by the name of Niceratus whose father made him learn the works of Homer by heart. The *Iliad* and *Odyssey* each contain twenty-four books, and each book averages more than 500 lines. Apparently this kind of feat was not exceptional among the ancient Greeks.

Even in more modern times, men have achieved remarkable feats of memory. When the Soviet dissident writer Alexander Solzhenitsyn was exiled to a Siberian labour camp for making a derogatory reference to Stalin in a letter, he spent much of his time writing books in his mind. He wrote twelve to twenty lines at a time on scraps of paper, learned them and destroyed the evidence. Once a month he recited all he had written — counting the lines as he went. On his release, Solzhenitsyn immediately committed 12,000 lines to print.

These two examples, separated by more than 2,000 years of human history, demonstrate how powerfully accurate the human memory can be with sufficient incentive. Even if we overlook the vital ingredient of the divine aid to ensure an accurate memory, we can surely expect that the disciples rehearsed the words of their Master over and over again until they could accurately recall his teaching. After all, what he really said was far more valuable than anything they could have invented.

Is it reasonable and possible?

The doctrine of verbal inspiration does not depend upon our being able to prove infallibly and conclusively our solution of every problem, but it does depend upon our being able to demonstrate that no statement of Scripture is, by any and every reasoning, inaccurate. If we can show that there is a reasonable and possible solution of each particular problem, then the doctrine of verbal and plenary inspiration stands intact. We must abandon our belief only when the Bible is proved, beyond all doubt and beyond all defence, to be in error at even one point. It was understanding this important principle that led Charles Haddon Spurgeon, the great English preacher of a century ago, to ignore the conclusions of the so-called 'higher critical' scholars who denied as many of the historical facts of the Bible as they possibly could. He knew that if he interpreted the Bible correctly it would never be proved wrong and that it was the arguments of the critics that would be found false. In this Spurgeon has been shown to be right.

Lies and more lies

While committed to the total accuracy of Scripture, verbal inspiration does not involve us in a belief that every part of Scripture is a proclamation of truth. For example, the Bible records evil acts and lies told by men. Herod claimed that he wanted to worship Christ (Matthew 2:8) but we know from his later action that this was a lie. Similarly, it is evident that certain statements of Job's friends, although they are accurately recorded, are contrary to truth. We know this because God himself said so (Job 42:7). However, we must only come to such a conclusion when there is clear biblical evidence to lead us there.

By the pen of two or more witnesses

Nowhere in the Bible is the doctrine of verbal inspiration so attacked as it is in the Gospels. The problem is that not only are there differences in the order of events, although the writers do not claim an exact chronological order for all the narratives, but there are also variations in the recorded words of our Lord.

At least these problems provide evidence that the Gospel writers often worked independently of each other. Many modern critics claim that they used the same sources for their stories and just altered and added to them here and there. This is clearly not so because if Matthew, Mark or Luke (John is generally considered to be an independent witness anyway) were each aware of the work of only one of the others, or if they used common source material, then it is quite impossible to imagine that they would not have noticed that their accounts here and there were open to misunderstanding, and they would surely have altered them to avoid the problem. It is a mark of inspiration that these three independent writers nowhere plainly contradict each other.

We might also wonder why God did not simply give us one Gospel account and then there could be no apparent contradictions. In the first place there is a good biblical principle that any matter should be established by two or three witnesses (Matthew 18:16; 1 Timothy 5:19; Revelation 11:3). By giving us four independent witnesses to the life and death of Christ, God has confirmed his Word in a remarkable way. Interestingly, however, the critics of the Bible spend their time focusing on the supposed contradictions, some of which we shall answer in the next chapter, but fail to be convinced by the evidence of the full agreement, even in detail, of the great majority of the records. Besides, if we had only one Gospel writer we can be sure that the critics would use this as strong evidence against the reliability of the Bible; they would claim that we cannot give credibility to a single source.

Harmonizing — right or wrong?

Some have trouble with the need to harmonize at all; they feel that the very need betrays a great weakness in the Bible and it would be so much better if there were no 'apparent' contradictions. In the first place many of the supposed contradictions would never be seen as such in any book other than the Bible. The high claim for the Bible made by the evangelical Christian invites opponents to prove it false. No other book has been subject to such demanding claims and minute inspection.

But why should we ever be embarrassed by the need to harmonize the Bible? When two honest witnesses stand in a court of law with two stories that do not agree in every detail, it is not immediately assumed that one is lying or that either is wrong; a perfectly reasonable explanation can show both to be true. The same is true when two of our friends give us different accounts of the same event. If the witnesses are known liars then I will certainly doubt them, but since no one has certainly proved the Bible wrong at any point where it can be checked, it has a right to be trusted.

Writing in his book *Tough Questions Christians Ask*, Kenneth Kantzer provides an excellent example from his own experience of how two apparently contradictory accounts can have a perfectly reasonable explanation. This is his story: 'Some time ago the mother of a dear friend of ours was killed. We first learned of her death through a trusted mutual friend who reported that our friend's mother had been standing on the street corner waiting for a bus, had been hit by another bus passing by, was fatally injured, and died a few minutes later. Shortly thereafter, we learned from the grandson of the dead woman that she had been involved in a collision, was thrown from the car in which she was riding and was killed instantly. The boy was quite certain of his facts, relayed them clearly, and stated that he had secured his information directly from his mother — the daughter of the woman who had been killed. No further information was forthcoming from either source. Now which would you believe? We trusted both friends, but we certainly could not get the data together. Much later, we were able to seat the mother and grandson in our living room. There we probed for a harmonization. We learned that the grandmother had been waiting for a bus, was hit by another bus, and was critically injured. She had been picked up by a passing car and dashed to hospital, but in haste, the car in which she was being transported to the hospital collided with another car. She was thrown from the car and died instantly. This story from my own experience presents no greater difficulty than that of any recorded in the Gospels.'

Progressive revelation

Our belief in the sufficiency of Scripture does not imply that any one part is necessarily sufficient by itself. There are stages of revelation. For example, the song of Deborah (Judges 5) and some of the psalms praying for punishment upon enemies (e.g. Psalm 109) may not be appropriate for a Christian congregation to sing as a curse upon human enemies. Jesus discouraged his disciples from copying Elijah (Luke 9:54-56) but this in no way condemns Elijah's action. David's method of killing his enemies (2 Samuel 8:2) is not a model for modern military commanders. The epistle of James is an important part of Scripture, but standing alone it is not the clearest book to teach the doctrine of justification by faith. There is a progression as God reveals more and more through the Scriptures. It is the whole Bible that is sufficient, not any one part.

Interpreting the Old by the New

An important principle in understanding the Bible is that since the New Testament is as much part of God's infallible revelation as the Old Testament, it is God's own commentary upon the Old Testament. There are a number of occasions when the New Testament makes statements and gives information about Old Testament characters or events that are found nowhere in the Old Testament. This is not a sign of error but is God's way of adding to our understanding of the Old Testament. For example, we learn much about Moses that is not revealed in the Old Testament (see Acts 7:22; Hebrews 11:24-27), including the names of the Egyptian magicians (compare 2 Timothy 3:8 with Exodus 7:11). We also learn facts about Elijah (James 5:17) and Lot (2 Peter 2:7-8) which are nowhere recorded in the Old Testament.

Be patient

We must never forget that even the number of alleged errors forms only a very small fraction of the whole Bible and that again and again seemingly unsolvable difficulties have been solved in the light of modern discoveries and the advance of knowledge. Therefore we would be justified in claiming that time will resolve the difficulties that still remain.

These principles must be kept in mind throughout the remainder of this chapter.

The actual words of Jesus

On the question of the differences in the recorded words of Christ, there are two points to bear in mind.

First of all, there is no reason why Christ could not have used a variety of words in his teaching, and have taught the same thing on a number of different occasions. The early church leader Origen once wrote, 'The Gospel writers are four, but the gospel is one.' Perhaps few, if any, of the recorded episodes contain all the words that our Lord spoke on any particular occasion; each writer therefore placed his emphasis upon a different part of Christ's teaching, and unless they are proved to be contradictory we simply add each contribution to the whole picture.

Second, this matter of different words attributed to Christ raises the question of whether in the Gospel records we have the exact words of Jesus, or his authentic voice without necessarily his exact words. It is the difference between what the scholars refer to as the *ipsissima verba Jesu* (the precise words of Jesus), or the *ipsissima vox Jesu* (the precise voice of Jesus). The difference may be subtle, but it can be important. Remember that we cannot be reading his actual words if he spoke in Aramaic, the disciples recorded his words in Greek and we are reading them in English! However, we are hearing his authentic voice if the words used by the disciples exactly express what he said. If my words are translated into a foreign language and when the translation is shown to me I recognize it is an accurate translation, I may quite truthfully say, 'Yes, those are my exact words.' We have our Lord's actual words only in the cry from the cross recorded in Matthew 27:46 and Mark 15:34.

Since languages can rarely be translated word for word, there are bound to be slight variations between the writers in their accounts of the same event. When the Holy Spirit reminded the disciples of everything Christ had said (John 14:26), he allowed them some liberty of expression whilst at the same time ensuring that they conveyed exactly the meaning of our Lord's words. Look back at the definition of 'inspiration' at the end of chapter 3. Remember that variation is not contradiction; if different words are occasionally used to report a saying of our Lord then we believe that they all help to give the full meaning of what he said.

Here are just two examples of the different words used for the sermons of Christ. In Matthew 6:11 our Lord taught the disciples to pray: 'Give us today...' In Luke 11:3 he taught: 'Keep on giving us each day...' The verb 'to give' is a completed form in Matthew and a continuous form in Luke. Similarly Matthew uses the word 'today' whilst Luke uses 'each day'. It is very likely that these represent two occasions when our Lord preached substantially the same sermon; if so, why should he not vary the emphasis on the second occasion? No contradiction is involved. Even if it can be shown that both records refer to the same occasion we must insist that our Lord simply repeated his teaching in a different form to give the fullest possible meaning. What is certain is that in both Gospels we can confidently say, 'These are the words of Jesus', since they are what he actually said and what he intended the Gospel writers to record.

Unacceptable solutions

Sources in error?

The writers of the Bible, and particularly of the Old Testament, used many sources for their material. 1 Chronicles 29:29 refers to the books of Nathan and Gad in addition to the book of Samuel. Similarly, Ezra and Nehemiah contain genealogies, letters of Persian kings and other documents, presumably copies from ancient libraries or 'archives'. In the New Testament Luke lays claim to careful and diligent search (Luke 1:1-4). It is sometimes suggested that these original sources contained errors and that when they were copied by the inspired writers of Scripture God did not consider it necessary to correct these defects. Matthew Henry, the wise and spiritual seventeenth-century Bible commentator, accepts this argument and in his comment upon some of the problems found in the genealogy of 1 Chronicles 8:1-32 suggests: 'There was no necessity for the making up of defects, no, nor for the rectifying of the mistakes, of these genealogies by inspiration: it was sufficient that he copied them out as they came to his hand, or so much of them as was requisite to the present purpose.'

But the question is, are there mistakes? It may not necessarily undermine the doctrine of inerrancy to admit that there are, and in the next chapter we shall see that when, for example, Joab reported the result of David's census to the king, the figure may only be an estimate. All the Scriptures do is accurately to report Joab's numbers. Certainly when we have the text of a letter by a pagan king, as in Ezra 7:11-26, the accuracy is limited to the reporting of that letter. In the unlikely event that it is one day proved beyond doubt that Artaxerxes had eight and not seven advisers (v.14) the error would be the king's and not Ezra's. However the weakness of this defence is that we cannot always be certain when a writer is quoting from documents or when he is receiving direct revelation from God; we have no right to assume he is using ancient records unless he specifically tells us so.

Others are not really troubled by what they consider to be minor errors here and there, since they consider them to be unimportant and they do not affect the doctrine of the authority of Scripture. But authority and inerrancy are necessarily related to each other and therefore no apparent error is unimportant.

Copyists' errors

Some find it easy to hide behind 'copyists' errors' and assume that any problem we cannot solve was not in the original writing, but has been introduced over the years as the Bible was copied. This is an attractive idea and to some certain extent the argument is allowable. For example, where one Hebrew letter can change the number twenty into thirty we may plead a copyist's error. But are we right to plead copyists' errors where a whole phrase or sentence is involved?

Even the great sixteenth-century Reformer John Calvin occasionally went too far in this direction. For example, during Stephen's sermon recorded in Acts 7, the Christian martyr claimed that Jacob came to Egypt with seventy-five souls (v.14) whereas according to Genesis 46:27 the number was seventy. Similarly in Acts 7:16 Stephen says that Abraham bought a tomb from the sons of Hamor at Shechem, whereas Genesis 23:9 claims that the patriarch bought the cave of Machpelah from 'Ephron son of Zohar'. Calvin resolved the first problem by suggesting that Stephen simply copied the erroneous number of seventy-five found in the Greek translation of the Old Testament (the Septuagint), and warns that Paul told us not to be too troubled by genealogies. The second discrepancy is dismissed by Calvin with the words: 'It is manifest that there is a mistake... Wherefore this place must be amended.' In the next chapter we shall suggest a more satisfactory solution to these two apparent mistakes. To admit occasional errors in the copying is one thing, but to allow errors in the original autographs is another.

The Bible and science

Many find difficulty in Scripture because, in places, it appears to be contradicted by modern scientific theories and knowledge. Our reply to this is that if current scientific knowledge is our standard for judging the accuracy of Scripture then we must abandon our belief in the virgin birth, the resurrection, the miracles of our Lord and the fact that in creation God made everything out of nothing. In these examples the most that any scientist can say is that he has never observed them to happen.

As Christians we believe that God can, and does, intervene in the universe he has made. A great weakness in many supposed scientific conclusions is that people forget that when a scientist says, 'We have never seen this happen and we cannot explain how it happens; therefore it has never happened,' he is coming to a very false conclusion. Scientists cannot say that a virgin birth, or a resurrection from the dead, or creation out of nothing is impossible; no scientist knows enough about the universe to say this. He can only say, 'I have never seen it happen, and I do not know how it could happen', but the conclusion is not 'Therefore it did not happen' — that would be a very unscientific and even dishonest conclusion.

To avoid a clash with science it is at times claimed that the Bible is not a scientific textbook and therefore it does not make scientific statements. Of course it is true that the Bible is not a scientific text-book if by that we mean it does not always describe scientific facts in the language of modern science. But if that is the definition of a scientific textbook then few scientific publications issued before the last fifty years can be described as scientific either. Scientific language and theories are constantly changing.

It is a fact that the Bible does make claims about subjects that are of great interest to the scientist. The origin of the universe is one obvious example; and so is its description of a universal flood. The Bible describes both of these in a plain straightforward manner, and in language that men in every generation can understand. All these are facts capable, in some measure, of scientific investigation. It is true that miracles are not easily open to scientific investigation and in this sense they may be 'unscientific'. However, that does not make them against or contrary to science, unless, that is, we make a god of science.

Science, by its very definition, can never reach a final statement. Fifty years ago scientists talked confidently of the laws discovered by Isaac Newton; then Einstein disproved many of them, and today some are trying to improve upon Einstein himself! It was once agreed that an atom was the smallest particle of matter and it was impossible to divide it; now every student of physics knows about the practical effects of splitting the atom! Science must always be ready to alter course when new facts demand such action. Revelation, on the other hand, is final. We therefore expect science, as it advances in knowledge, constantly to change and increasingly to support biblical statements. In this expectation we are not disappointed.

It is not our present concern to spend time considering the supposed scientific problems in biblical creation as described in the opening chapters of Genesis. All that we need to claim here is that many non-Christian scientists disagree with the modern theories of evolution as explanations for the origin of the universe, and that there are a large number of scientific books that defend biblical creation. To say that science has disproved the Bible, and especially the Genesis account of creation, is nothing less than a lie. The most we can say is that many scientists think the Bible to be wrong — but many do not think so. If we believe that revelation is more certain than science then we shall have no hesitation in accepting God's record rather than man's ideas.

Admittedly in the Bible there are some claims that have given its opponents an opportunity to dismiss its relevance. Here are just three.

The language of the Bible

It is often claimed that such expressions as 'the four corners of the earth' (Isaiah 11:12) and the 'pillars' of the earth (Psalm 75:3) reflect a primitive view that the earth was flat and supported by posts. Pictures are often drawn in text books to illustrate the simplistic Hebrew view! But if such a claim is made, then it must at once be accepted that 'the circle of the earth' (Isaiah 40:22) and Job's claim that God 'spreads out the northern skies over empty space; and suspends the earth over nothing' (Job 26:7) are statements full of modern scientific knowledge! It is wiser to take all these statements as poetic descriptions, but it is interesting, though hardly surprising, to note that critics ridicule those first two phrases and completely ignore the second two.

Strange incidents

Balaam's ass, Moses crossing the Red Sea, Elisha's floating axe-head and Jonah's big fish are all too absurd for many to accept. But what a man may think absurd is hardly a standard for judging the facts of the case. Perhaps Balaam, Moses, Elisha and Jonah would have considered it absurd to be told that man would one day walk on the moon, or walk in space a hundred miles above the surface of the earth, or live for weeks at the bottom of the oceans in a metal tube — even Jonah did not experience that! In fact an all-powerful God can do what he wants to and use whatever means he chooses.

The sun and moon standing still

Perhaps no two stories in the Bible have been so quickly dismissed as untrue as that of the sun standing still, recorded in Joshua 10:12-14, and the shadow going backwards in 2 Kings 20:11. We are told that, according to our present scientific knowledge of the universe, if the sun appeared to stand still this must mean that the earth had stopped its rotation round the sun and, as a consequence, the earth would be drawn into the sun and would be burned up. This miracle is therefore dismissed as impossible.

Sadly many Christians feel they must bow to this and they try to find another way of understanding the passage. Perhaps, they suggest, it is really just a poetic story? But our principles of hermeneutics (see chapter 14) will not allow this. Joshua is a book written as plain history and this story is written as plain history also. Then perhaps it was merely a day so full of activity that to Joshua it seemed that the sun had stopped? Even today we talk about 'time standing still'. But to argue like this does not take into account all that happened on that day! We shall survey briefly the events of Joshua 10.

Joshua was compelled by his treaty of peace to help the Gibeonites when they were attacked by five kings of the Amorites. He wanted to gain a complete victory, and to do this required careful strategy and plenty of time. Joshua acted quickly and marched his army through the night from Gilgal to Gibeon, a distance of about forty kilometres (twenty-five miles) on a 914 metre (3,000 feet) ascent.

The five kings panicked and fled on the road to Beth-horon. On this road God rained great hailstones on the retreating army, but Joshua's men, tired after a night march and a morning battle, required more time to catch up with the retreating Amorites. The hailstones halted the enemy and gave Joshua's men a much-needed rest; it is unlikely they returned to Gilgal at this point and verse 15 probably refers to the close of this long day.

Having cut off their retreat into Jerusalem, Joshua drove the Amorites a further twenty-six kilometres (seventeen miles) to Makkedah where the five kings were discovered hiding in a cave. Joshua sealed the cave and pressed on to Azekah, a further five kilometres (three miles) before returning to deal with the kings at Makkedah, and destroying the city itself (v. 28). At sunset Joshua was at Makkedah with his weary but victorious army (v. 27).

In one night and day Joshua had marched his men twenty-five miles up a 3,000 foot ascent, fought a battle, chased the retreating enemy a further twenty miles to Azekah, returned three miles to Makkedah and destroyed a city. We may compare this achievement with that of Sir Archibald Hunter who, when he set out to relieve the British Army at Mafeking, South Africa, in May 1900, started at four in the morning, marched his army until eight at night and covered thirty miles in those sixteen hours!

A closer parallel is the fact that a thousand years after Joshua the Roman legionary was not infrequently driven to cover thirty-six kilometres (twenty-two miles) in five hours and with a full pack weighing thirty kilograms (seventy pounds)! A forced march was well in excess of fifty kilometres (thirty-one miles) a day.

It is clear that the story of Joshua 10 demands a longer than usual day. An extra twelve hours would be sufficient — just! We cannot suggest the writer put all the details in to support a pretended miracle, because if this had been his intention he would have given us details of distances between towns and the height of Beth-horon above Gilgal; in fact we have to study carefully the passage, and the geography of the land, in order to realize just how much was achieved in one day.

We may note in passing that in 1890 the American astronomer and mathematician Professor Totten calculated the exact time of this 'long day'; his reckoning was confirmed by W. Maunders, a Fellow of the Royal Society of Astronomy at the Royal Observatory Greenwich, in his book *Astronomy and the Bible* published in 1908. In addition there are many independent records of a long day, particularly from Greece, Egypt and China. Herodotus, 'the father of history', lived in Greece about 480 B.C. and he informs us that priests in Egypt showed him records of a long day, which coincided with Joshua's time. Chinese writings place a 'long day' in the time of Emperor Yeo, a contemporary of Joshua. All this information is not conclusive proof, but it is sufficient to warn us that it is contrary to science to dismiss the story just because we find it hard to believe.

17.
Examples of supposed errors and contradictions

It is now time to turn our attention to some examples of supposed errors and contradictions in the Bible. These are divided into five areas for the sake of convenience.

Dates, numbers and family trees

It is claimed that in the Bible there are many chronological, numerical and genealogical inaccuracies — in other words, incorrect dates, numbers and family trees!

Much of the Old Testament is made up of lists, but do they have any relevance and are they to be trusted? Actually they are often very important not merely as historical records, but to establish relationships and the right to office; their accuracy therefore mattered in Old Testament society. One example is found in Ezra 2:61-63 where a group of priests 'searched for their family records but they could not find them and so were excluded from the priesthood as unclean'. Records were kept by the prophets (2 Chronicles 12:15) and this indicates the importance of the task. However, we have to be aware of the fact that sometimes gaps occur in these list. This is not evidence of error, nor is it unusual. Outside the Bible the family tree of King Esarhaddon, the King of Assyria and Babylon who is mentioned in 2 Kings 19:37, leaves out no fewer than sixty-two generations.

There are a number of problems, not all of which can be perfectly solved, but most can be solved. We shall now examine a few examples of some inconsistent numbers.

David numbering the people

The record of Joab's census of the fighting men in Israel and Judah shows a difference of nearly a quarter of a million men in the lists given in 2 Samuel 24:9 and 1 Chronicles 21:5! In Chronicles the number of men 'who could handle a sword' was 1,100,000 in Israel and 470,000 in Judah. In Samuel the number was only 800,000 in Israel and 500,000 in Judah. In resolving this difference there are two facts we must bear in mind.

In the first place, according to 1 Chronicles 27:24, Joab never completed his count, and his incomplete numbers were 'not entered in the book of the annals of King David'. This is because Joab knew that the king should never have ordered a census in the first place and he therefore carried out the order reluctantly and half-heartedly.

Secondly, according to 1 Chronicles 21:6, Joab did not include the tribes of Levi and Benjamin in the census 'because the king's command was repulsive to him'. Presumably this is why Chronicles records that the numbers were incomplete and the larger figure in Chronicles would include an estimate for these two tribes. The figure in Samuel ignores these two tribes altogether.

In either case, the figures are simply those given by Joab, with or without the estimate for Levi and Benjamin, and they need not be exact. The accuracy of the Bible extends only to the fact that these were the figures offered to the king; it does not guarantee that Joab got his sums right and since he did not complete his census he may have inflated the figures to impress the king.

David's famine

As a punishment for numbering the people, David was offered, among other choices, 'three years' of famine (1 Chronicles 21:12). But the account in 2 Samuel 24:13 refers to 'seven years' (see NIV footnote). The reconciliation is to be found in 2 Samuel 21:1. David had already suffered three years of crop failure, the results of which continued into the fourth year; the new period of three years would follow upon this. Since Chronicles does not mention the earlier famine there is no need for it to add those years to the proposed three.

Some scribal errors

As we noted in the previous chapter, there are occasions where it is not wrong to plead that a small error which has found its way into the text during the centuries of copying and recopying is sufficient to account for a difference. There are three reasons that lead us to this conclusion. Firstly, in all major areas of fact the Bible is never found to be in error and we never have to assume a copyist's mistake to solve a problem; therefore it is reasonable to assume that in details it was also originally free from error. Secondly, all the instances where we assume a copyist's error are in small details of numbers or an occasional word; mostly they are confined to the books of Samuel, Kings and Chronicles where we can cross-check with a similar passage in Scripture. The number of differences is very small indeed. Thirdly, when we remember the difficulty of copying words that have no vowels or punctuation (see chapter 12) then we can appreciate how easily an occasional mistake could have been made; in most cases just one letter can make a difference. Here are a few examples of copyist's errors.

1 Kings 4:26 and 2 Chronicles 9:25 both claim that Solomon had 12,000 horsemen, but whereas Chronicles speaks of 4,000 stalls for horses and chariots, Kings has the unusually large figure of 40,000. This figure is almost certainly incorrect, particularly since 1 Kings 10:26 refers to Solomon possessing 1,400 chariots which would be a reasonable figure to require 4,000 stalls for chariots and horses, allowing two horses to each chariot. In Hebrew 40,000 becomes 4,000 by writing the letter 'M' in place of the letter 'T' and they are very similar letters. 'M' is like this , Δ and 'T' is like this, U . Such a small mistake is easy to understand and in reading his text back, a scribe might well have read what he expected to see rather than what he had actually written — something we are all familiar with.

1 Kings 5:13-16 and 2 Chronicles 2:2. There are eight figures quoted in these passages; of these, two are mentioned only in Kings, two more are mentioned in both and agree exactly, the last one is mentioned in both, but Kings has 3,300 while Chronicles has 3,600; the difference between these two figures is the omission of the Hebrew letter ל (L). Since 2 Chronicles 2:18 repeats the 3,600 that is most likely to be the correct figure.

1 Kings 9:28 and 2 Chronicles 8:18. The difference between the 420 talents of gold from Ophir and the 450 talents is the difference between two very similar letters in the Hebrew.

2 Kings 24:8 is correct in giving the age of Jehoiachin as eighteen years when he came to the throne. But in 2 Chronicles 36:9 his age is given as eight years. Just one word has dropped out to cause this error, and it is an understandable error because the word following the one that is missing is very similar to it in appearance; the scribe's eye must have run along the line a little too fast!

In each of these examples we have been able to correct the scribal error by the Scripture itself. Sometimes we cannot do this. For example, in 1 Samuel 13:5 the incredible number of 30,000 chariots is given to the Philistine army. It is true that among all the records of chariots that we possess of this time, no army was ever able to put so large a number into battle; in every other case the number of horsemen always exceeds the number of chariots. Besides, we are immediately told that there were 'six thousand charioteers', and for this reason some manuscripts of the Greek translations of the Old Testament change the number of chariots to 3,000, which means changing just one Hebrew letter — another small scribal error.

Ornan's threshing-floor

There is a great difference between the 'fifty shekels of silver' in 2 Samuel 24:24 and the 'six hundred shekels of gold' in 1 Chronicles 21:25. But the first refers only to the price David paid for the 'threshing floor and the oxen' while the second refers to the price he paid for the 'site', that is the whole area of Mount Moriah; this was several acres in extent and the temple was later built on it (1 Chronicles 22:1).

The kings of Israel and Judah

There are differences in the total period covered by the kings of Israel and Judah if we simply add up separately the individual years of the kings. However, frequently the years are rounded up to the nearest year, so that a king who died in his fortieth year, even if only one month into it, would often be said to have reigned forty years. Similarly some kings acted as co-regents, reigning with their father. These small differences in reckoning make a considerable difference over a few centuries. We have already noted that chronologies were carefully and accurately recorded and preserved, which is clear from 2 Chronicles 12:15 where we are told that the records were written by 'Shemaiah the prophet and Iddo the seer that deal with genealogies'.

Similarly, some differences between Scripture dating and that of pagan records, and even differences within Scripture itself, can be explained simply by alternative methods of calculating the length of a reign. This variety presents a problem to historians even outside the Bible. For example, Cicero claims that Cyrus reigned thirty years from his joining Cyaxares; Ptolemy allows him only nine years from his defeat of Babylon; whilst Xenophon reduces this to seven years from the time Cyrus became sole monarch. Perhaps Ezra's dating (Ezra 1:1) is based upon this last approach.

War between Asa and Baasha

1 Kings 15:16,32 state clearly that there was war between these two kings all their days. But 2 Chronicles 15:19 claims: 'And there was no more war until the thirty-fifth year of Asa's reign.' It is likely that the difference lies in the use of the word 'war'. Although Israel under Baasha, and Judah under Asa, were constantly in a condition of threats and hostility, there was no major armed conflict until the thirty-fifth year of Asa's reign. Even today we use the term 'war' to cover both isolated guerrilla attacks and a full-scale military clash between two or more nations. In fact 1 Kings 15:17 tells us what was happening at this time: Baasha laid siege to Judah, preventing 'anyone from leaving or entering the territory'. There were no pitched battles and no declarations of war; instead there was an uneasy peace during which Baasha contained the movements of his southern neighbours.

There is also in these passages a possible scribal error. According to 1 Kings 15:33 and 16:8 Baasha began to reign in the third year of Asa and reigned about twenty-four years until the twenty-sixth year of Asa. But 2 Chronicles 16:1 says Baasha attacked Asa in the thirty-sixth year of Asa's reign. The simplest explanation is to admit a scribal error in the figure thirty-six (and similarly for thirty-five in 2 Chronicles 15:19). In the Hebrew it is a matter of writing thirty instead of twenty; the difference is between כ and ל .

The genealogy of Jesus

Some family lists are not intended to be complete. The genealogy of our Lord recorded in Matthew is grouped in three lots of fourteen. This reflects a tidy style but does not necessarily claim to be complete. When Matthew said Uzziah was born to Jehoram (Matthew 1:8) he knew perfectly well, for his Old Testament told him, that Ahaziah, Joash and Amaziah came in between. Matthew's list differs from Luke's only in this, that Matthew traces our Lord's descent through David to Joseph, the royal line. Luke traces it through Nathan to Mary, the natural line. Both are accurate, but the purpose of each is different. Incomplete family lists in Scripture are frequently taken as examples of errors, but we are perfectly entitled to claim that those lists are not necessarily intended to be complete.

The statement that one man was father of another may leave out many generations in between. One example among many is that in 2 Kings 22:2, where Josiah is said to have walked 'in all the ways of his father David'; but Josiah was the sixteenth generation from David and the writer of the book of Kings was well aware of this fact. Such deliberate shortening of lists is quite common even outside the Bible. As a matter of fact there is no Hebrew word for 'grandson' and therefore the only way to refer to a grandson many times removed was either to give all the fathers that came between or miss them all out and call him 'son'!

Gospel chronology

The different order of the stories recorded in the Gospels would only present an unanswerable problem if each writer claimed to give the exact order. In fact only Luke claims 'an orderly account', but even this cannot be pressed too far, for 'orderly' probably means simply 'with a meaningful order'. The Gospel writers chose to arrange their material according to their individual purpose; they sometimes grouped stories together that fitted a theme. In this sense they were 'redactors', or editors.

Historical errors?

150 years ago the Bible was assumed to be full of historical errors. But the work of archaeologists, and particularly of historians like Sir William Ramsay, has changed this assumption. One by one the details that were assumed to be errors were found to be true after all, as we saw in chapters 9 and 15. We need only take two examples here because they reflect upon the accuracy of our Lord's words. It becomes less and less easy now to find examples where even critical scholars are prepared to accuse the Bible of historical inaccuracy.

Slowly the critics are learning to treat the Bible with more respect.

Abiathar the high priest

Mark 2:26 quotes our Lord as asserting: 'In the days of Abiathar the high priest, he [David] entered the house of God and ate the consecrated bread.' This was at the time of David's visit to Nob. 1 Samuel 21:1 names the priest as Ahimelech. You will notice that he is not actually called the high priest in Samuel, though we may assume that he was. Was our Lord mistaken?

We know for a fact that Ahimelech's son, Abiathar, was with his father at this time and later was the only survivor of Saul's massacre of the priests of Nob (1 Samuel 22:20). Abiathar certainly became high priest on his father's death and in fact may well have been acting jointly with his elderly father at the time of David's visit. There would be nothing unusual in such an arrangement. Whether or not Abiathar was joint high priest at the time, our Lord's statement is perfectly correct in that the episode did take place 'in the days of Abiathar' who later became well known as the high priest in the time of David.

A similar situation arises in the New Testament when Luke speaks of both Annas and Caiaphas as high priest (Luke 3:2 and Acts 4:6), and John does the same (John 18:13,19,24). In fact Annas had been deposed by the Romans in A.D.15 and his son-in-law Caiaphas took the office. According to Jewish tradition the office of high priest was for life and thus even if he was deposed or functioned jointly with his successor, his title was retained.

Zechariah the son of Berakiah

Our Lord's reference to 'Zechariah, the son of Berakiah' in Matthew 23:35 appears to contradict 2 Chronicles 24:20 where he is called 'the son of Jehoiada'. Was our Lord confusing the Zechariah of Chronicles, who was murdered 'between the temple and the altar', with the Zechariah who preached at the time of Nehemiah and who is described as 'Zechariah son of Berekiah'? (Zechariah 1:1). Clearly Christ meant to refer to the Zechariah who was murdered, but did he get the wrong father?

There is little value in trying to find another Zechariah who was murdered in the temple and we may assume our Lord was referring to the biblical Zechariah of Chronicles. How then do we answer the apparent mistake of our Lord? In the first place, if he did make a mistake and confuse the two Zechariahs it is quite amazing that the Jews, to whom he was speaking at the time, did not correct him; this fact alone teaches us that the Jews knew perfectly well to whom he was referring and did not think his language strange.

We have already noted that there is no Hebrew word for 'grand-son' and if the Zechariah of Chronicles was in fact the grandson of Jehoiada —which is quite likely since 2 Chronicles 24:15 tells us that Jehoiada died at the age of 130 years — it would be natural for Chronicles to refer to them as father and son. An example of this is found in a statement of the other Zechariah. He calls himself 'the son of Berekiah, son of Iddo' (Zechariah 1:1) while in Ezra 5:1 and 6:14 he is called simply 'the son of Iddo' (NIV 'descendant'); in fact he was the grandson of Iddo. It is quite possible that Ezra used this term 'son of Iddo' to avoid confusion with the other Zechariah in Chronicles whose father was also a man by the name of Berekiah. After all, in chapter 15 we saw how for many years critics assumed Daniel 5:1 was in error because they had never heard of a man by the name of Belshazzar!

Some suggest that a scribe copying out the text of Matthew remembered the Zechariah son of Berekiah and erroneously inserted the name here. This is very unlikely since almost every Greek manuscript of this verse that we possess contains the words 'son of Berakiah'. The fact that only one old copy of *Codex Sinaiticus* omits these words shows just how careful the copyists were with their texts because it must have been a temptation to some to alter what appeared to be an error!

Mistaken quotations?

New Testament quotations of the Old Testament

The New Testament writers frequently used the Septuagint (the Greek translation of the Old Testament made in Alexandria between 250 and 150 B.C.) and sometimes this differs from the Hebrew Masoretic Text (see chapter 12). An example of this is in 1 Corinthians 2:9, where Paul writes, 'No mind has conceived what God has prepared for those who love him.' In the Hebrew of Isaiah 64:4

the verse ends: 'No eye has seen any God beside you, who acts on behalf of those who wait for him.' Paul's quotation is very close to the Greek Septuagint of Isaiah 64.

Elsewhere New Testament writers use the Hebrew where it differs from the Greek Septuagint. Sometimes there is a mixture. Matthew 12:17-21, for example, begins with the Hebrew, departs from both Hebrew and Greek versions in the phrase 'till he leads justice to victory' (v. 20) and concludes by quoting from the Greek!

At other times a phrase is inserted that does not appear in the Hebrew versions; for example in Hebrews 1:6 where the quotation from Deuteronomy 32:43, 'Let all God's angels worship him,' is in the Greek but not in the Hebrew. Occasionally one writer follows the Hebrew (e.g. Matthew 8:17 quoting from Isaiah 53:4-5) while another takes the same verse from the Greek (e.g. 1 Peter 2:24).

If we accept Paul's statement in 1 Corinthians 2:13 we shall have no difficulty in accepting the way the New Testament writers handled the Old Testament; the apostle's use of the Old Testament, whether they used the Hebrew or Greek version, was 'not in words taught us by human wisdom but in words taught by the Spirit'. The verbal inerrancy of Scripture leads us to believe that a change of words from the Hebrew to the Greek, when used by the New Testament writers, infallibly reflects the revelation of God through those words.

It is important to realize that nowhere does a New Testament writer contradict either the Greek Septuagint or the Hebrew Masoretic Text, though he may add to or interpret the one or the other. For example, in Hebrews 10:5, 'A body you prepared for me', is taken from the Greek of Psalm 40:6. The Hebrew reads: 'My ears you have pierced' (a reference to the bond-slave of Exodus 21:6). The familiar Jewish custom of the Hebrew Old Testament had no meaning to the Greek reading the Septuagint and thus the whole (a body) is put for the part (an ear). This is a problem familiar to anyone translating the Bible from one culture to another. The two expressions are complementary, not contradictory.

A problem arises in Hebrews 11:21 where Jacob is said to have blessed Joseph's two sons 'as he leaned on the top of his staff'. Admittedly the writer is not claiming to quote from the Old Testament, but in Genesis 47:31 the Hebrew Masoretic Text clearly informs us that Jacob 'bowed down at the head of his bed'. The difficulty arises in the fact that the Hebrew word for 'bed' has just three consonants in it: MTH, whilst the Hebrew word for 'staff' also has three consonants: MTH! Remember that until 600 years after Christ, the Hebrew was written without vowels and without spacing between the words (see chapter 15). Therefore the Masoretes could have rendered the same word either by 'bed' or 'staff'; the difference meant the addition of the vowel, 'i' or 'a'. Clearly the Massoretes chose the word 'bed' and assumed the vowel was 'i', whilst the translators of the Septuagint, working long before the Masoretes, chose the word 'staff' and assumed the vowel was 'a'. But which is right? The most straightforward conclusion is that since the word used in Genesis 47 could be either 'bed' or 'staff' the Masoretes made an error of judgement in their choice and the New Testament writer, directed by the Holy Spirit (1 Corinthians 2:13), gives us the correct translation. After all, whilst Genesis 47:31 was inspired by the Spirit (so the consonants are right), the Masoretes were not (therefore the vowels may be wrong).

Zechariah or Jeremiah?

In Matthew 27:9 an Old Testament quotation which appears to come from Zechariah is attributed to Jeremiah. But the passage in Zechariah 11:12-13 is considerably different from that in Matthew and since Matthew nowhere claims to be quoting from Zechariah, he may not be.

Probably the best explanation is to notice that in the *Babylonian Talmud* (a book of Jewish laws and teaching just before and after the birth of Christ) Jeremiah is placed at the head of all the prophets (compare Matthew 16:14); so Matthew may have used Jeremiah as the general heading, just as we might say, 'Samuel tells us,' using the title of the book, when we actually refer to the words of Saul or David recorded within the book of Samuel.

Paul's paraphrase

Romans 10:6-8 is hardly a literal quotation from Deuteronomy 30:11-14, but it is an excellent paraphrase; the apostle used that which suited his theme. It can only be shown as an example of a Bible mistake if it can be proved that Paul intended to quote exactly. Paul quoted neither from the Hebrew nor the Greek (though he possessed both). He paraphrased loosely to draw out the meaning.

Similarly Romans 11:8, 'God gave them a spirit of stupor', is a paraphrase of Isaiah 29:10: 'The Lord has brought over you a deep sleep.' Ephesians 4:8 is an even looser paraphrase of Psalm 68:18.

This paraphrasing by New Testament writers in no way affects the doctrine of verbal inspiration. The words that the apostles use to give the sense of an Old Testament passage are themselves God-breathed and are therefore exactly what God desired in order to draw out an accurate meaning of the words he first gave to the Old Testament prophets. This does not, however, mean that we can settle for a paraphrase rather than a translation of the Bible text since we cannot claim the same infallibility through the Holy Spirit that the apostles had.

Bible inaccuracies?

Our claim that the Bible never contradicts itself even though written by some forty different authors over a period of fifteen hundred years is of course challenged by its critics. We must consider some of the incidents that are supposed to show the Bible as a book disagreeing with itself.

The Egyptian cattle

An example of thoughtless criticism is the suggestion that since Exodus 9:6 records the death of all Egyptian cattle, none could have remained to be killed in verse 19. The answer is obvious: either the word 'all' in verse 6 is a general term which does not mean all without exception or, more likely, the Egyptians, having lost their animals, raided the land of Goshen and plundered the Israelite herds.

Problems in Deuteronomy

The critical scholars who deny that Moses was the author of the Pentateuch emphasize minor differences between the laws in Deuteronomy and those in Leviticus and Numbers.

The laws on tithes differ in Deuteronomy (12:6,17-19; 14:22-29; 26:12-15) from Numbers (18:21-31). The most simple reconciliation is that we have in Deuteronomy a 'second tithe' different from the first and to be given in different circumstances.

There are small differences in the laws governing firstlings (compare Deuteronomy 15:19-20 with Numbers 18:17-18), bondservants (compare Deuteronomy 15:12-18 with Exodus 21:1-6) and eating carrion (compare Deuteronomy 14:21 with Leviticus 17:15). But when looked at carefully, none of these presents a contradiction; they are easily reconciled as additions and small changes to previous laws in the light of a changed situation. Remember Deuteronomy was preparing the people for the settlement in the promised land of Canaan, whereas previously laws were concerned with the wilderness wanderings.

Goliath and his brother

1 Chronicles 20:5 informs us that in renewed fighting between Israel and the Philistines, during the reign of David, 'Elhanan the son of Jair killed Lahmi the brother of Goliath'; this Goliath is probably the giant David had killed as recorded in 1 Samuel 17. But 2 Samuel 21:19 appears to leave out the words, 'Lahmi the brother of', and the suggestion is that Elhanan killed Goliath himself. However, since the writer of Samuel has already recorded the death of Goliath (1 Samuel 17) he is unlikely to have forgotten this or to expect us to have done so. There are two possible explanations. The first is that the Philistine word 'goliath' may simply mean 'giant'; in this case the writer of Samuel having already spoken of the Goliath whom David killed, is content in 2 Samuel 21:19 to refer to this man as 'a goliath' knowing that we will not confuse the two. On the other hand the writer of Chronicles has not previously spoken of Goliath and therefore must be more careful to avoid confusion.

Another possible explanation is that 2 Samuel 21:19 betrays a scribe's attempt to correct a manuscript that was not clear at this point. It is a fact that the name Lahmi (used in 1 Chronicles 20:5) is identical in Hebrew to the last part of the word Bethlehem (used in 2 Samuel 21:19). If a copy of the text was a little unclear at this point it would be very easy for a scribe to confuse 'Bethlehem' with 'killed Lahmi'; the addition of one letter and a small change in writing two others alters 'killed Lahmi' into 'Bethlehem'.

Who incited David?

2 Samuel 24:1 records that 'the Lord' incited David to the disobedient action of counting the people of Israel. 1 Chronicles 21:1

speaks of Satan inciting him. Which is correct? It is only a failure to understand the relationship between the sovereign God and the work of Satan that causes a problem at this point. In 2 Corinthians 12:7-8 Paul speaks of the 'thorn in my flesh, a messenger of Satan', which he clearly saw as coming from the Lord. God's judgement or correction is sometimes seen when he allows Satan a limited 'free hand'. This is exactly what we find in the first chapter of Job.

Paul's testimony

Sometimes a less than careful translation can mislead us. In Acts 9:7 we are informed that those accompanying Paul on the road to Damascus heard a voice but saw no one; yet in his own testimony recorded in Acts 22:9 Paul maintained that they did not 'hear the voice of him who spoke to me' (NKJV). It is sufficient to know that the verb 'to hear' when followed by the accusative case may be taken to mean 'to understand'; and so it is translated in the New International Version. In Acts 9 with the genitive case they heard the sound of the voice, but in Acts 22 with the accusative case we are informed that they did not understand the voice. In other words, they heard a voice, but without understanding it. Besides it is hardly likely that Luke would have made such an elementary mistake within such a short space of writing! He was a careful historian, not a fool.

Paul's Old Testament history

Paul claimed in 1 Corinthians 10:8 that 23,000 died 'in one day' of the plague, whereas Numbers 25:9 refers to the number of dead as 24,000. Paul may well have been making an allowance for the leaders who were killed by the sword of the judges (see Numbers 25:4-5); presumably these were killed before the plague broke out and 23,000 died of the plague in one day. Numbers 25:9, as a matter of convenience, grouped the total number of deaths resulting from the plague. This convenient reporting is common enough today; no one is accused of error if he claims that 24,000 people died by an earthquake if in fact 1,000 of them died as a result of starvation or cholera after the earthquake.

In Galatians 3:17 Paul implies that the time from God's promise to Abraham in Genesis 12:7 to the giving of the law at Sinai was 430 years. In fact, according to Exodus 12: 40-41, 430 years was the

exact time that the Israelites lived in Egypt. But Paul, brought up as
a strict Jew who knew his Old Testament thoroughly (Philippians
3:5), was hardly likely to make such a simple mistake. A careful
reading of Galatians 3:17 will show that Paul actually says, 'the law,
introduced 430 years later...' The crucial question therefore is,
'Later than what?' Paul nowhere says, 'later than the first giving of
the promise to Abraham'. If in fact Paul means to imply 430 years
after the patriarchal period of Abraham, Isaac and Jacob, during
which time the promise was often repeated, this would bring us to
the beginning of Israel's exile in Egypt and would agree with
Exodus 12:40-41.

In passing we should notice that Genesis 15:13 and Stephen in
Acts 7:6 both refer to the period as one of 400 years. But this is
merely a rounding-off of the accurate figure in Exodus 12 and
Galatians 3. We speak of the Authorized Version of the Bible being
400 years old, whereas in fact it is nearly twenty years short of that.

Stephen's Old Testament history

Stephen's long sermon in Acts 7, based upon Old Testament history,
has been criticized at many points for its supposed errors. Before we
attempt to reconcile any of these we should not forget that Stephen
was speaking before the Jewish Council who knew the Old Testament Scriptures in detail and who would have challenged any
inaccuracies at once. However, it was not for this that they stoned
him, but because 'They could not stand up against his wisdom or the
Spirit by whom he spoke' (Acts 6:10).

Stephen implies that Abraham left Haran 'after the death of his
father [Terah]' (Acts 7:4). But Genesis appears to conclude that
Terah was 145 years old when Abraham left Haran (compare
Genesis 11:26 with 12:4) and we know that Terah lived to the age
of 205 years (Genesis 11:32). Thus he lived sixty years after the
departure of Abraham from Haran! There are two reasonable
suggestions to solve this problem.

The expression that Terah lived seventy years and then became
the father of Abraham, Nahor and Haran (Genesis 11:26) does not
mean that he had all three sons at that age! It means he was seventy
before he began to have these three. There is no reason to assume
that Abraham was the oldest, and these three sons may be listed
merely in the order of importance and not in order of birth. The

Scriptures often speak of 'Jacob and Esau', but that is not the order of their birth. Similarly in Genesis 25:13 we are told that the list that follows is given 'in the order of their birth', which implies that this is not necessarily the case elsewhere. We do know that Haran died before his brother Abraham (Genesis 11:28) which is at least an indication that Haran may have been older by many years. If all this is true, Terah could have been 130 years old when Abraham was born. We have looked at the subject of long life in Genesis in chapter 15.

On the other hand, Stephen may have intended merely to recount the details in the order in which they appear in Genesis. Genesis 11:32 and 12:1 need not be taken as an exact sequence, and if the Jews recognized this Stephen could safely follow the order as he recounted the history. Thus Stephen was saying in effect: 'After the Scriptures record the death of Terah, they then record the removal of Abraham from Haran.'

Another problem concerns the purchase of a field by Abraham. Stephen speaks of a tomb in Shechem which Abraham had purchased from the sons of Hamor (Acts 7:16); in this tomb Jacob and his sons were buried. But the only field that the Old Testament records Abraham buying was the field belonging to Ephron in Machpelah (Genesis 23:17). However, we may ask on what grounds we are to assume these two purchases were the same? Abraham purchased a field and cave in Machpelah in which he buried Sarah (Genesis 23), and in which he was himself buried (Genesis 25:9). He also purchased a tomb in Shechem (Acts 7). Jacob later purchased the entire field in which this was situated (Genesis 33:19; Joshua 24:32); in this cave in Shechem Jacob and his sons were buried.

Finally, in Acts 7:14 Stephen claimed that the number of Israelites that originally came into Egypt was 'seventy-five persons'. Genesis 46:27; Exodus 1:5 and Deuteronomy 10:22 all state that this figure was seventy. This is not a difficult problem to solve because the Greek translation of the Old Testament (the Septuagint) gives the number in Genesis 46:27 and Exodus 1:5 as seventy-five persons and Stephen was obviously following the Septuagint number. But does this mean that the Hebrew Old Testament was wrong? No, because in Genesis 46:20 a list of five grandsons of Joseph are added in the Greek Septuagint; these five are simply ignored in the Hebrew. In claiming that just seventy, or seventy-five, persons came into Egypt, both the Hebrew and Greek are

referring to those whom they considered important heads of house-
holds. In fact many servants and other great-grandchildren must
have come with them. The Hebrew Old Testament therefore lists
only the sons and grandsons of Jacob and the number is seventy
persons; the Greek Old Testament adds five great-grandsons. Both
are right!

Gospel contradictions?

In the previous chapter we noted that the Gospels are the chief
hunting-ground of Bible critics; they try to find errors everywhere.
That is just what Sir William Ramsay expected until the force of
truth convinced him otherwise.

The Sermon on the Mount

The differences between the sermon recorded in Matthew 5-7 and
that in Luke 6 present the critic with a reason for suggesting that we
have two contradictory accounts of the same event. However, it is
most likely that the two occasions are entirely different and that our
Lord preached the same sermon on two occasions — something
almost all preachers have done! This possibility is indicated by the
fact that whereas Matthew is clear that Christ preached 'on a
mountainside' (Matthew 5:1), Luke speaks of him standing 'on a
level place' (Luke: 6:17). Of course, the two phrases are not
necessarily exclusive of each other since you can find a level place
even on a mountainside. The healing of the centurion's servant that
follows in both Matthew and Luke does not prove the accounts are
of the same sermon because the Gospel writers were under no
obligation to keep the accounts in exact chronological order. In
Luke 7:1-2 the writer records: 'When Jesus had finished saying all
this in the hearing of the people, he entered Capernaum. There a
centurion's servant whom his master valued highly, was sick and
about to die...' Luke implies that the event followed on immediately. On the other hand, Matthew makes a more definite break
between chapter 7:29 and 8:5.

However, if it is insisted that these two accounts do refer to the
same sermon there still need be no problem in reconciling the
differences. In the previous chapter we discussed the subject of the

reported speech of Jesus. In any sermon the preacher will repeat the same teaching in different ways.

The centurion's servant

Matthew 8:5 informs us that the centurion came in person to Christ, whereas Luke 7:3 claims that he sent messengers. There is nothing in either account to forbid the possibility that when our Lord persisted in drawing near to the house the centurion came in person to repeat his request. Alternatively, the words 'came to him' in Matthew, which may be literally translated 'approached', may simply express the sending of messengers; just as we may speak of a nation's leader making an 'approach' to another head of state without necessarily going in person. Compare Matthew 11:2-3 where John sent two disciples to Jesus and the words literally read: 'And he said to him…'

The temptations of our Lord

Matthew and Luke reverse the order of the last two temptations, but this would only be a contradiction if both claimed to present the correct order. In fact each closes with the temptation suited to his theme — Matthew is presenting Jesus as king, while Luke presents him as man. Probably Matthew has the original order since he introduces his second temptation with 'then', while Luke connects the second and third merely with the word 'and'.

Blind Bartimæus

Matthew 20:30 mentions two blind men, while Mark and Luke refer only to one (Mark 10:46; Luke 18:35). Luke also states the episode took place as Jesus approached Jericho while Matthew and Mark claim he was leaving Jericho.

The first problem is easily resolved. Mark and Luke do not deny there were two men; they concern themselves only with Bartimæus. Perhaps he was a well-known figure either before or, more likely, after his healing. This is implied by Mark's reference to his father (Mark 10:46). In the same way Matthew refers to two demoniacs while Mark and Luke mention only one (compare Matthew 8:28 with Mark 5:2).

The second problem is more difficult because a plain contradiction in the location of the miracle appears to be involved. Many solutions have been put forward, but the two most reasonable are suggested here.

1. A possible understanding is that which reconstructs the events of Luke 18 and 19 in the following way. Our Lord entered Jericho and, although it was late, no one offered him hospitality for the night and he was therefore 'passing through' (Luke 19:1) on his way out of the city. As he was coming out of the city our Lord met Zacchæus, called him down from the tree and invited himself to stay at his home (Luke 19:5). It was as the party now turned to re-enter Jericho that Bartimæus and his companion were healed of their blindness. This perfectly accounts for the statement of both Matthew and Mark that the healing took place 'as Jesus and his disciples were leaving Jericho' (Matthew 20:29; Mark 10:46); if the healing took place immediately after the conversion of Zacchæus, while the astonished crowd were still gathered round our Lord and Zacchæus, then our Lord was both going out from and returning to the city.

The only remaining difficulty is why Luke should place the account of Zacchæus after that of Bartimæus when in fact it came first, especially when we know that Luke set out to give 'an orderly account' of our Lord's ministry. It is clear that the teaching given in Luke 19:11-27 was directly connected, not with the healing of Bartimæus, but with the conversion of Zacchæus; notice the important connecting phrase in verse 11: 'While they were listening to this...' Luke placed the story of Bartimæus outside its correct order in the events of that evening so that it would not separate the story of Zacchæus and the instruction that followed as our Lord returned to the home of Zacchæus. Neither Matthew nor Mark refers to Zacchæus and therefore they do not face the same problem of separating the two stories.

If it is objected that verse 28 implies that all this teaching took place as Christ finally left Jericho on his way to Jerusalem, we can only respond by saying that Luke must here be referring to the following day since the Gospel writer cannot be such a fool that he had so soon forgotten that our Lord invited himself to stay the night at the home of Zacchaeus! (v. 5).

2. Alternatively we may reconstruct the events in the following way. The blind men were sitting in the entrance of the city and began

calling to our Lord as he passed by. He took no notice and the crowd ordered them to be silent; such a refusal to stop and listen at once was not unusual in Christ's ministry when he wanted to draw out a stronger appeal to himself (see the story of the Canaanite woman in Matthew 15:21-28). Jesus entered the city, met Zacchæus and stayed with him for the night. During the evening or early morning the blind men crossed the city to renew their appeal as Jesus left in the morning. It was on this occasion that Jesus stopped and healed them.

This reconstruction assumes that the Gospel writers decided not to break up the story before and after our Lord's night in Jericho but to complete it as one event. It is most natural that Matthew and Mark should deal with it on the departure, since that is when the appeal was answered, and that Luke should deal with it on the entry, since that is when the appeal began and, as we have seen in the first suggestion, he wanted to keep it separate from the story of Zacchæus and the instructions that followed. If we take Luke 19:1, 'Jesus entered Jericho and was passing through', as a reference to the story of Bartimæus and not the story of Zacchæus, then we have Luke's way of telling us that the events he has just related actually took place as Christ came into and came out of the city — a perfect harmony with Matthew and Mark.

The cursing of the fig tree and cleansing the temple

Mark's account (Mark 11:11-14) states that after his triumphant entry into Jerusalem our Lord went into the temple and saw what was going on; as it was late he returned with his disciples to Bethany. The following morning he went up to the city, cursed the fig tree on the way, then drove out the money-changers from the temple. Matthew's account (Matthew 21:18-22) implies that he cleansed the temple on the day of his triumphant entry, returned to Bethany and the following morning cursed the fig tree.

But Matthew nowhere actually says our Lord cleansed the temple on the day of his triumphant entry. If we insert Mark 11:11 between Matthew 21:11 and 12 we have the correct order of events. The reference to the fig tree in Matthew 21:18 refers to the morning of the day he has just described. Note that Matthew does not say, 'next morning' but 'early in the morning'. It is perfectly natural for

him to record the chief activities of the day (vv. 12-17) and then slip
in a less significant event that happened earlier in the morning (vv.
18-22).

The parable of the vine-growers

In Mark 12:9 and Luke 20:15-16 our Lord answered his own
question at the conclusion of the parable: 'What will the owner of
the vineyard do to them? He will come and kill those tenants and
give the vineyard to others.' Matthew 21:41 records that the priests
and Pharisees responded to his question: 'He will bring those
wretches to a wretched end.' Which account is correct? Did Christ
answer his own question, or did the Pharisees answer it for him? It
is quite reasonable to assume that our Lord, having drawn the
answer from his hearers, repeated their answer for emphasis.

The parable of the sower

Matthew, Mark and Luke each use a different Greek word to refer
to those who respond to the word. Matthew uses 'understand'
(Matthew 13:23), Mark has 'accept' (Mark 4:20) and Luke adds
'retain' or 'hold fast' (Luke 8:15). But Jesus spoke in Aramaic and
thus we may safely assume that these three expressions (which are,
incidentally, a natural progression) express all that our Lord originally had in mind. We must never forget that the evangelical
doctrine of inspiration insists that the writers of Scripture were
governed by the Holy Spirit and 'No one knows the thoughts of God
except the Spirit of God' (1 Corinthians 2:11).

Peter's denial

The accounts of Matthew and Mark correspond exactly provided
that we do not assume that 'the servant girl' in Mark 14:69 is the
same as the one in verse 66, since Matthew refers to her as 'another
girl' (Matthew 26:71). We may harmonize Luke's account (Luke
22:54-62) in the following way. The second maid identified Peter to
the bystanders (Matthew 26:73 and Mark 14:69) and it was one of
the men who confronted Peter (Luke 22:58). After a while, Luke
says about an hour, the crowd challenged him again and all three

Gospels agree in detail here. There is nothing in John's account (18:17,18,25-27) that conflicts with the above. John merely adds details that came to him from his better acquaintance with the people involved.

The death of Judas

This is one of the most quoted incidents in an attempt to prove a contradiction in the Gospel accounts. The facts are that Matthew 27:5 reports on the end of the betrayer with the simple statement that 'He went away and hanged himself.' It is Luke who, in Acts 1:18-19, adds to Matthew's account and states that Judas 'bought a field' with his ill-acquired money. And so he did! Though it was never his intention; the priests made the purchase for him, as Matthew 27:6-10 informs us; they bought the very field in which he had committed suicide, and with his money. Sixteen hundred years ago Augustine resolved the only other difference in these two accounts by suggesting that when Judas hanged himself (Matthew 27:5) his body fell to the ground and broke open (Acts 1:18). A gruesome harmony — but why not?

The inscription on the cross

The form of the inscription varies in each of the four Gospels. Matthew 27:37 records: 'The written charge against him: This is Jesus, the King of the Jews.' Mark 15:26 has: 'The written notice of the charge against him read: The King of the Jews.' Luke 23:38 is similar, with the addition of one word (in the Greek): 'A written notice above him which read: This is the King of the Jews.' Clearly Mark went to the heart of the charge and ignored the rest; the others merely fill in. There is no conflict here. John 19:19, however, adds a much fuller record of the charge: 'Jesus of Nazareth, the King of the Jews.' The inscription was in three languages (John 19:20) and thus some variation in translation is perfectly normal. It is more than likely that Pilate himself was not consistent in using exactly the same inscription in all three languages. If John is reading from the Aramaic inscription then by the addition of the words 'of Nazareth' Pilate would have been deliberately insulting the Jews by suggesting that the Jewish king came from Nazareth.

John's timing

When John places our Lord's conviction at 'about the sixth hour' (John 19:14), he would seem to be in conflict with the other writers, who claim that at the sixth hour our Lord was already on the cross and the darkness had begun (Matthew 27:45; Mark 15:33; Luke 23:44). The Jewish day began at sunrise, about 6 a.m., and thus the sixth hour was midday. However, John was evidently using a Gentile time-scale which, like our own, began the day at midnight. Thus the trial and conviction took place around 6 a.m. and Jesus was crucified at 9 a.m. This harmonizes with the other Gospels. John's use of the Gentile-Roman clock is not unnatural since at the time of writing his Gospel he had been resident in Ephesus for many years and was writing particularly with Gentiles in mind.

The thieves on the cross

Matthew and Mark inform us that the two robbers crucified with our Lord ridiculed him (Matthew 27:44; Mark 15:32) but Luke elaborates this to show that one had second thoughts and was converted (Luke 23:39-43). Whether or not Matthew and Mark knew of this change is irrelevant; it clearly did not suit the purpose of the Spirit for them to record it. The value of these complementary accounts is that we know the repentant thief began by reviling Christ.

The resurrection of Christ

The variation in the Gospel accounts of what happened during the early dawn on that first Easter Sunday has led critics to conclude that here we are faced with irreconcilable contradictions. However, once we accept that each writer adds to the total picture, we may harmonize the Easter story in the following way.

Our Lord rose during the early darkness of Sunday morning. A violent earthquake petrified the guards and an angel came to roll back the stone so that the disciples would be able to go into the tomb; the angel then sat on a stone by the tomb (Matthew 28:2-4). All this happened before any of the women arrived.

From Matthew 28:4 we turn to John 20 for the next part of the story. Mary Magdalene was first on the scene. Perhaps she came just to satisfy herself that she knew the exact tomb or to make sure the

'We may harmonize the Easter story'

guards had done their duty. Whatever the reason, she came 'while it was still dark' and she appears to have come alone (John 20:1). At this time Mary saw the stone was removed, but nothing else. She returned at once to Peter and John, who apparently were not with the other disciples, and she poured out her tragic story: 'They have taken the Lord out of the tomb, and we don't know where they have put him.' The plural, 'We do not know...' may have no significance, or it may imply that Mary had roused some of the other women on her way back. Peter and John ran to the tomb, found it empty, and returned to their lodgings (John 20:3-10). Why they did not go at once to the other disciples remains a mystery, but these were hours of bewildering events and confused emotions and we hardly expect everyone to act with cold, logical reason.

Mary followed, and after the two disciples had left, two angels appeared to her (John 20:11-13). Shortly afterwards she met the Lord himself after 'thinking he was the gardener' in the twilight of the now breaking dawn (John 20:14-17). Mary returned to the rest of the disciples with her story (v. 18). Thus Mary was the first to whom Jesus appeared after his resurrection (Mark 16:9). The disciples were not greatly impressed with the story of one woman (Mark 26:11) and Peter and John were not present to confirm any part of it.

It was now 'just after sunrise' (Mark 16:2; Matthew 28:1; Luke 24:1). Mary retraced her steps towards the tomb in company with the other women. Mary must have met Mary the mother of James, Salome, Joanna, and possibly some others, as they were already on their way to the tomb with spices to anoint the body of the Lord (Matthew 28:1; Mark 16:1-2; Luke 24:1,10). We may expect Mary Magdalene to be a little distrustful of her recent experience, especially as she had met with such a cold response from the disciples. Whether or not she shared her news with the other women is a matter of opinion, but if she did, they were obviously no more persuaded than the disciples, for they began discussing how they could remove the heavy stone from the door (Mark 16:3). When they arrived at the tomb, the party of women discovered the stone was already rolled back (Mark 16:4; Luke 24:2). They went into the tomb and were mystified by the absence of the body (Luke 24:3-4).

Suddenly, and presumably before Mary Magdalene had time to say, 'I told you so', two angels appeared (Luke 24:4). Matthew 28:2 and Mark 16:5 refer only to one angel, presumably the one with whom they spoke. We may reasonably assume that the angel who rolled back the stone and terrified the guards (Matthew 28:2) was not apparent to the women when they first arrived, but was then joined by a second angel. The two angels then revealed themselves to the women inside the tomb, and the first angel spoke with them.

The angel reminded the women of the promise of the resurrection and told them to go and inform the disciples (Matthew 28:5-7; Mark 16:6-7; Luke 24:5-7). The women ran to tell the disciples (Mark 16:8; Luke 24:9). On the way they met the Lord and worshipped him (Matthew 28:8-10). It must have been an excited and highly emotional group of women that burst in upon the company of disciples that Mary had earlier left and, incredibly, they were no more convinced now than they were then (Luke 24:11). It was only at this point that the guards recovered their senses and reported the events of the night to the authorities (Matthew 28:11-15).

Later in the day the Lord appeared to the two walking to Emmaus (Mark 16:12-13; Luke 24:13-35). They returned to find the disciples listening to Peter, who had at last informed the group of his and John's early morning discovery (Luke 24:33-34). Even yet there was general unbelief (Mark 16:13). Towards the evening of this day our Lord appeared to the eleven and others as they were discussing during their evening meal (Mark 16:14; Luke 24:36; John 20:19).

Conclusion

There is no suggestion that in this chapter we have dealt with all the problems of the Bible! But it is certainly true that an attempt has been made to discuss those that are most difficult and to cover a fair sample. Even these supposed errors and contradictions form only a very small part of the Bible; whole pages and even chapters contain nothing that even the most severe critic could argue against. Not all the answers given may satisfy even the evangelical Christian who believes in biblical inerrancy, but remember the issue is not, 'Are our answers proved by every standard to be right, without a shadow of a doubt?' but simply, 'Are they reasonable?' If they are reasonable then they may well be right, and if they are right then no error or contradiction has been found in Scripture.

God's Word has stood against its critics for hundreds of years. The critics come, they criticize, they disagree among themselves, and they go; all they leave behind is a loss of secure faith and a lack of sincere interest in the Bible on the part of their converts. But for those who believe the Bible to be without error, and who believe it is God's clear revelation for modern man, it proves to be a reliable guide to the way of salvation and for every aspect of the Christian life.

18.
Blow-flies and the lion!

'Defend the Bible!' exclaimed the Victorian preacher Charles Haddon Spurgeon, 'I would as soon defend a lion.' No doubt he meant it, but writing in a preface to his commentary on Psalm 138 the same preacher concluded: 'Many modern critics are to the Word of God what blow-flies are to the food of men: they cannot do any good, and unless relentlessly driven away they do great harm.'

This book did not set out to defend the lion but it has tried to drive off a few blow-flies. The simple fact is that today there are many who claim to be 'Christians' but who do not believe in the inerrancy of the Bible or submit to its final authority. One third of Church of England bishops do not believe in the virgin birth of Christ or his resurrection; David Jenkins, Bishop of Durham, claimed the resurrection of Christ was 'merely a conjuring trick with bones'; 110 Bible scholars in America have voted out of the New Testament many of the parables Jesus told; and a North American professor, Robert Funk, confidently assures us that 'New Testament scholars have established beyond any reasonable doubt that the Jesus of the early Christian documents is to some extent a fiction of the Christian imagination.' When we abandon the Bible as our clear authority for what Christians believe then we are, as John Newton wrote 200 years ago, 'exposed to all the illusions of imagination and enthusiasm'. There are more blow-flies today than there were a century ago in the time of Spurgeon.

Today's agenda

The main item on today's agenda for the church is ecumenism: getting all 'Christian' churches together irrespective of what they believe, or even if they believe. In a forlorn hope of filling the churches, we are encouraged to unite and bury theology. Ecumenical advocates appear to have forgotten that the more important question to be asked today is not what will fill the churches but what emptied them in the first place. It was not two world wars, rising wages or modern technology that caused a decrease in people taking Christianity seriously, but the abandoning of the Bible as the Word of the living God. When the critics emptied the Bible of its meaning they emptied the churches of their members.

But if ecumenism is the agenda, it would appear that pluralism is the chairman! Today, everything anyone ever believed must be accepted as a serious contribution to our package of beliefs; exclusivism — the commitment to beliefs that exclude others — is outlawed. In today's world there seems to be little place for those who believe that the Bible alone has the truth, but there is plenty of room for those who believe that everybody else has!

In 1977 the Scottish theologian James Barr wrote a book called *Fundamentalism*. It was a strong attack against the evangelical view of the Bible which he regards as 'a pathological condition of Christianity'! He probably chose the word 'Fundamentalism' not because it was accurate but because it was the most insulting. Barr at least understands the commitment of the true evangelical to the Scriptures because he writes, 'To ask him [the evangelical] to modify his position is to ask him for something that he cannot perform' (p.17). Barr is right, we cannot modify our position any more than Martin Luther could when, on trial at Worms in 1521, he defended his commitment to the Bible by declaring: 'I am bound by the Scriptures ... and my conscience has been taken captive by the Word of God.'

However, as in the case of Luther, our refusal to modify our position is not based upon blind tradition or stubborn ignorance, but the force of the truth of God's Word itself. It persuades our minds and hearts by its own authority; the evangelical position is both reasoned and intellectually satisfying. In this book we have not avoided hard issues or ignored the challenges made against the authority of the Bible.

At a practical level James Barr admits, and laments, that the 'clergy' find it easier to present the biblical narratives as if they really happened. In this he is right, of course, and he reveals the weakness of a liberal attitude to the Bible. A writer to *The British Weekly* as long ago as September 1925 defended the evangelical attitude to the Bible by commenting that 'With a Bible under suspicion, a Christ shorn of the miraculous, and a Gospel which has to be preached, as donkeys eat thistles, "very carefully", the wonder is not that we lack leadership but that [we] should have anybody to lead.' When ordinary people read a book much of which is clearly written as history, they expect to be able to rely upon it as factual; just as ordinary people expect historical biographies to tell us the truth about the person concerned. Evangelicals are ordinary people.

The view of the Bible outlined in this book has been held by evangelical Christians throughout history. Above everything else it has been their trust in the Bible that has ensured that, apart from their many differences of opinion on other issues, evangelicals have remained evangelicals — and recognizably so.

The evangelical view of Scripture matters because, according to Christ, obedience to his words is a necessary description of what makes a true disciple. In Luke 6:46 we have a record of the words of Christ that set out his challenge like this: 'Why do you call me "Lord, Lord", and do not do what I say?' Something similar is also recorded in Matthew 7:21 and John 14:15. One of the most important questions we must answer is this: are these the words of Christ or not? If they are not then we can presume there are no words of Christ available to us and to which we must be obedient in order to be counted as true Christians. This is exactly where a liberal attitude to the Bible leads us: there is no final authority, no reliable words of Christ, no test by which we shall be judged, and nothing to obey. No wonder critics of the Bible think there will be atheists in heaven; in fact even that is a staggering statement of faith, since without a reliable Bible we cannot know whether there is a heaven to which anyone can go!

If you doubt the Bible, nothing, without exception, is reliable. On the other hand, if Luke 6:46 really does record the actual saying of Christ then somewhere there must be the words that he expects his present-day disciples to obey. If they are only to be found *among* the words attributed to him in the Bible then we are no wiser, and we may finally be judged for not obeying words that it was impossible for us to know whether or not he spoke in the first place!

In contrast to this, the evangelical is not a Christian with tentative opinions but with a certain faith in the certain authority of God. We believe that the 'Word of the Lord stands for ever' (1 Peter 1:25;

Isaiah 40:8; Psalm 119:89) and that is the Word we believe, preach, teach and obey.

A consistent view

The evangelical view of Scripture is consistent with the needs of man. Imagine that you are out walking in the country and you come to a crossroads. Unsure of your way, you discover that the signpost has blown down and is lying broken beside the road. How will you ever discover your route? With a moment's thought the answer is simple. So long as you know where you came from, you can stand the signpost up with the correct arm pointing down the road you have just walked and so determine which way you must go. If you know your origin, you can easily find your destination. One of the fundamental problems with modern man is that he is lost in the maze of life. He has no idea why he is here, where he is going, or even how he would get there if he knew where it was! The reason for this confusion is that he does not understand where he came from.

Our moral maze, with its cheap view of life, encourages us to kill 200,000 unborn babies each year in the United Kingdom alone, just because we don't want them. The chances of being killed by a terrorist in the United Kingdom is one in 420,000, but the chances of being killed in the womb of a British woman is one in five! Our moral maze leads to tragic inconsistencies in behaviour. As I write this, the nation mourns the death of a premature baby that weighed in at less than the weight of a can of Coke; doctors fought for its life, thousands prayed and a nation waited in hope. Yet every day hundreds of healthy and fully developed children are sucked from the womb, thrown into a plastic sack and burned in a hospital incinerator. It is called 'the woman's right'. Our moral maze advocates terminating the life of the elderly and incurably sick and treating moral issues as a free-for-all. Our moral maze is a direct result of our spiritual maze, and our spiritual maze is because we have lost sight of our origin and destination.

If we listen to the false scientists and assume our ancestors were monkeys, then we will behave like monkeys. On the other hand if we appreciate that we are created in the image and likeness of God, made by God and for God, then we will understand that we are

accountable to God and that we shall one day stand before him. All
this inevitably affects the way we live. Men and women are inwardly
crying out for spiritual and moral direction and they feel lost and
often hopeless; indeed without the clear direction of God's Word,
the Bible, that is exactly what people are — lost and hopeless. The
evangelical view of the Bible is consistent with our need to know our
origin and our destination.

Not only is the evangelical view of Scripture consistent with the
needs of man, but it is consistent with a Christian view of God. There
can be no understanding of God within the Christian faith that does
not view him as the sovereign Creator who made everything and
controls the universe he brought into being. To think of God as a
remote architect who created and then distanced himself from his
creation, and is therefore unknowable, is deism and not Christianity.
To think of everything as God and God as the great 'sum of all
things' without intelligence or personality is pantheism and not
Christianity.

The Christian God is personal, moral and involved in the world
he made. Like any engineer who knows best how his machinery
should be operated, so God the Creator has perfect plans for his
creation. He knows how the human race should live and behave for
its best welfare; he knows what is good and what is bad for mankind
spiritually, morally, socially and even economically. It is unthinkable that the God who knows best and has plans should either keep
them all to himself or allow his plans to be so jumbled in the process
of communication that they become unrecognizable. Can we imagine a medical scientist with a life-saving formula either keeping it to
himself or allowing a five-year-old boy to communicate the gist of
it to the waiting world?

If God is God, we would expect him to share with us both his bad
news and his good news with such accuracy that there could be no
mistake about his message. The evangelical view of the Bible is
therefore consistent with the Christian view of God.

The evangelical view of the Bible is also consistent with the
teaching of Scripture itself. In chapter 4 we noted that even the
German liberal critic Rudolf Bultmann had to acknowledge that
Christ believed the Old Testament to be trustworthy. The same can
be said of the apostles and in fact all the human writers of Scripture.
Throughout its pages the Bible never expresses one sentence or
word of doubt about either its divine origin or its absolute

trustworthiness; on the contrary, it constantly asserts both. 'Every word of God is flawless' is how Proverbs 30:5 sums up the attitude of the Bible towards itself. In the New Testament Peter says that the Word of God 'stands for ever' (1 Peter 1:25), and Christ himself promised that not the smallest part of it would disappear (Matthew 5:18).

Of course, the fact that the Bible claims to be the inerrant Word of God is not, in itself, necessary proof of the claim. In chapter 3 we discussed the value of self-witness, or self-authentication as it is known. But it is at least a fact of immense significance that a book written by forty different men over a period of fifteen hundred years should consistently maintain its total accuracy and divine authority, and that the writers do not question the authority of all the other books that make up this unique library. The evangelical view of the Bible is consistent with the Bible's own claim.

Unashamedly we can add that the evangelical view of Scripture is consistent with a thinking mind. I have frequently spoken to schoolchildren and students on the subject of a 'a book without error' and when I do so I always begin by outlining what I actually believe. Perhaps that is not the wisest way to start because it is evident that from then on many in the classroom, including members of staff, do not take me seriously. However, the stories of the life and work of Robert Dick Wilson and William Mitchell Ramsay, that we saw in chapter 9, are guaranteed to awaken an interest and sometimes a degree of respect.

Evangelicals are too often intimidated by the so-called scholarship of those who earn their living by promoting a negative view of the Bible. There is an almost unbelievable arrogance in the statements of some of the blow-flies attacking the Bible. One writer summarized the conclusions of the nineteenth-century critics like this: 'And moreover, these things are not in doubt; they are not hypothetical reconstructions or tentative suggestions, but truths as assured as anything ever can be in the sphere of literary research.' That was in a book entitled *Preface to Bible Study*! We may ask what Bible there is to study.

The world rejects biblical authority and ridicules the strong arguments in favour of it. By this point the reader should be secure in the knowledge that the intellectual arguments are not on the side of the critic. If men of the academic calibre of Wilson and Ramsay could declare, 'I give my students such an intelligent faith in the Old

Testament Scripture that they will never doubt them as long as they live,' and, 'Christianity did not originate in a lie, and we can and ought to demonstrate this, as well as to believe it,' then we have no need to be ashamed of our evangelical convictions about the Bible.

Of course, this is not to suggest that the Bible is just like any other book that can be prodded and probed by scholars until it yields the truth. On the contrary, the matters dealt with in the Bible are 'spiritually understood' and no amount of unaided reason and pure scholarship will lead a man or woman to the truth. However, we are prepared for the fact that when the Bible writes about history it may be fairly judged by the rules of reliable historical recording — and it will never fail to prove itself true.

J. B. Phillips said that no man with 'sense as well as faith' could accept an evangelical view of the Bible, but if he had troubled to read the works of Ramsay and many other scholars he might have agreed that you may press the words of the Bible to a degree beyond those of any other historian and they stand the keenest scrutiny and the hardest treatment. When the International Council on Biblical Inerrancy commenced in 1977, the board had no difficulty in recruiting scores of scholars from around the world to serve their educational programme. A selected list of academic books on the subject, each committed to the inerrancy of the Bible, amounted to almost a hundred titles. The evangelical view of the Bible is certainly consistent with a thinking mind.

Being an evangelical

So then, who is an evangelical? James Barr has no doubt that to be an evangelical is 'a pathological condition of Christianity', and another modern critic, David Edwards, refers to 'loud-mouthed Bible-bashers' whose belief, in his view, is 'a doomed and dangerous perversion of the faith'. But we do not take our definitions from the university gutter. Unfortunately, however, there is considerable confusion amongst Christians today, and even amongst evangelical Christians themselves, as to what exactly an evangelical is, but at least on the subject of Scripture there should be no reasonable doubt. Here are the four key words relating to the Bible that distinguish a true evangelical.

Inerrancy

The evangelical Christian believes that the whole Bible is true and trustworthy. Unfortunately we have been forced to define even these two words — true and trustworthy. Francis Schaeffer, you may remember from an earlier chapter, spoke of 'true truth' in an attempt to avoid any confusion because some who claim to be evangelical seem little bothered by the possibility of 'minor' errors in Scripture. The day has long since gone when we could talk and write of the 'divine inspiration and authority' of the Bible and assume that everyone understood this to mean that the Bible is God-given, wholly without error and the final rule for all that we believe and do.

'Inerrancy' is one word that still appears to mean what it says. The International Council on Biblical Inerrancy was set up in 1977 and by the time the work was closed down ten years later, in the belief that its goal of information and education had been achieved, the council had made a significant contribution to clarifying the evangelical position. Nineteen short statements formed the *Articles of Affirmation and Denial* (see Appendix I) and Article XII introduced the word 'inerrant': 'We affirm that Scripture in its entirety is inerrant, being free from all falsehood, fraud, or deceit. We deny that Biblical infallibility and inerrancy are limited to spiritual, religious or redemptive themes, exclusive of assertions in the fields of history and science...' There can be no understanding of the word 'evangelical' that denies the word 'inerrant'.

Sufficiency

Although the *Chicago Statement on Biblical Inerrancy* does not use the word 'sufficient', the phrase in Article V, 'We further deny that any normative revelation has been given since the completion of the New Testament writings,' is intended to make the same point. However, it is one thing to lay a claim to sufficiency and quite another to live so consistently with the teaching of the Bible that every part of our Christian life and belief is brought under its judgement. Writing in *Hermeneutics, Authority and Canon*, Don Carson comments that among evangelicals it is to our shame that 'We have hungered to be masters of the Word much more than we have hungered to be mastered by it' (p.47). It is not commentaries, councils or creeds that should mould our Christian beliefs, however valuable some of them may be, but the Word of God. *Sola Scriptura* was the watchword of the Reformation. This means that the Bible is sufficient for our guidance also. John Newton once wrote to a friend, 'We are directed to expect the teaching and assistance of the Holy Spirit only within the limitations and by the medium, of the written word.'

Unless we are prepared to make the unqualified claim that God's verbal, authoritative and inerrant revelation ended with the close of Scripture, then we cannot justifiably use the word 'evangelical' to describe our position.

Authority

Too often it has been assumed that to sign a statement of faith that reaffirms the inerrancy and authority of Scripture is enough for us to claim the title 'evangelical'. This is certainly not so. Evangelical Christians have always been men and women of action and not merely reaction. 'Evangelical' is a statement of how we live, not simply how we respond to false views of the Bible.

In 2 Samuel 23 the story is told of three of the bodyguards to King David of Israel. Long before he became king, David was 'holed up' in the cave at Adullam. King Saul was after his life and the invading Philistines had set up an outpost at Bethlehem. One burning day David stood at the entrance of the cave and in the blistering heat expressed a longing for a drink of water from the well near the gate of Bethlehem, the city of his childhood. Instantly the three warriors buckled on their armour and cut their way through the Philistine lines; whilst two kept guard, the third swung his container into the well and drew a flask of cool clear water. The three then fought their way out of the Philistine garrison and presented the fruit of their loyalty to David. If that is an illustration of our instant and fearless obedience to the Word of our God, then we can rightly be known as evangelical Christians — but not otherwise.

The life of the evangelical should be marked by a constant desire to conform to Scripture and this should be evident to everyone. The story is told of an Islamic trader who could not read a word of English but who kept a copy of the Bible beside him. He explained the reason for this: 'When I meet a trader who is unknown to me, I

put the Bible in his way and watch him. If he opens and reads it, I
know I can trust him; if he throws it aside with a sneer or a curse, I
will have nothing more to do with him.' If a person's life is not
governed and changed by the Bible, then he or she is not to be known
as evangelical. 'If you love me', said Christ to his disciples, 'you
will obey what I command' (John 14:15).

In his biography of England's national poet William Cowper,
Lord David Cecil commented upon Cowper's evangelicalism.
Although no friend of evangelical beliefs himself, Cecil was nevertheless compelled to an interesting conclusion about eighteenth-
century evangelicalism: 'In spite of its defects, its absurdities, one
cannot refuse the Evangelical one's admiration. For they imposed
a moral order on life... It alone among the philosophies of its time
took account of man's spiritual side... The compelling power of
their faith was shown by their actions. It was they who purified the
morals of English society, who founded modern philanthropy, who
stopped the slave trade. Nor could any creed less passionately
exclusive have so effectively inspired them. You must look only to
the cross to be a successful crusader.' It is the Word of God that leads
to the cross of Christ and makes evangelicals what they are:
'successful crusaders'. The 'successful crusader' is the evangelical
Christian under the authority of God's Word.

Interpretation

This may be an unexpected term to use in defining an evangelical,
but it is very necessary. Chapter 14 is easily one of the most
important chapters in this book. It is a tragedy that Christians who
claim to be evangelicals often treat the Bible as if they have the right
to make it say whatever they want it to. There are clear and vital
principles to follow when understanding God's Word; these have
been generally accepted by evangelicals and they guarantee that we
treat the Bible fairly, wisely and accurately. The danger comes
when, under the pressure of modern philosophy, so-called science,
the latest social fad or moral lapse, or the emotional pull of what we
think is fair or right or acceptable, we begin to twist the plain
teaching of Scripture.

There has rarely been a greater need for evangelicals to understand how to interpret the Bible, and to submit humbly to the rules.
What the Bible says about any subject may often be contrary to what

society says is right, and sometimes contrary to what we think is fair. However, the evangelical is not God's lawyer with a duty to defend the client and explain his actions in the best possible light. On the contrary, we are servants of the Sovereign Lord and our task is to publish his laws and proclaim his words — whatever he says. If we are to remain evangelical we must follow the well-trodden paths of hermeneutics — wherever they may lead. Plain honesty in interpreting the Bible is what all evangelicals must possess if they are to remain evangelical.

Inerrancy, sufficiency, authority and interpretation — is this all that can be said in our attempt to define and describe an evangelical? Not quite, but before we move on, it must be understood that what is true of the individual Christian is equally true of the community of Christians. Again, writing in *Hermeneutics, Authority and Canon,* Don Carson expresses his alarm at 'the diminishing authority of the Scriptures in the churches' (pp.47-48). Unless a local church believes, preaches and lives under the inerrancy, sufficiency and authority of Scripture, and interprets it wisely and sensibly, it cannot be called an evangelical church.

But there is more to it than that. If this is what we really believe about the Bible, certain things must follow.

Being a consistent evangelical

If this book leaves the reader with a dry, academic knowledge of the Bible, and no more, then it has largely failed in its purpose. We need to live and feel what we believe.

The evangelical loves the Bible

Writing of some of the characters in the church at Sandfields in South Wales where Dr Martyn Lloyd-Jones was minister from 1926 to 1939, his widow drew attention to William Nobes who, somehow managing on his meagre pension, would often be found sitting outside the entrance to the market chatting in his kindly way with any who had time to talk. When someone asked him about his family and relatives his contented reply was simply: 'There's just four of us now. My bed and my table, my Book and me!' Surely if King

David could say of the Old Testament, 'Oh! How I love your law' (Psalm 119:97), then those who possess and believe the completed verbal revelation from God should love both the Giver and his gift.

Some have charged evangelicals with 'bibliolatry', a strange and ignorant way of referring to the passionate love we have for the words our God has spoken. King David can presumably be charged with the same sin. When a young man loves to hear the voice of his fiancée, it is because he loves the words of the girl he loves. It is the same with the evangelical. Our most treasured earthly possession is the words of the God of heaven. In every century evangelicals have died rather than give up their right to own the words of God in their own language. John Huss died for this in Czechoslovakia early in the fifteenth century, and so did William Tyndale from England a hundred years later. It was this same love for the Word that caused Mary Jones to walk twenty-five miles across the Welsh mountains in search of a Bible in the summer of 1802. The same love motivated teams of young Christians in the former Soviet Union to construct the Kristiana Press and publish sheets of pages from the Bible at the risk of heavy fines and labour camps. We cannot be evangelical if we do not love the words of our Master.

The evangelical trembles at the Bible

Rajamani, who was used by God in a revival that touched India during the 1940s, asked that on his grave only one simple sentence should be written: 'Here lies the body of a man who trembled at the Word of God.' In that simple epitaph Rajamani calls our attention to Isaiah 66:2: 'This is the one I esteem: he who is humble and contrite in spirit, and trembles at my word.'

Those who understand the importance of the Bible and take its message seriously will never make jokes about it, or treat it casually; it is an awesome thing to read what God says. An absence of holy awe when we listen to God's Word read or preached betrays our slovenly attitude to the voice of God. We are happy to talk of the power and authority of God's Word providing it is safe and directed elsewhere. In the same way we can admire sheet-lightning for its power and beauty, because it is safe. Forked-lightning is dangerous — it may hit us. The Bible is forked-lightning, and the Christian who never trembles at the Word of God betrays his profession.

346   *Nothing but the truth*

The evangelical values the Bible

Speaking to the Church Pastoral Aid Society on 8 May 1862, Lord
Shaftesbury, the evangelical earl, declared: 'Depend upon it, my
friends, that there is no security whatever except in standing upon
the faith of our fathers, and saying with them that the blessed old
Book is "God's Word written", from the very first syllable down to
the very last, and from the last back to the first.'

Do we believe that the Bible is 'God's Word written' from the
first syllable down to the very last, and from the last back to the
first? If so, it should be evident to all how much we value 'the
blessed old Book'. Paul urged Timothy to place a high priority in
his ministry upon 'preaching the Word' and 'the public reading of
Scripture' (2 Timothy 4:2; 1 Timothy 4:13). If those two things are
not central to evangelical worship then, again, we betray our
profession. Sadly in some congregations that claim to be evangelical, more attention is given to the imaginations of men's minds than
to the revelation of our God; and even those congregations who
boast of the importance of the Word often listen to its reading with
half a mind and to its exposition with less.

Privately we may be little better. To value the Bible must mean
that we read it, unless we treat it as a lucky talisman. But the
ignorance of professing Christians today of the content of the Bible
reveals our true attitude to it. In April 1990 *Christianity Today*
published the results of a survey by the Barna Research Group in the
United States. Only 18% of Christians read their Bible daily, 37%
read it once or twice a week, another 18% read it between three and
six times a week and 23% did not read it at all! What the definition
of the word 'Christian' was we are not told, nor how many of them
would claim the title 'evangelical', but at least 30% of non-
Christians said they read their Bible. These figures were reflected in
the answer to the question whether or not there is a Book of Thomas
in the Bible. 22% of Christians thought there was and 13% did not
know! Similarly 27% thought Jonah was not a Bible book and
another 12% had no idea. 11% believed Isaiah to be in the New
Testament and 13% did not know. Even half the non-Christians
knew where to find Isaiah in the Bible! How valuable is the Bible to
a 'Christian' who rarely reads it and cannot even locate one of its
major prophets?

If the evangelical is described by the value he or she places upon the Bible, how many evangelicals are left after a few simple tests have been applied to us?

The evangelical shares the Bible

Evangelicals are a people known to use the Bible in their preaching, evangelism and discussions. Billy Graham's well-known phrase, 'The Bible says,' became an evangelical watch-word from the middle of this century. Of course, there is a danger in simply throwing texts about like a soldier lobbing mortars at random, but at least the evangelical knows where his authority lies. Whilst the liberal critic timidly offers his opinions and suggestions, the evangelical can boldly declare: 'This is what God says.' The books, tracts, sermons and debates of evangelicals are woven with the unbreakable thread of biblical authority; the evangelistic call is to 'the obedience that comes from faith' (Romans 1:5) and that obedience is not following a preacher but a commitment to God through his Word.

More than in any other way, the longing of evangelicals to share their faith is seen in their eagerness to translate the Bible into every language known to men. This has been true for centuries. All the Reformation Bible translators, like Wycliffe, Huss, Groote, Luther and Tyndale, were men of evangelical commitment and zeal. So were many of the eighteenth and nineteenth-century pioneer missionaries like William Carey and Henry Martyn. Historically, if evangelicals had not taken up Bible translation who would have the Bible in their own language today? What has motivated evangelicals to share the Bible is well summed up in the words of John Wycliffe in the fourteenth century, who believed the Scriptures to be 'the faultless, most true, most perfect and most holy law of God, which it is the duty of all men to learn to know, to defend, and to observe'.

The Wycliffe Bible Translators is an interdenominational and international agency dedicated to the translation of the Bible into all languages where Scriptures are needed — irrespective of population size. It has 5,600 members and members in training working worldwide in hundreds of the 6459 known languages. To date the Wycliffe Translators have published New Testaments in 333 languages and are actively involved at present in 863 languages. Many thousands of Scripture portions are being produced. Since their beginning nearly fifty years ago they have been involved in over 1300 languages. The need for Bible translation reaches right round the world, from the Veps and Karelians on the Russian-Finnish border in the north to the Aborigines of Australia in the South, and from the Mongolians and sixteen million Zhuang people in China to the East and the Beaver and Dogrib people of Canada in the West. In the former Soviet Union alone, Bible translation work is required for fifty to a hundred groups of people. But the cost is high, and even with computer technology a team may still have to dedicate fifteen years of their lives in order to produce a New Testament in a language that may not have been written down until they started their work. Every Wycliffe Bible Translator is wholly committed to the evangelical view of Scripture — and they are only one of several evangelical groups providing God's Word for a lost world.

The Waorani Indians of Ecuador's rain forest now have the New Testament in their own language. Once known as the Aucas, in 1956 they murdered five missionaries who had come to give them God's Word. On 11 June 1992 the Wycliffe Bible Translators presented the first Waorani New Testament to the tribe in a service attended by many villagers. Included in the service were three of the men who speared the five missionaries; these men are now elders in the local church.

Returning from their Babylonian exile in the year 537 B.C., the Jews were described as 'a people of the Book'. Having lost the temple and all its ceremonies and with the priesthood scattered, the faithful Jew clung to the words of his God revealed in the Old Testament Scriptures. Evangelicals are similarly a people of the Book. We do not rely upon sacrifices or ceremonies, buildings or church organizations, a central priesthood or church politics. The evangelical has only one clear and infallible guide and that is the Holy Spirit leading and directing through his Word — the Bible. When Paul urged the Galatians to 'keep in step with the Spirit' (Galatians 5:25) he was not expecting the Christians to watch for visions, interpret dreams, listen in to 'voices', or relay the 'infallible' impressions of their mind. By keeping in step with the Spirit he meant quite simply that they were to obey the words the Spirit has already given. Since the last message came in revelation to the apostle John almost two thousand years ago, the Christian community has possessed an infallible, inerrant and complete Bible. We should love the Book, fear it, value it, share it — and above all we should obey it.

'Every word of God is flawless;
　　He is a shield to those who take refuge in him.
Do not add to his words,
　　or he will rebuke you and prove you a liar'

(Proverbs 30:5-6).

Appendix I
The Chicago Statement on Biblical Inerrancy

In 1977 the International Council on Biblical Inerrancy was formed in the United States of America under the chairmanship of James Boice with a council of sixteen. Concerned at the erosion of a belief in the authority and accuracy of Scripture, the ICBI set out to provide conferences and publications that would explain the evangelical position on inerrancy. After ten years of vigorous work the council considered its work complete and the organization closed down.

From the start the ICBI intended to be international and interdenominational in its representation. Membership of the council and forty-six strong advisory board included: Edmund Clowney, James Packer, Roger Nicole, Jay Adams, Norman Geisler, Kenneth Kantzer, James Kennedy, John MacArthur, John Montgomery and Luis Palau.

The following statement set out the council's commitment to biblical inerrancy.

Preface

The authority of Scripture is a key issue for the Christian Church in this and every age. Those who profess faith in Jesus Christ as Lord and Saviour are called to show the reality of their discipleship by humbly and faithfully obeying God's written Word. To stray from Scripture in faith or conduct is disloyalty to our Master. Recognition of the total truth and trustworthiness of Holy Scripture is essential to a full grasp and adequate confession of its authority.

The following Statement affirms this inerrancy of Scripture afresh, making clear our understanding of it and warning against its denial. We are persuaded that to deny it is to set aside the witness of

Jesus Christ and of the Holy Spirit and to refuse that submission to the claims of God's own Word which marks true Christian faith. We see it as our timely duty to make this affirmation in the face of current lapses from the truth of inerrancy among our fellow Christians and misunderstanding of this doctrine in the world at large.

This Statement consists of three parts: a Summary Statement, Articles of Affirmation and Denial, and an accompanying Exposition [the Exposition is not printed here]. It has been prepared in the course of a three-day consultation in Chicago. Those who have signed the Summary Statement and the Articles wish to affirm their own conviction as to the inerrancy of Scripture and to encourage and challenge one another and all Christians to a growing appreciation and understanding of this doctrine. We acknowledge the limitations of a document prepared in a brief, intensive conference and do not propose that this Statement be given creedal weight. Yet we rejoice in the deepening of our own convictions through our discussions together, and we pray that the Statement we have signed may be used to the glory of our God toward a new reformation of the Church in its faith, life, and mission.

We offer this Statement in a spirit, not of contention, but of humility and love, which we purpose by God's grace to maintain in any future dialogue arising out of what we have said. We gladly acknowledge that many who deny the inerrancy of Scripture do not display the consequences of this denial in the rest of their belief and behaviour, and we are conscious that we who confess this doctrine often deny it in life by failing to bring our thoughts and deeds, our traditions and habits, into true subjection to the divine Word.

We invite response to this statement from any who see reason to amend its affirmations about Scripture by the light of Scripture itself, under whose infallible authority we stand as we speak. We claim no personal infallibility for the witness we bear, and for any help which enables us to strengthen this testimony to God's Word we shall be grateful.

A short statement

1. God, who is Himself Truth and speaks truth only, has inspired Holy Scripture in order thereby to reveal Himself to lost mankind through Jesus Christ as Creator and Lord, Redeemer and Judge. Holy Scripture is God's witness to Himself.

2. Holy Scripture, being God's own Word, written by men prepared and superintended by His Spirit, is of infallible divine authority in all matters upon which it touches: it is to be believed, as God's instruction, in all that it affirms; obeyed, as God's command, in all that it requires; embraced, as God's pledge, in all that it promises.

3. The Holy Spirit, Scripture's divine Author, both authenticates it to us by His inward witness and opens our minds to understand its meaning.

4. Being wholly and verbally God-given, Scripture is without error or fault in all its teaching, no less in what it states about God's acts in creation, about the events of world history, and about its own literary origins under God, than in its witness to God's saving grace in individual lives.

5. The authority of Scripture is inescapably impaired if this total divine inerrancy is in any way limited or disregarded, or made relative to a view of truth contrary to the Bible's own; and such lapses bring serious loss to both the individual and the Church.

Articles of affirmation and denial

Article I
We affirm that the Holy Scriptures are to be received as the authoritative Word of God.

We deny that the Scriptures receive their authority from the Church, tradition, or any other human source.

Article II
We affirm that the Scriptures are the supreme written norm by which God binds the conscience, and that the authority of the Church is subordinate to that of Scripture.

We deny that Church creeds, councils, or declarations have authority greater than or equal to the authority of the Bible.

Article III
We affirm that the written Word in its entirety is revelation given by God.

We deny that the Bible is merely a witness to revelation, or only becomes revelation in encounter, or depends on the responses of men for its validity.

Article IV
We affirm that God who made mankind in His image has used language as a means of revelation.

We deny that human language is so limited by our creatureliness that it is rendered inadequate as a vehicle for divine revelation. We further deny that the corruption of human culture and language through sin has thwarted God's work of inspiration.

Article V
We affirm that God's revelation in the Holy Scriptures was progressive.

We deny that later revelation, which may fulfil earlier revelation, ever corrects or contradicts it. We further deny that any normative revelation has been given since the completion of the New Testament writings.

Article VI
We affirm that the whole of Scripture and all its parts, down to the very words of the original, were given by divine inspiration.

We deny that the inspiration of Scripture can rightly be affirmed of the whole without the parts, or of some parts but not the whole.

Article VII
We affirm that inspiration was the work in which God by His Spirit, through human writers, gave us His Word. The origin of Scripture is divine. The mode of divine inspiration remains largely a mystery to us.

We deny that inspiration can be reduced to human insight, or to heightened states of consciousness of any kind.

Article VIII
We affirm that God in His Work of inspiration utilized the distinctive personalities and literary styles of the writers whom He had chosen and prepared.

We deny that God, in causing these writers to use the very words that He chose, overrode their personalities.

Article IX
We affirm that inspiration, though not conferring omniscience, guaranteed true and trustworthy utterance on all matters of which the Biblical authors were moved to speak and write.

We deny that the finitude or fallenness of these writers, by necessity or otherwise, introduced distortion or falsehood into God's Word.

Article X
We affirm that inspiration, strictly speaking, applies only to the autographic text of Scripture, which in the providence of God can be ascertained from available manuscripts with great accuracy. We further affirm that copies and translations of Scripture are the Word of God to the extent that they faithfully represent the original.

We deny that any essential element of the Christian faith is affected by the absence of the autographs. We further deny that this absence renders the assertion of Biblical inerrancy invalid or irrelevant.

Article XI
We affirm that Scripture, having been given by divine inspiration, is infallible, so that, far from misleading us, it is true and reliable in all the matters it addresses.

We deny that it is possible for the Bible to be at the same time infallible and errant in its assertions. Infallibility and inerrancy may be distinguished, but not separated.

Article XII
We affirm that Scripture in its entirety is inerrant, being free from all falsehood, fraud, or deceit.

We deny that Biblical infallibility and inerrancy are limited to spiritual, religious, or redemptive themes, exclusive of assertions in the fields of history and science. We further deny that scientific hypotheses about earth's history may properly be used to overturn the teaching of Scripture on creation and the flood.

Article XIII
We affirm the propriety of using inerrancy as a theological term with reference to the complete truthfulness of Scripture.

We deny that it is proper to evaluate Scripture according to standards of truth and error that are alien to its usage or purpose. We further deny that inerrancy is negated by Biblical phenomena such as a lack of modern technical precision, irregularities of grammar or spelling, observational descriptions of nature, the reporting of falsehoods, the use of hyperbole and round numbers, the topical arrangement of material, variant selections of material in parallel accounts, or the use of free citations.

Article XIV

We affirm the unity and internal consistency of Scripture.

We deny that alleged errors and discrepancies that have not yet been resolved vitiate the truth of the claims of the Bible.

Article XV

We affirm that the doctrine of inerrancy is grounded in the teaching of the Bible about inspiration.

We deny that Jesus' teaching about Scripture may be dismissed by appeals to accommodation or to any natural limitation of His humanity.

Article XVI

We affirm that the doctrine of inerrancy has been integral to the Church's faith throughout its history.

We deny that inerrancy is a doctrine invented by Scholastic Protestantism, or is a reactionary position postulated in response to negative higher criticism.

Article XVII

We affirm that the Holy Spirit bears witness to the Scriptures, assuring believers of the truthfulness of God's written Word.

We deny that this witness of the Holy Spirit operates in isolation from or against Scripture.

Article XVIII

We affirm that the text of Scripture is to be interpreted by grammatico-historical exegesis, taking account of its literary forms and devices, and that Scripture is to interpret Scripture.

We deny the legitimacy of any treatment of the text or quest for sources lying behind it that leads to relativizing, dehistoricizing, or discounting its teaching, or rejecting its claims to authorship.

Article XIX

We affirm that a confession of the full authority, infallibility, and inerrancy of Scripture is vital to a sound understanding of the whole of the Christian faith. We further affirm that such confession should lead to increasing conformity to the image of Christ.

We deny that such confession is necessary for salvation. However, we further deny that inerrancy can be rejected without grave consequences, both to the individual and to the Church.

Appendix II
The Bible in the British Museum —
a tour guide

Introduction

The British Museum contains a wealth of exhibits and information that are related to our study of the Bible. The following tour covers all the most significant items. The information is correct as at the beginning of 1993 but it is not uncommon for items to be changed or sent out on loan to other museums. The fact that something is listed in this tour is no guarantee that you will be able to view the item, or that it will be in the place indicated here. However, you are advised to read through these notes beforehand in order to acquaint yourself with the theme of the tour. You would be wise to take this book with you.

Bags will be searched by security at the entrance and you can then leave them in the cloakroom. Travel light around the museum; there is a lot of walking. A pencil and paper, these notes and a pocket Bible are all you need to carry. You are allowed to take photographs (hand-held only) in the museum.

Please note that throughout the tour you must not touch exhibits or lean on the glass display cases. The eagle eye of the attendants will see to it that you are soon corrected if you do!

There are hundreds of interesting exhibits in the museum, and many indirectly connected with the Bible that are not mentioned in these notes. You are advised to resist the temptation to stray from the route; if you do, you will never complete it. Doubtless you will make a note of areas you would like to return to some other time.

Visitors are not infrequently confused by the room numbering in the museum. It will help you to remember that whenever you see a room number it refers to the room you are currently in — not the one you are about to enter.

Much of the text here is repeated from earlier chapters in this book; this is to avoid the inconvenience of constantly referring back. However, some items are more fully explained in the book, and the index will help you to identify this.

We begin from the entrance hall and turn right into the British Library Galleries (Room 30 — see chapter 12).

Our first stop here will be to see the two Greek codices of the Bible, *Codex Sinaiticus* and *Codex Alexandrinus*. They are displayed side by side and are two important documents. The word 'codex' means book. They are both written in the 'uncial' Greek (capital letters). *Sinaiticus* was discovered in 1859 at a monastery on Mount Sinai. It contains part of the Old Testament and the entire New Testament. You can see that it is in excellent condition and is dated around the middle of the fourth century A.D. The copy is open at Luke 22:20-23:14. *Alexandrinus* was presented to King Charles I of England by the Patriarch of Alexandria in 1627. It is thought to have been copied between 350 and 450 A.D. The New Testament is not complete. The copy is open at the end of Acts and the beginning of James. These are two of the oldest Greek manuscripts of the Bible.

Close by you will find a case labelled 'Bibles' which displays examples of papyrus and vellum. Papyrus was made from the pith of reeds and was the first paper to be used; vellum was the leather from young animals. Obviously papyrus was cheaper but less durable; originally all our Bible was written on either papyrus or vellum. Part of a third-century copy of the *Gospel of Thomas* (this is a *pseudepigrapha,* or false writing) and part of a fifth-century Latin translation of Genesis by Jerome are on papyrus. The *Purple Gospels* is a sixth-century Greek uncial. Notice the abbreviated divine names are picked out in gold. Matthew 26:61-65 is displayed.

We now turn our attention to Bible translations, and briefly survey how our Bible came to us. Behind *Sinaiticus* and *Alexandrinus* is the Bible case containing the *Wessex Gospels* (see chapter 13).

As the Christian gospel spread across the Roman world, so the Bible spread with it. At first, the Bible that was common in western Europe was the translation of Jerome completed by the year A.D. 405. Jerome's translation was in Latin, because that was the language used in Europe for both official and church business. Jerome's translation was known as the Vulgate, a word taken from the Latin for common or popular. The Latin Vulgate was faithfully copied all over the Roman Empire.

But a Bible in Latin was of little use to English-speaking people. The language which was spoken by the Anglo-Saxon people of Britain before the Norman conquest of 1066 is known as Old English. It was so different from our modern English that it is virtually another language.

Alfred the Great should not only be remembered for burning the cakes, building a navy and beating the Danes; he was a just and educated king whose Christian faith was real. How much translation Alfred undertook himself and how much his scholars did for him is uncertain, but in addition to the translation of many good books into English, he had the Ten Commandments and other parts of Exodus and Acts translated. He is said to have been engaged in a translation of the Psalms when he died in 901.

The *Wessex Gospels* are the first example we possess of a translation of the Gospels into Old English, and they are dated some time after the death of Alfred in the tenth century. This copy was once owned by Thomas Cranmer (Archbishop of Canterbury at the time of the Reformation in the sixteenth century). It is a twelfth-century copy of the tenth-century translation. It is open at the beginning of Luke's Gospel.

Room 30a is behind you and the first display case contains an important item, *The Lindisfarne Gospels*. There is nothing more of especial interest for our tour in this room. Whilst the Latin translation continued to circulate, sometimes a helpful monk would add an English translation to it. The *Lindisfarne Gospels* are perhaps the most famous example of this. They were originally copied towards the end of the seventh century, and 250 years later an obliging priest named Aldred added a literal Anglo-Saxon translation in the Northumbrian dialect between the lines. It is therefore an 'interlinear' version. Notice the beautiful art-work in this copy.

Leaving this room go straight ahead into the King's Library (Room 32 — see chapter 12).

The first case on the left contains a tenth-century copy of the Hebrew Pentateuch (Genesis to Deuteronomy). This is written in Masoretic

Hebrew. By the tenth century A.D. the Jewish Masoretes had completed their work of adding vowel signs to the Hebrew as a way of preserving the correct pronunciation of the sacred text; before this written Hebrew only had consonants and people learnt the pronunciation by practice in the school and synagogue. The vowels, or 'points', are all those dots and dashes inside and underneath the letters.

Other cases contain various versions (translations) of the Bible during the early centuries.

Further down on the right you will find a case displaying writing materials. In Case 1 notice the *'Ostraca'*. You will meet this kind of writing again in Room 24 (Ancient Palestine). In Case 2 there is a fifteenth-century leather scroll in unpointed Hebrew.

Halfway down the King's Library, on the right, is the collection of the English Bibles dating from the time of the Reformation (see chapter 13).

The first exhibit (Case 1) is a copy of Wycliffe's Bible. John Wycliffe was born around the year 1324 and early turned his pen against the abuses of the church of Rome both in its theology and its practice. Aided by Nicholas of Hereford and John Purvey, Wycliffe completed the translation of the Bible from the Latin Vulgate before his death in 1384. It was the first complete Bible in the English language.

The church responded in alarm, and in 1394 a bill was presented to Parliament forbidding anyone to read the Bible in English without a bishop's licence. The effect of the Bible was to bring both revival and reformation into the nation, and the later revision of Wycliffe's Bible by John Purvey enjoyed great popularity throughout the fifteenth century. However, the law was applied so vigorously that by the early sixteenth century Wycliffe's Bible was scarce. All copies of Wycliffe's Bible were written by hand because there were no printing presses. The copy you are looking at is open at Hosea 1.

Tyndale's *Cologne Fragment* (1525) is next. William Caxton set up his printing-press close by Westminster Abbey in 1476 and the first paper-mill was established in England in 1490, within a year or two of William Tyndale's birth. Tyndale, a graduate of Oxford and Cambridge, slipped across to the continent in 1524 because no bishop in England would give him permission to translate and publish an English Bible. In 1525 the press of Peter Quentel in Cologne was printing Tyndale's New Testament; however, the

work was discovered when the printing had proceeded no further
than Matthew 22. This *Cologne Fragment* was bound into a quarto
edition. It was the first printed English New Testament and the first
to be translated from the Greek. In 1526 the complete New Testament was printed from Worms. (The Baptist College in Bristol has
the only known complete copy of this.)

Coverdale's Bible of 1535 (Case 1) and Matthew's Bible of 1537
(Case 2) were both circulating in England a year after Tyndale's
martyrdom in 1536 'with the Kinges most gracyous lycense'. John
Rogers, the editor of 'Matthew's Bible', was the chaplain at the
English House in Antwerp where Tyndale lodged and he was
converted through Tyndale's preaching.

Miles Coverdale was given the task of revising Matthew's Bible
so that the king's order of 1538 could be obeyed that every parish
church in the country should display a copy of the Bible 'of the
largest volume in English'. This was the Great Bible of 1539 (Case
2). In fact the Great Bible was merely a revision of Tyndale's
translation of the New Testament.

The Reformers who were forced to escape to Geneva during the
persecution of Queen Mary from 1533 prepared their own translation, known as the Geneva Bible and published in 1560 (Case 2).
Even this used Tyndale as its basis. The Geneva Bible was the Bible
of the later Reformers, the Puritans, the Pilgrim Fathers who sailed
to America in the Mayflower in 1620 and even of Shakespeare. It
was so popular that it was still being printed in 1644, thirty-three
years after King James had ordered a new translation in 1611, the
Authorized Version (Case 3). Notice the original spelling!

We now leave the King's Library and climb the East Stairs.

As we do so, our minds must slip back centuries before Christ. At
the top of the stairs pause to read the first two pages of chapter 15
as an introduction to archaeology.

Archaeology is the science of reading history from the 'leftovers' of previous civilizations. It involves uncovering the remains
of buildings and of household bits and pieces, and learning from
them who the people who used them were, and when and how they
lived. Archaeology has been called 'the study of durable rubbish.'

*Turn left and walk through Room 52, the Iranian Room, into Room
51.*

On the left is Case 9, 'The Achaemenians'. It contains the Cyrus Cylinder (item no.6).

In 2 Chronicles 36:23 and Ezra 1:2 we read, 'This is what Cyrus king of Persia says: "The Lord, the God of heaven, has given me all the kingdoms of the earth and he has appointed me to build a temple for him at Jerusalem in Judah. Anyone of his people among you — may the Lord his God be with him, and let him go up..."'

For years it was assumed that no pagan king would have referred to the Jewish God in the terms described here. The same was said of the decree of Darius recorded in Ezra 6. When archaeologists discovered the clay Cyrus Cylinder critics were forced to change their minds. The cylinder marks the triumph of Cyrus over Babylon and part of it reads: 'I am Cyrus, king of all, the great king, the mighty king, king of Babylon, king of Sumer and Akkad, king of the four corners of the earth...' The cylinder describes his victory over Babylon in 539 B.C. and how he allowed the nations to rebuild their temples. He does not refer to the Jews here, but the cylinder confirms the policy described in Ezra 6:3-5.

This clay cylinder is written in the Babylonian cuneiform (square-ended) script. You will see a lot more of this as we continue. The writing was pressed into soft clay which was then baked hard in the sun. This was a heavy and cumbersome way of storing official documents, but excellent for the archaeologist as they were virtually indestructible.

Case 11 contains a seal of Darius I, 521-486 B.C. (item no. 44). Item no 38 is also inscribed to 'Darius, Great King'. Beside it is a picture of a rock-carving commemorating the accession of the same king; notice the prisoners of different nations parading before him. This is the king referred to in Ezra 4:5 etc. and the first verses of Haggai and Zechariah. This carving was cut into a massive rock face west of Tehran and 300 feet above ground level. In 1802 a German schoolmaster deciphered the hieroglyphics and discovered in the Persian cuneiform writing the names of Darius and Cyrus. In 1835 Major General Sir Henry Rawlinson completed the work of writing out the text and this helped with the understanding of the more complicated Babylonian cuneiform script.

Return through Room 51 into Room 52.

As you leave Room 51, examine the relief panel, in the centre of the room entrance. This panel of glazed brick once adorned the palace of Darius in Susa. Imagine the splendour of a palace decorated with wall panels like these.

On the right just before you exit from Room 52 notice the large picture of an excavation of a ziggurat — a word that means temple, or mountain peak. These were places of worship in the ancient world, and Abraham would have been familiar with the ziggurat at Ur dedicated to the moon god, Sin.

Continue through into Room 65 but do not delay here. Continue into Room 56, Early Mesopotamia.

You will need to spend a short while in this room picking out the objects of most interest to you. All that you see here would be familar to Abraham. In fact most of it comes from around 2500 B.C., 500 years prior to the patriarch.

In Genesis 11:31 we read, 'Terah took his son Abram ... and his daughter-in-law Sarai ... and together they set out from Ur of the Chaldeans to go to Canaan. But when they came to Haran, they settled there.'

Between 1922 and 1934 Sir Leonard Woolley excavated the site of Ur, the city of Abraham's birth, and his discoveries revealed the advanced state of civilization there even centuries before Abraham. The patriarch may well have lived in a two-storey brick house with a lobby, courtyard, kitchen and toilet, bedrooms and reception rooms; Sarah could have been accustomed to wearing beautifully intricate head-dresses and jewellery such as you see here.

Tablets of clay and a small square-ended spatula were the paper and pencil of Abraham's day; baked hard in the sun, the completed document would last almost indefinitely. Thousands of these official records reveal a bustling city of merchants and business men trading across into Syria and down to the Persian Gulf; they record purchases, marriages, and all the events of the life of a busy city. You will find many of these official documents in this room. Some came from the 'Ministry of Agriculture' and detailed the size and yields of certain fields; others were business contracts, and one is a letter of complaint that the wrong quality copper had been sent in response to an order! There were even tablets used by the teachers to help children learn to read and write — these were of immense help to the archaeologists!

The priests were busy with their elaborate duties at the gigantic temple (ziggurat) of the moon god, Sin. Their strong attachment to the cultic superstitions are clearly displayed in this room under 'Babylonian Science and Literature'.

Obviously Abraham, thought by some to be a primitive nomadic tribesman, came from a city of culture and comforts. Cities of the same date, excavated in the same region, reveal that these people had a correct understanding of mathematics and geometry, including the theory of Pythagorus, nearly fifteen hundred years before the Greek philosopher wrote it down!

Many of the items displayed in this room, including the headdresses and jewellery, come from the royal graves at Ur. One of them is known by the macabre name of 'the Great Death Pit'. In addition to the burial chamber of the king, the bodies of six guards were found together with the remains of sixty-eight richly clothed attendant women. Small cups beside each body imply that, having taken their station, they drank a fatal poison with the intention of accompanying their king into the next world. See the case on your immediate right as you enter the room 'the King's Grave'.

This room is full of 'Abrahamic flavour'. Wander around and notice the jewellery, games and official records of state bureaucrats. It all gives you a sense of what Abraham and Sarah left behind. About the year 2000 B.C. wandering Amorites overran Ur and settled in the city (see Genesis 10:16 and 13:18; 14:13). Possibly Abraham made an alliance with the Amorites, and Genesis 14 reveals the turbulent life of the nomadic tribes that Abraham exchanged for the comparative security of the great city civilization. Hammurabi, whose law codes are referred to in this room, was one of the most powerful of the Amorite kings.

As you move towards Room 57 notice the case on your right displaying the history of writing. Do not enter Room 57 but return to Room 63, Antiquities from Egypt.

We are now experiencing the culture of Israel in Egypt from the time of Joseph for 400 years until the exodus in the time of Moses.

Cases 164-165 contain an example of brick-making, including a brick stamped with the name of Rameses II. It is made of mud from the River Nile amd chopped straw (see Exodus 5). In this room there are also displays of food and wooden models, often found in Egyptian tombs, illustrating various occupations that would have been familiar to the Israelites at the time when they were slaves in Egypt from about 1900 to 1450 B.C.

As you leave Room 63, notice the head-rests in the case on your left. They give a vivid explanation of the otherwise strange practice of Jacob who took a stone and 'put it under his head and lay down to sleep' (Genesis 28:11). Apparently this was considered much cooler than lying directly on the ground or a mattress of straw.

Continue into Rooms 61 and 60.

The book of Genesis closes with the words: 'Joseph ... was placed in a coffin in Egypt.' Joseph, as a man of high rank, and his father Israel would have been embalmed and 'mummified' exactly as you see examples in these rooms (see Genesis 50:2-3,26). His body would have been placed in a great wooden coffin (or perhaps a stone one like those we shall see later in Room 25) and we may wonder whether his coffin included the elaborate drawings and plans to direct the spirit of the deceased to the underworld, or whether he had left instructions that these were unnecessary!

When you have wandered around the Egyptian rooms for a while to gain an impression of the life of Joseph and the Israelites in Egypt, turn into Room 59 and from there left into the Nimrud Ivories (Room 58).

In 1 Kings 22:39 we are told that Ahab built a palace and inlaid it with ivory. In addition to being the wife of Ahab, King of Israel, Jezebel was also a Phoenician princess, and the Phoenician craftsmen were experts in the art of carving ivory. From the time of King Solomon onwards, ivory was a symbol of wealth and when the monarchy divided, both Israel and Judah squandered their riches in this way. Ruins at Samaria, where Ahab and Jezebel lived, have revealed hundreds of fragments of ivory, and larger items also, many of them intricately carved; archaeologists believe these date from the time of Ahab, that is, about 860 B.C. Among the items of tribute that the Assyrian king Sennacherib claims Hezekiah sent to him at Nineveh are 'ivory-decorated beds and ivory-decorated armchairs, elephant hide and tusks...' It was this wasteful luxury that the prophet Amos vigorously condemned in his ministry (see Amos 3:15; 6:4). Significantly, critics once scoffed at the idea of

Ahab making an ivory palace. They had assumed this meant a palace of solid ivory, whereas we now know that the custom was to overlay wood with carved ivory. This fact is well illustrated in Room 58. See especially Case 10, 'Ivories for furniture'.

Room 57 is the Syrian Room.

Notice in Case 12 (on the right as you enter) the small pottery urns. These contain the remains of children burned as sacrifices to the goddess Tanit (or Astarte). God warned against this gruesome and cruel practice in Deuteronomy 18:9-10, but it was widespread throughout the east from the seventh to the second centuries B.C. (see 2 Kings 23:10 where the god Molech is mentioned).

Return through rooms 57, 58, 59 and proceed down the West Stairs and into Room 24 which is immediately ahead at the bottom of the stairs on the ground floor. This is the room of Ancient Palestine.

The second display case on your left contains fragments from the 'Amarna letters'. These clay tablets were discovered at Amarna in Egypt in 1887 and were unusual because they were written in the cuneiform script which was not used in Egypt — so they were clearly a long way from their home. In fact they were letters sent to Egyptian kings from Palestine in the fourteenth century B.C. at the time when the Hebrews were settling in the land of Canaan. The writer refers to the troublesome 'Hapiru' who were wandering the land and settling. Some think this is a reference to the Hebrews, but since the name is now known to be widespread throughout the ancient east, it is likely that the name describes wandering nomads and the title 'Hebrews' may have been derived from this word.

The third display case on your left contains ivories from Samaria and can be linked with those discoveries displayed in Room 58 above. Notice also the jewellery. Other cases display typical lamps and pottery from Palestine at the time of the monarchy.

The last case on the left contains pottery fragments, including a message scribbled in ink on a broken pot. The name '*ostraca*' describes this (item no.21). During the last days of Judah, Nebuchadnezzar of Babylon was systematically destroying the cities of Palestine, and the net was tightening round the city of Jerusalem and its king Zedekiah (2 Kings 24 to 25). Jeremiah reports: 'The army of the king of Babylon was fighting against Jerusalem and the other cities of Judah that were still holding out — Lachish and Azekah. These were the only fortified cities left in Judah' (Jeremiah 34:7). This fragment is part of a military dispatch written from an officer in an outpost, to the commander at Lachish.

To the right as you enter this room there is a relief of Tiglath Pileser III, the King of Assyria in the eighth century B.C. Kings of both Israel and Judah paid tribute to him (see 2 Kings 15:29; 16:7-18). This relief pictures the capture of Ashtaroth Karnaim in Gilead (see 2 Kings 15:25-29).

In the case nearby is a jar found in the Qumran caves near the Dead Sea in 1947 (see chapter 12). These jars contained literature from the Essene Community that lived in the Dead Sea area 150 years before Christ. Many of the scrolls were Old Testament books, including a complete book of Isaiah.

Room 25 contains many sculptures and stone coffins from Egypt.

The large central bust of Rameses II is considered by many to depict the Pharaoh of the Exodus. This is unlikely since a date around 1280 B.C. involves such difficulties in harmonizing the biblical chronology that an earlier date, around 1440, is preferable.

Almost at the end of this hall on the right is the Rosetta Stone. This creates considerable interest. Discovered by a French officer in 1799 in the western Delta of Egypt, it was surrendered to the British and came to the British Museum in 1802. The stone is carved on black basalt and is valuable because it contains two forms of ancient Egyptian writing, and one section of Greek. The Greek is part of a decree issued by Ptolemy V in 196 B.C. The Egyptian writing, once deciphered, helped scholars to understand ancient Egyptian writing. It has no direct interest for us in a Bible-related tour.

Just opposite the Rosetta Stone you will find an 'Egyptian King List — Ancient Egyptian History'. Normally this is the kind of exhibit you will pass by as 'boring', but look carefully at this one. Notice that from the eighteenth-century dynasty list the names of a number of kings are omitted, including Akhenaten and the famous Tutankhamun. The reason for this is that Akhenaten became a monotheist and thus betrayed the national religion. For this crime he was treated as if he did not exist! What is the value of this information? Some critics will tell us that the story of the repentance of Nineveh in the time of Jonah must be fabricated since there is no such reference in the Assyrian records. However, any king who turned to the God of the Jews would cetainly have the records of his reign destroyed. In the same way we do not expect the records of Egyptian history to account for the Exodus described in Exodus 14:23-28, nor the records of Sennacherib to mention the virtual annihilation of his army at the walls of Jerusalem recorded in Isaiah 37:36 — humiliating defeats for the Egyptians and Assyrians.

Walk to the end of Room 27.

Beside the souvenir shop in the left corner is a relief of Shalmaneser III. This is the King of Assyria (858-824 B.C.) in the time of Ahab, Kng of Israel. (It is not the Shalmaneser referred to in 2 Kings 17:3 and 18:9; that is Shalmaneser V). Although Shalmaneser III is not mentioned in the Old Testament, he refers to Israel in his own records as we shall see.

Just outside the shop notice the stela of Ashurbanipal II — a fine example with good detail.

Between the two winged lions turn into Room 19, Nimrud.

As you do so, notice the massive gates from the palace of Ashurbanipal.

The walls of Room 19 are decorated with the sculptures from the palace of Ashurbanipal II (883-859 B.C.). This King of Assyria is possibly mentioned in Ezra 4:10, but the significant item in this room is the Black Obelisk in the centre of the room. The story behind this great chunk of polished basalt is interesting (see chapter 15).

Jehu (2 Kings 9:14) was not from royal descent, but he was a soldier who butchered his way to power as King of Israel. Having killed both the Kings of Israel and Judah he doubtless felt a little uneasy about some of the enemies he had made! A strong friend and ally would be a wise policy; but where would he find one?

In 1845 a young and inexperienced archaeologist, Henry Layard, ran out of money, packed his horse and rode miserably away from the site he and his team had been digging on the banks of the River Tigris in Assyria. No sooner had he left than a workman caught up with him and urged him to return to the site because a block of black polished basalt stone had been found lying in a trench. It measured two metres high and was carved with pictures and writing on all four sides. The 'Black Obelisk' (an obelisk is just a shaped block of stone, generally tapering at one end) proved to be a stone cut to commemorate the triumphs of the Assyrian king, Shalmaneser III. Part of it depicts rulers in national costume bringing tribute to the king. The second row of the panel facing Room 20 shows a kneeling figure in Israelite dress with the inscription above which reads: 'Tribute of Yaua, son of Humri: I received silver, gold, a golden bowl, a golden beaker, golden goblets, golden pitchers, lead, a royal staff, a javelin.' This is 'Jehu the son of Omri'. In fact Jehu is the fourth in line of descent from Omri, who was the founder of this dynasty. Behind the kneeling Jehu is a line of his servants laden with the items of tribute. This is how Jehu found an ally! But the story is not ended there, because in order to make a friend of Shalmaneser, Jehu abandoned Hazael of Damascus (in Syria). Hazael is also mentioned on the obelisk, but he had resisted the Assyrian king. For this treachery Jehu and Israel paid dearly in later years, as 2 Kings 10:32 reveals.

Exit from Room 20 and turn left into Room 16 towards the stairs leading down to the Basement level — but stop at the head of the stairs.

You are standing in front of the great king Sargon. In the year 721 B.C. Sargon became King of Assyria; he continued the siege of Samaria begun by Shalmaneser V and the city was destroyed (2 Kings 17:5-6). For years the critics doubted that a king by the name of Sargon ever existed because the only reference to him came in Isaiah 20:1 and it was assumed that Sargon was an invention of the prophet's fanciful imagination.

In 1843 a French archaeologist, Paul Botta, started digging at a town called Khorsabad, twenty-two kilometres (fourteen miles)to the north of Nineveh. He discovered a great palace guarded by huge human-headed winged bulls nearly five metres high (you are probably leaning against them right now — stand back and admire them!). The walls were lined with great slabs of stone carved with pictures and cuneiform writing — the square script of ancient Babylon, Assyria and Persia. The writing proved that Botta had discovered the palace of King Sargon. He is now one of the best-known Assyrian kings and was one of the most powerful rulers in the ancient world.

Of the many documents left behind by Sargon, one contains a reference to his defeat of Samaria: 'In the first year of my reign I beseiged and conquered Samaria... I led away captive 27,290 people who lived there.' In fact it was Sargon's predecessor Shalmaneser V, referred to in 2 Kings 17:3-4 and 2 Kings 18:9, who began the siege; however, he died after two years and Sargon completed the work and took full credit for it! Interestingly in 2 Kings 17:6 and 18:10, when the fall of Samaria is recorded after the three-year siege, the name of Shalmaneser is not repeated because it was Sargon who finally broke the Israelite capital. We have an incredible store of knowledge of this man including the fact that one of his daughters was both a priestess and a poetess!

The statue of Sargon is facing the crown prince Sennacherib.

Walk between the winged bulls and turn left into Room 17, the Lachish Room.

In Isaiah 36:1-2 we read, 'Sennacherib, King of Assyria, attacked all the fortified cities of Judah and captured them. Then the king of Assyria sent his field commander with a large army from Lachish to King Hezekiah at Jerusalem.'

In the year 701 B.C. Sennacherib, the powerful King of Assyria, sent a massive army against Jerusalem when Hezekiah rebelled against him. The details are recorded in 2 Kings 18-19; 2 Chronicles 32; Isaiah 36-37. Sennacherib left his own account on a clay prism just 37.5 centimetres high. It was discovered in 1830 at Nineveh by Colonel Taylor, the British resident in Baghdad, and is therefore known as the Taylor Prism. The Taylor Prism has been in the British Museum since 1855 — it is in Room 89 and we will refer to this shortly.

Sennacherib records details of his campaign against the Hebrew king. Although unable to take Jerusalem itself, he destroyed the surrounding country and spoke of shutting up Hezekiah in his royal city 'like a caged bird', adding, more for the benefit of his own conceit than for historical fact, 'The terrifying splendour of my majesty overcame Hezekiah. The warriors and select troops [Arabs and mercenaries?] he had brought in to strengthen his royal city Jerusalem, did not fight.'

Sennacherib also adds that he laid siege to forty-six Judean cities and carried off 200,150 people of all ranks from Judah and that Hezekiah sent tribute after him to his royal city in Nineveh; this is clear evidence that the Assyrian king did not enter Jerusalem to carry off plunder for himself. In fact he is careful never to claim that he entered Jerusalem, and in the victory room in his palace at Nineveh, it is the defeat of Lachish, not Jerusalem, that illustrates his victory over the Hebrews. This all fits exactly the biblical record. The story of the defeat of Lachish was carved into stone and it occupies the room in which you are now standing. This is a vivid picture of the siege of Lachish and as you move along the wall, the following description may help you to identify the battle details.

The battle for the strategic city of Lachish begins in the second panel on the wall facing you. Notice the ranks of archers, with quivers stuffed with arrows, firing over the walls into the city; some kneel, protected by the tall leather shields of the javelin throwers. Behind them are the bearded artillery men with long pointed helmets wielding their sling and carrying a spare stone in their left hand; they keep up a barrage of small but lethal missiles. The storm-troopers with flat helmets are scaling the walls, firing arrows as a protective shield as they advance. The air is thick with missiles. The siege-engines trundle up the earth and stone ramps right up to the walls of the city. Each engine encloses an archer, a man to guide the 'tank' and a 'fireman' who, with great ladles of water, douses the constantly falling fire-torches of the defenders as they try to set fire to the protective leather covering of the battering ram.

The defenders, for their part, are desperately hurling their fire-bombs and rocks upon the attackers; some are falling over the wall, victims of advancing archers. At the bottom of the panel is the gruesome scene of those who tried to escape the city and have been impaled on long stakes in the sight of the defenders. Groups of prisoners, men, women and children clinging to their mothers, are led away; the spoils of war follow them on camels and in heavily laden ox-carts. The leaders of the city are spread-eagled and flayed alive, whilst others are summarily executed. King Sennacherib himself took part in this siege and he is seen receiving the defeated prisoners as he sits upon his high throne. The inscription reads: 'Sennacherib, King of the world, King of Assyria, on a seat he sat and the booty of Lachish before him it passed.' The king's chariot and bodyguard are below and behind him. Notice how the king's face has been hacked out — probably the work of a Babylonian soldier when Nineveh itself was destroyed in 612 B.C!

As you follow the relief round you will notice the plan of the base camp with priests offering sacrifices to their gods and the servants busy in their tents. This is the end of the Lachish sequence.

The remaining panels depict Assyrian cavalry, slingers and archers, and prisoners being led away under the watchful and taunting eye of the Assyrian guards; the prisoners are playing their lyres, which is reminiscent of Psalm 137.

Before you leave this room notice the glass case containing items found at Lachish. The octagonal prism describes Sennacherib's campaigns, including Lachish. This is not the Taylor Prism.

As you exit from Room 17 via the way you came in and walk between the winged bulls, notice the large inscription to your left in the alcove. This includes the detail of the tribute sent to Sennacherib by Hezekiah after the Assyrian's enforced withdrawal from Jerusalem (see Isaiah 37:36-37).

The stairs to your left, beside the Sargon relief, will lead down to Room 89.

Here you will find the Taylor Prism, or Sennacherib's Prism, in a case on the left. It is on this prism that Sennacherib describes how he shut up Hezekiah like a bird in a cage.

Return to the West Stairs via Rooms 20-21. These rooms depict Nineveh in the time of Sennacherib.

We now turn to the New Testament.

Go down the West Stairs and after the first flight of stairs turn left into Room 12.

Of interest in this room is the base of one of the columns of the Temple of Diana in Ephesus. This is from the old temple which was one of the seven wonders of the world. Doubtless Paul himself stood and looked at this column (see Acts 19).

Continue down the stairs into Room 78, Classical Inscriptions.

Here is another item connected with the Acts of the Apostles. Luke, the author of the Acts of the Apostles, was well acquainted with all the political arrangements in the various provinces of Asia and he reveals this by his correct use of titles for the local dignitaries. Here are just a few examples: at the time Paul was in Cyprus a proconsul was in charge and, although there had been many changes, Luke used exactly the correct title when referring to Sergius Paulus (Acts 13:7). Philippi was accurately described as a Roman colony whose officials are referred to as '*stratagoi*' or magistrates (16:38). In Ephesus the 'officials of the province' are called the 'Asiarchs' (19:31), exactly the people we now know controlled religious affairs. At Malta the '*protos*' (28:7) is the 'chief official'. Small things? Perhaps, but these are facts that would not have been known to later generations and are therefore clear evidence that Luke was an eyewitness of all that he recorded.

In this room you will find the Politarch Inscription (see chapter 9, under William Ramsay). At Thessalonica (now Salonika) the reference to the 'politarchs' or 'city officials' (17:6) is well attested by inscriptions from that town and we know that the city had five politarchs in the first century. The first word in this inscription (which is written in Greek uncial — capital letters) is from the verb *politarcheo*, to act as a politarch. Four of the men listed in this inscription as politarchs bear the names of men recorded in the New Testament — Sosipatros and Lucius (lines 1, 2 — see Romans 16:21), Secundus (line 2 — see Acts 24:4) and Gaius (line 5 — see Acts 20:4). They are not the same men, but these names were common at that time.

Retrace your route up the West Stairs and you will come to the centre of Room 25. Turn right here and go to the end of the room, and then left to the Book Room. This will lead you back to the Main Entrance Hall. From the main entrance it is a short step up the main stairway to the Wolfson Gallery, Room 70.

In this room you will find the busts of many of the Roman emperors of the New Testament period. Caesar Augustus was the first of the emperors, and arguably the greatest. In office for forty-one years, he claimed to have found Rome brick and left it marble. He was the emperor at the time of our Lord's birth and the one who ordered the census (Luke 2:1).

Room 69 contains a cabinet entitled 'Gladiators'. One of the worst features of Roman life was the brutal use of men in the public arenas to satisfy the lust for violence and blood. By the end of the second century B.C. public displays were so common that the Emperor Trajan held a festival that lasted 117 days during which almost 5,000 pairs of gladiators fought in the arena. Animal hunts were popular in the arena and criminals and Christians were thrown to the wild animals for the sport of the crowds. There is an allusion to all this by Paul in 1 Corinthians 15:32. Christians went to the arena for their refusal to swear allegiance to the emperor. Clay lamps and models depict the contests which became illegal after A.D. 400, largely through Christian influence. Other items in this room display something of life in the Roman Empire during the New Testament time.

Address of the museum:

British Museum
Great Russell Street
London WC1 3DG
Telephone: 071 580 1788

General index

This index does not include words that are found within quotations from the Bible, nor does it include the names of Bible books when they are used in connection with a Scripture reference. Information on both of these will be found by using the Scripture index. Also, the country is generally put for the language and culture; thus 'Egypt' includes 'Egyptian'. Hebrew and Aramaic are exceptions to this. Proper names, especially Bible characters, are only indexed where there is a significant mention.

The index does not cover Appendix II, the tour guide to the British Museum, as information in this section is likely to date more quickly than the rest of the text, owing to frequent changes of displays in the museum, and much of the material is in any case repeated elsewhere in the main text.

Scripture index